Emerging Technology for Managers: Effective Management in the 21st Century

Second Edition

Cengage

Australia • Brazil • Canada • India • Mexico • Singapore • United Kingdom • United States

Cengage

Emerging Technology for Managers: Effective Management in the 21st Century, 2e

Rahul Dubey

For product information and technology assistance, contact us at **asia.infoindia@cengage.com**

For permission to use material from this text or product, submit all requests online at **www.cengage.com/permissions**

ISBN-13: 978-93-6053-975-7
ISBN-10: 93-6053-975-9

Cengage Learning India Pvt. Ltd.
T-303, 3rd Floor
DAV Complex, Plot 3
Mayur Vihar Phase 1
Delhi 110091

Cengage is a leading provider of customized learning solutions with employees residing in nearly 40 different countries and sales in more than 125 countries around the world. Find your local representative at: **www.cengage.com.**

Cengage is committed to creating inclusive and diverse products, including perspectives that represent the diversity of people across all backgrounds, identities, opinions, and experiences. If you have any feedback related to this, please contact us at **support.cengage.com.**

To learn more about Cengage products, platforms and services, visit **www.cengage.co.in.**

Printed by:
VA Global
Ground Floor, Plot No. 41, Pocket J, Sector-2, Bawana,
DSIDC, Delhi-110039

Print Number: 01 Print Year: 2025

To

My Family and Friends

Foreword

Atul Pandey, B.E. (IIT—Roorkee) & MBA (IIM—Lucknow)

Founder, **Eternity Solution Corp**—*an organization focused toward helping individuals and organizations leverage the limitless human potential*

The Backdrop Technology has been an inseparable part of human evolution from time immemorial. In every era of human history, the quest to assert the power of human thinking led to the evolution of technologies needed by the society in that time. While there are innumerable technologies supporting our lives today, the role and share of information or digital technology has perhaps been the sharpest considering the rate at which it is becoming an indispensable part of our lives. What is even more striking is how it is reshaping every other industry with its presence, promise, and potential. The DNA of human progress is getting recoded within the two inseparable strands of physical and digital technologies. And we have barely begun to unlock and unleash its potential.

These technologies are still emerging!

The Problem While this evolution and acceleration of technology and human life is exciting, it also poses several problems for the professionals who are looking to embrace and leverage the power of the digital world. The rate at which the digital stack is growing and transforming makes it difficult to track what to really learn and focus on! The speed at which companies are developing their own offerings on these stacks poses yet another dilemma, which one to go after? Some companies are focusing on big data, some on AI/ML, some on cybersecurity, some on cloud infrastructure, and some on sensors or robotics. The list is endless!

To compound it further for the digital technology aspirants, there are two distinct 'islands' where they may find themselves with respect to their current capabilities. One island is that of developers or coders who are quite adept at getting into the gut of the individual components of the stack. However, most of them miss the big picture of application—the larger, business use cases where these could be applied; an understanding of the value that their code can unlock. On the second island could be found professionals such as MBAs who are more equipped to think about the big (business) picture, business use cases, and value proposition, and, therefore, what solutions are needed to unlock that value. However, these professionals are not equipped with the basic understanding of the digital technology and its working, which makes them ill-prepared to envision, propose, and create technology-led business solutions.

There are three distinct gaps that need to be bridged for these professionals, which are largely unaddressed today.

Gap 1 At one end, there are a bunch of technology courses, workshops, books, and programs that jump into coding and the detailed constructs without spending any time on the core (basic) concepts. While this may work well for people who are already good at coding, it does not help one who is new to technology from a non-technical background. Even the courses that profess to teach the beginners do it by presenting the codes without clarifying the concepts, thus creating copycat coders, for the most part. The *Whys* behind the *Hows* are missed.

Gap 2 The second gap is at the other end of the spectrum! A lot of *business* books on technology talk about product management, portfolio management, technology business cases, business and architecture frameworks, but miss the technology basics. Although good for people with a management background, they do not augment their knowledge and insight in knowing the technology stack beyond, mere, some terms and hype statements.

Gap 3 The third gap has been about creating a space or lab that can bring these two sets of professionals together! Letting people interact and dissolve their gaps of understanding! In work teams, they can experiment with the actual technology—code and application—and learn from their experience, observations, and mistakes; and overcome those mistakes by referring backward and discussions on the basics.

The Answer This book by Dr Dubey does just that—addresses these-very gaps head-on! It aims to bridge and connect the two islands. It establishes a solid foundation of the core concepts behind each emerging technology and its applicability in business solutions. The coverage of each topic is thoughtful in terms of providing a great starting point and then inducing them to think and expand on those concepts through their own reflections. The language is easy to read and the book relates to the real world, which would help in smooth absorption and assimilation of these concepts, which are not easy to grasp at the outset, especially for non-technology business professionals. The book takes these enablement means a step further by creating a space for the readers to experiment with the concepts, thereby building the much-needed tech mental muscle on an ongoing basis.

I have known Dr Rahul Dubey for more than a decade, not only as a professional, thinker, and an educator but also as an inspiring *change agent*. I hope the readers of this book are also 'infected' by his 'open-minded' thinking, passion for understanding technology, and looking 'beyond' to its business application as he makes the world of technology simple to understand, relatable, and useful for business managers.

Atul Pandey

Belmont, San Francisco Bay Area, CA

Previously, two decades in the technology services industry, in sales and delivery leadership role, with clients in industry segments including manufacturing, hi-tech, retail & CPG, and banking & financial services.

Atul's passion is to decode the nuances of human behavior and help individuals and organizations to recode a greater roadmap of possibilities by unlocking and unleashing their untapped potential through a structured and scientific approach enabled by the limitless power of human knowledge and core values.

Contact: https://www.linkedin.com/in/atulcp/

Preface to the Second Edition

In the book, *The World Is Flat: A Brief History of the Twenty-first Century*, Thomas L. Friedman talks about globalization. Amongst other aspects, he describes the ways the distribution of knowledge and technology has created equal opportunities in many different countries across the world. Now, the world is conducive to technology sharing. Using the Internet, *emerging technologies* such as Cloud Computing and Generative AI have become accessible across the world concurrently. A person living in Silicon Valley gets access to a Generative AI dialogue model on the same day as a person living in Bangalore, India. This does not stop at computing; it also includes communication technologies such as 5G.

These (emerging) technologies have become a part of our lives. We hardly think about the technology that enables an app on our smartphone. In the book, we cover several, or rather most, emerging technologies around us. Each topic has the potential to be a book in its own right. Here, instead of delving deep into the technology itself, we provide an overview of the technology and the business applications of the same. This includes Big Data, Internet of Things (IoT), Cloud Computing, Blockchain, Machine Learning, Deep Neural Network, sensors, robotics, and computer vision. To make technology relatable, each topic of the book has discussions on possible use cases, an experiment section to grok the technology, and also Python code snippets to put some technologies to work. The material covered in the book is suitable for a wide audience: readers with or without a technical background. There is a new technology that has taken the world by storm—Generative AI. This technology will impact many areas. It makes you feel like Aladdin with your own personal Genie. But, you have to be specific in what you are looking for; otherwise the Genie cannot help you. Generative AI is like any other tool from the past, such as Computer Aided Design (CAD). The tool can help you do your work faster; but you need to know what you are doing! We lightly tread on the use of Generative AI, with some example prompts. The reader is encouraged to experiment on their own on the best way to use Generative AI.

You may be familiar with the quote, "The whole is greater than the sum of its parts." This quote is often attributed to the Greek philosopher Aristotle and it signifies that a system is more than the aggregate of its individual components. In context to this book; the emerging technologies that we discuss have a synergistic effect, and have provided mankind with many useful applications. The ideas presented in the book not only help businesses, they also help cities, countries, schools, hospitals, and similar institutions manage their operations effectively. I had a great time writing this book; exploring and learning new facets of technology and applications. Once I learn about a new technology, I can spot it being used in various applications. I do hope that after reading the book, you will become more mindful about the technologies around you and maybe create a new killer application with them. A good deal of learning is embedded in the exercises section of each chapter. Feel free to contact me (https://www.linkedin.com/in/rahul-dubey-phd-ab39863/) with your suggestions and feedback.

Rahul Dubey

March 2025, Cupertino, California

Preface to the First Edition

Technology has evolved immensely in the last two decades. The growth of the Internet, wireless communication, cloud computing, artificial intelligence, AI-based analytics, and visualization technologies have all contributed to more efficient business processes.

The objective of this book is to give an overview of the business applications of the latest technologies such as Big data analytics, Cloud computing, Blockchain, Machine Learning (ML), Artificial Intelligence (AI), Deep Neural Networks (DNN), IoT & IIoT, and Visualisation technologies.

Even though many of these technologies may sound esoteric; it is possible to harness their power by calling a few simple software functions. Python code snippets are used to demonstrate this. This book takes you on a journey of how contemporary technology can be used for business processes. Rather than going deep into technical detail, this text provides a concise view of emerging technologies and their relevance to modern-day businesses.

Using the content presented in this book, the readers can understand the basics and potential applications of emerging technologies. By demonstrating how these technologies fit together in a business framework, this text prepares the student or professional to independently explore further on, and also to form simple architectures by putting together different technologies for a particular use case.

We hope that this easy-to-read book will be an interesting read and a starter for students as well as industry professionals. Any suggestions for improvement are welcome.

Rahul Dubey

December 2022, California

About the Author

Rahul Dubey, PhD, is a member of technical staff at a global training solutions company and is based in the San Francisco Bay Area, USA. He possesses a mix of academic and industrial experience. He started his career as an application engineer for factory automation and participated in the design of control systems for various industries, such as textiles, tires, petrochemicals, cement, and automotive. Subsequently, for a decade, he was a faculty member at multiple universities and taught courses on industrial automation, embedded systems, and digital design.

Acknowledgments

My experience of writing a book follows the Gartner hype cycle. There is a technology trigger which gets me started. It is followed by a phase of inflated expectations. Midway in the book writing process, I go through a trough of disillusionment. With some portion of the book completed, I start seeing hope in finishing it and that leads me to the slope of enlightenment. Finally, with a deadline to honor, I become productive and start putting together content.

Some parts of what I have said in the previous paragraph are not exactly true, but you get the picture! Book writing is a strenuous journey with its set of highs and lows. Understanding, kind people are needed to complete the journey. My family—mother, younger brother Rohit, wife Sulekha, and daughters Aditi and Avni—gracefully gave me the needed time and space to work on the book. In this time, I also found support from a new family member—my son-in-law Shubham, who frequently asked me about the progress and patiently listened to me describing it in great detail.

My father's friend PK—Dr Prabhat Kumar Dubey—speaks highly about my books and encourages me to write. Similarly, my maternal uncle, Mr R.S. Mishra, got some stories I had written as a boy, typed and bound in the form of a book! Both of them, like so many others, have lasting positive impressions and silently motivate.

I sincerely thank Mr. Atul Pandey for accepting my request to write a foreword to the book. Many times forewords tend to be perfunctory; but Atul has given the topic of emerging technologies a great deal of thought and has created an engaging foreword.

This book is the result of excellent support from the team at Cengage India. They are a group of responsive, considerate, and talented people. *The weariness of a journey is forgotten upon reaching the destination*. What remains in the mind are fond memories of the travel. Book writing is a similar journey.

I wish to thank the Almighty for making the journey memorable.

Rahul Dubey

Brief Contents

Detailed Contents

CHAPTER 1

Introduction to Emerging Technologies and Their Applications

CHAPTER OUTLINE

1.1 Evolution of New Technologies
1.2 Combine Material Flow with Data
1.3 Challenges of E-Commerce Business Enterprise
1.4 Bird's-Eye View of Emerging Technologies
1.5 Mapping Emerging Technologies to Business Requirements
1.6 Real-World Use of Emerging Technologies
1.7 Grokking Technology Using Python
1.8 Explore and Experiment
1.9 Organization of Content

LEARNING OBJECTIVES

After reading this chapter, you will be able to:

- understand evolution of new technologies
- enumerate needs of contemporary business
- learn about challenges for businesses in new economy
- get a bird's-eye view of emerging technologies
- map emerging technology to business requirements

Effective Management Using Emerging Technologies

In 1999, Bill Gates and Collins Hemingway wrote a book "Business @ the Speed of Thought." The book discussed how business and technology are integrated, and how digital infrastructures and information networks can benefit modern businesses. Today, all businesses use emerging technologies to remain relevant, efficient and cost-effective. It is, therefore, imperative that employees and C-level executives understand and use technology for their businesses effectively.

1.1 | Evolution of New Technologies

Computers, communications and algorithms, have seen a great deal of change since the mid-1990s. Several new innovations such as e-mail, Internet, revival of AI algorithms, and cloud computers have changed the world in many ways. Not only has it changed the way we interact with each other (using social media), but it has also changed the way we conduct business. Emerging technologies play a role in new (or greenfield) businesses, and also make an important contribution to existing business. This book explores these emerging technologies and their impact on businesses.

Let us pause and try to understand what effective management is. Intuitively, effective management of a process or system is related to optimized cost, better operational efficiency, and its sustainability. To illustrate how effective management is applied to an application, we will consider the case of a parking garage (Fig. 1.1). These parking garages have become commonplace in many parts of the world and can be seen at shopping malls, airports, downtowns, and tourist places. A driver takes a ticket from a kiosk as he/she drives into the parking garage. When the driver returns to the parking after paying the parking charges at a kiosk, the boom gate opens. A surveillance camera checks for the license plate of the car and opens the gate automatically or the driver is requested to deposit the paid ticket into the exit kiosk. This entire automated process of letting a car in, collecting the required parking fee, and recording the exit of a car is managed by minimal human intervention. It provides effective management in the following ways:

- Recording license plate of each car at the entry and the exit
- Keeping track of the number of cars in the parking at any given time
- Knowing precisely the duration of parking of each car
- Correlating the time and the day with occupancy

How does emerging technology enable this seemingly trivial parking operation? There are several mature technologies working under the hood. These include the following:

- Database
- Machine learning and artificial intelligence

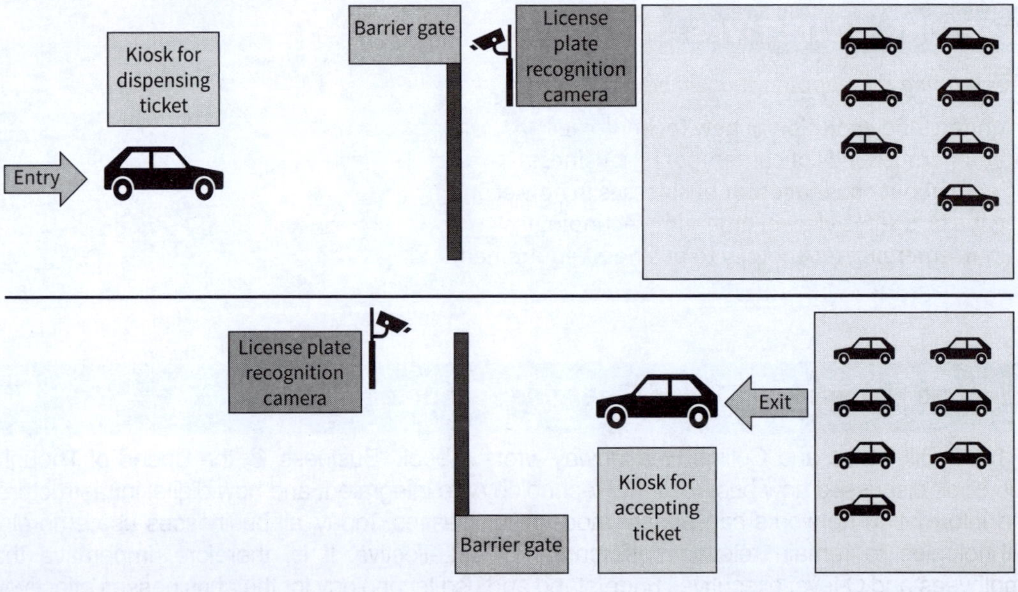

Fig. 1.1 An automated parking garage setup

- Internet of Things
- Computer vision
- Digital Transaction
- Barrier gate automation

The use of emerging technology leads to the following benefits

Better decision-making Contemporary technologies provide businesses with access to real-time data and analytics, enabling them to make better-informed decisions. With these technologies, businesses can track Key Performance Indicators KPIs and other important metrics and adjust their strategies in real-time. On a special weekend, the automated parking lot may offer discounts or decide to raise prices.

Cost-effectiveness As briefly mentioned earlier, emerging technologies automate tasks, reduce errors, and improve efficiency, which results in cost-effective operation.

Enhanced customer service In case a customer needs assistance with their parking ticket, the parking lot Websites and businesses can leverage emerging technologies like chatbots, voice assistants, and other AI-powered tools to offer better customer service. These tools provide instant support to customers and improve overall customer experience.

1.2 | Combine Material Flow with Data

Let us examine the material and data flow in a modern industry. We track produce from the farm where food items are grown and track their journey from a manufacturing plant to the retail store. Some of these goods may also be transported to warehouses or fulfilment centers. Based on where the customer buys the product from, the goods are either shipped directly to the consumer or sent to retail outlets.

The flow of physical goods is associated with data that accompanies these goods. The manufacturing plant uses several emerging technologies to keep track of the raw products, maintain manufacturing throughout to match demand, and use technology to optimize production.

Table 1.1 shows the material and data flow for a perishable food product. Modern businesses combine material flow with suitable data. This helps in optimizing the supply chain. Consider both Table 1.1 and Fig. 1.2 to understand how material and data travel together. Over the last few years, this approach to use data-material together has become the standard. Think of any contemporary business process (such as on-line food delivery service) and you will be surprised to see how intertwined physical goods and data are.

Table 1.1 Example of material-data flow

Material Flow	Data Flow
Get seeds and grow produce on farm	Log seed vendor and variety
Package, tag and transport produce after harvesting	Create shared, secure tag for traceability
Accept produce at factory and start processing	Software to ensure consistent product quality by maintaining proper temperature, pressure, and speed control of machinery.
Ship processed food in temperature controlled trucks	Monitor temperature of truck through its journey
Product transferred to refrigerated units at retail store	Share data of product sales with the supplier and within the retail store

1.3 | Challenges of E-Commerce Business Enterprise

As seen in Fig. 1.2, a modern e-commerce enterprise is complex and expected to be nimble and highly synchronized. The diagram shows a simplified view of the supply chain of a perishable products company. The raw material is produced in a farm, then processed in a factory and subsequently stored in a warehouse before being shipped to retail stores using refrigerated trucks. The entire operation is monitored with the help of data that is aggregated in a centralized cloud computing setup. Patterns in consumer preference is quickly recognized and the entire supply chain is adjusted to meet the new demand. This is easier said than done. There are several challenges that need to be overcome. These include:

(a) Making sense and learning from data
There is data everywhere. It is in all shapes and sizes: videos, images, and text data. Data comes from production, product social media Websites, sales prediction, and accounts. The challenge is to ingest and timely extract value from large data.

(b) Data connectivity and security
Secure data transactions between servers and devices using the Internet. Product traceability from different suppliers.

(c) Availability of flexible computing infrastructure
It is difficult to foresee computational needs of a company. Seasonal product demand means fluctuating requirements of computers and data services.

(d) Logistics
Reliably ship orders across cities, states, or countries.

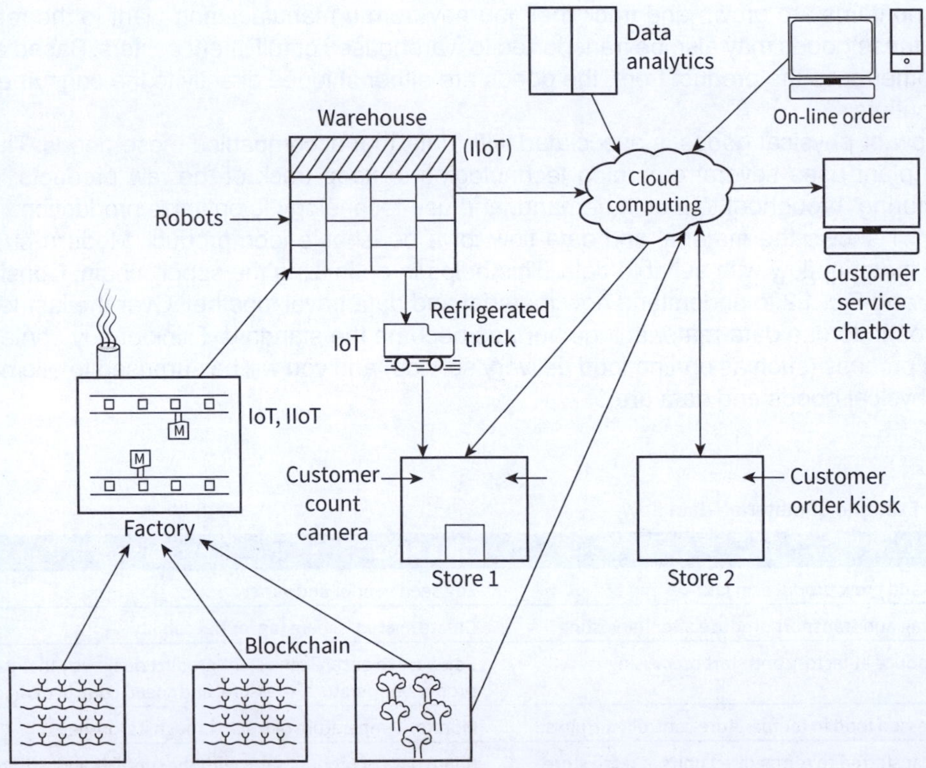

Fig. 1.2 Diagram of a modern-day enterprise—Flow of data and goods between different business units

These challenges affect both small- and large-scale corporations. A small-scale corporation can offer goods and services to a larger customer base, if it surmounts the challenges mentioned above.

In this scenario, emerging technologies has acted as a great leveler. It has given small entrepreneurs and start-ups a level playing field. The accessibility and cost-effectiveness of new technology is able to address most of the challenges listed earlier.

1.4 | Bird's-Eye View of Emerging Technologies

Now, we take a brief look at some emerging technologies. These technologies have evolved and matured quickly in the last two decades. They provide production ready solutions for today's businesses.

(a) **Internet**
Worldwide connectivity of people and businesses. Offer your product to prospective customers across the world.

(b) **Cloud computing infrastructure and services**
Flexible computer infrastructure, which is billed based on usage. Managed services to address frequently used business needs, such as data storage, Web and mobile, data analytics, and authorized secure access.

(c) **Ability to connect with remote devices**
With the help of Internet of Things (IoT), it is possible to monitor and track perishable goods in transport. Similarly, with the help of the Industrial Internet of Things (IIoT), unattended infrastructure is monitored by use of low power, long-range communication protocols.

(d) **AI algorithms to extract value from data**
AI algorithms offer multiple techniques to analyze data—computer vision models to classify and detect objects, natural language processing (NLP) models to parse text, analyze time-series data, carry out anomaly detection, and provide predictions based on past data. Many of these pretrained AI models are used for data analytics, factory shop floor, retail shop, and Websites.

The most important aspect of these emerging technologies is its ease of access and affordability. Few decades ago, it was only the large corporations who could have inhouse computing systems. Today, most businesses can easily access technologies for effective management. Some of these technologies are the following:

Artificial Intelligence (AI) AI is used by businesses to automate customer service interactions, improve inventory management, and optimize logistics operations. Chatbots are increasingly being used by businesses to handle customer inquiries, while AI-powered algorithms are being used to analyze customer data and provide personalized product recommendations.

Internet of Things (IoT) IoT enables businesses to monitor and track assets, improve supply chain management, and increase efficiency. Sensors are placed on equipment to monitor usage and detect malfunctions, while smart devices can be used to track inventory levels and automate ordering.

Augmented Reality (AR) AR improves customer experiences and product visualization. It is used to provide customers with virtual try-on experiences when shopping for clothes or cosmetics, or to visualize furniture or home décor in a virtual room.

Blockchain Blockchain uses distributed ledger technology to improve transparency, reduce fraud, and improve supply chain management. Many industries use blockchain to track the origin and movement of goods, ensuring that they are authentic and free from counterfeit.

Robotics Robotics automates manufacturing processes, improves quality control, and reduces costs. Modern factories use different types of robots to assemble products, inspect them for quality, and perform routine maintenance tasks.

Table 1.2 Mapping business needs to emerging technologies

Business Requirement	Technology to Assist
Precision agriculture for farming	Use computer vision and deep learning to detect and spray herbicides on weeds
Ways to accurately track farm produce	Distributed ledger based blockchain
Monitor cold chain for perishable produce	Use IoT technology
Share manufacturing best practices between different plants	Internet of Things (IoT) and Industrial Internet of Things (IIoT)
Store and process data from various operations at a centralized location	Cloud computing resources and services
Extract meaningful information from data about customer preferences, demand, engaging with customer and optimizing manufacturing operations	Use of Artificial Intelligence (AI) technology

All technologies listed above provide multiple benefits. Even though we have just spoken about the use of technology in a garage parking lot and a typical farm-to-table scenario, these technologies contribute to effective management in any business in the following ways:

Streamlining operations Emerging technologies like automation, AI, and ML can help businesses automate their operations, reduce manual tasks, and increase productivity.
Improving customer experience Technologies such as chatbots, virtual assistants, and personalization algorithms help businesses enhance their customer experience by providing personalized recommendations, 24/7 support, and faster response times.
Enhancing data analysis Big data and analytics can help businesses analyze customer behavior, market trends, and operational data to make informed decisions and improve business strategies.
Enabling remote work Emerging technologies like video conferencing, cloud computing, and collaboration tools help businesses facilitate remote work and improve communication among team members.
Increasing data transaction security Technologies such as blockchain, biometrics, and cybersecurity software help businesses secure their data and prevent cyberattacks.

1.5 | Mapping Emerging Technologies to Business Requirements

In the earlier section, we talked about a few requirements/challenges facing e-commerce companies. Let us try and map these requirements/challenges to emerging technologies. We start at the bottom of the chain (the farm) and end at the retail store. Table 1.2 encapsulates some items of this mapping.

Even though we have barely started our discussion on emerging technologies, we get a sense from Table 1.2, how it can help modern businesses. We will continue to elaborate on this table in different chapters of the book.

Every business requirement may or may not benefit from technology. In 1966, Abraham Maslow wrote "If the only tool you have is a hammer, it is tempting to treat everything as if it were a nail." Each business process is unique and all relevant aspects need to be considered before applying technology.

1.6 | Real-World Use of Emerging Technologies

Before we delve into the details of how these technologies work and their use, let us take a brief look at how some successful modern businesses use them effectively. This compilation on how businesses use contemporary technology is collated from information available in the public domain.

Amazon Amazon transformed the retail industry with its use of emerging technologies such as AI, big data analytics, and warehouse robotics. These technologies have enabled Amazon to provide personalized recommendations to customers, streamline its supply chain operations, and improve its warehouse management.

Netflix Netflix uses ML algorithms to analyze user data and provide personalized recommendations to its users. This has helped the company to understand its customers, retain its users, and increase customer satisfaction.

Google Google has used ML to improve its search algorithms and provide more relevant search results to users in different applications such as YouTube, Maps, and Travel.

Uber Uber revolutionized the transportation industry with its use of emerging technologies such as GPS and its smart phone app. Both technologies have enabled Uber to provide a seamless experience to its customers and improve the efficiency of its operations.

Tesla Tesla disrupted the electric vehicle industry with its use of emerging technologies such as AI and big data analytics. Similar technologies have enabled Tesla to develop its Autopilot driver assistance system. Also, remote software updates to cars have decreased the need to recall cars for improvements.

McDonald's McDonald's uses AI and big data analytics to analyze customer data and personalize its menus. This helps the company maintain customer loyalty and increase its revenue.

Taking a closer look at the companies listed above, you will notice that companies such as Tesla started the use of emerging technologies to differentiate themselves in the automotive market, while others such as Netflix and McDonald's used it for staying relevant. Let us now talk about companies that have leveraged technology to change their business model.

Netflix Netflix started as a DVD rental service but faced a significant challenge when video streaming became popular. To address this challenge, Netflix invested in big data analytics and ML algorithms to improve its recommendation engine. The company's investment paid off, and it became the leading video streaming service in the world.

Domino's Pizza In the mid-2000s, Domino's Pizza was struggling to compete with other fast-food chains. The company invested in emerging technologies such as mobile apps and digital ordering systems. With these technologies, Domino's was able to improve its customer experience and increase sales.

Walmart Walmart was facing tough competition from e-commerce giants like Amazon, but the company started to embrace emerging technologies such as big data analytics, ML, and AI to optimize its supply chain and improve its customer experience. This helped Walmart to increase its efficiency and compete more effectively in the digital age.

Many companies in India use emerging technologies for effective management of telecommunications infrastructure, logistics, manufacturing, and customer engagement. A partial indicative list of such companies is mentioned here.

Reliance Jio The telecom company Reliance Jio revolutionized the Indian telecom industry by leveraging emerging technologies like 4G, 5G, and IoT. The company has disrupted the market with its low-cost data plans and has become the largest mobile telecom player in India.

Flipkart The Indian e-commerce giant Flipkart uses big data analytics to understand customer behavior and preferences. This has enabled the company to offer personalized recommendations and targeted promotions, which has helped to increase customer engagement and loyalty.

Mahindra & Mahindra The automobile company Mahindra & Mahindra has used data analytics to improve its manufacturing processes and supply chain management. It is also incorporating Advanced Driver Assistance Systems (ADAS) technology in its vehicles to improve road safety.

HDFC Bank HDFC Bank has leveraged AI and ML to improve its customer service and fraud detection. The bank has been able to offer personalized banking services and has significantly reduced the risk of fraud.

Every chapter of the book ends with technology applications from the real world. I encourage you to read the resource provided and then populate the use case template to solidify your understanding of the application and related technology.

1.7 | Grokking Technology Using Python

Certain ideas are best understood by trying them out. In the spirit of this philosophy, we will demonstrate several emerging technologies with the help of Python code snippets (20 lines or less). Python provides a high level of code abstraction; this results in concise and simple code to understand important ideas of emerging technology.

All code snippets presented in the book are available as Google Colaboratory notebooks and can be accessed through the Cengage Digital App. If you are new to Python, please spend some time to go through Appendix A—a quick overview on Python. Feel free to use the code presented in this book as a starting point for experimentation. Extend the existing code with your own ideas! If you think Python or programming is not your strong suit, you can consider tools such as Orange (https://orangedatamining.com/) that can help create graphical data flows by using Python under the hood.

Competence in Python is not a prerequisite to understand and learn emerging technologies. It does help in experimenting with ideas and putting together applications using different technologies. With a little effort and knowledge of Python syntax you can get the Generative AI tool to create Python code for your requirements.

1.8 | Explore and Experiment

Most chapters of the book contain steps on how to explore and experiment different aspects of emerging technologies. Ideas such as generating customized quick response (QR) codes, accessing sensors on a smartphone, installing Python packages to program drones are presented in different chapters of the book. In the future, more ideas in this section will be added using the Cengage Digital App. The exercises section also contains a resource describing the use case for a particular technology. This resource can be in the form of a YouTube video or a writeup. Using the resource, you are the supposed to create a brief use case. In the process of generating the use case, you will understand the relationship between the technology and the use case better; it will also open new application ideas for you. Most contemporary AI technologies use the same approach: *learning by example*.

Speaking of learning by example and AI, I recommend that you experiment with Generative AI prompts. Generative AI is a great learning tool for both work and education. As per the Microsoft Copilot frequency asked questions webpage[1], it can help with the following:

- Understand the implications of a decision: 'What are the pros and cons of offline marketing strategies?'
- Learn new skills: 'What are the top five things I should know when managing a large project?'
- Analyze data: 'If we're forecasting 7% EPS growth this coming quarter, how does our internal forecast compare with EPS growth in the top US public CPG companies?'
- Summarize a work PDFs open in Edge: 'Recap the findings of this internal cybersecurity report and the top three concerns' or 'What are best practices for addressing these kinds of security issues?'
- Write better code faster: 'Write a regular expression in Python that matches e-mail addresses'

Like many large language models (LLMs) based dialogue tools, Microsoft Copilot offers support for a variety of prompts. Some of these prompts are mentioned in Fig. 1.3. By setting the

[1]Frequently asked questions about Copilot, https://learn.microsoft.com/en-us/copilot/faq (accessed 18 December 2023).

conversation style to more precise; the LLM model relies on referenced facts when it generates answers. It is up to the user to validate and cross-check AI model responses before using it in a real-world scenario.

For each chapter in the book, I present some sample Generative AI conversations to demonstrate how it can help get a better understanding of the topics discussed. The examples are indicative; I encourage you to try out your own prompts, and accelerate your learning. Sample prompts are created by the author and answers presented are generated by Microsoft Copilot.

Generative AI tools available from companies such as Microsoft, OpenAI, Google, and Meta are functionally quite similar. Even though the prompts and responses mentioned in the text use the Microsoft Copilot tool, generative AI tools from other companies are likely to provide comparable interaction.

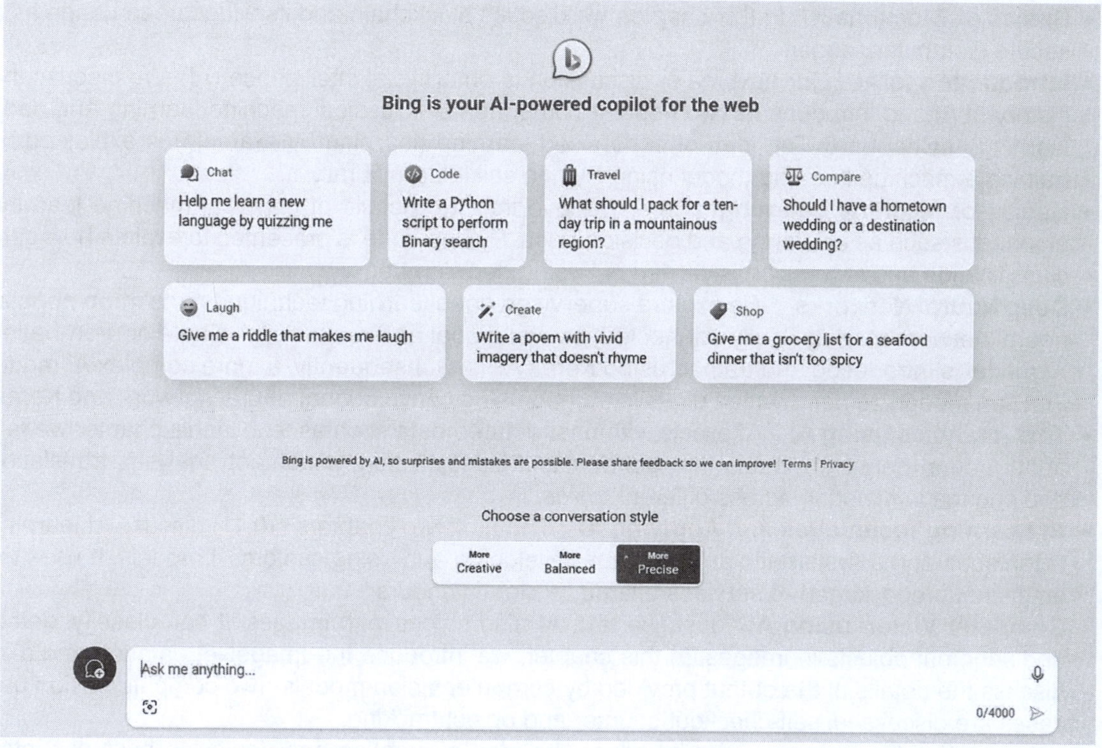

Fig. 1.3 Microsoft Bing AI-powered Copilot for experimenting with Generative AI

1.9 | Organization of Content

In the book we will use examples to understand how existing and new businesses can take advantage of emerging technology. Different chapters of the book will help in connecting the pieces of the technology puzzle together. It is important to keep in mind that each topic or chapter can be an entire book in its own right. Our objective for most chapters is to present the basics of the technology and enable experimentation with executable Python code.

- **Big Data Overview and Analysis** Our journey starts with big data. Here we explain the explosion of data, its characteristics and different sources that contribute to it. We also discuss different types of databases that store tabular and non-tabular data. The chapter includes

Python code snippets to demonstrate structured query language (SQL) and use of application programming interfaces (APIs).

- **Internet of Things (IoT) and Industrial IoT (IIoT)** Here we explain the data pyramid of an IoT system. Data from multiple edge devices flows through a gateway to a server (cloud computer). Data packets from hundreds of edge devices get shared and assimilated for informed decision making. The chapter also contains Python code for setting up an IoT publisher, subscriber-based system.
- **Overview of Cloud Computing Services** The next stop in our journey focuses on cloud computing. In this chapter we explain the evolution of cloud services; study differences between various types of cloud setups, and discuss key services offered by the cloud. We further elaborate on cloud usage by discussing details of cloud deployment, and cost metrics for different services. The chapter ends with a discussion on cloud service architecture diagrams.
- **Basics of Blockchain** In this chapter, we discuss blockchain and its widespread usage as a secure distributed ledger.
- **Introduction to AI** Our next major discussion is on artificial intelligence (AI). We discuss the history of AI and introduce its two popular components—classical machine learning and deep learning in Chapter 6. The idea of supervised learning (learning by example) is explained by training a machine learning model using Python scikit-learn library.
- **Basics of Machine Learning** Here, we dive into the details of classical machine learning algorithms such as clustering and decision trees. Python code is presented to explain how data classification and regression is carried out using decision trees.
- **Deep Neural Networks** We explore supervised deep learning techniques and three popular neural network models—fully connected, convolutional and recurrent. A single neuron-based AI model is introduced and trained using Keras APIs. Subsequently, a more complex AI model that can recognize handwritten digits is trained using convolutional neural network and Keras.
- **Text Analytics using AI** AI excels with unstructured data such as text. In this chapter we talk about neural network models that perform text classification, sentiment analysis, translation and engage in dialogue across different topics.
- **AI Learning Techniques and Applying AI** The next two chapters (10,11) discuss AI learning techniques and a systematic approach for developing and using custom AI models. It uses examples of prepackaged AI services offered by cloud vendors.
- **Computer Vision using AI** Just like text, AI also shines with images. It can classify, detect and segment objects in images. In this chapter, we introduce the ImageNet dataset, and also discuss the details of the output provided by computer vision models. Two computer vision use cases are discussed: self-checkout counter and object tracking.
- **Visualization Techniques** We introduce the idea of creating and deploying business intelligence dashboards to display data in real-time. These dashboards also provide event-based notifications based on the data being ingested. The chapter includes an explanation of how augmented, virtual and mixed reality technologies help in decision making process by adding or creating computer generated relevant details.
- **Edge Computing** For many applications, the computer system is located close to where the data is generated. A smart traffic light is an example of such an application. This chapter discusses gateways/edge devices that can process data locally and send output data packet to cloud servers.
- **Intelligent Sensors, Drones, and Robotics** We turn our attention from software and AI to hardware systems in Chapters 15 and 16. The two chapters discuss the eyes/ears (sensors) and the arm/legs (actuator) of a system. Video sensors, drones and robots leverage computer vision capability derived from AI and are widely used in warehouses, security and logistics.
- **Cybersecurity** Towards the end of the book (in Chapter 17), we talk about the real possibility of cyber-attack threats to connected computer systems and share ways to guard against these.

- **Synthesizing Ideas using Emerging Technologies** The last chapter of the book (Chapter 18) puts together all the learning from different chapters of the book to understand how it helps solve complex use cases such as: ride-sharing, logistics, e-governance, smart cities, and precision agriculture. A short section at the end discusses some recommendations on creating your own disruptive application.
- **Prototyping Ideas for Societal Good** The last chapter of the book discusses how ideas are converted to products. It uses examples of ideas that benefit society. A simple diagram, along with a table on use of technology provide a starting point to translate an idea to reality.

1.10 | Conclusion

This chapter provides a roadmap to contextualize use of emerging technologies such as cloud computing, IoT, and AI for business applications. We created an exemplar framework to understand how goods and data flow in a modern enterprise and how emerging technologies can help. These technologies are employed by several companies to effectively manage complex manufacturing, logistics, and retail operations. It is not necessary to understand the nitty gritty of each technology; it is important to understand its existing and potential applications.

Exercises

A. Short-answer Questions

1. Give an example of how businesses make use of e-mail to interact with customer.
2. Create a timelog of an e-commerce order lifecycle. This would track an order from order to delivery.
3. Enumerate data associated with a single online order such as a food delivery order.
4. Assume a food delivery company logs GPS locations of all food deliveries. Provide one use of this location data.
5. Mention three products that require refrigerated transport.
6. In the automated parking garage use case, explain how emerging technologies provide a better user experience.
7. Give an example of a multinational company that uses emerging technology effectively to increase its business.
8. Describe an example of an Indian company that effectively uses emerging technology.
9. Find out and list business applications that use Python. Explore Python.org website to get more details.
10. Provide an example of how you personally use emerging technology to optimize your work/life.

B. Long-answer Questions

1. Using a diagram, explain the flow of data and goods when you place an order for a laptop computer on a Website such as Amazon. Include as many details as you can.
(Hint: Use of one-time password (OTP) to ensure delivery to the right person.)
2. Enumerate the software services you think are needed to successfully complete the transaction of part A.
(Hint: Start by software needed to send an e-mail acknowledging the order. End by software needed to create and post an invoice for the laptop to your Amazon account.)
3. Discuss in detail an emerging technology application that impressed you.
(Hint: Example—The first time you carried out a financial transaction using a smartphone.)
4. Study the business and manufacturing model of an automotive company. Prepare a table along the lines of Table 1.2 to map the business requirement to a technology that assists it.

C. Explore and Experiment

1. Make a list of companies that you think use emerging technologies such as AI, IoT, data analytics, or robotics. If you are not sure about the use of a particular technology, use the Internet to research and confirm.
2. Try out Python code from Appendix A.
    1. Access the Python code using Colab notebook link.
    2. Run the code given in the notebook.
    3. Modify/update code to increase your confidence with Python.
3. The prompt in Fig. 1.4 is used to supplement the idea presented in Table 1.2 of the text. Here, Generative AI enumerates business requirements along with emerging technologies for a logistics application.

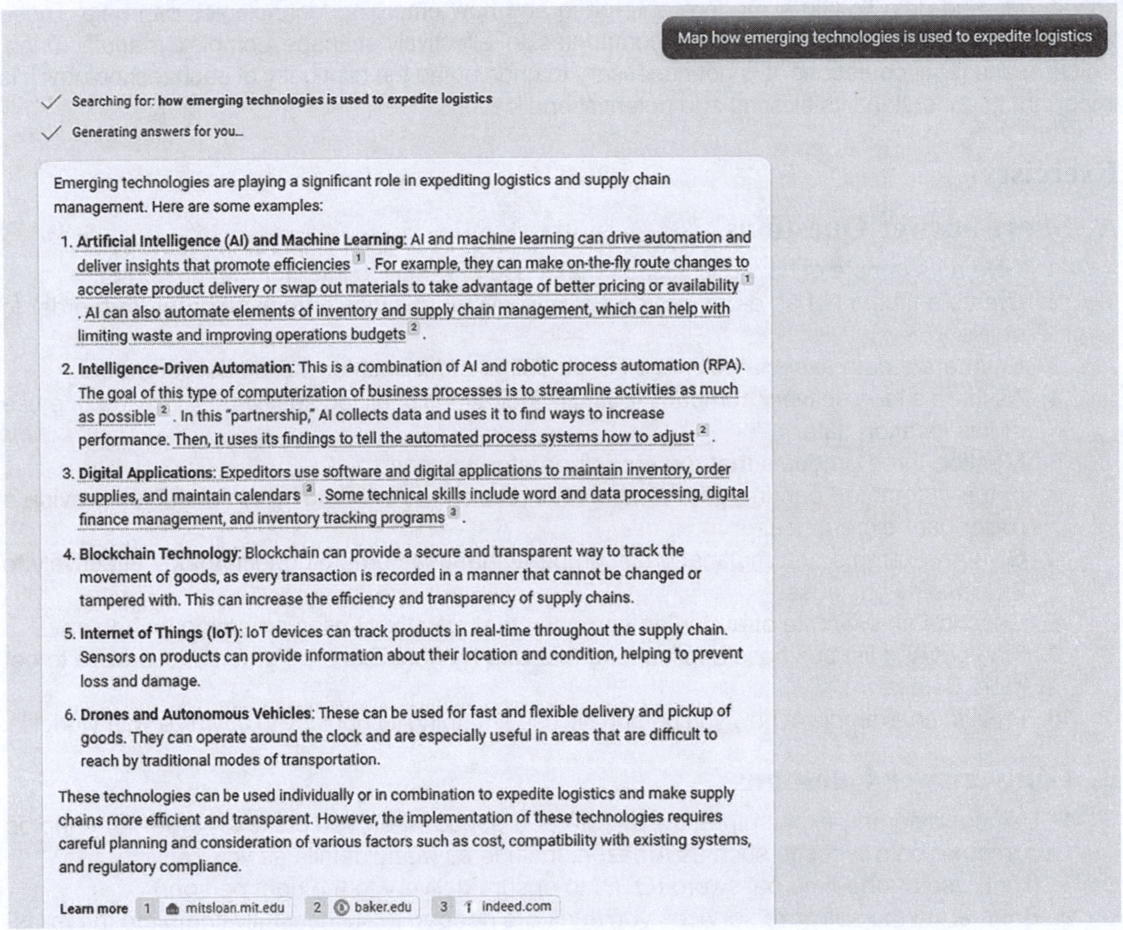

Fig. 1.4 Generative AI's referenced answer on use of technology for logistics use case

D. Generate Use Case on How Emerging Technologies Work Together

Use Case: E-commerce and Supply Chain

Brief description: The recent pandemic has accelerated the use of technologies that deliver products to the doorstep. Watch both videos in the resources section below, and put together a use case on efficient supply chains. Try to correlate this Table 1.1 and Fig. 1.2 of the chapter.

Resources

Walmart: How Walmart Is Automating Its Supply Chain to Deliver the 'Perfect Order' I WSJ Shipping Wars.
YouTube Link: https://www.youtube.com/watch?v=Nf-P-qNej3c
Here's How Your Package Ordered Online Gets to Your Doorstep I The Quint
YouTube link: https://www.youtube.com/watch?v=AnYrQt2uh_E

Template for Creating Use Case on Supply Chain Management

Define goal and purpose	Goal statement
	Identify stakeholders
	Define scope
Details to include in use case	Capture how technology helps business process
	Keep use case findings description textual, with a few simple flowcharts if needed
	Focus on describing how technology benefits the use case
Future applications	Mention any new applications that can leverage the technology used

Suggested Reading

1. Paige Baltzan, Business Driven Technology, 8th edition, McGraw-Hill.

CHAPTER

2

Big Data Overview and Analysis

CHAPTER OUTLINE

LEARNING OBJECTIVES

After reading this chapter, you will be able to:

- identify sources of big data generation (volume)
- understand the need for timely processing of data (velocity)
- distinguish different kinds of data (variety)
- learn the basics of structured query language (SQL) and non-SQL (NoSQL) constructs

Effective Management Using Data Analytics

Data storage and analysis is one of earliest uses of computers. Over the years the importance of data has only grown. Modern day businesses use computers for storing customer details, employee details, inventory details, manufacturing plant records and much more. Data analysis is the hidden engine that keeps modern enterprises running. It assists in taking informed decisions and reveals patterns in business operations.

You may have heard of the term *data-driven decision-making*. It is often used to explain the value of data in a modern business. Most operations in a business setup either generate or consume data. This has led to creation of large amounts of data, often referred to as big data. Big data is characterized by three prominent features—volume, velocity, and variety. In this chapter, we will study these features in context to traditional and e-commerce-based businesses. Data features such as volume, variety, and velocity are commonly used by businesses in different ways. Let us discuss them by using some examples.

The volume of data is the amount of data that businesses collect and store. Big data analytics tools are used by businesses to analyze large volumes of data, such as customer behavior, sales data, and social media interactions. For example, a retail business can analyze the volume of sales data to identify top-selling products, trends, and consumer preferences. This information is used to optimize inventory management and marketing strategies.

Variety refers to different types and formats of data that businesses collect and store. Businesses can use data mining tools to extract insights from different types of data, such as text data, images, audio, and video data. For example, a social media platform can analyze the variety of user-generated content to understand user behavior, preferences, and sentiments. This information is then used to improve user engagement and experience.

Velocity of data is related to the speed at which data is generated and processed. Businesses use real-time analytics tools to process and analyze data as it is generated, such as in the case of streaming data or sensor data. For example, a transportation business can use the velocity of sensor data from vehicles to optimize route planning, maintenance schedules, and fuel efficiency.

Businesses leverage the above-mentioned features of data to gain insights, improve decision-making, and enhance business performance, aptly known as data-driven decision-making.

2.1 | Sources of Data (Volume)

Large quantity of data is produced by numerous sources. A sensor in a factory, a mobile phone, or Web-related activity on a computer generates a steady flow of data. A steady trickle of data from millions of sources adds up very quickly. Often, it is easy to remain oblivious to the data devices and humans continue to produce and consume. Some sources of data include,

- Location (GPS) data captured by delivery and ride-sharing companies
- Sensors that capture process data in factories
- Online browsing data from business Websites
- Social media data
- Data generated by business processes within a corporation—such as customer feedback, sales, demand, customer inquiries, and many more.

It is quite a challenge to accurately quantify the amount of data that is generated on a daily basis. Even if we obtain that number, the next job is to find out how much of that data is useful. It turns out that much of the data is repetitive or redundant data. Data scientists parse data and analyze it for business insights.

2.2 | Different Kinds of Data—Numbers, Text, Audio, and Video (Variety)

Data is broadly categorized as structured, semi-structured, and unstructured data. Structured data uses some kind of a *schema* and is in the form of tables (spreadsheets), while unstructured data is in the form of text, images, video, and audio. Semi-structured data does not follow a rigid or fixed tabular structure and is not stored in conventional databases. Unstructured data such as video and audio are stored as binary large objects or BLOBs. Each object includes the data, metadata, and a

Table 2.1 Data types—structured, semi-structured, and unstructured

Data Format	Type	Data Source Example
Text and numbers	Structured	Tables, spreadsheets from internal processes.
JSON (JavaScript Object Notation) open-source text format, CSV (comma separated values)	Semi-structured	GPS location of a cellphone tower
Pure text	Unstructured	Customer feedback, social media
Video	Unstructured	Analytics from retail store, manufacturing plant, automation
Audio	Unstructured	Call center customer interaction

unique identifier that applications use for easy access and retrieval. Table 2.1 provides examples of these three data types.

2.2.1 Working with Different Data Types

We will now discuss ways to work with different data types—structured, semi-structured, and unstructured. Data gathered in a business system can be stored in two places—close to the place where data is generated (the edge) or on the cloud computer. The steps for setting up and working with a database is the same for both platforms—edge and cloud.

Data is stored in the following three formats in a supported database.

1. SQL tables (structured)—e.g., MySQL, SQLite, MariaDB, PostgreSQL
2. NoSQL format (semi-structured)—e.g., MongoDB
3. Blobs or objects (unstructured)—images, video, etc.

We start our discussion with two popular database types—relational database (often referred to as SQL database) and non-relational database (often referred to as NoSQL database). Both SQL and NoSQL databases support Create, Read, Update, and Delete (CRUD) operations with data.

For the purpose of understanding, we will use MySQL as an example of a relational database. MySQL[1] is a fast, multi-threaded, multi-user, and robust SQL (Structured Query Language) database server. If you prefer to work with a free and open-source equivalent of MySQL, try out MariaDB.[2] Both MySQL and MariaDB share common commands. Figure 2.1 shows a functional diagram of data from edge devices getting stored in a relational database. This data is later used for analysis and machine learning. The software used to store, manage, query, and retrieve data stored in a relational database is called a *relational database management system* (RDBMS).

2.2.2 Functionality Offered by Structured Query Language (SQL)

SQL is the most widely used database language. It is designed to work with SQL databases mentioned earlier. Its salient features include,

(a) Non-proprietary. SQL became a standard of the American National Standards Institute (ANSI) in 1986.

(b) Easy to learn

(c) Powerful. It is possible to carry out complex database operations by using simple SQL commands.

[1]https://www.mysql.com/ (accessed 3 June 2023).
[2]https://mariadb.org/ (accessed 3 June 2023).

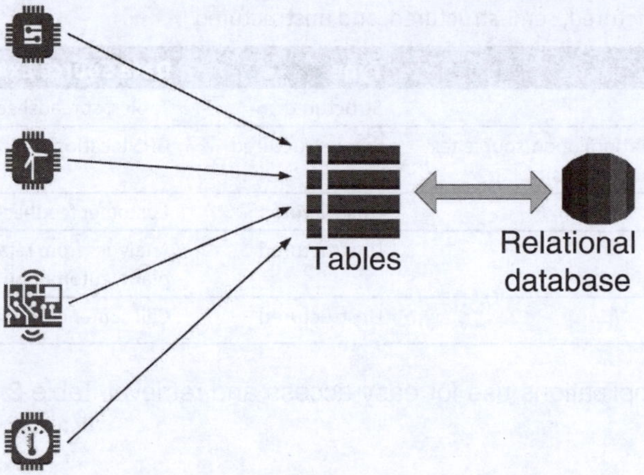

Fig. 2.1 Data from multiple devices stored in a database by use of tables

SQL allows users to carry out several operations on tabular data. In the next section, we will explain how these operations are carried out by describing how temperature sensor data is saved/queried from a structured database.

2.2.2.1 Basic structure of an RDBMS

Data in an RDBMS is stored in database objects called *tables*. The table consists of related data entries in the form of rows and columns (Fig. 2.2). Each column of a table is also known as a *field* and may consist of a sensor ID, name of the sensor, sensor location, time, date, the temperature reported by the sensor, and so forth. Later we will see, how this stored data is accessed by using a weather website.

Each row of the table is called a *record*. The record is a horizontal entry in a table and usually consists of one complete set of reading from the sensor.

It is important at this time to put forth an explanation for the NULL value in a database. A database field that is blank (has no data entry) is a NULL value. An entry of zero or a space does not mean it is NULL.

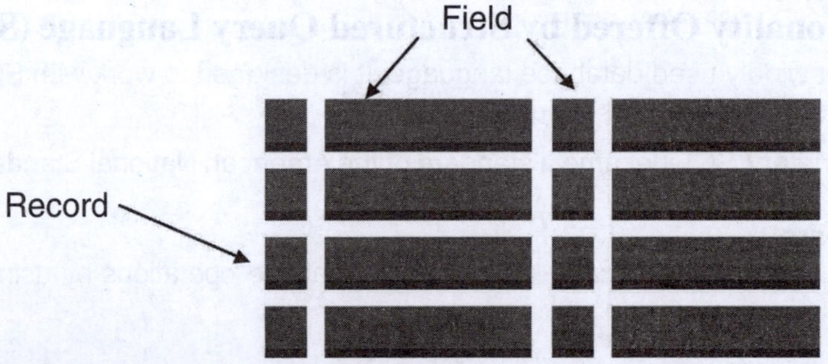

Fig. 2.2 Basic structure of a database table—values are stored using record and field

2.2.2.2 Constraints on data

SQL offers the possibility to impose constraints on data, which gets recorded in the table. The constraints can be in the form of a data type. This improves the accuracy and reliability of the data that is recorded. Column/field- or table-level constraints can be imposed on the data.

2.2.2.3 Syntax of SQL

We will now demonstrate how SQL constructs are commonly used. For this, we create a hypothetical database for storing real-time weather data. The SQL statements start with a keyword—CREATE, USE, SHOW, DROP, SELECT, INSERT, UPDATE, DELETE, ALTER—and end with a semi-colon ';'.

The SQL keywords are case insensitive. Both *CREATE* and *create* statements have the same effect. This does not apply to table names. Table *SENSOR* is different from a table called *sensor*.

Let us create a test database called sensor for recording temperature values.

You can recreate the steps by installing MySQL database on a local computer using instructions provided in the Digital App. Alternatively, you can choose to follow along to understand the commands to interact with a SQL database.

```
$ mysql> CREATE DATABASE sensor;
```

CREATE is a case-insensitive keyword which creates a case-sensitive database by the name of *sensor*.

You should now see

```
Query OK, 1 row affected (0.00 sec).
```

You can check for the creation of the database by using:

```
$ mysql> show databases;
```

Switch to that database:

```
$ mysql> USE sensor;
```

You should see Database changed.

EXAMPLE 1

Create a table to store sensor data. The name of the table is SENSOR_WEATHER and is part of database sensor.

Solution Let us first create a table which acts as a framework for accepting temperature data from different locations. This table can be part of a weather-station database. We use the CREATE TABLE statement for this purpose. The syntax of the CREATE TABLE is as follows:

```
CREATE TABLE table_name(
column1 datatype,
```

(Continued)

```
column2 datatype,
column3 datatype,
   .....
columnN datatype,
   PRIMARY KEY( one or more columns )
);
```

In our table, we use two IDs—the ID of the location and the ID of the reading. Each temperature reading is logged with a current time timestamp.

```
CREATE TABLE SENSOR_WEATHER(
    ID INT NOT NULL AUTO_INCREMENT,
    REMOTE_ID INT,
    AMBIENT_TEMPERATURE DECIMAL(6,2) NOT NULL,
    CREATED TIMESTAMP NOT NULL DEFAULT CURRENT_TIMESTAMP,
    PRIMARY KEY (ID)
  );
```

You should now see Query OK, 0 rows affected (0.05 sec). The table created using the above-mentioned command can be seen by using the DESC command, as follows:

```
mysql> DESC SENSOR_WEATHER;
```

Field	Type	Null	Key	Default	Extra
ID	int (11)	NO	PRI	NULL	auto_ increment
REMOTE_ID	int (11)	YES		NULL	
AMBIENT_ TEMPERATURE	decimal (6,2)	NO		NULL	
CREATED	timestamp	NO		CURRENT_TIMESTAMP	

```
4 rows in set (0.00 sec)
```

Press Ctrl - D or type exit to quit MySQL.

Accessing the structured query language database using Python

We installed the Python MySQLdb module when we installed the MySQL software. A quick check of this installation is done with the help of the following code in the Python shell environment:

```
>>> import MySQLdb    # Case sensitive
```

If the code completes without an error, the MySQLdb module is correctly installed.

The Python standard for database interfaces is the Python DB-API. This DB API provides a mechanism for working with databases using Python structures and syntax wherever possible. The API provides the following functionality:

- Importing the API module
- Acquiring a connection with the database
- Issuing SQL statements and stored procedures
- Closing the connection

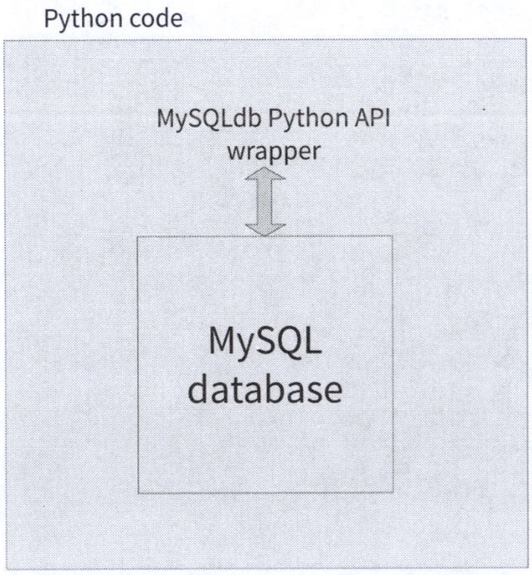

Fig. 2.3 Connecting Python to MySQL using MySQLdb application programming interfaces

Connecting to the database using MySQLdb API

Before connecting to a MySQL database using MySQLdb API (as seen in Fig. 2.3), make sure of the following:

- You have created a database sensor.
- You have created a table SENSOR_WEATHER in the database sensor.
- This table has fields ID, REMOTE_ID, AMBIENT_TEMPERATURE, CREATED time.
- User ID "root" and "password" are set to access the sensor.
- Python module MySQLdb is installed properly on your machine.

Populating the database

Let us insert some temperature data points in the database (Listing 2.1). This ensures that the Python–SQL connection is working and we also get a database to experiment with.

Listing 2.1 Connecting to a SQL database and inserting a record into a database called sensor

```
#!/usr/bin/python

import MySQLdb

# Open database connection
db = MySQLdb.connect("localhost","root","","sensor" )

# prepare a cursor object using cursor() method
cursor = db.cursor()

# Prepare SQL query to INSERT a record into the database.
sql = """INSERT INTO SENSOR_WEATHER (ID,REMOTE_ID,
        AMBIENT_TEMPERATURE) VALUES ('1', '40', 20.82)"""

try:
   # Execute the SQL command
```

(Continued)

Listing 2.1 (*Continued*)

```
        cursor.execute(sql)

13.     # Commit your changes in the database
        db.commit()
14.
    except:
15.     # Rollback in case there is any error
        db.rollback()
16.     print ('error - database not updated')

17. # disconnect from server
18. db.close()
```

The following code uses APIs to connect to the database using a hostname, user ID, password (which is not used in our example), and the database name. The SQL *insert* command is used to populate data fields and *cursor.execute(sql)* executes the SQL command. In case there is an error, data from the *insert* command is not committed to the database and a fault message is displayed.

The user can check to see if a record is correctly inserted into the table, by using either the *describe* or the *select* keyword, as shown in Fig. 2.4.

Line 4 from Listing 2.1 shows the need to login to MySQL database. Multiple users can use a MySQL database (see Fig. 2.5). Single-user embedded databases also exist. An example of such a database is SQLite which is built into all smartphones.

```
mysql> SELECT * FROM SENSOR_WEATHER;
+----+-----------+---------------------+---------------------+
| ID | REMOTE_ID | AMBIENT_TEMPERATURE | CREATED             |
+----+-----------+---------------------+---------------------+
| 1  |        40 |               20.82 | 2017-03-30 21:21:39 |
+----+-----------+---------------------+---------------------+
1 row in set (0.00 sec)
```

Fig. 2.4 Data inserted in the table SENSOR_WEATHER

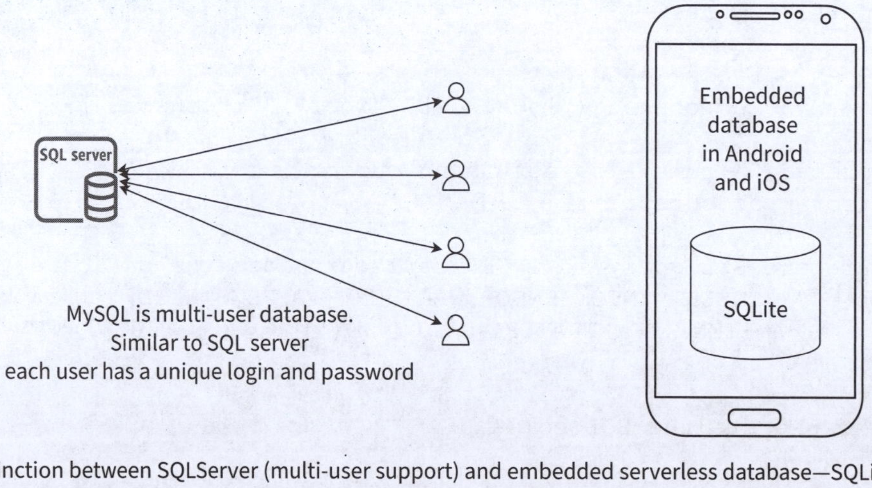

Fig. 2.5 Distinction between SQLServer (multi-user support) and embedded serverless database—SQLite

Creating a pseudo sensor for populating the database

Sometimes data scientists do not have access to actual sensor data or real data of the application. In such cases, pseudodata can be generated using random or known data patterns. The Python code (Listing 2.2) shown next uses the range function to generate temperature data points and inserts generated values in the sensor database. The range (20,40,5) function on line 4, populates the database table with values starting from 20 and increments by 5.

Listing 2.2 Inserting several records in the sensor database using Python MySQLdb API

```
01.  #!/usr/bin/python

02.  import MySQLdb
03.  import time

04.  sensor_value = range(20,40,5)

05.  # Open database connection
06.  db = MySQLdb.connect("localhost","root","","sensor" )

07.  # prepare a cursor object using cursor() method
08.  cursor = db.cursor()

09.  for n in sensor_value:

10.  # Prepare SQL query to INSERT a record into the database. The record is
11.  # value of n

12.    sql = """INSERT INTO SENSOR_WEATHER (REMOTE_ID, AMBIENT_TEMPERATURE)
13.        VALUES ('40','%d' )""" % (n)

14.    print (sql)
15.    time.sleep(1)

16.       try:
17.            # Execute the SQL command
             cursor.execute(sql)

18.          # Commit your changes in the database
             db.commit()

        except:
19.            # Rollback in case there is any error
               db.rollback()
20.     print ('error - database not updated')

21.  # disconnect from server
22.  db.close()
```

The last eight values of the table (ID 10–17) (Fig. 2.6) are inserted by the Python script mentioned in Listing 2.2. The script generates two sets of four values at an interval of 1s.

Querying data from a SQL database

Data assimilated in a database is useful if we can sort it using various criteria. Suppose we wish to know the time when the ambient temperature exceeds 25 degrees.

SQL simplifies the task of finding data from a database table through the use of the SELECT command. The SELECT command follows the syntax of the form:

```
SELECT column1, column2,columnN
FROM table_name
WHERE [condition]
```

We use the SELECT command in the next example to sort data where the ambient temperature is greater than 25 degrees (Fig. 2.7). The columns mentioned in the SELECT command are displayed as part of the result.

As discussed earlier, SQL supports Create, Read, Update, and Delete (CRUD) operations. Frequently used SQL commands to carry out CRUD operations are enumerated in the Table 2.2.

It is possible to transfer data stored in comma separated value (CSV) files to a relational SQL database. Please read section A.6 of the Python appendix which provides sample code to write a csv file to a SQLite database. There is also sample code which does the following using Python DB-API 2.0:

– Create a SQLite database
– Create table inside it
– Populate data table
– Retrieve data from the table using SQL query

ID	REMOTE_ID	AMBIENT_TEMPERATURE	CREATED
1	40	20.82	2017-03-30 21:21:39
2	40	25.82	2017-03-30 21:52:38
3	40	30.60	2017-03-30 22:11:54
4	40	28.44	2017-03-30 22:17:40
5	40	32.90	2017-03-30 22:28:41
6	40	32.90	2017-03-30 22:33:25
7	40	32.90	2017-03-30 22:33:34
8	40	35.00	2017-03-30 22:43:05
9	40	35.00	2017-03-30 22:44:32
10	40	20.00	2017-03-30 22:46:27
11	40	25.00	2017-03-30 22:46:28
12	40	30.00	2017-03-30 22:46:29
13	40	35.00	2017-03-30 22:46:30
14	40	20.00	2017-03-31 01:16:19
15	40	25.00	2017-03-31 01:16:20
16	40	30.00	2017-03-31 01:16:21
17	40	35.00	2017-03-31 01:16:22

17 rows in set (0.00 sec)

Fig. 2.6 View of the populated table generated using the code from Python code in Listing 2.2

```
mysql> SELECT AMBIENT_TEMPERATURE, ID, REMOTE_ID, CREATED
    -> FROM SENSOR_WEATHER
    -> WHERE AMBIENT_TEMPERATURE > 25;
+---------------------+----+-----------+---------------------+
| AMBIENT_TEMPERATURE | ID | REMOTE_ID | CREATED             |
+---------------------+----+-----------+---------------------+
|               25.82 |  2 |        40 | 2017-03-30 21:52:38 |
|               30.60 |  3 |        40 | 2017-03-30 22:11:54 |
|               28.44 |  4 |        40 | 2017-03-30 22:17:40 |
|               32.90 |  5 |        40 | 2017-03-30 22:28:41 |
|               32.90 |  6 |        40 | 2017-03-30 22:33:25 |
|               32.90 |  7 |        40 | 2017-03-30 22:33:34 |
|               35.00 |  8 |        40 | 2017-03-30 22:43:05 |
|               35.00 |  9 |        40 | 2017-03-30 22:44:32 |
|               30.00 | 12 |        40 | 2017-03-30 22:46:29 |
|               35.00 | 13 |        40 | 2017-03-30 22:46:30 |
|               30.00 | 16 |        40 | 2017-03-31 01:16:21 |
|               35.00 | 17 |        40 | 2017-03-31 01:16:22 |
+---------------------+----+-----------+---------------------+
12 rows in set (0.00 sec)
```

Fig. 2.7 Sorting data in a MySQL table using the SELECT command

Table 2.2 CRUD commands for SQL

Operation	SQL Command Example
Create	CREATE database, CREATE table, INSERT INTO
Read	SELECT * FROM <table name>;
Update	UPDATE table_name SET column1 = value1, column2 = value2, ... WHERE condition;
Delete	DELETE FROM table_name WHERE condition;

2.2.2.4 NoSQL databases

NoSQL databases are non-relational databases. NoSQL allows data to be represented in different formats. Some commonly used NoSQL data models include document, graph, key-value, and columnar. Check out this short introduction to NoSQL.[3] NoSQL databases are designed to handle semi-structured data that do not fit well into the traditional table-based relational database structure. A semi-structured data format (such as a JSON string) is stored in a NoSQL database. The position of the International Space Station (ISS) can be represented as a JSON object (see Fig. 2.8) and saved in a NoSQL database.

[3]What is NoSQL?, https://www.mongodb.com/nosql-explained (accessed 6 December 2022).

```
{"timestamp": 1489958241,
 "message": "success",
 "iss_position":
  {"latitude": "-41.8377",
   "longitude": "-148.3470"}
}
```


Fig. 2.8 Position of ISS as a JSON string. This string is obtained by querying ISS locator application programming interface (API)

Table 2.3 Terminology of SQL vis-à-vis the NoSQL database

SQL	MongoDB
Table	Collection
Row	Document
Column	Field
Primary Key	ObjectId
Index	Index
View	View
Nested Table or Object	Embedded Document
Array	Array

Table 2.4 NoSQL support for CRUD operations

Operation	NoSQL Command Example (MongoDB)
Create	db.collection.insertOne() db.collection.insertMany()
Read	db.collection.find()
Update	db.collection.updateOne() db.collection.updateMany() db.collection.replaceOne()
Delete	db.inventory.deleteMany({})

Take a look at Table 2.3 to understand the terminology of SQL vis-à-vis the NoSQL database. We use the MongoDB[4] commands to explain the working of a NoSQL database. Even though semi-structured data is different from tabular data, it still follows the same basic CRUD operations for transacting data to/from a database. Frequently used CRUD commands to transact data in a NoSQL environment are listed in Table 2.4.[5]

Let us understand two popular data types that can be stored using NoSQL format.

Document-oriented data: Document-oriented databases store each document as a separate entity, allowing for more flexible and efficient data storage and retrieval. NoSQL databases like MongoDB are commonly used to store document-oriented data, such as JSON or XML documents. This type of data is commonly used in content management systems, e-commerce applications, and social media platforms.

Time-series data: Time-series databases store data based on time stamps, allowing for efficient and fast analysis of data over time. Time-series databases are used in a variety of industries and

[4]MongoDB, https://www.mongodb.com/ (accessed 3 June 2023).

[5]MongoDB CRUD operations, https://www.mongodb.com/docs/manual/crud/ (accessed 4 June 2023).

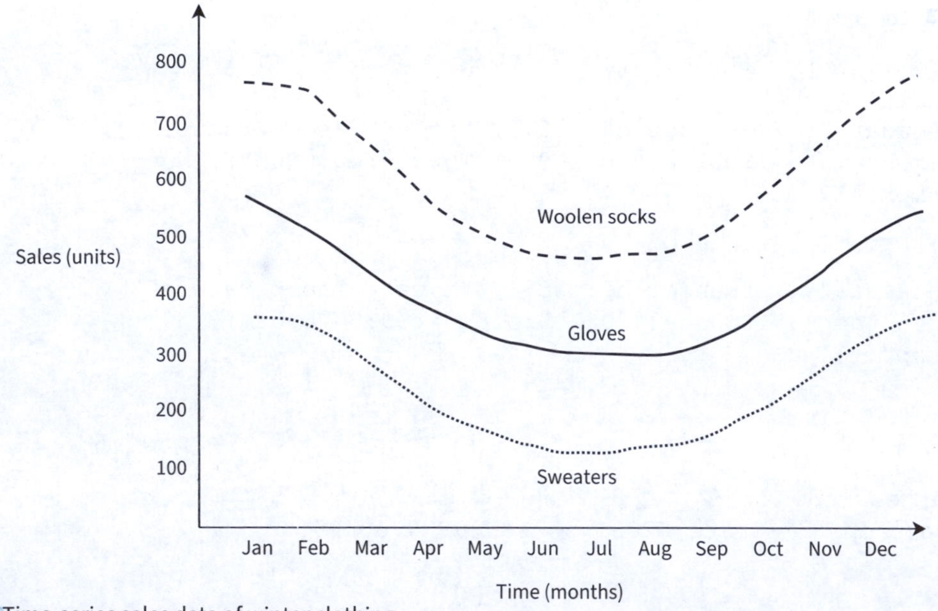

Fig. 2.9 Time-series sales data of winter clothing

businesses to store and analyze large amount of time-series data. Time-series data refers to data that is collected over time and is typically used to track trends and patterns. Examples of time-series data include stock prices, weather data, sensor data from IoT devices, and social media metrics. Time-series databases often come with built-in visualization tools that allow users to create charts and graphs. A simple time-series graph of sales data of woolen garments is shown in Fig. 2.9.

Industries that use time-series databases include finance, healthcare, energy, and manufacturing. In finance, time-series databases are used to store and analyze stock prices, while in healthcare, they are used to monitor patient data over time. In the energy sector, time-series databases are used to track energy usage and performance, while in manufacturing, they are used to monitor production processes and equipment performance. Listing 2.3 shows MongoDB

Listing 2.3 MongoDB[6] time-series API. (a) Create time-series collection. (b) Insert measurements into time-series collection. (c) Query time-series collection database

```
db.createCollection(
  "weather",
    {
      timeseries: {
        timeField: "timestamp",
        metaField: "metadata",
        granularity: "hours"
      }
    }
  )
```

(a)

(*Continued*)

[6]Create and Query time-series using MongoDB, https://www.mongodb.com/docs/manual/core/timeseries/timeseries-procedures/ (accessed on 7 June 2023).

Listing 2.3 *(Continued)*

```
db.weather.insertMany( [
  {
    "metadata": { "sensorId": 5578, "type": "temperature" },
    "timestamp": ISODate("2021-05-18T00:00:00.000Z"),
    "temp": 12
  },
  {
    "metadata": { "sensorId": 5578, "type": "temperature" },
    "timestamp": ISODate("2021-05-18T04:00:00.000Z"),
    "temp": 11
  }
])
```

(b)

```
db.weather.findOne({
  "timestamp": ISODate("2021-05-18T00:00:00.000Z")
})
```

(c)

time-series APIs for creating a database called weather, inserting records into the database and querying the database for temperature data. The APIs for time series database of MongoDB are similar to the NoSQL APIs. Shortly, we will discuss how SQL can also be used to work with a time-series database.

2.2.2.5 Storing unstructured binary data

Unstructured data such as images, video, Web hosting, storage for backup data is stored as binary large object or blob. In a cloud-computing environment, these objects are stored in buckets and are accessible over the Internet. The AWS Simple Storage Service-S3[7] is a Web-based database service. The pseudo code in Listing 2.4 demonstrates how binary data is uploaded to an AWS-S3 database using the Python environment.[8] We will discuss more about Python APIs in the chapter on cloud services.

Listing 2.4 Uploading binary data to a cloud database

```
import boto3

# Create an S3 client
s3 = boto3.client('s3')

filename = 'image.jpg'
bucket_name = 'my-bucket'

# Upload the given file
s3.upload_file(filename, bucket_name, filename)
```

[7]Amazon S3, https://aws.amazon.com/s3/ (accessed on 7 June 2023).

2.3 | Data Generation Rate and Processing Time (Velocity)

Data is generated at different rates. A sensor in a factory may generate hundreds of samples every second, while the customer feedback data on a retail Website may be created every 10 minutes. If we go back and take a look at the material and data diagram we have introduced in Chapter 1, there is one aspect worth noticing. Remember, we mentioned that all data are not useful. Most data is repetitive and routine. It does not make sense to transfer repetitive and routine data to a central location for storage or analysis. As a result, there are edge computing nodes (shown as dotted boxes in Fig. 2.10) that locally store and process data. This setup is referred to as distributed storage and processing. Analytics extract the gist from locally produced data and send it to the cloud. Distributed storage can easily deal with data generated at high rates.

Let us consider an example for local data storage and processing. Suppose a company wishes to find out footfalls in a retail store. It uses cameras to monitor people and AI to count people in camera frames. Instead of sending a video stream to a central database, it sends data packets containing the number of people counted every hour during a business day. This is much more efficient. Big data for a modern enterprise can reside at multiple places. It can be located on on-premise data centers, cloud storage, or may be split between on-premise and cloud.

To summarize, these are some reasons for locally storing and processing most data.

- Less requirement of internet bandwidth
- Privacy of data
- Data gets analyzed at the source and action is taken locally

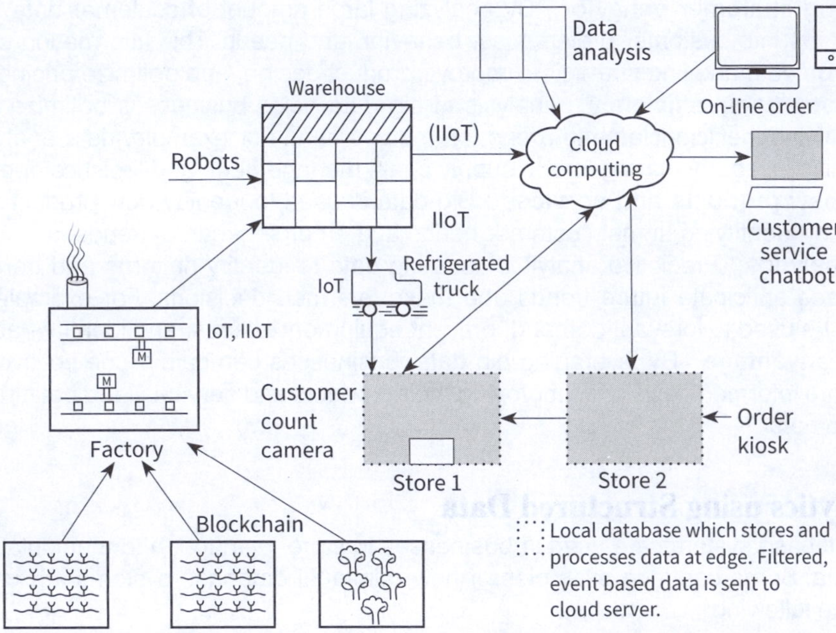

Fig. 2.10 Big data for modern enterprise

[8]'Representational State Transfer', *Wikipedia*, 2004, available at https://en.wikipedia.org/wiki/Representational_state_transfer (accessed on 6 December 2022).

Table 2.5 Data analytics and response to different types of data

Data Source	Velocity (Data Rate)	Data Analytics	Response (Turnaround Time)
Sensor connected to a critical machine	High	Check for Anomaly.	Attend immediately if anomaly detected
Video stream to assure worker safety	High	Safety detection using AI	React quickly to get worker out of harm's way
Customer feedback on product	Low (text)	Determine severity of complaint	Respond within 24 hours. For human well being related cases, respond at the earliest.

There is another aspect to data. It has to do with the urgency of its processing. Some data can be unattended for days, while some data require immediate attention. The urgency or importance of data does not necessarily have to be tied to its velocity. But it is definitely a challenge to deal with high-speed important data. Table 2.5 provides some examples of data sources and their expected reaction times.

2.4 | Analytics Using Big Data

At the start of this chapter, we talked about data-driven decision-making. Let us now understand how big data enables data-driven decision-making. To reiterate, big data refers to the large and complex data sets that businesses generate and collect from various sources, such as customer transactions, social media, sensors, and other digital channels. Big data is analyzed to gain valuable insights and informed business decisions. Here are some ways big data analytics is useful for businesses:

Understanding customer behavior By analyzing large amount of customer data, businesses can gain insights into customer preferences, behavior, and needs. This information can be used to develop targeted marketing strategies, improve product design, and optimize pricing strategies.
Improving operational efficiency Analysis of big data helps businesses optimize their operations by identifying inefficiencies and areas for improvement. For example, data analytics can be used to optimize inventory management, supply chain management, and logistics operations.
Developing new products and services Big data is used to identify new product and service opportunities by identifying unmet customer needs and emerging market trends.
Predictive analytics Predictive analytics uses big data to identify patterns and trends that can help businesses anticipate future trends and make informed decisions. For example, predictive analytics can be used to forecast demand, prevent equipment failures, and identify fraud.
Competitive advantage By leveraging big data, businesses can gain a competitive advantage by making more informed decisions, improving their products and services, and better understanding their customers.

2.4.1 Analytics using Structured Data

Relational database systems are used in businesses to store, manage, and manipulate tabular or structured data. Some common examples of how relational database systems are used in businesses are the following:

Customer Relationship Management (CRM) CRM systems use relational databases to store customer data, including contact information, transaction history, and customer interactions. This information is used to develop targeted marketing campaigns, provide personalized customer service, and analyze customer behavior.
Human Resources (HR) HR departments utilize relational databases to manage employee information, including personal information, employment history, and performance evaluations.

Database is used to manage employee benefits, track training and development, and perform performance analysis.

Inventory Management Relational databases are very useful in managing inventory, stock levels, orders, and shipments. SQL queries about inventory levels helps track product availability, and manage supply chain logistics.

Finance and Accounting Finance and accounting departments use relational databases to manage financial data, including transaction history, budgets, and financial statements. Information from database is used to perform financial analysis, forecast revenue, and monitor expenses.

e-Commerce Online retailers use relational databases to manage product data, orders, and customer information. SQL queries are used to track inventory levels, process orders, and personalize the online shopping experience.

Some frequently used SQL queries to retrieve or write data from a relational database that holds customer-related data are enumerated in Listing 2.5. SQL queries can be embedded as part of Python DB-API to interact with relational databases such as MySQL and SQLite.

Listing 2.5 Commonly used SQL commands for basic analytics. Example follows the command description

```
SELECT: Retrieve data from a database table.
Example:
SELECT * FROM customers;

WHERE: Filter data based on a condition.
Example:
SELECT * FROM customers WHERE age > 30;

INSERT: Insert data into a database table.
Example:
INSERT INTO customers (name, age, email) VALUES ('Raj Kumar', 35,
'raj.kumar@example.com');

UPDATE: Update data in a database table.
Example:
UPDATE customers SET age = 36 WHERE name = 'Raj Kumar';

DELETE: Delete data from a database table.
Example:
DELETE FROM customers WHERE age < 18;

JOIN: Combine data from two or more tables based on a related column.
Example:
SELECT orders.order_id, customers.name, orders.order_date
FROM orders
JOIN customers
ON orders.customer_id = customers.customer_id;

GROUP BY: Group data based on a specific column.
Example:
SELECT category, COUNT(*) as count FROM products GROUP BY category;
```

(Continued)

Listing 2.5 *(Continued)*

```
ORDER BY: Sort data based on a specific column.
Example:
SELECT * FROM customers ORDER BY name ASC;

LIMIT: Limit the number of rows returned by a query.
For example:
SELECT * FROM customers LIMIT 10;

HAVING: Filter data based on a condition after grouping.
Example:
SELECT category, AVG(price) as avg_price
FROM products
GROUP BY category
HAVING AVG(price) > 50;
```

2.4.2 Data Analytics for NoSQL Database

NoSQL databases are designed to store semi-structured data and do not follow the traditional tabular structure of relational databases. As a result, NoSQL queries are different from SQL queries. Instead of using a structured query language like SQL, NoSQL databases use various APIs for querying data.

The examples presented in Listing 2.6 provide basic syntax to query a NoSQL database. There are sample databases available on the internet,[9] which you can experiment with. These queries are

Listing 2.6 Examples of NoSQL queries using MongoDB Commands. The query is shown in bold.

```
Retrieve data from a collection:
db.orders.find({});
NoSQL query to retrieve all data from the "orders" collection in a
MongoDB database.

Filtering data using the $match:
db.orders.aggregate([
   { $match: { order_date: { $gte: ISODate("2022-01-01"), $lte:
ISODate("2022-12-31") } } }
]);
NoSQL query to filter data from the "orders" collection in a MongoDB
database where the order date is between January 1, 2022, and December
31, 2022.

Aggregating data using the $group operator:
db.products.aggregate([
   { $group: { _id: "$category", total_sales: { $sum: "$sales" } } }
```

[9]Sample Datasets, MongoDB, https://www.mongodb.com/docs/atlas/sample-data/ (accessed on 10 June 2023).

Listing 2.6 *(Continued)*

```
]);
In this case, the NoSQL query groups data from the "products" collection
in a MongoDB database by category and calculates the total sales for
each category.

Joining data using the $lookup:
db.customers.aggregate([
   { $lookup: { from: "orders", localField: "id", foreignField:
"customer_id", as: "orders" } }
]);
For this example, NoSQL query joins data from the "customers" and
"orders" collections in a MongoDB database based on the customer ID
and returns all customers with their associated orders.

Updating data in a collection:
db.customers.updateOne({ id: 1 }, { $set: { address: "123 Main Street" }
});
This NoSQL query updates the address of the customer with ID 1 in the
"customers" collection in a MongoDB database.
```

the stepping stones for complex data analytics. Some commonly used MongoDB commands are enumerated in Table 2.6.

By installing the PyMongo package, you can interact with a NoSQL (MongoDB) database from Python. To do so, you would have to connect with the MongoDB server ('mongodb://localhost:27017/') and then provide details of the database name and collection. Once you connect to a MongoDB database, you can insert documents into a collection, and query all documents in the collection.

A time-series database[10] (TSDB) is a type of database that is optimized for storing and retrieving time-stamped data. Some frequently used queries for working with TSDBs are mentioned in Listing 2.7. These queries help extract items of interest from the database.

Table 2.6 Frequently used NoSQL queries using MongoDB commands

Command	Description
Find	Searches for data in a NoSQL database
Update	Updates data in a NoSQL database
Delete	Deletes data from a NoSQL database
Aggregate	Performs aggregation operations like counting, summing, grouping, etc. on the data in a NoSQL database

[10]InfluxDB (Time-series database), https://www.influxdata.com/ (accessed on 4 June 2023).

Listing 2.7 Generic SQL queries for a time-series database (TSDB)

```
Inserting data: Insert data into a TSDB.
Example query:
INSERT INTO <table_name> (timestamp, value) VALUES (<timestamp>, <value>);

Querying data for a time range: Retrieve data for a specific time
range.
Example query:
SELECT * FROM <table_name> WHERE timestamp >= <start_time> AND time-
stamp <= <end_time>;

Aggregating data: Aggregate data over a certain time period.
Example query:
SELECT AVG(value) FROM <table_name> WHERE timestamp >= <start_time>
AND timestamp <= <end_time> GROUP BY time(<time_period>);

Interpolating missing data: Fill in missing data in a time series.
Example query:
SELECT time, IFNULL(value, LAG(value) OVER (ORDER BY time)) as value
FROM <table_name>;

Creating a time bucket: Time bucket to group data into regular intervals.
Example query:
SELECT time_bucket(<interval>, timestamp) AS time_bucket, COUNT(*)
FROM <table_name> GROUP BY time_bucket;

Filtering data by tags: Filter data by tags associated with it, the
following query can be used:
SELECT * FROM <table_name> WHERE <tag_name> = '<tag_value>';
```

2.5 | Working with Data and Application Programming Interfaces

An application programming interface (API) allows different software systems to interact and exchange data with each other; making it easier to develop new applications and services.

To explain APIs, it is helpful to use an analogy. Think of an API as a waiter in a restaurant. Just as a waiter takes orders from customers and communicates them to the kitchen, an API takes requests from software applications and communicates them to other systems. The API acts as a middleperson, providing a standard interface for different applications to communicate with each other, regardless of the programming language or platform used.

APIs can be used in a variety of ways, such as integrating with third-party services, enabling mobile app development, automating business processes, and more. By providing an easy way for different applications to interact to each other, APIs help businesses streamline their operations, improve customer experiences, and drive innovation. Many APIs connect to databases to provide requested information. Some popular APIs used in the tech industry are mentioned in Table 2.7.

Table 2.7 APIs used to connect with common web services

API Type	Description
Twitter API	Obtain Twitter's data and features, such as retrieving tweets or sending tweets.
Facebook API	Access Facebook's data and features, such as retrieving user information or posting on a user's behalf.
YouTube API	Integrate YouTube videos and features into their applications and Websites.
Amazon Web Services (AWS) API	Retrieve data on AWS services and resources, such as EC2 instances or S3 buckets.
Stripe API	Integrate payment processing into their applications and Websites.
Spotify API	Get access to Spotify's music data and features, such as retrieving playlists or searching for tracks.
Twilio API	Integrate SMS and voice messaging into their applications and Websites.
GitHub API	Get access to GitHub's data and features, such as retrieving repository information or creating issues.

2.5.1 Application Programming Interface (API) and JSON

Web service APIs that adhere to the *representational state transfer* REST architectural constraints are called RESTful APIs. HTTP-based RESTful APIs are defined with the following structure.

1. Base URL, such as http://api.example.com/resources/
2. An Internet media type that defines the state transition data elements. The current representation tells the client how to compose requests for transitions to all the next available application states.
3. Standard HTTP methods (OPTIONS, GET, PUT, POST, and DELETE).

JavaScript Object Notation or JSON is a lightweight data-interchange format. This format is easy for humans to read and write. It is also easy for machines to parse and generate. NoSQL databases are best suited to store and query JSON data. A JSON structure starts and ends with curly brackets '{' and '}'. The data in the form of a string value pair is accommodated within these curly brackets. String and value are separated by a colon ':'. More than one string value pairs are separated by a comma ','.

An example of the JSON string-value pair data structure is seen here.

```
{
"firstName": "Rajesh",
"lastName": "Kumar",
"age": 25,
"email":"Rajesh@kumar.com"
}
```

2.5.2 API and REST API

As mentioned earlier, API refers to a set of protocols or functions that work as tools to access and use the features of a software. As an example, consider the access of a database that records and maintains the position of the International Space Station (ISS). If someone wishes to know the current position of the ISS, there is an API just for this purpose. The API returns the current latitude and longitude of the ISS along with the Unix timestamp for the time of the location. This unsecure API has no inputs. The API can be accessed through the following Website: http://api.open-notify.org/iss-now.json

The JSON output from the API is as follows:


```
{"timestamp": 1489958241,
 "message": "success",
 "iss_position":
  {"latitude": "-41.8377",
   "longitude": "-148.3470"}
}
```


We have a Python program in Listing 2.8 that accesses this API every 2 seconds. The code uses the *requests* module to access the ISS location API and store the JSON content in a file (mentioned in the code as LatLonLog.txt). The content of the saved file is seen in Table 2.8.

Experiment with the code in Listing 2.8 and also understand the following processes from the code:

- How a text file gets created in the append mode
- How a JSON string gets parsed and data of interest is extracted and written to a file

Listing 2.8 API request to obtain position of International Space Station (ISS)

```
import requests
from time import sleep

url = "http://api.open-notify.org/iss-now.json"

f = open ("LatLonLog.txt", "a")

f.write ("Timestamp"+ "\t"+ "Longitude" + "\t" + "Latitude" + "\n")

for i in range (1,10):
    r = requests.get(url)
    j = r.json()

    time = j['timestamp']
    lon = j['iss_position']['longitude']
    lat = j['iss_position']['latitude']
    f.write (str(time) + "\t" + str(lon) + "\t" + str(lat)+"\n")
    sleep(2)

f.close()
```

Table 2.8 Content of LatLonLog.txt file as captured by the Python program

Timestamp	Longitude	Latitude
1524084499	−104.4489	51.1840
1524084501	−104.2520	51.1659
1524084503	−104.0553	51.1475
1524084505	−103.8586	51.1287
1524084507	−103.6131	51.1047

Table 2.8 *(Continued)*

Timestamp	Longitude	Latitude
1524084509	−103.4169	51.0851
1524084511	−103.2209	51.0651
1524084513	−103.0250	51.0448
1524084515	−102.8293	51.0242

Listing 2.9 Sample Python code to demonstrate SQLite database access using Flask server and web API

```
01.  from flask import Flask, jsonify
02.  import sqlite3

03.  app = Flask(__name__)

04.  @app.route('/api/v1/sensor/temperature /all', methods=['GET'])
05.  def api_all():
06.        conn = sqlite3.connect('sensor_database.db')
07.        # Create a cursor object
08.        cursor = conn.cursor()
09.        all_nodes = cursor.execute('SELECT * FROM temperature;').
           fetchall()
10.        return jsonify(all_nodes)

11.  if __name__ == '__main__':
12.       app.run(debug=True)
```

We will now consider a simple example using Listing 2.9 to explain how a database can be queried using a web API. Let us assume we have an SQLite database (sensor_database) that has a table (temperature) that contains the temperature recorded by different sensor nodes. If we wish to access the temperature recorded by all nodes through a web server interface, we use an API route (/api/v1/sensor/temperature/all). When the Flask web server receives this API request (line 4), it calls function api_all (line 5) that connects to a database (line 6) and then executes a SQL query (line 9) to obtain temperature data. The output from this query contains all records from the temperature table, which is converted to JSON format (line 10) and returned to the user who sent the API request.

2.5.3 Accessing Weather Data using APIs

The weather data Website[11] provides access to a database that has data on weather conditions across the world (Fig. 2.11). A user sends an API request[12] using a predefined syntax to access the database. Python code in Listing 2.10 is used to request weather conditions of Bangaluru. The API response is a JSON file, mentioned in Listing 2.11. Each API request is mapped to either a SQL or a NoSQL query that is passed on to the database.

[11]Free weather API, https://open-meteo.com/ (accessed 10 June 2023).

[12]API documentation, https://open-meteo.com/en/docs (accessed 10 June 2023).

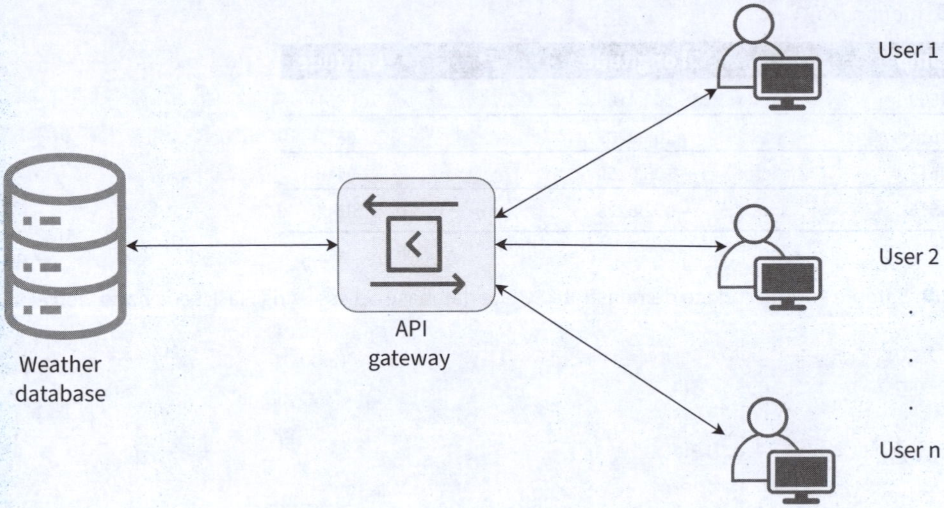

Fig. 2.11 Set-up of a weather database, accessible by multiple users through an API gateway

Listing 2.10 Weather information API from open-meteo.com

```
import requests
import json

#Bangaluru latitude= 12.97N and Longitude:77.59E

r = requests.get('https://api.open-
meteo.com/v1/forecast?latitude=12.97&longitude=77.59&current_
weather =
    true&hourly=temperature_2m,relativehumidity_2m,windspeed_10m')
parsed = json.loads(r.text)
print (json.dumps(parsed, indent=4))
print ('Status code', r.status_code)
```

Listing 2.11 JSON output when API request from Listing 2.9 is executed


```
{
   "latitude": 13.0,
   "longitude": 77.625,
   "generationtime_ms": 0.20301342010498047,
   "utc_offset_seconds": 0,
   "timezone": "GMT",
   "timezone_abbreviation": "GMT",
   "elevation": 914.0,
   "current_weather": {
      "temperature": 25.8,
      "windspeed": 13.5,
```

Listing 2.11 *(Continued)*

```
      "winddirection": 261.0,
      "weathercode": 3,
      "is_day": 1,
      "time": "2023-06-08T04:00"
   },
```

Many businesses have data on operations, inventory, and payroll stored in databases. Intranet- or Internet-based APIs provide access to relevant information from the database.

2.6 | Conclusion

In this chapter we talked about how data is created and analyzed in large volumes to facilitate modern business operations. We discussed three important aspects of data—volume, variety, and velocity. Businesses that understand and effectively use data are more likely to be successful. Building on the idea of data analytics, we presented frequently used SQL, NoSQL, and time-series database queries. When accessing a database through the internet, queries are formed by parsing data contained in the API.

Exercises

A. State True/False

1. Image data is structured data.
2. Customer feedback written as a paragraph is unstructured data.
3. Edge storage and processing of data prevents transfer of large volumes of data to a central location for storage and processing.

B. Short-answer Questions

1. If the process of creating a product-identification number takes 500 bytes (100 bytes from 5 production stages), calculate data produced in 30 days if 20 products are produced every hour in the factory.
2. List the data types needed to store patient information and test reports in a hospital computer.
3. Which SQL command is used to query data from a relational database table?
4. List different commands for updating a NoSQL database collection.
5. Give examples of data that needs to be stored in a time series database.
6. Mention a relational database for a single-user/embedded application.
7. What type of database is better suited for data in JSON format? Structured or unstructured?

C. Long-answer Questions

1. Give an example of a use case where it is beneficial to locally store and process data. Also give an example of a use case where it is a necessity to bring data to a central repository.
2. Research and list examples of databases to store structured, semi-structured, and unstructured data.
3. Consider a large business that you understand well. Create a database schema (table names, fields, data types, and the relationships between these entities) for capturing important information about the business—such as employee data, inventory, financial information and information about vendors.

4. An employee at a retail store needs to find out from the warehouse database if a certain shirt in a certain size is available. Assume the warehouse relational database consists of a table called *shirts*. The table has three columns—type, size, and quantity. Write an SQL query to find out if the desired shirt is available in the warehouse.
5. A retail store has a SQL database containing the expiry dates of perishable edible items. Create a SQL query that will inform the store manager of products that are reaching their expiry dates in a month. The manager can then put these items on sale.

D. Explore and Experiment

1. Install Sqlite3 tools[13] on your desktop computer and create databases, table and query them using SQL commands.
2. Set up a NoSQL database on your computer and save weather data to it. Acquire weather data using open-meteo.com APIs.
3. Practice NoSQL queries using online MongoDB playground.[14] Access the template multiple collections, which provides two collections to experiment with.
4. The following three prompts experiment with generating SQL tables for a retail store (Fig. 2.12); sample NoSQL employee data (Fig. 2.13) and a sample sales spreadsheet for a supermarket chain (Fig. 2.14). Generative AI is also able to form SQL/NoSQL queries; something you can try out on your own!

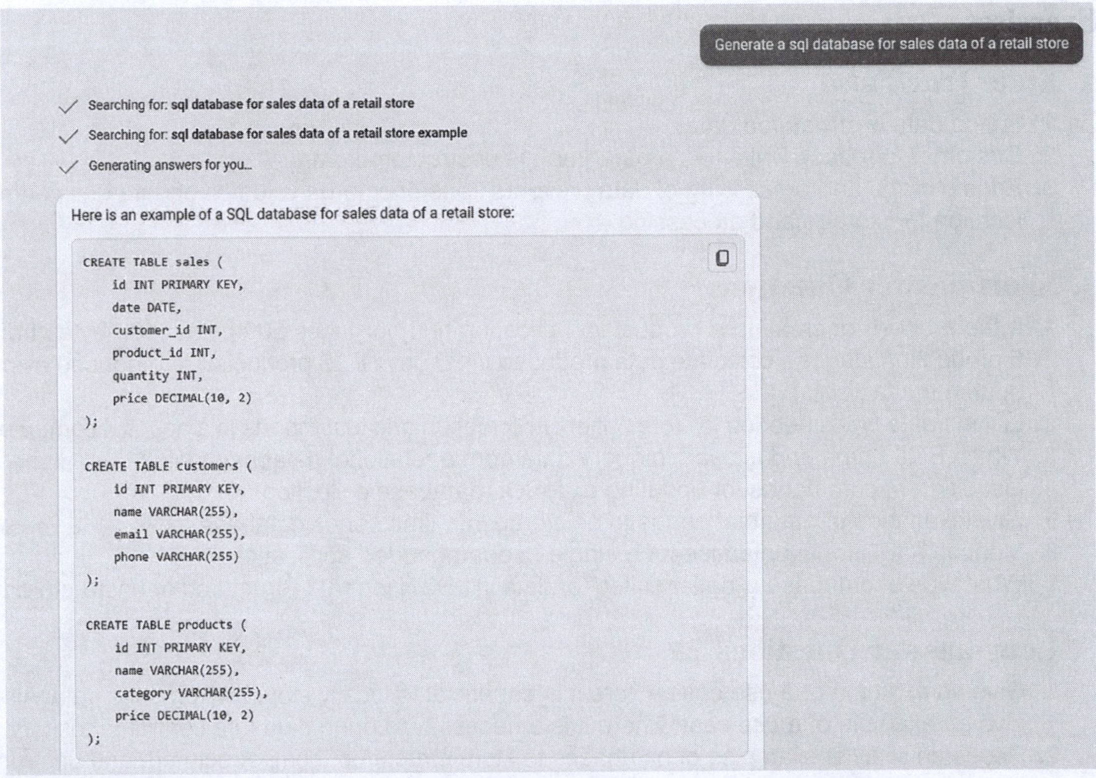

Fig. 2.12 Prompt for creating SQL database, consisting of three tables—sales, customers, and products

[13]Sqlite Tutorial, https://www.sqlitetutorial.net/download-install-sqlite/ (accessed 8 June 2023).
[14]MongoDB playground, https://mongoplayground.net/ (accessed 10 June 2023).

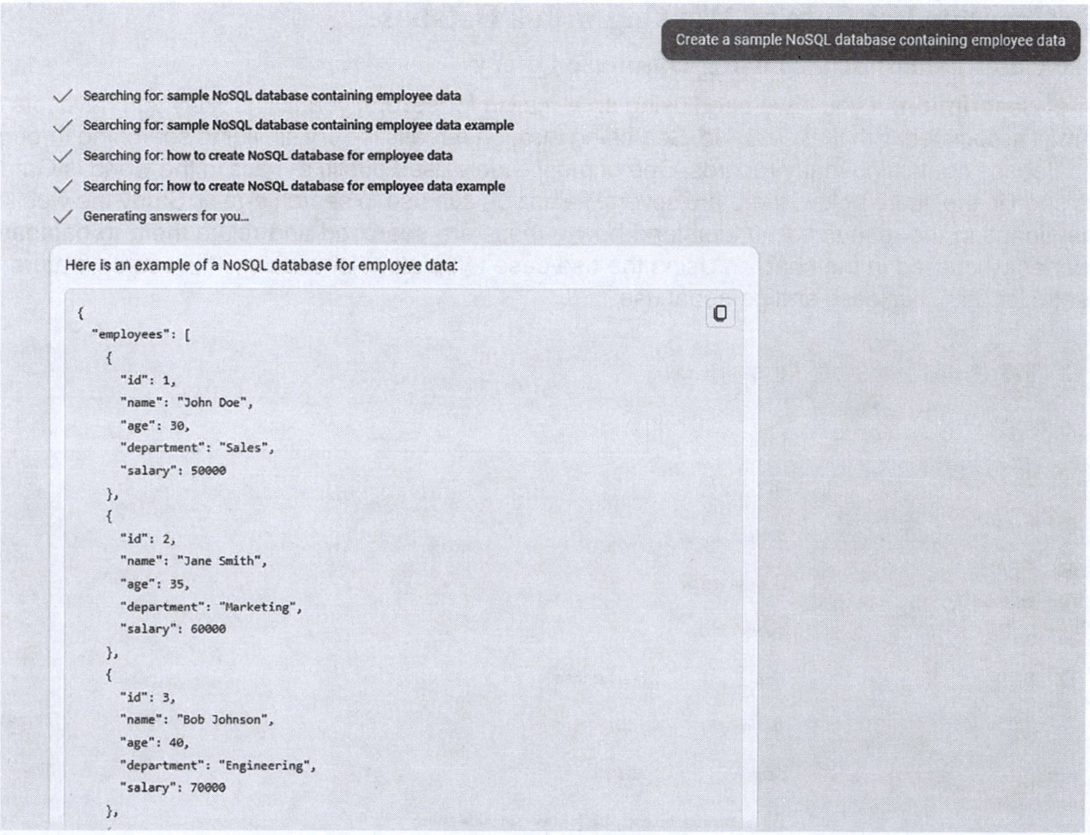

Fig. 2.13 Generative AI created NoSQL sample database consisting of employee data

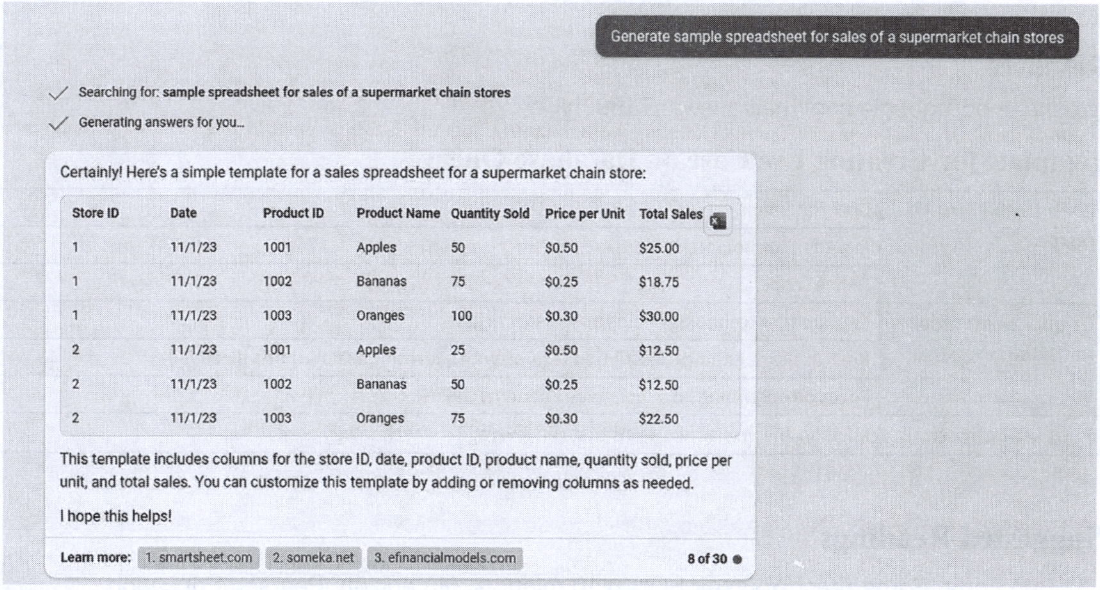

Store ID	Date	Product ID	Product Name	Quantity Sold	Price per Unit	Total Sales
1	11/1/23	1001	Apples	50	$0.50	$25.00
1	11/1/23	1002	Bananas	75	$0.25	$18.75
1	11/1/23	1003	Oranges	100	$0.30	$30.00
2	11/1/23	1001	Apples	25	$0.50	$12.50
2	11/1/23	1002	Bananas	50	$0.25	$12.50
2	11/1/23	1003	Oranges	75	$0.30	$22.50

Fig. 2.14 Sample downloadable sales spreadsheet for a supermarket chain

E. Generate Use Case on Working with a Database

Use Case: E-mail Search using Database Query

Brief description: If you have been using an e-mail id for several years, it is likely you have lots of e-mail associated with that e-mail id. Searching through e-mails is very similar to searching through a database containing many records. One of most widely used public e-mails in the world is Gmail. As seen in the figure below, there are several fields you can use to search e-mail. Study the weblink mentioned in the resource to understand how e-mails are searched and relate them to database queries discussed in the chapter. Using the use case template, discuss why this search feature is useful for both: business and personal use.

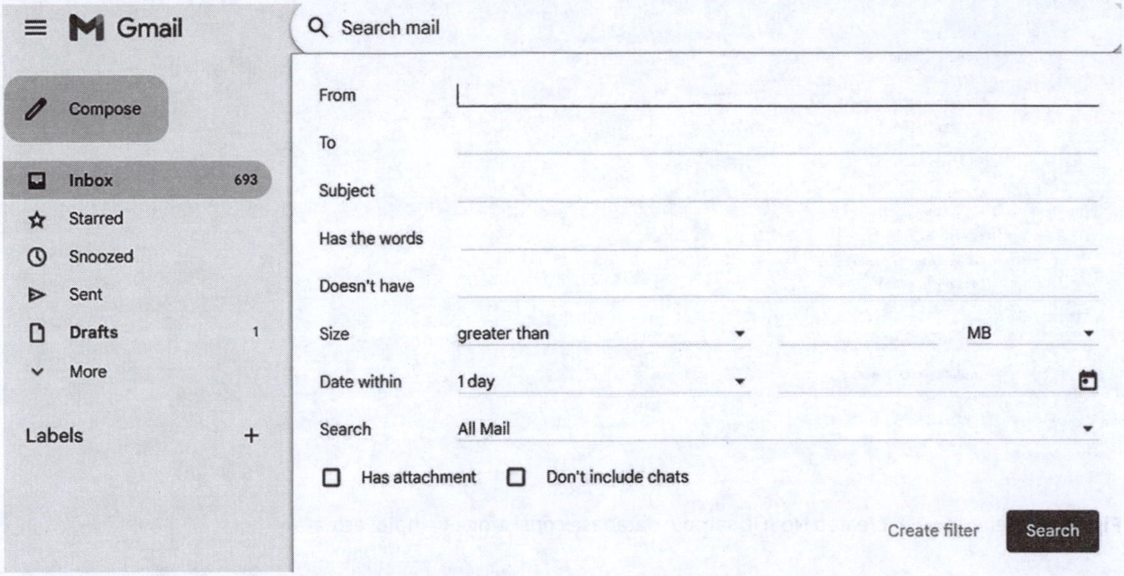

Resource

https://support.google.com/mail/answer/7190?hl=en

Template for Creating Use Case on Database Query

Define goal and purpose	Goal statement
	Identify stakeholders
	Define scope
Details to include in use case	Capture how technology helps business process
	Keep use case findings description textual, with a few simple flowcharts if needed
	Focus on describing how technology benefits the use case
Future applications	Mention any new applications that can leverage the technology used

Suggested Readings

1. Ben Forta, Sams Teach Yourself SQL in 10 minutes, 5th edition, Pearson Education.
2. Dan Sullivan, NoSQL for Mere Mortals, Addison-Wesley Professional.

CHAPTER 3

Internet of Things

CHAPTER OUTLINE

LEARNING OBJECTIVES

After reading this chapter, you will be able to:

- identify the three building blocks of IoT—thing or edge device, communication network, and cloud-based data aggregator/analyzer
- understand use of data acquired from IoT devices
- apply IoT technology to business use cases/applications

Effective Management Using Internet of Things

Businesses and governments need to monitor processes and systems across different regions. For example, a government needs to know the state of food grains stored in different silos across the country. If the grains are rotting or getting eaten by rodents; timely action can help cut down losses. IoT makes this feasible by monitoring each silo and transmitting its data to a central server.

3.1 | Overview of Internet of Things

The landscape of IoT is understood by looking at the different areas it impacts. IoT is used to monitor and optimize resource utilization in cities, buildings, transport, health, energy, living, and in many more areas. Present-day IoT technology is an amalgamation of sensors, actuators, communication,

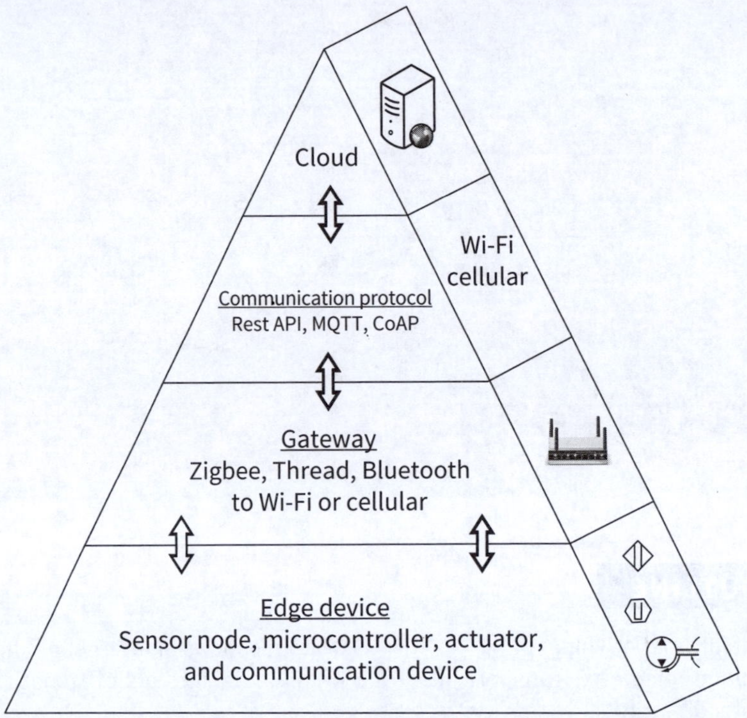

Fig. 3.1 IoT pyramid

Note: REST API, Representational State Transfer Application Program Interface; CoAP, Constrained Application Protocol; MQTT, Message Queuing Telemetry Transport; IoT, Internet of Things.

and computing technologies. For several years, these technologies were independent domains. Information and communication technologies first came together as ICT, and now the edge devices have joined to form the concept of IoT.[1]

The resources needed for a typical IoT application can be viewed from the perspective of a pyramid (Fig. 3.1). Different layers of pyramid transfer data from edge devices to the central cloud computer, which is a data aggregator. Let us break down the functionality of each layer of the IoT pyramid. We start with the bottom most layer which consists of edge devices. These devices can be located inside a factory in the form of a surveillance camera or as sensors mounted on transport vehicles. Numerous edge devices connect to a gateway or a hub. The hub or gateway can have local intelligence to control the edge devices or it may simply collate and forward the information to the cloud computer.

Based on the location of the edge device, different communication mediums are used to transmit information from the gateway to the cloud. If the gateway device is located in an area where WiFi is available, the gateway module transmits the data through WiFi.

Let us dive a little deeper to understand the three building blocks of IoT. The IoT represents the synergy between the following:

1. Things or devices
2. Communication networks (WiFi, Zigbee, LoRa, cellular)
3. Cloud-based computing

[1]The Industrial Internet of Things (IIoT) is similar to IoT in many ways. Most of the discussion is applicable to both IoT and IIoT.

3.1.1 Thing/Edge Device

The thing or edge device can be a sensor, actuator, or both. Most edge devices are based on small computers or microcontrollers and are capable of doing some preliminary processing before transmitting information to the next step of the IoT pyramid. To become a part of an IoT system, the edge device must be registered before the device can be used. There is a registry on the cloud computer which holds the information about each thing or device. Each device is identified with the help of custom attributes which are submitted at the time of registration. Devices are also associated with certificates for secure communication and client identities.

3.1.2 Device Gateway

The device gateway provides connectivity for the edge device to the cloud computer. It can be thought of as an edge device data aggregator and transmitter. It collates data from multiple edge devices and then forwards it to the cloud computer, using one of several protocols. A Bluetooth gateway collects data from Bluetooth devices and transmits the information to the Internet. Common protocols include the Hypertext Transfer Protocol (HTTP) using Representational State Transfer (REST), Message Queuing Telemetry Transport (MQTT) protocol, and the Constrained Application Protocol (CoAP).

3.1.3 Cloud Computing and IoT

The cloud computer is the data aggregation point for device data. It ingests data coming from hundreds, thousands, or millions of things/devices and stores them in a database. Machine learning or AI algorithms then work on the obtained data to extract meaningful trends and insights. IoT services offered by the cloud include a structured query language (SQL) based rules engine to extract data from device message payloads.

3.1.4 Examples of IoT Systems

Before we move further, let us consolidate our understanding of IoT components by a real-world example. Some of you may be aware about Apple AirTags.[2] If you do not know, please visit the link mentioned in the footnote.[3] An AirTag is a Bluetooth-based edge device, which is provisioned by pairing with the owner's iPhone. The AirTag sends a secure message to every iPhone it comes across. Each iPhone thus acts as a gateway device. Whenever an iPhone receives a secure message from an AirTag, it sends the AirTag's location to a Website (on a cloud computer) accessible by Find My app.[4] See Fig. 3.2 to visualize the communication between AirTag, iPhone, and cloud application.

Now assume you left your briefcase under a table (with an AirTag) at a coffee shop. Someone with an iPhone happens to walk by the table. The AirTag would securely communicate with the iPhone and update its location on the cloud. When you start searching for your briefcase and go to your iPhone's Find My app, you would see the briefcase showing up at the coffee shop location. In this example, all three components of an IoT system worked together to help locate a missing item.

Another IoT ecosystem that is becoming popular is LoRaWAN. LoRaWAN (Long Range Wide Area Network) is a Low Power Wide Area Network (LPWAN) protocol designed to connect devices over long ranges with low power consumption. It enables devices to send small data packets wirelessly over long distances, typically ranging from a few kilometers in urban areas to tens of kilometers in rural areas.

The LoRaWAN protocol operates in the license-free spectrum bands of different countries; which means that anyone can use the protocol without the need for a license. LoRaWAN operates in

[2]This example is not meant to promote Apple products. It is purely to map functionality of IoT components with a simple use case.
[3]Apple AirTags. https://www.apple.com/airtag/ (accessed 8 November 2022).
[4]Find My app. https://apps.apple.com/us/app/find-my/id1514844621 (accessed 8 November 2022).

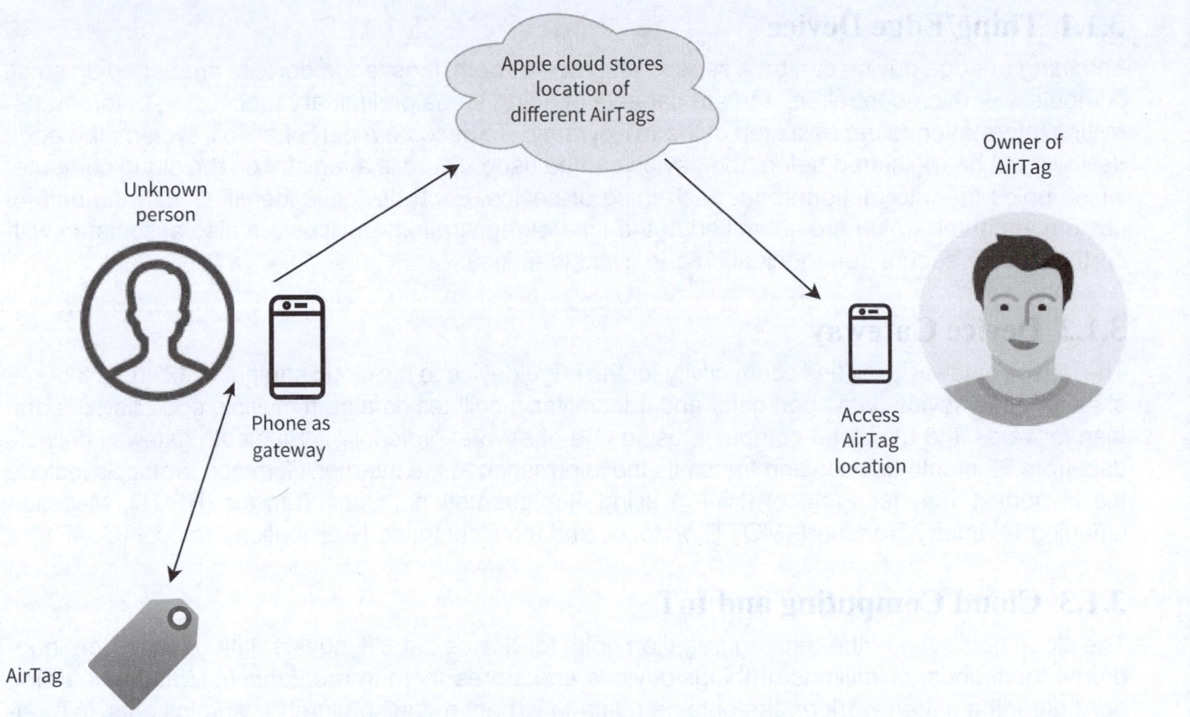

Fig. 3.2 Example of AirTag[5] to explain working of IoT system components

three different frequency bands: 433 MHz, 868 MHz, and 915 MHz. The choice of frequency band depends on the country or region where the network is being deployed.

Just like the IoT framework we discussed earlier, the LoRaWAN network architecture consists of three main components: end devices, gateways, and cloud servers (Fig. 3.3). A LoRaWAN device connects to a LoRaWAN gateway and the gateway connects the device to a larger server which Web APIs can access. End or edge devices are the devices that collect data and send it to the

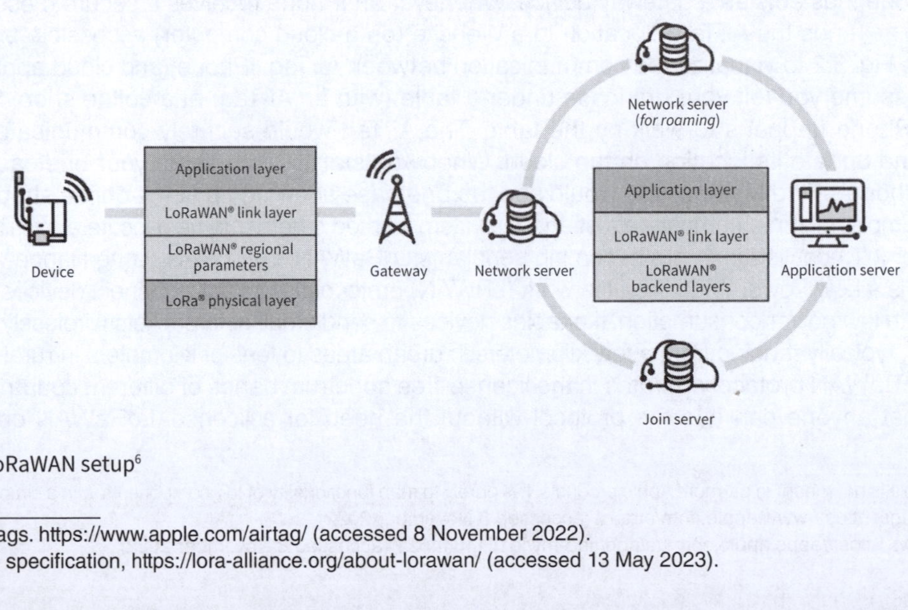

Fig. 3.3 LoRaWAN setup[6]

[5]Apple AirTags. https://www.apple.com/airtag/ (accessed 8 November 2022).
[6]LoRAWAN specification, https://lora-alliance.org/about-lorawan/ (accessed 13 May 2023).

gateways. Gateways receive the data from the end devices and forward it to the network server. The network server manages the network and the communication between the gateways and the end devices. Setting up a LoRaWAN system consists of the following steps:

- Obtain LoRaWAN-enabled hardware, such as a LoRaWAN gateway and LoRaWAN sensors.
- Configure the gateway with the appropriate network settings and security keys.
- Configure the sensors with the appropriate network settings and security keys.
- Develop or obtain software to receive and interpret the sensor data sent via LoRaWAN.
- Deploy the LoRaWAN enabled sensors in the desired location.
- Monitor the sensor data and adjust settings as needed.

Keep in mind that the specific steps may vary depending on the hardware and software being used, and the specific use case for the LoRaWAN network. LoRaWAN protocol based IoT system is suited for applications, where edge devices are located kilometers apart and transmit small data packets.

Now that we have a decent understanding of the three components that make an IoT system, let us go ahead and apply it to our business use case. In our hypothetical business setup (Fig. 3.4), we can use IoT for the following applications:

(a) Farming Assist precision farming
(b) Manufacturing Industrial management and predictive maintenance
(c) Logistics Tracking products in transit
(d) Retail Inventory and warehouse inventory management

IoT and IIoT edge device locations include refrigerated trucks that carry perishable products, freezers in the retail stores, and sensor feedback from hundreds of factory equipment for predictive maintenance. Before designing an IoT system, the motivation of an IoT system needs to be clearly spelled out. Connecting sensors to an edge or a cloud computer does not necessarily make a meaningful IoT system. The designers of an IoT system should have a clear idea about how they

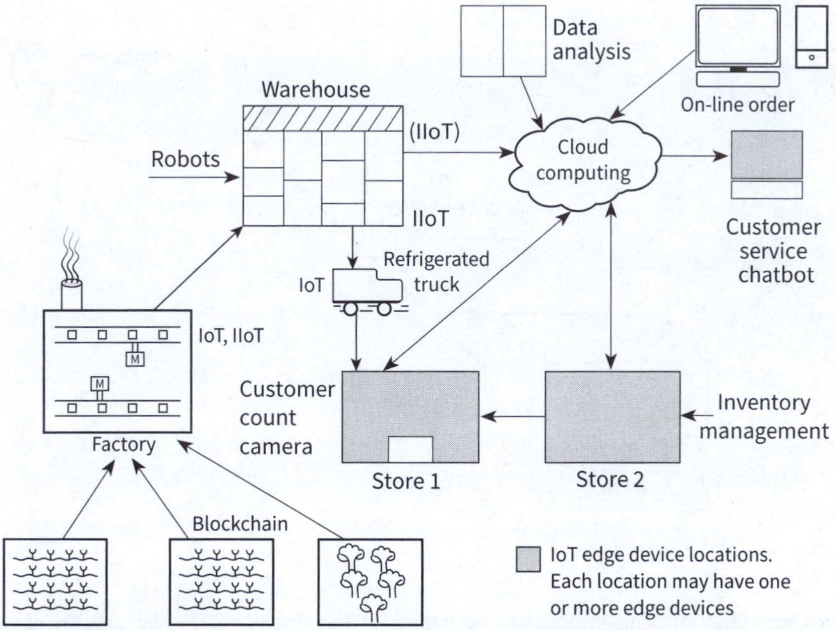

Fig. 3.4 IoT and IIoT edge device locations

intend to use the data gathered from the different sensors. A good starting point to evaluate IoT data usage, is to think from the perspective of time-based data analytics. This is presented in Table 3.1.[7]

The first column of Table 3.1 describes the analysis of data which is non-real time and has been collected in the past. This type of data is suited for using as training data for machine learning algorithms. It can also be used to investigate the root cause of problems/incidents that have already occurred. The second column of the Table describes an IoT system which evaluates and acts on real-time data. A rules engine describes the algorithm on how to act on real-time data. The last column of the timescale explains how the collected data can be used to predict future events. AI algorithms can ingest the data and explore if the symptoms of a looming fault can be detected at an early stage.

In practice, IoT edge devices do not send out large volumes of data to cloud computers. Local action and analytics is performed at the edge and only a summary data packet is communicated (Fig. 3.5). Data payloads sent from IoT devices are lightweight—bytes to kilobytes.

Table 3.1 Time-based data analytics of data gathered from IoT devices

Past (Diagnostic)	Present (Real-Time)	Future (Predictive)
Descriptive	Rules Engine	Predictive
Diagnostic	Real-time Analysis	Prescriptive
	Used to Determine	
What happened?	What is happening?	What could happen?
Why did it happen?		What should happen?

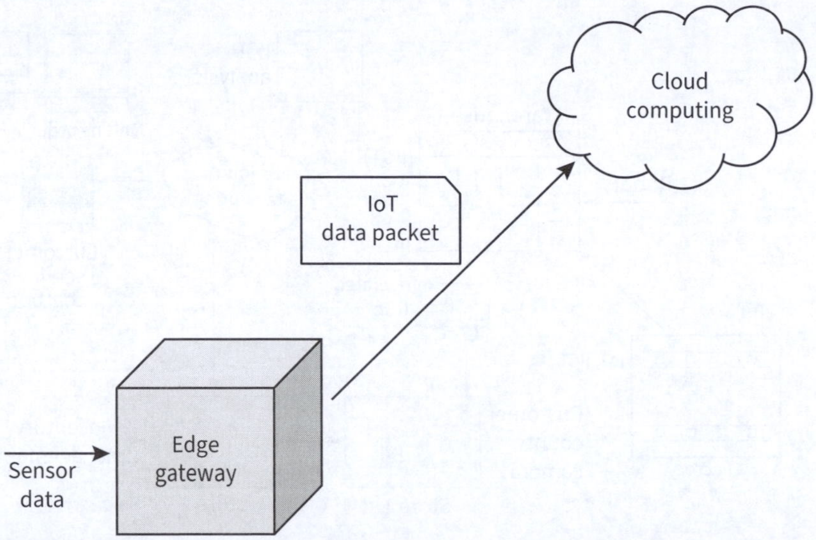

Fig. 3.5 Data payloads from IoT devices

[7]Bruce Sinclair, IoT Inc: How Your Company Can Use the Internet of Things to Win in the Outcome Economy, United States, McGraw Hill 2017.

3.2 | Message Queue Telemetry Transport Protocol

The Message Queue Telemetry Transport (MQTT) is a lightweight publish/subscribe messaging protocol, originally created by IBM and Arcom in around 1998. The protocol was designed to asynchronously transfer data from oil pipelines to satellites. Since a satellite link was not always available, the protocol envisioned the need of a local broker or server, which could hold and forward messages to and from clients (oil pipeline sensors). In contemporary terminology, the clients are often referred to as publishers (if they produce data) or as subscribers (if they consume data).

Conventional protocols (such as client–server) have a direct connection set up between the client and the server. If a sensor or sender needs to send data to multiple receivers, it needs to individually communicate with all receivers (Fig. 3.6). This kind of setup works well in applications such as in the case of electric energy meters communicating with an energy utility company.

Let us consider a smart home automation use case to demonstrate Client–Server-Based IoT Application. Here, a homeowner can control their home lighting system remotely using a mobile app. In the pseudocode (Listing 3.1), a hypothetical API is defined and used. This API exists on a Website and is accessed by the light switch via home WiFi or cellular internet connection. Using a mobile device, a user accesses the API and posts a payload to it. The payload in our example is to turn on the light. If the Website API successfully processes the request, it generates a code of 200. This code is communicated to the user as a confirmation.

The client–server code and protocol works well when one-to-one connectivity is needed. In the example the one-to-one connectivity is between the user and the light. For applications where a single stream of data needs to be viewed or used by multiple users, a different model is needed. MQTT uses the idea of a broker/server to route information from the sender to the receiver. It uses a publisher–subscriber model to disseminate information (Fig. 3.7).[8]

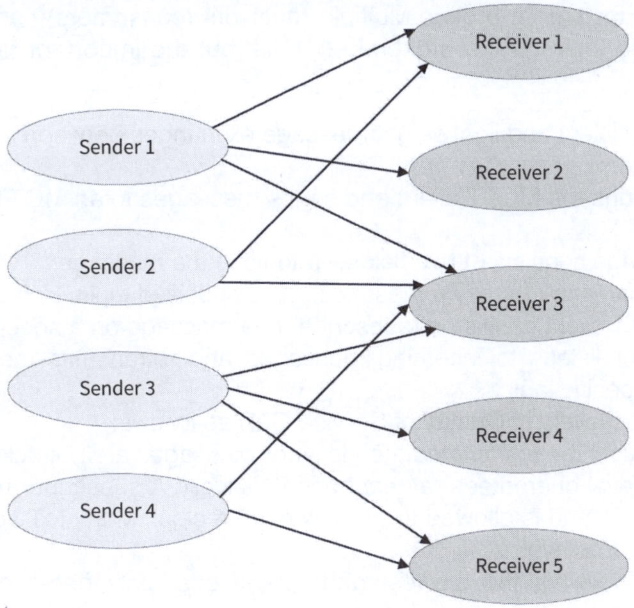

Fig. 3.6 Client–server communication methods (HTTP and Constrained Application Protocol)

[8]Some examples of the publish–subscribe model include YouTube channels, e-mail services, and so on. Every time a new YouTube video is posted (published), all subscribers are notified.

Listing 3.1 Pseudocode to control a light using client-server (HTTP) protocol

```
import requests

# Define the API endpoint (hypothetical)
api_url = 'http://home-automation-api.com'

# Define the payload
payload = {'light': 'on'}

# Send the HTTP POST request to turn on the light
response = requests.post(api_url + '/light', data=payload)

# Check the response status code
if response.status_code == 200:
 print('Light turned on successfully')
else:
 print('Error turning on light')
```

Features of MQTT

In contrast to a client–server protocol, for a producer-consumer protocol (such as MQTT), data is shared between one producer and several consumers. This is illustrated in Fig. 3.7, which shows the broker can be hosted on the cloud or on the IoT gateways. A producer (sender node) writes data to a designated topic on a broker. Multiple receivers (consumers) can access the data by subscribing to a given topic on the broker. Let us list out the important features of the MQTT protocol.

1. MQTT provides efficient and lightweight message exchanges between edge devices (clients–senders or receivers).
2. An edge device runs the MQTT client and sends messages to an MQTT broker located on a server.
3. The MQTT message consists of two fields—a topic and a message.
4. An MQTT client can send (publish) messages on a specified topic.
5. Similarly, an MQTT client can listen (subscribe) to a message on a specific topic.
6. The MQTT broker listens to incoming messages and retransmits messages to the client subscribed to a specific topic.
7. MQTT allows three levels of Quality of Service QoS as follows:
   (a) **QoS 0** This level means “immediate” delivery. Messages are not acknowledged.
   (b) **QoS 1** This level guarantees “at least once” delivery. A subscriber may get the message more than once and is allowed to acknowledge receipt. Many IoT service providers such as AWS use QoS level 1.
   (c) **QoS 2** This level is the slowest and guarantees “only once” delivery. A four-stage handshake mechanism is used for delivery.
8. MQTT supports the birth and last will testament (LWT). A new device sends its birth message the first time it comes online. If the device is offline because the connection with the broker has timed out, the broker acts on the device’s LWT. As an example, a device’s LWT may be to SMS someone indicating its offline status.

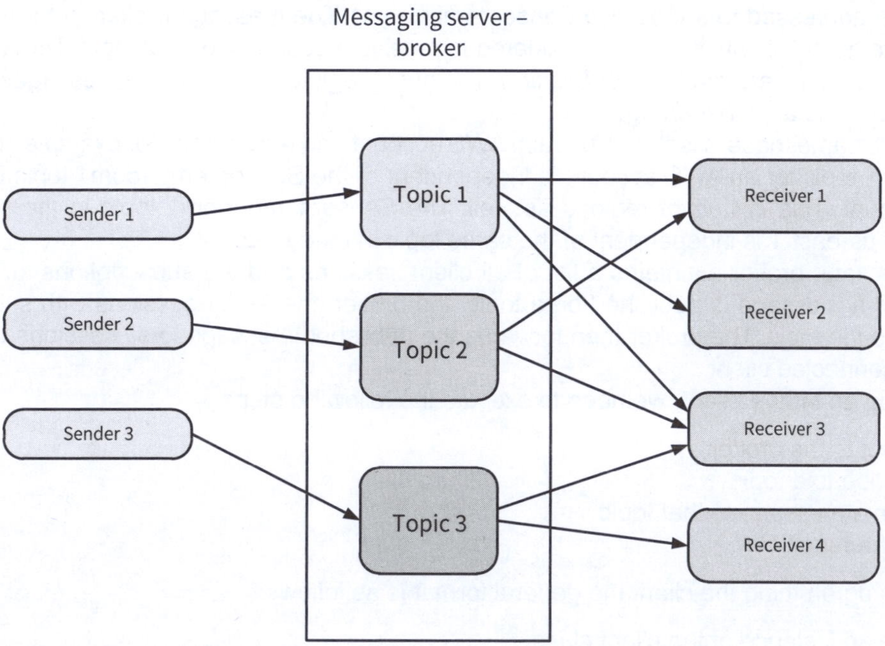

Fig. 3.7 The publisher–subscriber network of MQTT based on messaging server–broker

Table 3.2 Comparison of MQTT and HTTP

	MQTT	HTTP
Design orientation	Data centric	Document centric
Pattern	Publish/subscribe	Request/response
Complexity	Simple	More complex
Message size	Small, with a compact binary header just two bytes in size	Larger, partly because status detail is text-based
Service levels	Three quality of service settings	All messages get the same level of service
Extra libraries	Libraries for C (30 KB) and Java (100 KB)	Depends on the application (JSON, XML), but typically not small
Data distribution	Supports 1 to zero, 1 to 1, and 1 to *n*	1 to 1 only

Table 3.2 compares the salient features of MQTT and HTTP.

An IoT device can send text or binary (e.g., a photo) data. As long as the client can parse the data type, the device can send it. MQTT cloud brokers support a few kilobytes of payload but the theoretical maximum is 256 MB.

To create an MQTT ecosystem, the following components are put in place:

1. MQTT Broker (can be hosted locally or on a cloud server)
2. MQTT Client (which can publish and subscribe to topics)

The AWS IoT message broker is a publish–subscribe broker service that enables sending and receiving of messages to and from the AWS IoT. When communicating with AWS IoT, a client sends a message addressed to a topic like Sensor/temp/room1. The message broker, in turn, sends the message to all the clients that have registered to receive messages for that topic. The act of sending the message is referred to as *publishing*. The act of registering to receive messages for a topic filter is referred to as *subscribing*.

The topic namespace is isolated for each AWS account and region pair. For example, the Sensor/temp/room1 topic for an AWS account is independent of the Sensor/temp/room1 topic for another AWS account. This is true of regions as well. The Sensor/temp/room1 topic in the same AWS account in us-east-1 is independent of the same topic in us-east-2.

The message broker maintains a list of all client sessions and the subscriptions for each session. When a message is published on a topic, the broker checks for sessions with subscriptions that map to the topic. The broker then forwards the published message to all sessions that have a currently connected client.

To set up an MQTT client, we need to execute the following steps:

(a) Connect to the broker
(b) Subscribe to a topic
(c) Publish a message to that topic
(d) View the result

When programming the client the general format is as follows:

(a) Create an instance of the client class
(b) Create a connection to the broker
(c) Subscribe to messages
(d) Publish messages

EXAMPLE 1

Write a Python Paho-based MQTT code to understand the concept of the topic, publish, and subscribe.

Solution IoT data from devices is communicated to other devices or cloud servers using MQTT protocol. As discussed, this protocol uses publish–subscribe topology to communicate data between devices that produce data and that consume data. Python code uses a public broker hosted by Eclipse[9] to demonstrate the concept of topic, publish and subscribe. There are two call back functions. These functions activate when a new connection is received (*on_connect*) or when a new message is received (*on_message*). First code demonstrates publisher functionality (Listing 3.2). Here a value is published to a topic, hosted by the broker. The value of the *counter* variable is published to the topic *city/street/cars.* When we subscribe to the topic *city/street/cars*, we are able to see the value of the counter (from the broker) and print it out. This is mentioned in the subscriber part of code (Listing 3.3). We use Colab to demonstrate this code as it has access to the public broker (test.mosquitto.org) through the Internet.

Check the of working publisher, subscriber, and broker IoT nodes as shown in Fig. 3.8.

- Execute the publisher Python code from Listing 3.2 in Colab environment. The code publishes a counter value to the topic "**city/street/cars**". The counter value increments every second, five times.

[9]MQTT Broker, https://test.mosquitto.org/ (accessed 6 December 2022).

Listing 3.2 MQTT code that publishes a value to a topic on a broker

```
import paho.mqtt.client as mqtt #import the client
import time
def on_connect(client, userdata, flags, rc):
 m="connection received with result code " + str(rc)
 print(m)
def on_message(client1, userdata, message):
 print("message received ,str(message.payload.decode("utf-8"))")

broker_address= "test.mosquitto.org"

#create new instance
client = mqtt.Client()

#attach connect to callback
client.on_connect= on_connect

#attach message received to callback
client.on_message=on_message
time.sleep(1)

#connect to broker
client.connect(broker_address)

#start the loop
client.loop_start()
counter =0

time.sleep(1)
counter += 1
client.publish("city/street/cars", counter)
time.sleep(1)
counter += 1
client.publish("city/street/cars", counter)
time.sleep(1)
counter += 1
client.publish("city/street/cars", counter)
time.sleep(1)
counter += 1
client.publish("city/street/cars", counter)
time.sleep(1)
counter += 1
client.publish("city/street/cars", counter)

client.disconnect()
client.loop_stop()
```

- Now execute the subscriber Python code in Colab mentioned in Listing 3.3 on another computer with a different Gmail id login. The subscriber code will show updated values of the topic "city/street/cars". The subscriber obtains values from the Mosquitto test broker, which acts as a messaging server.

Listing 3.3 MQTT subscriber loop to read a topic from the broker

```
import paho.mqtt.client as mqtt #import the client

import time

def on_connect(client, userdata, flags, rc):
 m="connection received with result code " + str(rc)
 print(m)

def on_message(client1, userdata, message):
 print("message received " ,str(message.payload.decode("utf-8")))

broker_address= "test.mosquitto.org"

#create new instance
client = mqtt.Client()

#attach connect to callback
client.on_connect= on_connect

#attach message received to callback
client.on_message=on_message
time.sleep(1)

#connect to broker
client.connect(broker_address)
#start the loop
client.loop_start()

#continously poll topic "city/street/cars" for updates

while true:
 client.subscribe("city/street/cars")

client.disconnect()
client.loop_stop()
```

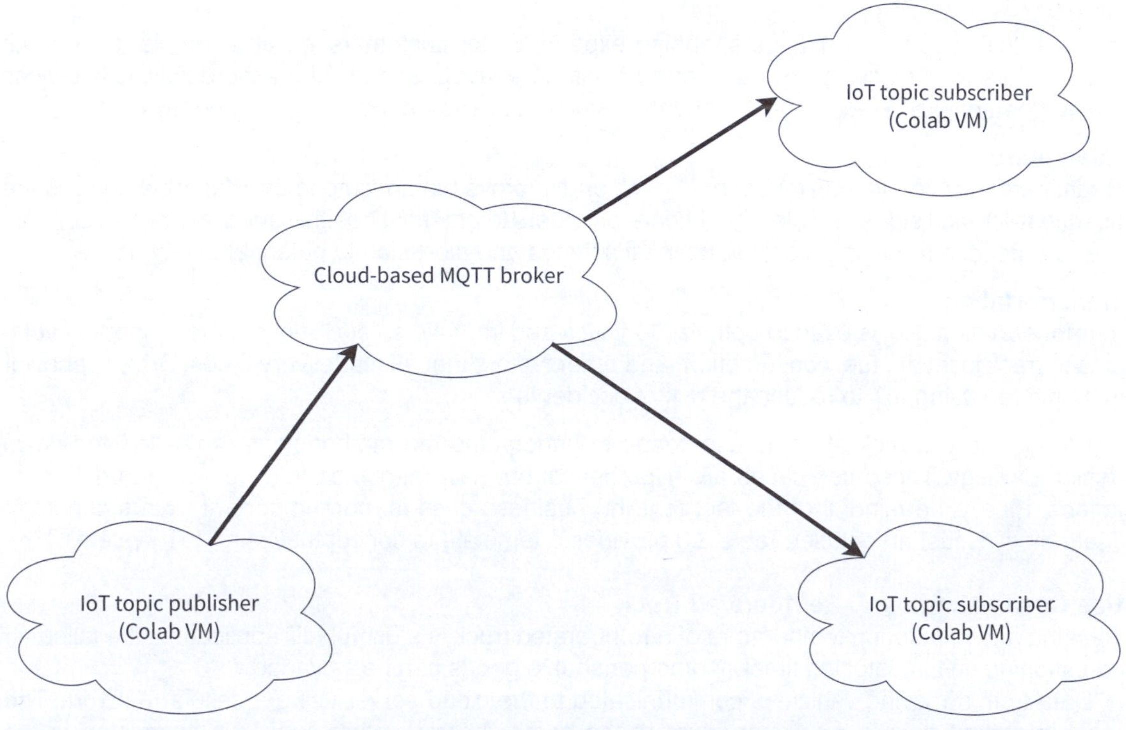

Fig. 3.8 Working of IoT broker, publish, and subscribe nodes using cloud hosted Colab virtual machine (VM)

This type of edge AI can be used in various business scenarios, such as predictive maintenance for industrial equipment or real-time monitoring of health data in healthcare settings. Multiple subscribers can subscribe to one or more topics from one or more publishers.

3.3 | Applications of Internet of Things

Applications of IoT and IIoT have become increasingly popular across various industries. A digital replica of the IoT device is stored on the cloud computer. This replica is known as the the Digital Twin of the IoT device and is used to study the behavior of the IoT device. The Digital Twin does not need to communicate continuously with the IoT device. It stores salient attributes of the IoT device, as and when it is able to receive a data packet from it. Several related Digital Twins form a fleet of IoT devices, and help in understanding data trends and in modeling the behavior of the IoT device. Let us discuss some examples of how businesses use IoT and IIoT:

Manufacturing
IIoT is used to connect machines and devices to a centralized system, allowing for real-time monitoring and controlling of the production process. For example, sensors can be placed on machines to collect data on temperature, vibration, and other factors that can affect production. This data is used to optimize production, reduce downtime, and improve quality control.

Agriculture
IoT is used to collect data on soil moisture, temperature, and other environmental factors that affect crop growth. The collected data is used to optimize irrigation, fertilizer application, and other aspects of crop management. IoT sensors are used to monitor the health and well-being of livestock.

Retail

In retail, IoT is used to enhance shopping experience for customers. As an example, stores can use sensors to track customer traffic and adjust store layout and staffing accordingly. IoT devices provide personalized recommendations to customers based on their shopping behavior.

Healthcare

Healthcare uses IoT to monitor patient health and improve patient outcomes. Wearable devices are used to track vital signs and alert healthcare providers to potential health issues. IoT based sensors are also used to monitor patients in hospital settings and alert staff to potential safety risks.

Transportation

In transportation, IoT is used to optimize logistics and improve safety. Sensors are placed on vehicles to track location, fuel consumption, and other factors that affect delivery times. Driver behavior is monitored using IoT to reduce the risk of accidents.

We now take a look at some use cases to understand the methodology of the IoT top-down design strategy. These use cases are hypothetical but have attributes from real-world implementations. Please be mindful of the fact that the business case is more important than technology. Technology is just an enabler. Table 3.3 provides a template to conceptualize an IoT system.

Use Case—Monitoring Refrigerated Truck

Tracking and monitoring temperature of a refrigerated truck is a useful IoT application. If a failed air conditioning unit is detected timely, some perishable goods can be salvaged.

Data from a moving vehicle is communicated to the cloud server using a cellular network. The most important data is the temperature of the cargo. A temperature sensor is connected to the gateway module. To transmit vehicle operation data, on-board diagnostics (OBD) port is connected to the gateway. The OBD port transmits vehicle dashboard data along with its location (using global positioning system or GPS) to the cloud. All relevant information is populated in Table 3.4.

Table 3.3 Template for planning an IoT system

Sample IoT Application	
Data Analytics	Plan for data usage—based on Table 3.1
Gateway/Communication	Evaluate power, range and availability of communication options. Cellular connectivity may not be available at all locations
Edge Devices	Enumerate edge devices/sensors needed for application

Table 3.4 IoT system planning for refrigerated truck

Vehicle Telematics for Refrigerated Truck	
Data Analytics	• Check for temperature variations during transit • Provide alerts if the vehicle travels beyond a certain route-GeoFencing (real-time) • Coordinate roadside assistance in case of vehicle problems (Realtime) • Use vehicle diagnostic data to preempt failures (diagnostic, predictive)
Gateway/Communication	• Cellular connectivity from the vehicle to the cloud-3G or LTE • Service is provided by cellular network providers
Edge Devices	• Temperature sensor close to cargo • Refrigeration unit diagnostics • Global positioning satellite (GPS) Sensor • Connectivity to On Board Diagnostics (OBD) port. Collect information from the vehicle dashboard-odometer, engine temperature, alarms/warnings, etc.

A real-world IoT system monitors a fleet of such trucks and not just one. Each truck has a unique ID and its edge device would populate a database on a central computer with data on temperature, refrigeration unit diagnostics, and GPS coordinates with date and timestamp.

3.4 | Industrial Internet of Things

Industrial Internet of Things (IIoT) is an extension of IoT and is used to optimize industrial processes and prevent breakdowns. Existing systems are IIoT-enabled by adding sensors and gateway as part of retrofitting. New machines have preinstalled sensors and gateways. As an IIoT use case, let us consider monitoring of a back-up diesel generator (DG). First, we populate Table 3.5 with information about parameters that need to be monitored using sensors. At the same time, we also create a plan on how to use data from the DG in the data analytics section of the table.

An existing DG is retrofitted with a cellular gateway device, which connects to existing sensors on the DG (such as battery, fuel level, and others) as shown in Fig. 3.9.

Table 3.5 Industrial internet of things requirements for diesel generator monitoring

Diesel Generator Monitoring System	
Data Analytics	Storage: Operation data for efficiency monitoring Analyse: Any faults based on vibration, sound Actionable items: Communicate with user on low fuel level, or weak battery
Gateway/Communication	Cellular
Edge Device	Sensors: Vibration, sound, fuel level, battery Actuator: Alarms on local control panel

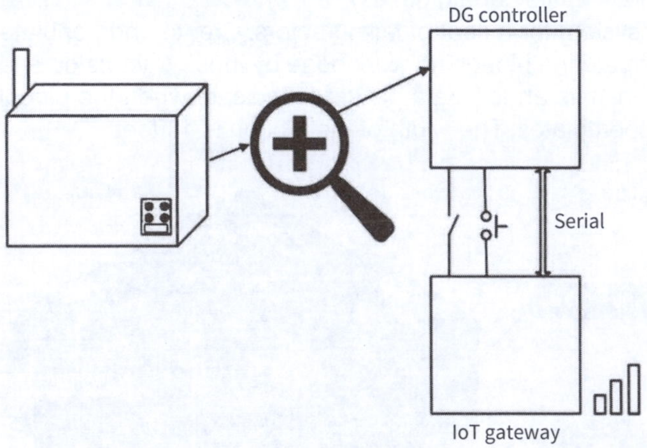

Fig. 3.9 Providing IoT connectivity and services to a diesel generator

3.5 | Conclusion

IoT and IIoT technologies help businesses connect to remote devices. These devices track product movement, detect faults in machinery, and help connect the dots by getting data from far flung locations. An IoT system based on the templates discussed in the chapter can be used to create meaningful IoT applications.

Exercises

A. State True/False

1. IoT devices communicate with server or cloud computer.
2. Data acquired from IoT devices is used for diagnostic or predictive decision making.

B. Short-answer Questions

1. Is Apple AirTag an edge device or gateway?
2. Research and find out if data flows from Apple cloud to an AirTag. If it does, what do you think it is used for?
3. Preventive maintenance of motors in an IIoT application is diagnostic, real-time or predictive?
4. Give an example of a client–server protocol.
5. Give an example of a publisher–subscriber protocol.
6. What does Quality of Service—QoS 1 of MQTT protocol guarantee?
7. Create a MQTT topic naming convention for monitoring number of people in different rooms of a building.
8. Provide an application where client–server protocol is better than publisher–subscriber protocol.
9. Explain how an AirTag can be used to locate misplaced airline luggage.

C. Long-answer Questions

1. In many developing countries, food grain stored in godowns or silos gets eaten by rodents or just rots. Develop an IoT system that can detect rotting grain or rodents which can trigger an alert message for the staff of these godowns. Fill in Table 3.6 on food grain monitoring with your ideas. Use Fig. 3.10 to see an example of a real-world food grain monitoring system. (Hint: Rotting grain emits certain gases)
2. Design an IoT system for a fleet of farm tractors. Create and populate Table 3.2 for this application to estimate the ploughing work done by these tractors on a farm by using IoT data. Each tractor transmits an IoT data packet to indicate when the plough is in use along with GPS location coordinates. The width of the plough is 15 feet.

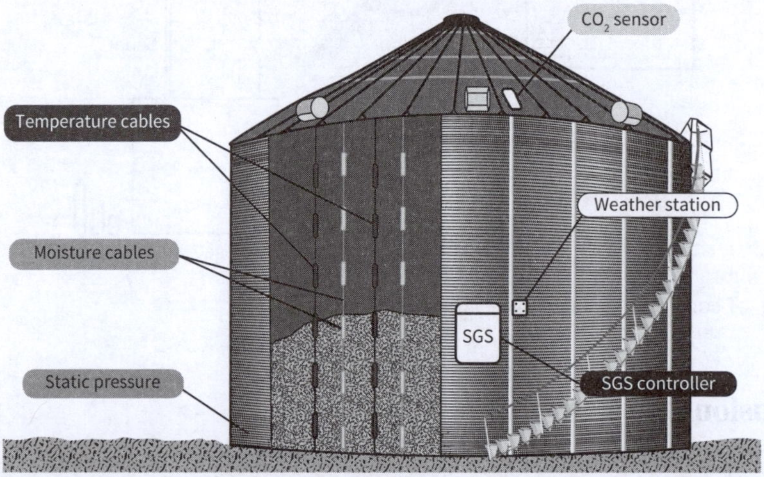

Fig. 3.10 Smart grain monitoring example

Source: Smart Grain Solutions, available at https://www.smartgrainsolutions.com/for-the-farm, accessed on 26 August 2018

Table 3.6 Template for food grain monitoring IoT system

Food Grain Monitoring	
Cloud Processing	Storage Analysis Actionable items
Gateway/Communication	Connectivity Gateway
Edge Device	Sensors Edge processing Actuator

3. Think of an industrial IoT application (like the diesel generator monitoring system) that can benefit from IoT technology. Describe your application and give reasons why it would benefit from IoT.
4. Learn about the working and applications of IoT protocol called Matter. Explain how Matter based applications differ from LoRAWAN based applications.

D. Explore and Experiment

1. Execute MQTT publisher and subscriber codes on different computers (with internet connectivity) to understand how multiple users can subscribe and access a given topic.
2. If you or a friend has access to an AirTag ecosystem and an AirTag, place the AirTag inside a package and track its movement. Understand the frequency of its location update and compare it to how often it comes in range to an iPhone.
3. Telecom vendors (source: https://www.timesnownews.com/technology-science/reliance-jio-unveils-jiomotive-affordable-4g-gps-tracker-for-cars-with-theft-alert-article-105023303) provide 4G GPS trackers for automobiles. These trackers connect to the OBD port of the automobile and can transmit vehicle information along with its location. Try out one of these trackers to implement geo-fencing or monitor rash driving.
4. Remote medical monitoring is an upcoming IoT application. Generative AI code (Fig. 3.11), generates a sample IoT data packet, using JavaScript Object Notation (JSON) format.

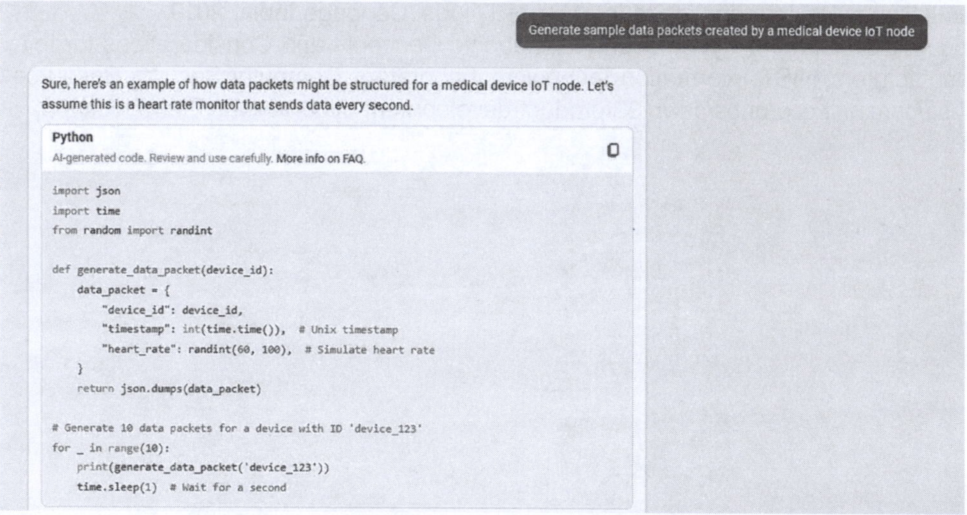

Generate sample data packets created by a medical device IoT node

Sure, here's an example of how data packets might be structured for a medical device IoT node. Let's assume this is a heart rate monitor that sends data every second.

Python

AI-generated code. Review and use carefully. More info on FAQ.

```python
import json
import time
from random import randint

def generate_data_packet(device_id):
    data_packet = {
        "device_id": device_id,
        "timestamp": int(time.time()),  # Unix timestamp
        "heart_rate": randint(60, 100),  # Simulate heart rate
    }
    return json.dumps(data_packet)

# Generate 10 data packets for a device with ID 'device_123'
for _ in range(10):
    print(generate_data_packet('device_123'))
    time.sleep(1)  # Wait for a second
```

Fig. 3.11 IoT data packet generation for heart rate monitoring

E. Generate Use Case for an IoT System

Use Case: Smart Door Bell

Brief description: Smart door bells use a camera to detect people/packages and send out a text or an e-mail notification. These doorbells act as IoT edge devices and share data with a cloud computer. The cloud server stores video when an event is triggered (such as person/package/animal detected) and informs the user. The IoT gateway for the smart door bell is usually the home WiFi router.

Use the following product webpages to understand more about smart door bells and then create a use case using the template below.

Resources

Nest doorbell: https://store.google.com/us/product/nest_doorbell?hl=en-US&pli=1
Ring doorbell: https://ring.com/products/video-doorbell-v2?msclkid=e27c07e7d35b139f58aa62856ccc7add

Template for Creating Use Case on Smart Door Bell

Define goal and purpose	Goal statement
	Identify stakeholders
	Define scope
Details to include in use case	Capture how technology helps business process
	Keep use case findings description textual, with a few simple flowcharts if needed
	Focus on describing how technology benefits the use case
Future applications	Mention any new applications that can leverage the technology used

Suggested Readings

1. Bruce Sinclair, IoT Inc.: How Your Company Can Use the Internet of Things to Win in the Outcome Economy, United States: McGraw Hill, 2017.
2. Claire Rowland et al., Designing Connected Products, Cambridge: O'Reilly, 2015.
3. Rahul Dubey, An Introduction to Internet of Things, Cengage India, 2019.
4. Product Development Cybersecurity Handbook: Concepts and Considerations for IoT Product Manufacturers, NIST, Information Technology Laboratory, Computer Security Resource Center, https://csrc.nist.gov/pubs/cswp/33/product-development-cybersecurity-handbook/ipd

CHAPTER 4

Overview of Cloud Computing Services

CHAPTER OUTLINE

LEARNING OBJECTIVES

After reading this chapter, you will be able to:

- understand emergence of cloud computing
- distinguish between different cloud services and deployment models
- learn how different services work together
- understand how a cloud architecture is set up
- estimate pricing of services provided by cloud setup

Effective Management Using Cloud Computing

Most businesses rely on some sort of compute for their operations. If this is expensive to setup and difficult to scale; businesses will have a tough time. Cloud services provides low-cost, scalable compute that is accessible and easy to setup. It therefore plays a key role for many start ups and established businesses.

4.1 | Introduction

As we progress in our journey of interconnecting different parts of a modern business, we now discuss a crucial component that serves as a hub or the brains of a system. For many businesses across the globe, the Cloud computing setup plays this role. So what exactly is cloud computing?

The official definition from the National Institute of Standards and Technology (NIST)[1]:

> Cloud computing is a model for enabling ubiquitous, convenient, on-demand network access to a shared pool of configurable computing resources (networks, virtual machines, storage, applications, and services) that can be rapidly provisioned and released with minimal management effort or service provider interaction.

To elaborate on this definition, we list the main features of cloud computing as the following:

- Pooled computing resources available to subscribing users
- Use of virtual servers (physical computer server divided into multiple unique and isolated servers) to maximise hardware utilization
- Elastic scaling up or down of compute resources based on business needs
- Automated (software script based) management of virtual machines
- Billing based on resources used

First, let us understand the role of computer servers in a typical business environment. We use the setup from Chapter 1 to see how computers help. Data from different parts of the business gets stored and analyzed by computers. From Fig. 4.1, we see data being generated from retail stores (customer footfalls, items sold, and so on), warehouses, factories, supply chain, logistics operations (using IoT), e-commerce, and customer support. Data from various operations are all stored on computer servers. This includes data from operations, sales, logistics, e-commerce and customer support. In our material and data flow setup of a modern industry, computers connect different parts of the business. They serve as the data store, web server, IoT device hub, and data analytics platform. There are companies which use the cloud for all the services we just mentioned, while some

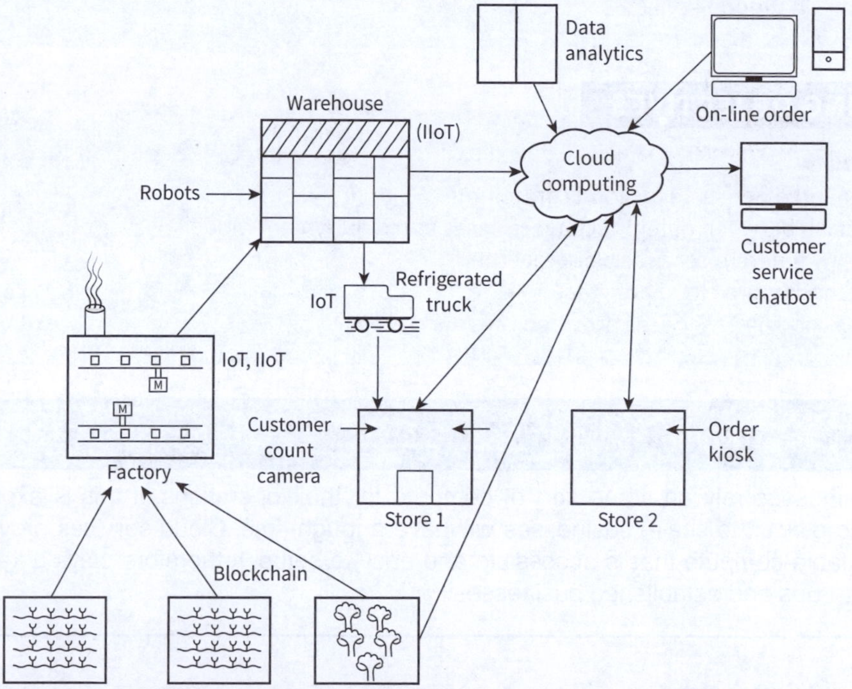

Fig. 4.1 Data from various operations stored on computer servers

[1]The NIST Definition of Cloud Computing, https://nvlpubs.nist.gov/nistpubs/legacy/sp/nistspecialpublication800-145.pdf (accessed 9 November 2022).

may prefer an on-premise or hybrid solution. Irrespective of the computer setup a business uses, it is imperative that data is not only stored but also timely analyzed for taking business decisions.

If you give this some thought, you will realize that these business requirements existed long before cloud computing entered the picture. So how did businesses gather and use data prior to 2006? (the first cloud computing company Amazon Web Services (AWS) started operations in 2006).

The business world used on-premise computing to store and analyse business data. Each location would have its own computer system that would use modems and dedicated phone lines to relay information between offices across cities, states, and countries. This infrastructure was expensive, not simple to set up, and required constant attention (software updates, 24 × 7 power supply, hardware upgrades). Based on our introductory discussions on cloud computing, we know that the user pays only for the time that a resource is used or accessed. As seen in Fig. 4.2, the cost of using a cloud computer would be lower than an on-premise setup if the computing load was intermittent.

Before we move on to describe cloud services in greater detail, let us briefly talk about applications and scenarios where on-premise compute services are still used.

High security In some cases, applications may require a higher level of security than can be provided by cloud services. In these cases, on-premise services may be a better choice since they provide complete control over infrastructure and can provide higher levels of physical and logical security.

Performance Certain applications require very low-latency and high-bandwidth connectivity. For these applications, on-premise services are a better choice since they provide dedicated resources that are not shared with other users, leading to better performance.

Compliance Some industries have strict compliance requirements that dictate where data is stored and processed. In such applications, on-premise services are suitable since they provide more control over the location and management of data.

Legacy applications Certain applications may not be designed to work in a cloud environment, or may require significant modification to work properly in a cloud environment. In these cases, on-premise services are a better choice to avoid the cost and complexity of migration.

Cost-effective for long-term use In some cases, on-premise services may be more cost-effective in the long run for applications that require constant use and do not require dynamic scaling. For example, if an organization has a stable, predictable workload that requires significant computing resources (unlike in Fig. 4.2, which shows intermittent load), it may be more cost-effective to purchase and maintain on-premise infrastructure.

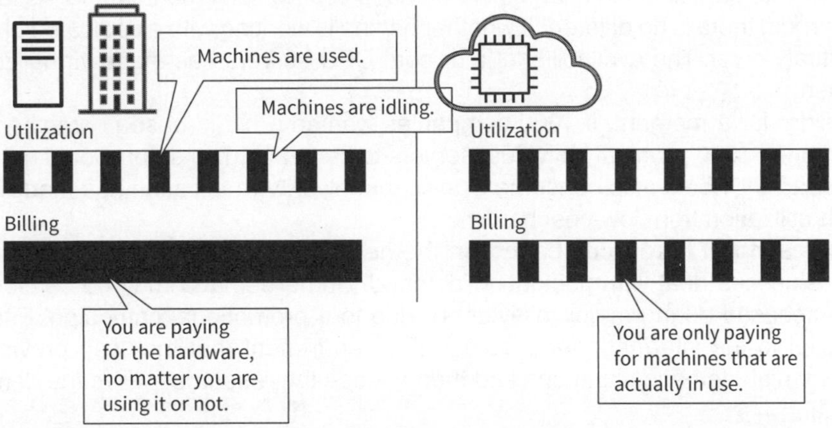

Fig. 4.2 Difference in cost (billing) when running intermittent load using on-premise and cloud computer

4.2 | Cloud Computing Basics

The spoke and hub model of computing is not new. In this model, the compute resources are at a centralized location (hub); while the terminals that access the compute resources are located at a distance (spokes). In the early days of mainframe computers, multiple users from across the company logged into a single computer. This computing framework lasted for several decades, till personal computers (PC) had enough computing and memory resources. This led to individuals using PCs instead of centralized computers. With the availability of low-cost and ubiquitous cloud computing resources (such as Google Workspace), many individuals started using the cloud for documents, spreadsheet, storage, and several other services. A full circle to mainframe like computing! There is a notable difference between the mainframe and the contemporary internet era. Each day billions of data requests are handled by millions of servers inside data centers.

It is important to keep in mind that cloud computing did not appear out of nowhere. It is the culmination of several technological advances. These advances include virtualization technology, high-speed data connectivity, computing, storage hardware, network hardware, high availability, remote operation and management, and access security.

To continue our discussion on different features of cloud computing, we now individually discuss each of them.

(a) Pooled computing resources

Why is pooling of computing resources relevant or useful? It has to do with economics. One of the biggest advantages of using pooled resources is the shift of capital expenses (CAPEX) to operational expenses (OPEX). A small company with a great idea and a credit card can provision the computing resources they require. This lowers the financial barrier for startups and gives them peace of mind that they can provision other resources (the pool is not going to run dry) as and when needed.

The second important aspect of pooled resources has to do with economies of scale. Large companies have the deep pockets to purchase goods in bulk, which reduces the unit cost of a product. With pooled resources, cloud service providers are able to provide low-cost computing (computing, storage, power, and network capacity) to all their customers. This works to everyone's advantage.

In a self-hosted or on-premise model, the business has to pay for hardware, computer software licences, and other fixed costs which need to be paid upfront.

(b) Use of server virtualization

Using software, virtualization partitions a physical computer server into several virtual servers. These servers participate in a large pool of resources available on demand. As far as the user is concerned, there is no difference whether he/she is working with a dedicated physical server or a virtual server. The availability of multicore CPU servers has made virtualization easy to implement.

Consider for a moment, if 1000 companies wanted a cloud-based computer server. This would require 1000 physical individual servers to be set up. The setup would not only take up lots of space, it would also consume significant power. Virtualization has made it possible to get high utilization from low-cost hardware.

(c) Elastic scaling of resources based on the needs of business

Most businesses deal with fluctuating demand. Some demand may be seasonal (such as items purchased during major festivals) or due to a promotional campaign. Either way, it is a big relief to the information technology (IT) department that they can provision a server quickly for high demand situations and then release the resources when the demand returns to normal.

(d) Automated (software script based) management of virtual machines
In continuation to our earlier point on elastic scaling of resources, a question would arise about its implementation. The good news is that this does not need to be done manually. An IT engineer can write a code (or script) to add additional cloud servers in response to growing demand, and these resources can be scaled back when certain conditions are met.

(e) Billing based on resources used
The idea of metered billing is very intuitive. When you travel in a taxi, you pay for the distance travelled. In a hotel, you pay for the number of days you stayed. This idea is now extended to cloud computing. Subscribers pay for the machines, storage or the service they use. Most cloud pricing plans mention cost/hour for compute, and cost/gigabyte (GB) for storage/access.

Cloud Deployment Models

There are three types of cloud deployment models—private, public, and hybrid. A business can use one or a combination of these three kinds of deployment options. We use NIST's[2] definition of cloud deployment models.

Private cloud

The cloud infrastructure is provisioned for exclusive use by a single organization comprising multiple consumers (e.g., business units). It may be owned, managed, and operated by the organization, a third party, or some combination of them, and it may exist on or off premises.

Public cloud

The cloud infrastructure is provisioned for open use by the general public. It may be owned, managed, and operated by a business, academic, or government organization, or some combination of them. It exists on the premises of the cloud provider.

Hybrid cloud

The cloud infrastructure is a composition of two or more distinct cloud infrastructures (private, community, or public) that remain unique entities, but are bound together by standardized or proprietary technology that enables data and application portability (e.g., cloud bursting for load balancing between clouds).

The public cloud is by far the most commonly used cloud deployment model. Based on our understanding of computing so far, let us enumerate the advantages of a public cloud setup.

- It is cost efficient due to economies to scale.
- It provides reliable operation as each data-center is designed for 24 x 7 and 365 days of service. In case of failure of a resource, it is possible to transfer the application or service to other available servers.
- Offers unlimited storage and compute. Due to interconnection of worldwide data-center locations (Fig. 4.3), a subscriber does not run into capacity limitations.
- Ease of access due to Internet connectivity. A developer or user can access cloud servers from anywhere in the world.

There are many analogies to compare public and private clouds. One popular analogy is the comparison to individual's transportation. One can own a car (private cloud), lease a car (public cloud), or use a taxi (serverless functions[3]) to go from point A to point B. The other analogy is

[2]Cloud deployment models, https://nvlpubs.nist.gov/nistpubs/legacy/sp/nistspecialpublication800-145.pdf (accessed 9 November 2022).

[3]We will discuss more about serverless functions in the next sections.

Fig. 4.3 AWS cloud infrastructure locations spread across the world (Microsoft and Google have a similar network of cloud infrastructure resources)

mentioned in Table 4.1. One can own a house (private cloud), rent a house (public cloud), or use Airbnb (serverless functions) for accommodation.

Table 4.1 Analogy of private and public cloud services with accommodation

Hosting Choice	Suitable For	Analogy
Private cloud	Long-term fixed needs	Have your own home
Using a virtual machine on a public cloud	Medium or short term variable needs	Rent/lease a house
Use functions (serverless) approach on a public cloud	Event triggered requirements	Use Airbnb

When making a decision on which cloud deployment model to use, it is important to understand the tradeoffs for each setup mentioned.

4.3 | Cloud Service Models

Cloud computing has evolved considerably. It not only offer servers, database, storage, but also offers services that can be configured and used by businesses. An example of such a service would be training of AI models or carrying out data analytics on stored data.

NIST[4] succinctly defines three major cloud services as follows:

Infrastructure as a Service (IaaS)
The capability provided to the consumer is to provision processing, storage, networks, and other fundamental computing resources where the consumer is able to deploy and run arbitrary software, which can include operating systems and applications. The consumer does not manage or control the underlying cloud infrastructure but has control over operating systems, storage, and deployed applications, and possibly limited control of select networking components (e.g., host firewalls).

Platform as a Service (PaaS)
The capability provided to the consumer is to deploy onto the cloud infrastructure consumer-created or acquired applications created using programming languages, libraries, services, and tools supported by the provider. The consumer does not manage or control the underlying cloud infrastructure including network, servers, operating systems, or storage, but has control over the deployed applications and possibly configuration settings for the application-hosting environment.

[4]Cloud service models, https://nvlpubs.nist.gov/nistpubs/legacy/sp/nistspecialpublication800-145.pdf (accessed 9 November 2022).

Software as a Service (SaaS)

The capability provided to the consumer is to use the provider's applications running on a cloud infrastructure. The applications are accessible from various client devices through either a thin client interface, such as a Web browser (e.g., Web-based e-mail) or a program interface. The consumer does not manage or control the underlying cloud infrastructure including network, servers, operating systems, storage, or even individual application capabilities, with the possible exception of limited user specific application configuration settings.

If you take look closely at Fig. 4.4(b), you will see that the cloud service provider manages everything for the SaaS model, everything (besides application and data) for the PaaS model, and is responsible for providing basic hardware setup (virtualized server, storage, and networking) in the IaaS model. It is up to the customer to choose one or a combination of these models for their application.

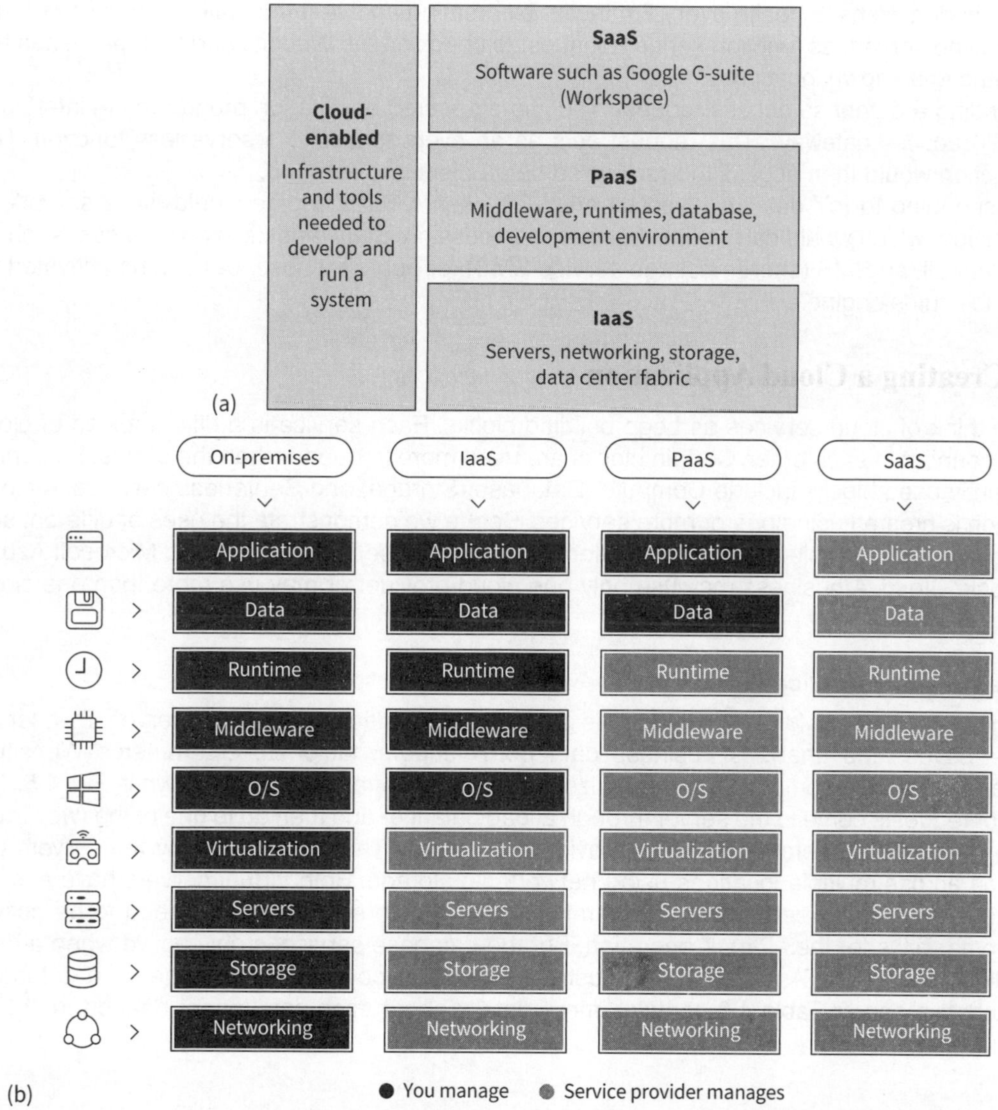

Fig. 4.4 (a) Cloud-based service model. (b) Who manages what in different service models—on-premise, IaaS, PaaS, and SaaS

Function as a Service (FaaS)

A new service model was introduced by AWS in 2014. It is known as FaaS or serverless function service. Even though it uses a managed server under the hood, the running cost of maintaining the server is not borne by the subscriber. We had briefly talked about this in Table 4.1, where we referred to the use of serverless functions as renting an Airbnb. You use it by calling a function that in turn may access a database. Serverless functions are written in multiple programming languages such as Node.js, Java, Go, Python, and many more.

Most virtual cloud dedicated servers (such as one running a Website) are usually active (and billed) all the time. Serverless services provide an option to react to a sporadic or periodic event by running certain cloud services, without having to lease a virtual server and keep it running all the time. This results in substantial cost savings.

Some examples on possible use of serverless functions:

(a) Monitoring Website health every 5 minutes by creating an event that calls a serverless function. The serverless function sends a request to check on the Website and then publishes the metric to a known location.

(b) Sending a database access request by using a secured application programming interfaces (API) access gateway.[5] This request acts as an event to invoke a serverless function. The function would then access the requested data object and respond.

(c) Responding to IoT data received by an IoT broker. A rules engine would fire a serverless function, which would carry out subsequent processing. Simple notification services (such as an e-mail, an SMS (short message service SMS), or publish–subscribe) can be activated by an IoT rules engine.

4.4 | Creating a Cloud Application

One can think of cloud services as Lego building blocks. Each service is a different kind of block and can connect to each other. Certain blocks are used more frequently than the others. Examples of frequently used blocks include Compute, Database, Storage, and Serverless services. A cloud application is created using one or more services. Before we demonstrate the uses of different services, have a look at Table 4.2. It lists functionally equivalent services from AWS, Microsoft Azure, and Google Cloud. A business may use only one cloud provider or may use more than one cloud providers for redundancy purposes.

Server as a Cloud Application

A common requirement for any business is an internet connected computer server. The server acquires, saves, and analyzes business data from vendors, factories, e-commerce Websites, stores, and so forth. A computer server realized using cloud infrastructure is shown in Fig. 4.5.

Data or requests come to the server through a load balancer and then go to one of the two virtual servers. Two servers operating together provide redundancy. The files needed by the servers are distributed across multiple locations using network file storage. Both virtual servers have access to a database for data read and write operations. Since both servers always need to be active, the customer pays for their 24 × 7 operation. But the database service is only active when a data transaction takes place. As a result, the customer does not pay a 24 × 7 charge for a database connected to a server. Table 4.3 contains more details about each component needed to set up this cloud server.

[5]The gateway provides a RESTful API for mobile and Web applications to access other cloud services.

Table 4.2 Cloud services offered by different providers

Functionality	Amazon Web Services (AWS)	Microsoft Azure	Google Cloud Platform
Linux and Windows virtual servers	Amazon elastic compute cloud (EC2)	Azure VMs	Google Compute Engine
Relational database (structured)	Amazon relational database service (RDS)	Microsoft Azure SQL database	Google SQL
Functions (which do not require a server)	Amazon Lambda	Azure Functions	Google Cloud Functions
Non-relational key-value database (semi-structured)	Amazon DynamoDB	Cosmos DB	Google Cloud Bigtable
Object store/ file storage	Amazon simple storage service (S3)	Azure Blob Storage	Google Storage
Artificial intelligence and machine learning	Artificial intelligence machine learning		

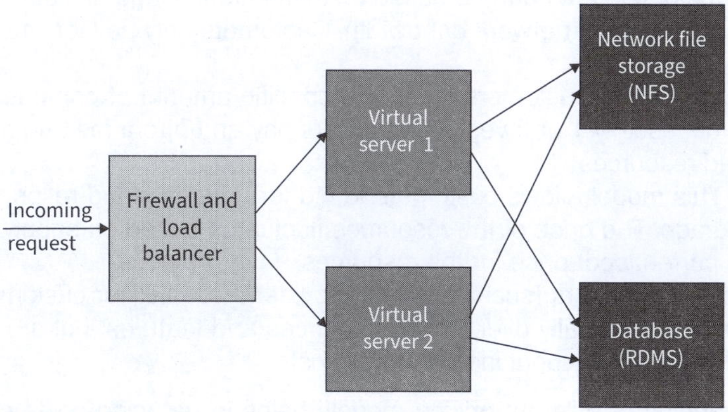

Fig. 4.5 Cloud computing components needed to set up a redundant server

Table 4.3 Cloud service components for setting up a server

Cloud Service	Functionality	More Details
Firewall and load balancer (LB)	Use-defined rules for incoming and outgoing traffic for each resource	Managed fault tolerant service (SaaS)
Virtual machines (VMs)	User can install needed software—Virtual Linux or Windows	Part of IaaS
Network file system (NFS)	Store and access files from multiple virtual machines	Uses Network File System (NFS)v4.1 protocol
Relational database (RDBMS)	Managed service with access to MySQL (or equivalent) database	Cloud provider manages backups, updates, and replication (SaaS)

Estimating cost for cloud services: All cloud services do not use a single billing metric. Data access, virtual server, load balancer have their own unique characteristics and are therefore billed accordingly. Table 4.4 shows the billing metric for the frequently used cloud services. When usage of cloud services is unchecked, many companies get exorbitant bills. Dedicated professionals are now employed by corporations who periodically review and study cloud usage pattern

Table 4.4 Cost metric for commonly used cloud services

Service	Billing Metric
Database access	Storage and minutes or hours of usage
Object storage	Storage usage (MB, GB, etc.) and traffic
Virtual Machine/Server	Minutes or hours of usage
Load balancer	Traffic and minutes/hours of usage
Content Delivery Network (CDN)[6]	Traffic

and charges. Based on their findings, they gently nudge different departments (such as ones using expensive compute resources for AI model training) to use compute resources from a cost-effective pricing model. For a business, it is therefore important to understand different pricing models offered by cloud computing service providers. Some of the most common pricing models are:

Pay-as-you-go Customers are charged based on their actual usage of cloud resources, such as computing power, storage, and network bandwidth. Customers only pay for what they use, with no upfront costs.

Reserved instances Here, customers reserve a specific amount of computing resources for a certain period of time, usually 1 or 3 years. Customers pay an upfront fee and a discounted hourly rate for the reserved resources.

Spot instances This model allows customers to bid for unused cloud resources, such as computing power or storage. The price of the resources fluctuates based on supply and demand, and customers pay the current spot price for the resources.

Free tier Many cloud providers (such as AWS) provide a free tier for customers to try out their services. These free tiers typically offer limited resources and features, but are a good way to get started with cloud computing without incurring any costs.

A good understanding of different pricing models helps in reducing costs of cloud computing services. Each pricing model discussed earlier can be effective in certain scenarios. Here are some simple recommendations which can help in cost-effective use of cloud services.

- **Reserved instances** Reserved instances allow users to pay a lower hourly rate for cloud resources if they commit to using them for a longer period, that is, for typically 1 or 3 years. This can save you a significant amount of money compared to using on-demand instances.
- **Autoscaling** Autoscaling enables you to automatically adjust the amount of computing resources based on the demand of your application. This allows you to avoid overprovisioning and wasting resources, while also ensuring that your application can handle spikes in traffic.
- **Spot instances** Spot instances allow you to bid for unused cloud resources, which can be significantly cheaper than on-demand instances. This approach can save you money, but it requires that you can tolerate some degree of unpredictability in your computing resources.
- **Cost optimization tools** Many cloud providers offer cost optimization tools that can help identify areas where costs can be reduced. These tools provide recommendations on which resources to optimize or turn off and also provide insights into how to better use cloud resources. This may sound counterintuitive as to why would a cloud service provider help a customer to reduce cost of cloud services? It builds credibility and fosters long-term partnership.

[6]Content Delivery Network (CDN) is a network of servers that transmit all kinds of media and content.

- **Resource tagging** Resource tagging enables you to categorize and organize your cloud resources based on various criteria, such as environment, project, or owner. This can help you better understand your cloud resource usage and identify opportunities to optimize your usage.
- **Usage review** Regular review of cloud resource usage can help you identify areas where you can reduce costs. This can involve turning off unused resources, resizing resources based on demand, or adjusting your pricing model.

4.5 | Setting Up Cloud Services

Even though it is unlikely you will ever need to set up a cloud service (like a virtual server) on your own, it is useful to have an idea of how it is done.

- The administrator remotely configures virtual servers and each cloud service to be used. This is done using an API for each service (see Fig. 4.6). Both the virtual server and services reside on the same cloud. But they are not on the same hardware. This distinction is explained using two clouds. One for services and other for the virtual server.
- The server interacts with the outside world using HTTP requests. Each request gets processed by using a service API if needed. This is seen in Fig. 4.7. To further elaborate on this, let us assume the user's HTTP request is for an image file. The server interacts with file storage service and passes details of the requested image file. It gets back the file from the file storage service and serves it to the user. The virtual server is always active, while the services get used (billed) based on how often the server interacts with them.

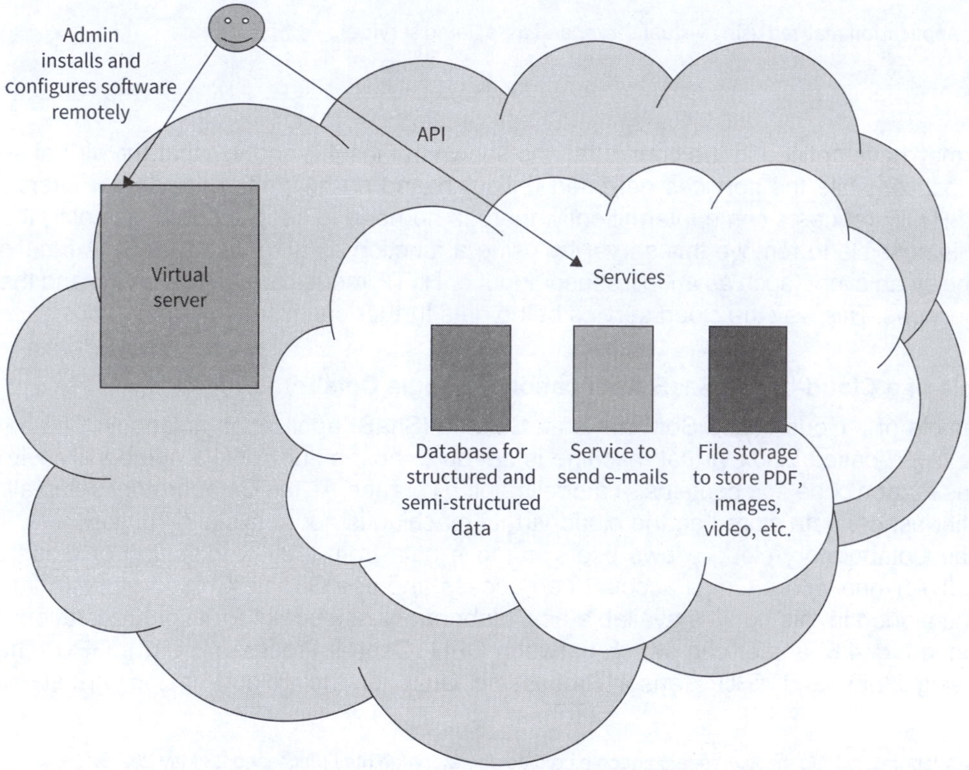

Fig. 4.6 Remotely configured virtual servers and cloud services

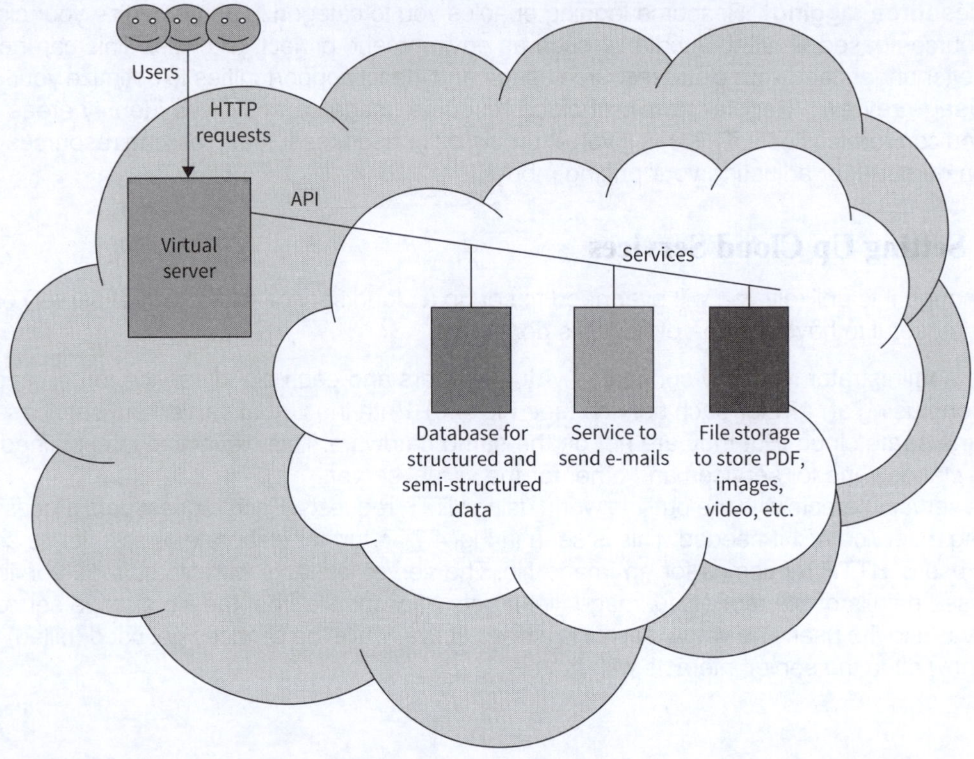

Fig. 4.7 Application realized using virtual server and associated services

You may have noticed in the configurations shown in Figs 4.6 and 4.7 that the virtual server is always active, while the services get used (billed) based on how often the server interacts with them. If HTTP requests come intermittently, there is no need to keep a server listening the entire time. It is possible to remove this server by using a function as a service (FaaS). A function gets triggered by an event (such as an IoT sensor input or HTTP request on API gateway) and then calls other services. This way the cloud service setup gets further optimised in terms of cost.

Example of a Cloud-based SaaS Application—Google Colaboratory

An example of a cloud-based Software as a Service (SaaS) application is Google Colaboratory.[7] Here, a cloud-based Linux virtual machine is set up to host a Jupyter-like notebook environment that runs Python code and contains AI model training libraries. As the Colaboratory setup allows for a free tier usage, data stored on the cloud virtual machine is not persistent. To work with relevant data, the Colaboratory cloud allows users to move data from their workstation or Google Drive (Fig. 4.8). Anyone with a Gmail account can access and use Google Colaboratory. In fact, most code mentioned in this book is available as Colaboratory notebooks for experimentation. As can be seen in Fig. 4.8, a user can switch between CPU (Central Processing Unit), GPU (Graphical Processing Unit), and TPU (Tensor Processing Unit) for their cloud-hosted virtual machine.

[7]Google Colaboratory FAQ, https://research.google.com/colaboratory/faq.html (accessed 23 May 2023).

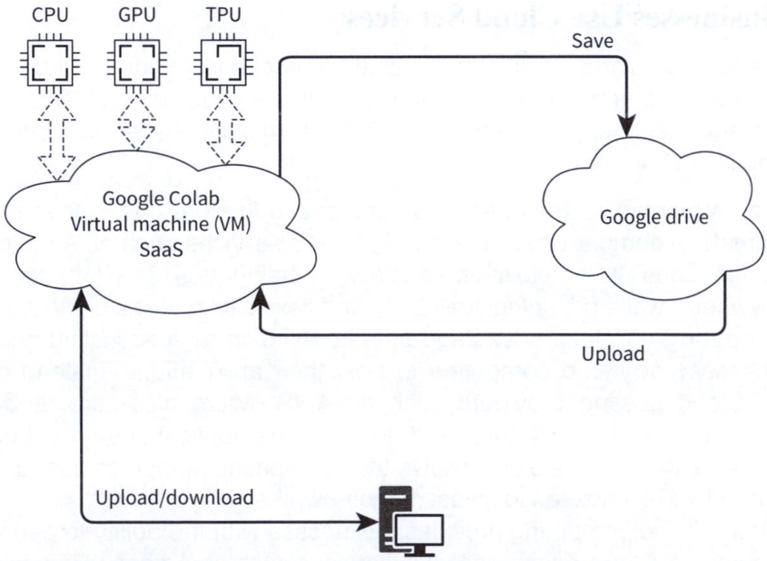

Fig. 4.8 Cloud setup for Google Colaboratory

```
1   !nvidia-smi

Thu May 18 15:49:13 2023
+-----------------------------------------------------------------------------+
| NVIDIA-SMI 525.85.12    Driver Version: 525.85.12    CUDA Version: 12.0     |
|-------------------------------+----------------------+----------------------+
| GPU  Name        Persistence-M| Bus-Id        Disp.A | Volatile Uncorr. ECC |
| Fan  Temp  Perf  Pwr:Usage/Cap|         Memory-Usage | GPU-Util  Compute M. |
|                               |                      |               MIG M. |
|===============================+======================+======================|
|   0  Tesla T4            Off  | 00000000:00:04.0 Off |                    0 |
| N/A   35C    P8     9W /  70W |      0MiB / 15360MiB |      0%      Default |
|                               |                      |                  N/A |
+-------------------------------+----------------------+----------------------+

+-----------------------------------------------------------------------------+
| Processes:                                                                  |
|  GPU   GI   CI        PID   Type   Process name                  GPU Memory |
|        ID   ID                                                   Usage      |
|=============================================================================|
|  No running processes found                                                 |
+-----------------------------------------------------------------------------+
```

Fig. 4.9 GPU usage details of a cloud-based machine—Google Colaboratory

For most applications, the CPU-based option works best. AI model training applications require use of GPU or TPU. When using GPU as the processor of the Colaboratory virtual machine, the user can monitor various parameters of the GPU. These parameters consist of GPU temperature, utilization, power usage, memory usage, and details about the process that is engaging the GPU. These details are shown in Fig. 4.9.

4.6 | How Businesses Use Cloud Services

One of the ways to understand usefulness of cloud services is to find out how businesses use it. Businesses use cloud computing for a variety of purposes, including data storage, application hosting, and data analytics. Here are some examples of how businesses use cloud computing from various cloud service providers:

- **Data storage** Many businesses use cloud computing to store and manage large amount of data. For example, a company can use cloud storage services such as Amazon S3, Microsoft Azure, or Google Cloud Storage to store and back up their data. This allows them to access their data from anywhere, while providing scalability and flexibility in terms of storage capacity.
- **Application hosting** To take advantage of features such as autoscaling and pay-as-you-go model, businesses use cloud computing to host their applications, instead of hosting them on-premises. Cloud hosting providers such as AWS, Microsoft Azure, and Google Cloud Platform provide businesses with the ability to host their applications on virtual servers in the cloud. Cloud allows them to scale up or down their computing resources based on demand, and reduces the need for businesses to invest in their own hardware.
- **Data analytics** Cloud computing provides businesses with the ability to perform data analytics on large datasets. Cloud-based analytics services such as Amazon Redshift, Google BigQuery, and Microsoft Azure Synapse Analytics allow businesses to store and analyze their data in the cloud. Central repository of data allows businesses to gain insights from their data and make data-driven decisions.
- **Disaster recovery** Businesses use cloud computing as a disaster recovery solution. By replicating their data and applications to the cloud, businesses ensure that their data and applications are safe in the event of a disaster, such as a natural disaster or cyberattack. Cloud-based approach provides businesses with peace of mind and reduces the risk of downtime.
- **Collaborative working** Cloud based services enable collaborative work by allowing remote and secure access by developers located in different regions of the world. The recent pandemic underscored this inherent advantage of cloud computing.

Many businesses have benefited from cloud services. Cloud services helps businesses improve their scalability, flexibility, and cost-effectiveness, and provides them with access to advanced technologies such as AI, big data analytics, and IoT. Few examples of businesses (based on information in the public domain) that use cloud services include the following:

- **Netflix** Netflix has been able to rapidly expand and scale its business thanks to cloud services. It uses AWS to store and stream its video content to millions of viewers worldwide.
- **Airbnb** Airbnb uses AWS to provide a seamless experience for its users. The company uses cloud services for everything from hosting its Website and mobile app to managing its reservations and payments systems.
- **Spotify** Spotify uses cloud services to store and stream its music content to millions of users worldwide. It uses Google Cloud Platform (GCP) to host its music catalog and streaming platform.
- **Slack** Slack is a cloud-based communication and collaboration platform that has become increasingly popular in recent years. The company uses AWS to host its platform and to provide real-time messaging, file sharing, and video conferencing capabilities to its users.
- **Intuit** Intuit, a financial software company, uses cloud services to power its products and services. Under the hood, the company uses AWS to host its QuickBooks Online platform, which allows small businesses to manage their finances online.

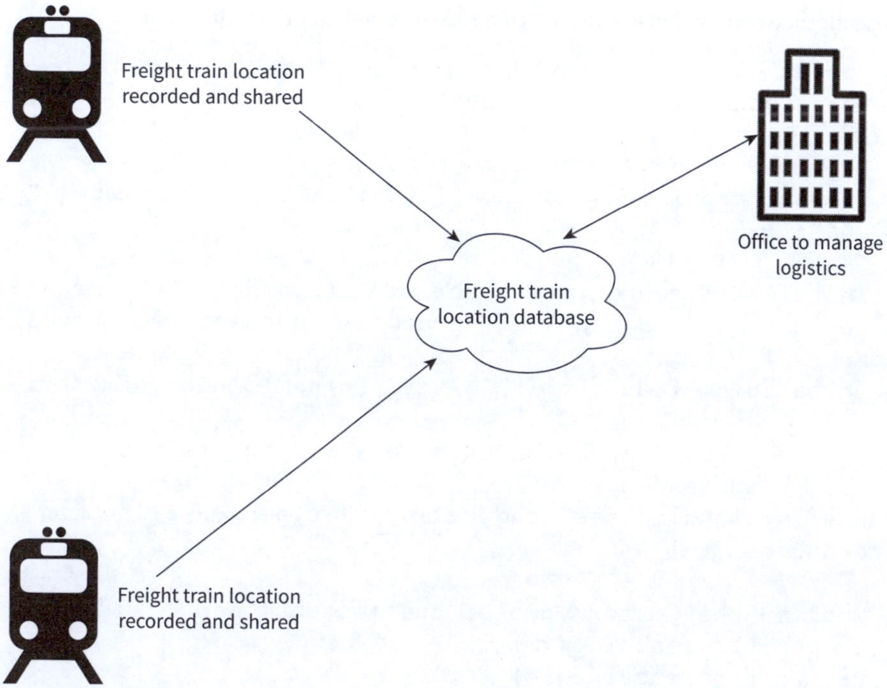

Fig. 4.10 Cloud database for disseminating information about rail asset management

- **Siemens**[8] Among many applications such as factory automation, Siemens uses AWS to deliver its Railigent application to rail operators. The application collects data from live trains (Fig. 4.10) and helps operators make data-driven decisions to ensure the safety and efficiency of their rail networks. Real-time information about train locations is populated in a cloud database
- **Dabur**[9] Microsoft Azure provides IoT, AI, and ML services to Dabur. By using Azure Hybrid Benefits (AHUB) for non-SAP workloads, Dabur has achieved cost savings by reducing energy costs of on-premise servers. This was made possible by using on-demand cloud services.

4.7 | Pseudocode for Engaging Cloud Services

In Section 4.4, we discussed how a virtual server is set up and configured to support several services. The pseudocode in Listing 4.1 demonstrates how a user might connect to a cloud provider, provision a new virtual machine instance (lines 4, 5), install and configure HTTP server software, upload html files (lines 7–9), create a load balancer to distribute traffic across instances (lines 12,13), monitor resource performance (lines 15,16), and scale up or down the number of instances as needed (lines 18,19). Scaling will start a new virtual machine (up to a maximum of 10)

[8]Use of AWS Cloud by Siemens, https://aws.amazon.com/solutions/case-studies/innovators/siemens/ (accessed 4 June 2023).
[9]Microsoft Azure services at Dabur, https://customers.microsoft.com/en-us/story/1629404334086631466-dabur-consumer-goods-azure-en-india (accessed 4 June 2023).

Listing 4.1 Pseudocode to provision a virtual machine instance with Ubuntu installation

```
// Connect to cloud provider
cloud = connect(cloud_provider)

// Provision a new virtual machine instance
vm = cloud.provision_instance({type: "t2.micro", image: "ubuntu-
 18.04"})

// Install and configure web server software on the instance
vm.run_script("sudo apt-get update && sudo apt-get install -y
 apache2")
vm.upload_file("index.html", "/var/www/html/index.html")

// Create a new load balancer to distribute traffic
// across instances
loadbal = cloud.create_load_balancer({type: "application",
 instances: [vm]})

// Monitor the performance of the instance and load balancer
cloud.monitor_resource(vm)
cloud.monitor_resource(lb)

// Scale up or down the number of instances as needed
cloud.scale_instances(lb, min: 1, max: 10, metric: "CPU",
 threshold: 80)
```

when CPU utilization crosses predefined threshold of 80 percent. The specific syntax and commands used will depend on the cloud provider and the services being used, but the basic principles of provisioning and managing resources in the cloud remain the same.

All cloud service providers have a Python Software Development Kit (SDK) to interact with different services. AWS Python SDK is called Boto3.[10] Boto3 allows Python developers to write software that makes use of AWS services like Amazon S3, EC2, CloudWatch, Lambda, DynamoDB, and more. The purpose of this section is not to discuss details of Boto3, but to explain how cloud services can be provisioned and used with the help of Boto3. The Boto3-based pseudocode presented in Listings 4.2 and 4.3 assumes that you have already set up your AWS credentials for Boto3 to use.

Listing 4.2 uses Boto3 to first list all the available metrics and makes a request to obtain the average CPU utilization metric of a virtual machine. The next pseudocode (Listing 4.3) demonstrates how to setup Function as a Service (FaaS). The function can be executed in response to an event and can invoke other cloud services. As discussed earlier, this is a cost-optimized approach, since it does not require use of a dedicated virtual machine.

[10]AWS SDK for Python, https://aws.amazon.com/sdk-for-python/ (accessed 10 June 2023).

Listing 4.2 Pseudocode to obtain average CPU utilization of virtual machine

```
01.  import boto3
02.  import datetime

03.  # create a CloudWatch client
04.  cloudwatch = boto3.client('cloudwatch')

05.  # list metrics
06.  response = cloudwatch.list_metrics()
07.  print(response['Metrics'])

08.  # get metric statistics
09.  response = cloudwatch.get_metric_statistics(
        Namespace='AWS/EC2',
        MetricName='CPUUtilization',
        Dimensions=[
        {
            'Name': 'InstanceId',
            'Value': 'INSTANCE_ID'
          },
        ],
        StartTime=datetime.datetime.utcnow() -
                                     datetime.timedelta(minutes=5),
        EndTime=datetime.datetime.utcnow(),
        Period=60,
        Statistics=['Average',]
        )
10.  print(response['Datapoints'])
```

Listing 4.3 Pseudocode to define a function called "my-function," mention the runtime (Python 3.7), indicate timeout. This is an example of Function as a Service (FaaS)

```
import boto3

# create a Lambda client
lambda_client = boto3.client('lambda')

# create a new function
response = lambda_client.create_function(
 FunctionName='my-function',
 Runtime='python3.7',
 Role='arn:aws:iam::ACCOUNT_ID:role/lambda-role',
 Handler='lambda_function.lambda_handler',
 Code={
 'ZipFile': b'bytes',
 },
```

(Continued)

Listing 4.3 *(Continued)*

```
 Timeout=60,
 MemorySize=128
)
print(response)

# invoke a function
response = lambda_client.invoke(
 FunctionName='my-function',
 Payload='{}',
)
print(response)
```

4.8 | Reading Cloud Service Architecture Diagrams

Cloud service architects connect different services together and by gluing using software APIs. Since each service has potentially dozens or hundreds of APIs; we are not going to discuss API details. To explain a real-world application that uses multiple cloud services, we will take the help of architecture diagrams. These diagrams pictorially tell the story of how data flows between physical devices and different cloud services. All cloud providers have icons representing different services that they support. Here we use AWS cloud service architecture diagrams for explanation. Once you understand one, you can quickly understand architecture diagrams from other cloud service providers.

Figure 4.11 shows the use of cloud services for a ports and inland logistics facility. You can see how CCTVs are used for surveillance purpose and video data frames are parsed using an AI computer vision service known as Amazon Rekognition. Data from the terminal is stored in an object database (S3) while real-time operational and financial data is stored in NoSQL database (DynamoDB). A customer facing Website uses an API gateway to access data and provides information to truckers and customers. Within the port a business intelligence tool (QuickSight) uses data from the database to populate data metrics for effective management of the port.

Figure 4.12 shows the use of IoT MQTT protocol to collect temperature data from four different pumps. This data is saved to a time-series database (Timestream) and is also provided to a dashboard (Grafana). An AI model (Lookout for Equipment) is used to parse the incoming data for any anomaly in the pump temperature.

The last cloud service architecture (Fig. 4.13) is of an intelligent retail supply chain. Each number mentioned in the figure represents an operation that triggers dataflow within the interconnected cloud services setup. Following is the description of the dataflow for intelligent supply chain documented by AWS.[13]

1. Suppliers receive the purchase order (PO) and demand signals and raise Order Received, Order Shipped, Autonomous System Numbers (ASN), and Invoice events.
2. The logistics provider receives driver alerts, and sends Order Loaded, Location, and Temp sensor readings.
3. Consumers receive estimated time of arrival (ETA) notifications and origin provenance, and in turn send the Order Delivered notice.
4. Stores and warehouses receive ASN notifications and Order Received notifications, and raise Order Received, Order Shipped, Put Away, Pick-Pack, and Dispatch notifications, and invoice events.

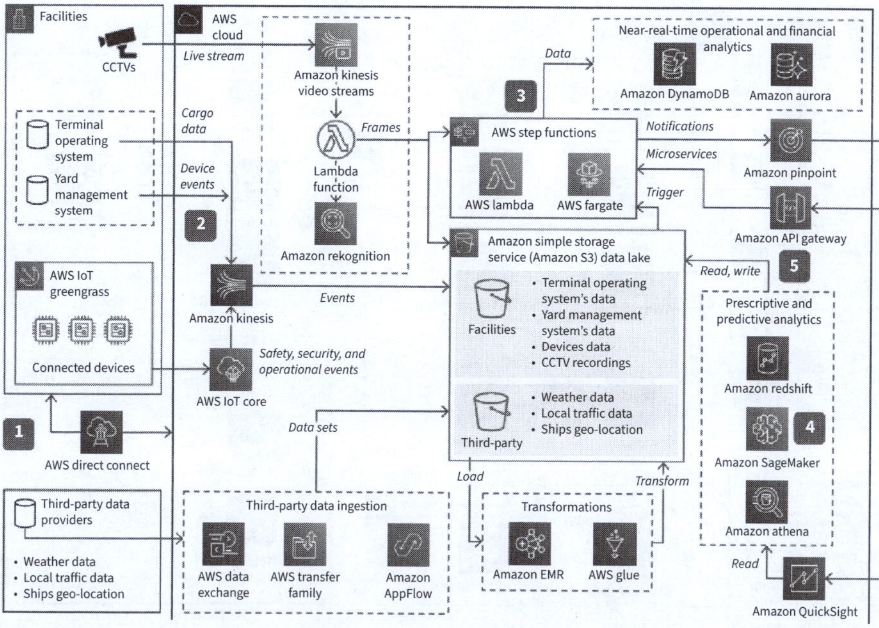

Fig. 4.11 Cloud service architecture diagram showing data platform for ports and inland logistics facilities[11]

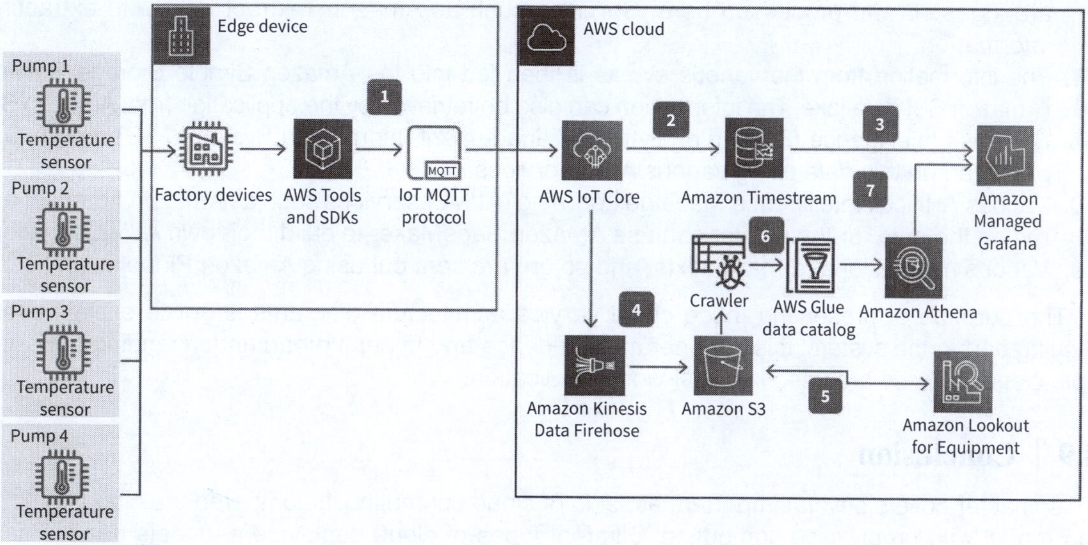

Fig. 4.12 Cloud service architecture diagram showing M-enabled predictive maintenance[12]

[11]AWS Reference Architecture for Ports and Inland logistics, https://d1.awsstatic.com/architecture-diagrams/ArchitectureDiagrams/data-platform-for-ports-ra.pdf?did=wp_card&trk=wp_card (accessed 4 June 2023).

[12]AWS reference architecture for predictive maintenance, https://d1.awsstatic.com/architecture-diagrams/ArchitectureDiagrams/machine-learning-enabled-predictive-maintenance-ra.pdf?did=wp_card&trk=wp_card (accessed 4 June 2023).

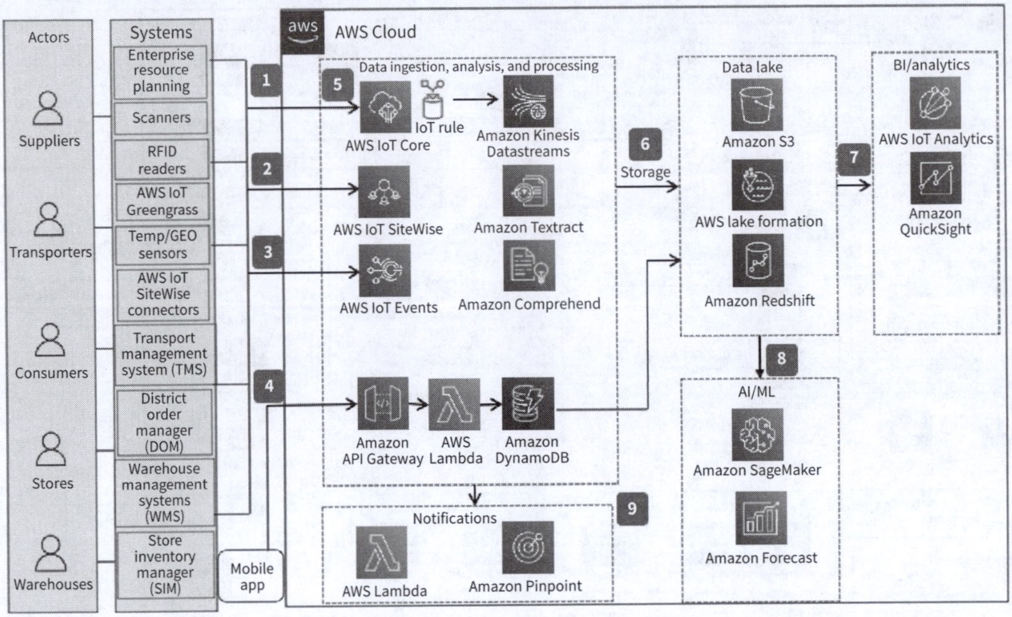

Fig. 4.13 Cloud service architecture diagram showing intelligent supply chain – retail[13]

5. Data ingestion and processing—Events from the various sources (systems and devices) are ingested and processed here. Services such as Amazon Textract help with extracting information.
6. The information from the various events is then fed into the Amazon Simple Storage Service (Amazon S3) data lake. The information can also be retrieved by the application from Amazon S3.
7. Business Intelligence (BI) and analytics—Management Information System (MIS) reports are produced on this data using various AWS services.
8. Various Artificial Intelligence/Machine Learning (AI/ML) services such as Amazon Forecast are run on the data, or the retailer can use Amazon SageMaker to build their own AI/ML services.
9. Various notifications (e-mails, texts, and so on) are sent out using Amazon Pinpoint services.

The purpose of presenting these cloud service architecture diagrams is not to explain every moving part in the system. It is to generate confidence and to get a broad understanding how multiple cloud services are used in a real-world application.

4.9 | Conclusion

This chapter covers several important aspects of cloud computing. It compared the cloud computing model with on-premise computing. Different types of cloud deployment models (IaaS, PaaS, SaaS, and FaaS) are presented. To set up real-world applications, different deployment and service models are put together. Cost optimization of cloud services is briefly discussed by use of function as a service (FaaS) concept. Python APIs in form of pseudocode are presented to demonstrate provisioning of a virtual machine, gathering metrics and setting up FaaS. The chapter ends with a discussion of reading cloud service architecture diagrams.

[13]AWS reference architecture for intelligent supply chain – retail, https://docs.aws.amazon.com/architecture-diagrams/latest/intelligent-supply-chain-retail/intelligent-supply-chain-retail.html?did=wp_card&trk=wp_card (accessed 4 June 2023).

Exercises

A. State True/False

1. On-premise computing services can scale quickly with demand.
2. Cloud service companies provide cloud infrastructure in different countries across the world.
3. Three leading public cloud computing companies in the world are Amazon, Microsoft, and Google.

B. Short-answer Questions

1. If a virtual cloud server costs ₹30/hour, calculate its annual running cost.
2. Briefly explain use of FaaS to contact a logistics operator (truck driver) when temperature inside refrigerated truck starts to rise.
(Hint: Use IoT temperature sensor input as a trigger.)
3. Enumerate the different cloud services associated with your Google (Gmail) id.
4. What is the billing metric used by a cloud-based database access service.
5. Give an example of a cloud-based SaaS application that you have used.
6. Mention the name of the AWS Python software development kit (SDK) package that is needed to provision and setup cloud services.
7. A business requirement states a new virtual machine to be spun up if the CPU utilization goes above 70 percent. Which line/parameter in Listing 4.1 needs to be modified to meet this requirement.

C. Long-answer Questions

1. Discuss a scenario when on-premise computing is better suited for a business as compared to cloud computing.
2. Map business requirements to cloud based services for the business setup we discussed in Fig. 4.1. Explore the Website of a public cloud service provider and fill in Table 4.5. We have partially filled in some cells of the table. Populate the shaded cells.
3. Create a cloud service architecture diagram using different cloud services for an automated parking garage setup (discussed in Chapter 1).
4. Identify two companies for each type of cloud deployment: on-premise, hybrid and cloud. Give reasons why each company uses a particular type of cloud deployment.

Table 4.5 Mapping business needs (Fig. 4.1) with cloud services

Business Need	Computing Requirement	Cloud Service
Monitor farm produce for predicting production, use precision farming techniques	Use computer vision to techniques at the edge for estimation and precision farming	Train computer vision models on cloud and deploy them on computers in the farm
Monitor footfalls and inventory in retail stores	Use computer vision for people counting, local database for store inventory	
E-commerce Website	Manage customer profiles, products ordered and payment gateway	
Monitor factory operations	Update data related to production, raw material, wastage, personnel....	
Analytics of data saved in structured database		
Website chatbot for simple customer interaction		

D. Explore and Experiment

1. Create a free account using a major cloud service provider[14] and experiment with setting up a virtual machine and different types of databases (structured, semi-structured, and unstructured).
2. Find out the RAM and hard disk capacity offered by the free version of Google Colaboratory virtual machine.
3. The Generative AI prompt in Fig. 4.14 enumerates real world examples of Cloud-based Software as a Service (SaaS).

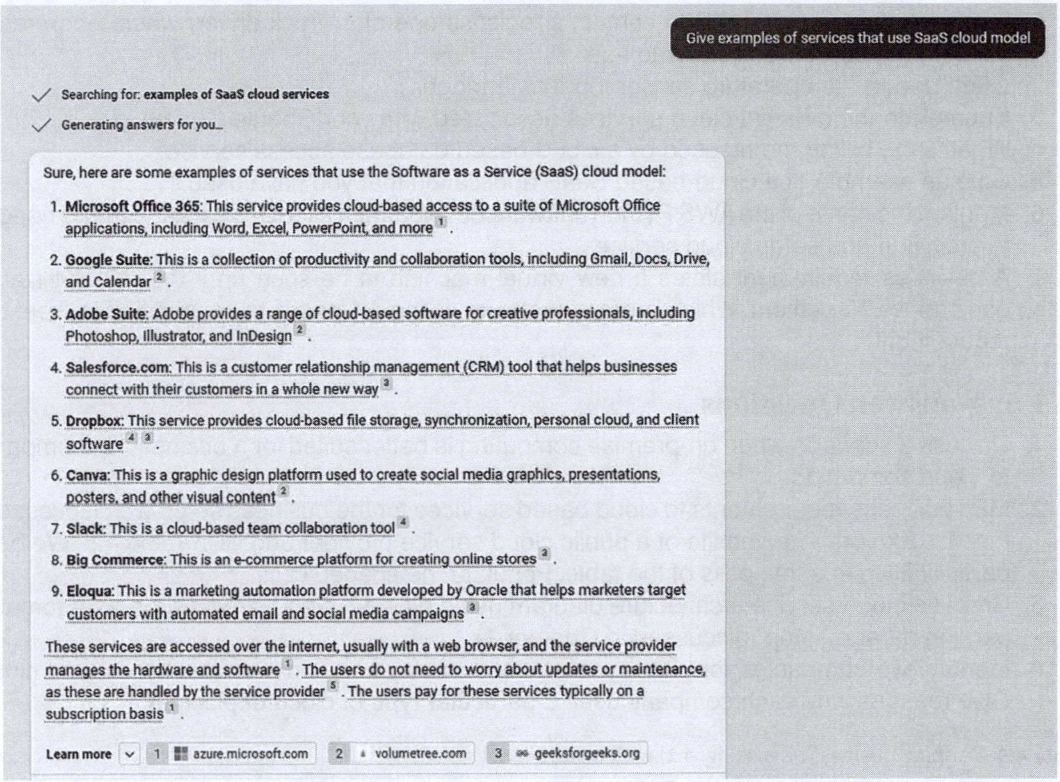

Fig. 4.14 Using Generative AI to list SaaS applications

E. Generate Use Case on Cloud Services (Learning by Example)

Use Case: Cloud Services for Managing Cold Chain

Brief description: The function of a cold chain is to provide constant temperature to a perishable commodity as it travels using different modes of transport and across long distances. The air-conditioning company Carrier, uses different cloud services (IoT, analytics and machine learning) to monitor and maintain a cold chain. Use the resources listed below to understand how cloud-based services are used for this purpose. Document the cold chain use case using the template given below.

[14] AWS Free Tier, https://aws.amazon.com/free/ (accessed 2 June 2023).

Resources

https://aws.amazon.com/campaigns/carrier/
YouTube: https://www.youtube.com/watch?v=QJfegmsMzXw&t=728s
AWS re: Invent 2020: How Carrier is transforming the cold chain to reduce food & medicine waste

Template for Creating Use Case for Cloud Services

Define goal and purpose	Goal statement
	Identify stakeholders
	Define scope
Details to include in use case	Capture how technology helps business process
	Keep use case findings description textual, with a few simple flowcharts if needed
	Focus on describing how technology benefits the use case
Future applications	Mention any new applications that can leverage the technology used

Suggested Reading

1. Wittig & Wittig, Amazon Web Services in Action, 3rd Edition, Manning.

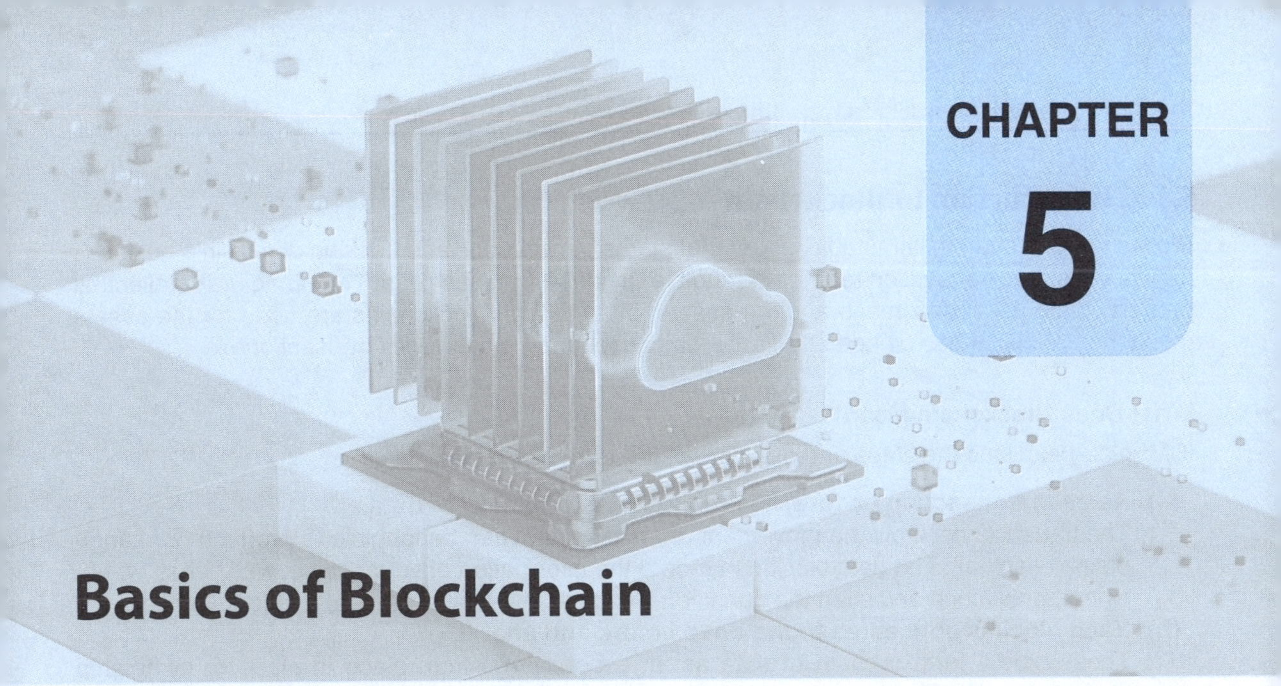

CHAPTER

5

Basics of Blockchain

CHAPTER OUTLINE

5.1 Introduction to Blockchain
5.2 Salient Features of Blockchain
5.3 Application of Blockchain to Business
5.4 Implementing Blockchain Technology

LEARNING OBJECTIVES

After reading this chapter, you will be able to:

- understand the concepts and benefits of blockchain
- apply blockchain to business applications

Effective Management Using Blockchain

The world is digital. All transactions are carried out digitally. Simple transactions such as going to a store and purchasing an item are logged to the store's computer server. When you go to return an item, the store looks up the receipt/membership number to verify the transaction. If the store were to lose the electronic record of the purchase, there is little one can do.

Let us now consider a scenario where multiple entities are involved. Suppose there is a car that has been sold multiple times. During each sale, the car's details (mileage, engine condition, tires, etc.) are recorded. If the fourth owner of the car has suspicions about the car's true odometer reading, they can go and access the one computer that maintains the record. But there is a possibility that the records may have been tampered with. It is therefore important that transactions are not stored on a single system, but are securely saved across multiple computers.

Millions of business transactions take place every day across the world. A secure mechanism to timestamp and save each transaction in a distributed ledger is needed for transparency and confidence in digital transactions.

5.1 | Introduction to Blockchain

Blockchain is a shared, immutable ledger that stores transactions and tracking details in a business network. It stores transaction records of tangible (a house, car, cash, land) or intangible (intellectual property, patents, copyrights, branding) assets. Even though blockchains are used for the assets mentioned above, it has gained popularity for its use for cryptocurrency transactions.

What Does Blockchain Mean?

IBM[1] nicely explains the steps and meaning of the term blockchain.

(a) As each transaction occurs, it is recorded as a "block" of data.
The transactions show the movement of an asset that can be tangible (a product) or intangible (intellectual). The data block can record the information of your choice: who, what, when, where, how much and even the condition—such as the temperature of a food shipment.

(b) Each block is connected to the ones before and after it.
These blocks form a chain of data as an asset moves from place to place or ownership changes hands. The blocks confirm the exact time and sequence of transactions, and the blocks link securely together to prevent any block from being altered or a block being inserted between two existing blocks.

(c) Transactions are blocked together in an irreversible chain: a blockchain.
Each additional block strengthens the verification of the previous block and hence the entire blockchain. This renders the blockchain tamper-evident, delivering the key strength of immutability. This removes the possibility of tampering by a malicious actor—and builds a ledger of transactions you and other network members can trust.

At the heart of blockchain is the distributed ledger technology (DLT). This is a peer-to-peer network consisting of replicated data (in different nodes) without the need for a central administrator (Fig. 5.1). All member nodes (computers) are interconnected and have their own data storage for independently recording transactions. A new event gets recorded in the blockchain, by having each node agree on the outcome. When consensus is reached, each node records the transaction data into its copy of the ledger. The Linux Foundation's Hyperledger Fabric is the market leading open source technology that is used for blockchain applications.

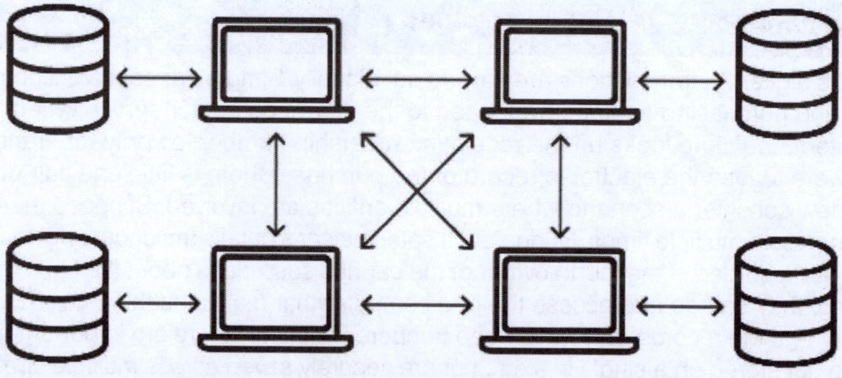

Fig. 5.1 Distributed ledger framework (based on Hyperledger Fabric) for blockchain

[1]https://www.ibm.com/topics/what-is-blockchain (accessed 14 November 2022).

A blockchain fabric network[2] consists of the following building blocks:

Peer nodes Execute chaincode, access ledger data, endorse transactions and interface with user applications
Ordered nodes Ensure validity of the blockchain and deliver agreed (consensus) transactions to the peers of the network
Membership service providers Implemented as a Certificate Authority, managing X.509 certificates to authenticate member identity and roles.

Some features of hyperledger fabric as spelled out by IBM[3]

(a) Permissioned network Establish decentralized trust in a network of known participants rather than an open network of anonymous participants.
(b) Confidential transactions Expose only the data you want to share to the parties you want to share it with.
(c) Pluggable architecture Tailor the blockchain to industry needs with a pluggable architecture rather than a one-size-fits-all approach.
(d) Easy to get started Program smart contracts in the languages your team works in today, instead of learning custom languages and architectures.

IT system integrators and cloud service providers assist in setting up a blockchain network for businesses. They install needed software on peer, ordered nodes and parse X.509 certificates to authenticate member identity.

5.2 | Salient Features of Blockchain

There are several features that contribute to blockchain's functionality. Some of these features are reiterated here:

Consensus Ensures agreement between member nodes before creation of block
Consensus process ensures shared ledgers are updated with a block of data only after the transaction is validated by all participants.
Replication Ensure ledger update for all participants
Once data blocks are approved, they are created across all participants in the network. This ensures there are no accidental (or intentional) data tampering. A decentralized setup provides transparency among all parties in a business network.
Immutability Ensures transparency
All blockchain transactions are immutably recorded with a time and date stamp. This provides confidence to members when they view the entire history of a transaction. Immutability eliminates any possibility of fraud.

5.3 | Application of Blockchain to Business

Blockchain has an inherent feature to provide trustworthy transactions. Many businesses use this in multiple ways. Blockchain technology has a wide range of use cases in business. Few examples of how businesses use blockchain are mentioned here:

[2]Hyperledger project: https://en.wikipedia.org/wiki/Hyperledger (accessed 15 November 2022).
[3]Hyperledger features: https://www.ibm.com/topics/hyperledger (accessed 15 November 2022).

- **Supply chain management** When applied to our farm to retail setup, blockchain helps create a tamper-proof, transparent supply chain by tracking the movement of goods from the manufacturer to the end customer. This helps businesses ensure the authenticity and quality of their products, as well as prevent counterfeiting and fraud.
- **Digital identity** Blockchain also creates a decentralized, secure digital identity system. This helps businesses verify the identities of their customers and employees, and provide a more secure and efficient way of managing access to sensitive information and resources.
- **Financial services** DLT of blockchain is used in financial services for a range of applications, including cross-border payments, trade finance, and asset tokenization. By using blockchain, businesses reduce the time and cost of financial transactions, increase transparency, and improve security.
- **Smart contracts** Blockchain enables creation and enforcement of smart contracts. These contracts are self-executing that automatically execute when certain conditions are met. This is used for a range of applications, including supply chain management, financial services, and real estate.

The most intuitive application for blockchain is track and trace. It fits very nicely with the business setup we have been discussing so far. A component or a subsystem supplied by one or multiple vendors is tracked and traced through its journey to the consumer. Figs. 5.2 and 5.3 (scenario from AWS[4]) show the flow of goods and information before and after implementation of blockchain.

Challenges without the blockchain-based track and trace are the following:

- No insight available on movement of goods
- Unknown sourcing concerns
- Interaction with manufacturer's fragmented data systems
- Non-real-time logistics update
- In the absence of timely data, wholesalers either overstocked or stockout
- Minimal insight into the supply chain for the consumer

Benefits provided by blockchain in a track and trace application are the following:

- Reduced need for a regulator
- Automated real-time logistics update
- Product authenticity
- Optimal stock at wholesaler based on demand
- Supply chain insight for the consumer

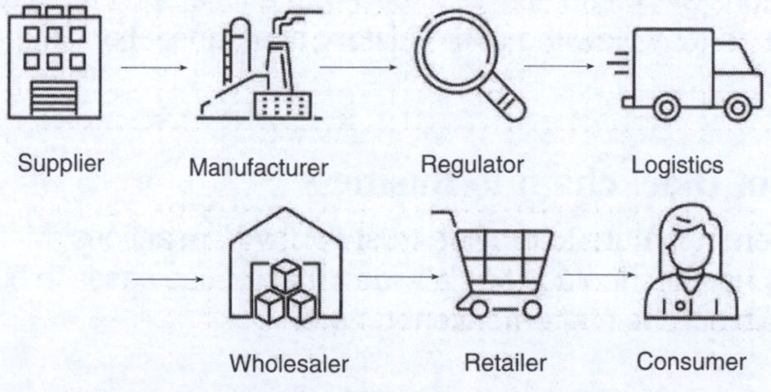

Fig. 5.2 Flow of goods from supplier to consumer

[4]Track and trace using blockchain, https://aws.amazon.com/blockchain/ (accessed 15 November 2022).

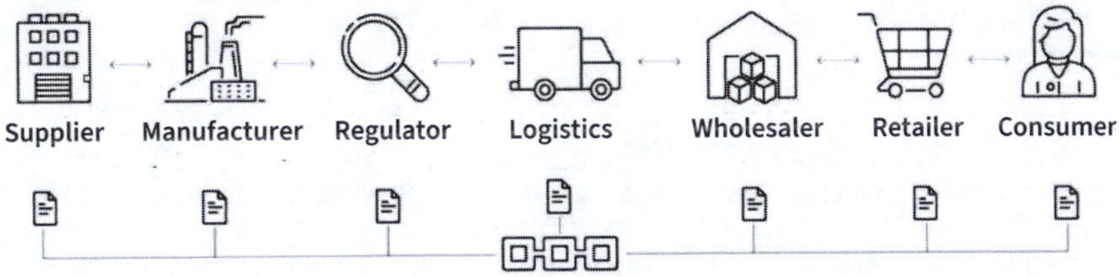

Fig. 5.3 Benefits of using blockchain to track and trace flow of goods from supplier to consumer

Table 5.1 Use cases of blockchain

Application	How Blockchain Helps
Supply chain	Blockchains improve supply chain processes by increasing transparency and traceability of transactions
Trading and asset transfer	Transactions using Hyperledger Fabric network process electronically (without lengthy paper-work), providing immediate feedback on its success or failure
Insurance	Blockchain prevents insurance fraud by ensuring claims are processed once and proceeds are given to the right person (by incorporating use of identity verification)
Food, medicine	Contaminated food and substandard medicine are traced and removed from shelves and pharmacies using blockchain

All these benefits translate to smoother business transactions for business entities operating in different parts of the world. Its use leads to greater efficiency by eliminating duplication of effort. In the real world, Blockchain technology is applied to supply chain, food distribution, financial services, government, retail, and more. Some example use cases are mentioned in Table 5.1. The list of applications mentioned in Table 5.1 is not comprehensive. Any process that needs multinodal verification benefits from blockchain.

5.4 | Implementing Blockchain Technology

In the previous chapter on cloud computing, we mentioned that the cloud offers a great platform to get started with a minimum amount of investment. Many cloud providers offer blockchain as a service. The steps employed for setting up a decentralized blockchain service are as follows:

- Choose an open-source blockchain framework. Join either a public network or create a new private network
- Invite members to join a private network
- Provision peer nodes that will store copy of distributed ledger
- Deploy decentralized applications. Carry out transactions without a centralized authority.

Blockchain is implemented using cloud services in several ways and depends on the specific requirements of the application. Some possible configurations include:

- **Cloud-based blockchain platforms** Cloud providers such as AWS, Azure, and IBM offer blockchain platforms that allow developers to build, deploy, and manage blockchain networks

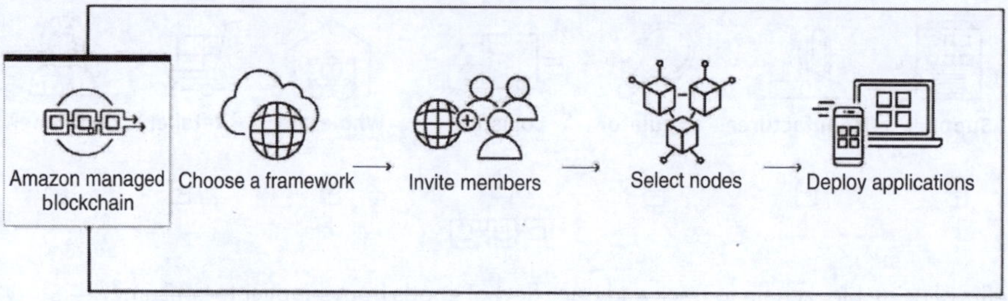

Fig. 5.4 Deploying blockchain using AWS-managed blockchain service

on the cloud. These platforms provide pre-built templates and tools for creating and configuring the blockchain network, as well as APIs and SDKs for integrating with other cloud services.

- **Blockchain infrastructure** Another option is to use cloud infrastructure services to host the blockchain network, such as virtual machines, containers, or serverless functions. This approach provides more flexibility and control over the blockchain implementation, as developers can customize the environment and resources according to their needs.
- **Blockchain-as-a-service (BaaS) providers** BaaS providers are third-party companies that offer blockchain services on the cloud, typically as a managed service. These providers handle the deployment, scaling, and maintenance of the blockchain network, while allowing customers to focus on developing and deploying their applications.

Managed blockchain services use tested deployment templates that makes the process of setting up blockchain fast and simple. An example of AWS-managed blockchain service is seen in Fig. 5.4.

Implementing a blockchain from scratch is a complex task that requires a deep understanding of cryptography, data structures, and distributed systems. Here is a simplified code example in Python[5] that implements a basic blockchain:

Listing 5.1 Class to define a new block, new transaction and generates hash

```
01.  import hashlib
02.  import json
03.  from time import time

04.  class Blockchain:
05.  def __init__(self):
         self.chain = []
         self.current_transactions = []

          # Create the starting block
         self.new_block(previous_hash=1)

06.  def new_block(self, previous_hash=None):
        block = {
             'index': len(self.chain) + 1,
```

[5]Simple Blockchain code in Python, https://www.geeksforgeeks.org/create-simple-blockchain-using-python/ (accessed 10 June 2023).

Listing 5.1 *(Continued)*

```
             'timestamp': time(),
             'transactions': self.current_transactions,
             'previous_hash': previous_hash or self.hash(self.chain[-1]),
  }

         # Reset the current list of transactions
         self.current_transactions = []

         # Append the block to the chain
         self.chain.append(block)

         return block

07.   def new_transaction(self, sender, recipient, amount):
        self.current_transactions.append({
            'sender': sender,
            'recipient': recipient,
            'amount': amount,
          })

      return self.last_block['index'] + 1

08.   # A static method is a method that belongs to a class rather than
09.   # an instance of a class
10.   @staticmethod
11.   def hash(block):
         # Convert the block dictionary to a JSON string and hash it
         # using SHA-256
         block_string = json.dumps(block, sort_keys=True).encode()
         return hashlib.sha256(block_string).hexdigest()

12.   @property
13.   def last_block(self):
         return self.chain[-1]
```

The code in Listing 5.1 defines a Blockchain class with three methods: new_block (line 6), new_transaction (line 7), and hash (line 11). A new block is created and added to the chain using the new_block method. Similarly, a new transaction is added to the current list of transactions using a new_transaction. The hash method (line 11) uses SHA-256 (a cryptographic hash function) to produce a 256-bit hash value for any input data. The hash value is used to verify data integrity, secure password storage, and digital signatures. To use this code, we create an instance of the Blockchain class and start adding transactions and blocks. The code in Listing 5.2 creates a new instance of the Blockchain class (line 2), adds a new transaction (line 4), mines a new block, and prints the current chain (line 9). This simple example of a blockchain does not include features, such as consensus mechanisms, peer-to-peer networking, or validation of transactions and blocks. When executed, the code

Listing 5.2 Creation of blockchain instance and adding a transaction to it

```
# Create a new instance of the Blockchain class
blockchain = Blockchain()

# Add a new transaction
blockchain.new_transaction('Alice', 'Bob', 30)

# Mine a new block
last_block = blockchain.last_block
previous_hash = blockchain.hash(last_block)
block = blockchain.new_block(previous_hash)

print(blockchain.chain)
```

Listing 5.3 Output from Listing 5-2

```
[{'index': 1, 'timestamp': 1686715036.083373, 'transactions': [],
'previous_hash': 1}, {'index': 2, 'timestamp': 1686715036.083373,
'transactions': [{'sender': 'Alice', 'recipient': 'Bob', 'amount':
30}], 'previous_hash': '4e509186b74d4b9433a02cc0379422ebcb7c15f4ae-
07d5a3539938db40c60f64'}]
```

produces the transaction record captured in Listing 5.3. The new transaction consisting of sender (Alice), recipient (Bob), and amount(30) is added to the chain. Timestamp and hash are also added to the transaction records. In the record, we observe that the transaction is recorded as index 2. It contains information of the sender, recipient and the amount. The hash digest of the transaction is also saved along with a timestamp.

5.5 | Conclusion

In the world of e-commerce, blockchain brings a sense of order and security. Open source Hyperledger fabric combines public or private computer nodes to create a blockchain network. A node gets to create a transaction only with the consensus of member nodes. The transaction is immutable and is stored with date and time stamps on peer nodes. Many business processes stand to benefit from blockchain's distributed ledger framework.

Exercises

A. State True/False

1. Blockchain use Distributed Ledger Technology—DLT.
2. Blockchain is only used for cryptocurrency trading.
3. Blockchain transactions are immutable.
4. Track and trace only works for perishable goods.
5. Cloud service providers do not provide managed blockchain services.

B. Long-answer Questions

1. Devise a blockchain-based strategy to track and trace farmer's produce from farm to storage silos, processing plants, cold chain all the way to retail store. If there are reports of contamination of produce in a city, how would blockchain be used to identify and remove produce of the infected batch from other stores.
2. Identify a business that you think would benefit from the blockchain. Prepare a scheme detailing the processes of the business that would participate in the blockchain and the data they will commit to the blockchain network. Explain how when the business benefits from blockchain.

C. Explore and Experiment

1. Create a simple blockchain using Python code.[6] Study reference code and interact with the Flask Web server (localhost, port 5000) in the code using methods *mine_block* and *get_chain*. Refer to the Colab notebook for Chapter 5, if you need help with running this code.
2. Figure 5.5 shows a Generative AI prompt to create details of an exemplar blockchain transaction. The data generated from the transaction consists of information of the sender, receiver, amount, data on farm goods and hash value of transaction.

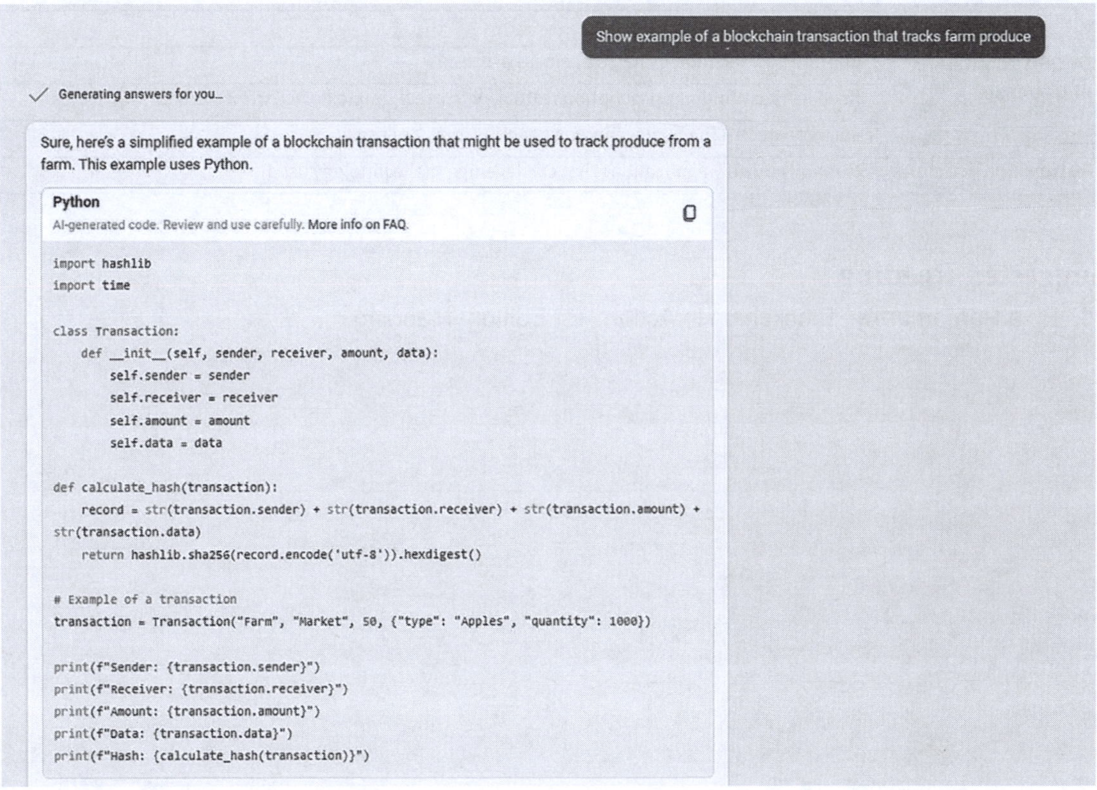


```
import hashlib
import time

class Transaction:
    def __init__(self, sender, receiver, amount, data):
        self.sender = sender
        self.receiver = receiver
        self.amount = amount
        self.data = data

def calculate_hash(transaction):
    record = str(transaction.sender) + str(transaction.receiver) + str(transaction.amount) +
str(transaction.data)
    return hashlib.sha256(record.encode('utf-8')).hexdigest()

# Example of a transaction
transaction = Transaction("Farm", "Market", 50, {"type": "Apples", "quantity": 1000})

print(f"Sender: {transaction.sender}")
print(f"Receiver: {transaction.receiver}")
print(f"Amount: {transaction.amount}")
print(f"Data: {transaction.data}")
print(f"Hash: {calculate_hash(transaction)}")
```

Fig. 5.5 AI generated *Transaction* class and *transaction* instance object to record a blockchain transaction

[6]Create simple blockchain, https://www.geeksforgeeks.org/create-simple-blockchain-using-python/ (accessed 8 June 2023).

D. Generate Use Case on Blockchain Based Supply Chain

Use Case: Tracking Coffee Beans Using Blockchain

Brief description: Coffee beans are grown in different parts of the world. Raw beans sourced from each region is handled by farmers, graders, roasters, and packers before making it to the market or the café. Use the resources mentioned below to understand how blockchain is used to track each batch of coffee beans across its journey to you. Use the template below to create a use case for this blockchain application.

Resources

YouTube:

AWS re:Invent 2020: Nestlé brings supply chain transparency with Amazon Managed Blockchain
https://www.youtube.com/watch?v=P6vPvZ0-7dY

AWS re:Invent 2019: Enterprise solutions with blockchain: Nestlé, Sony Music, & Workday
https://www.youtube.com/watch?v=UxroP6xf9ZM

Template to Generate Use Case on Blockchain

Define goal and purpose	Goal statement
	Identify stakeholders
	Define scope
Details to include in use case	Capture how technology helps business process
	Keep use case findings description textual, with a few simple flowcharts if needed
	Focus on describing how technology benefits the use case
Future applications	Mention any new applications that can leverage the technology used

Suggested Reading

1. Bina Ramamurthy, Blockchain in Action, 1st Edition, Manning.

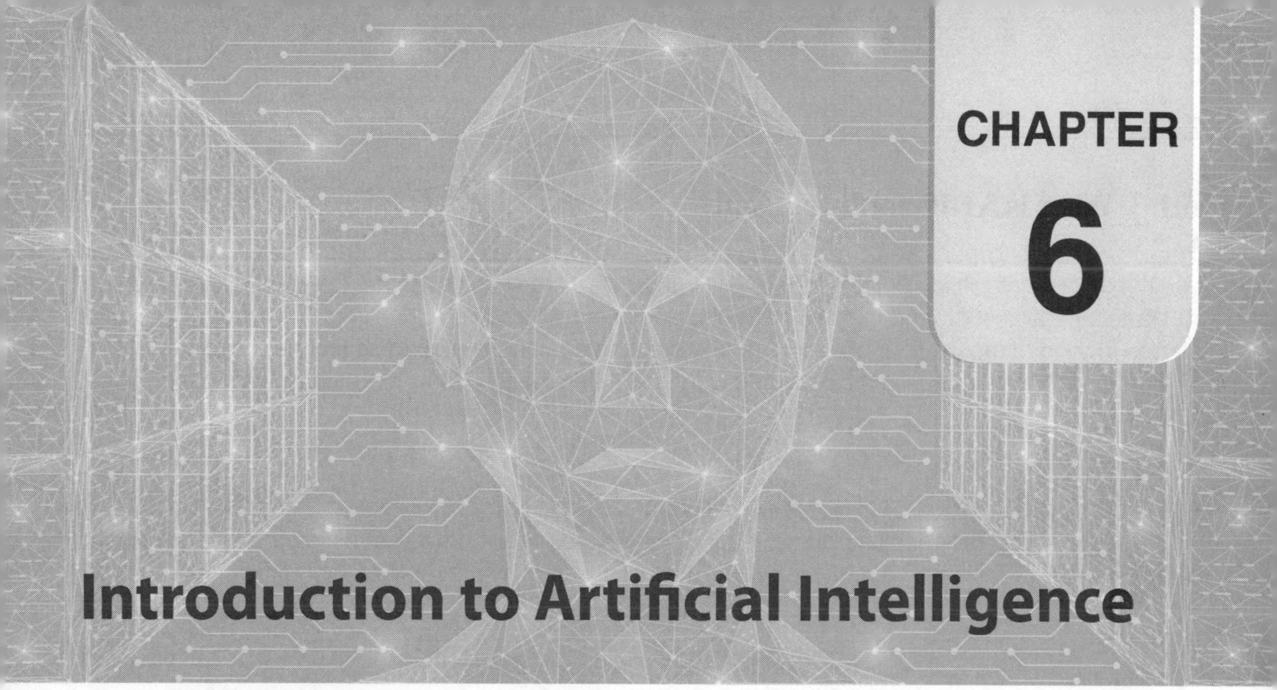

CHAPTER

6

Introduction to Artificial Intelligence

CHAPTER OUTLINE

LEARNING OBJECTIVES

After reading this chapter, you will be able to:

- understand the definition of a machine being artificially intelligent
- understand the techniques used to make a machine artificially intelligent

Effective Management Using AI

There are certain tedious tasks that humans do not wish to do. Some of these tasks include answering predictable and mundane questions (chatbots), driving on a long stretch of highway everyday (autonomous vehicles), or looking for anomalies in data or images 24×7 (anomaly detection). These tasks do not require creativity or creation of new algorithms.

Contemporary AI-enabled systems (with their limitations) serve the requirements of these applications and constitute the low hanging fruits of AI technology. Many business processes stand to benefit from AI technology.

6.1 | What is Artificial Intelligence

The idea of creating machines that have human-like intelligence has been around for a long time. Please see the timeline of artificial intelligence (AI)[1] to understand mankind's obsession with AI. Research on AI started in earnest around the 1950s. Groups of scientists at different universities around the world started looking at the way our brains work and creating analogous electronic (computer) models.

Before we travel far, let us make a distinction between the following three commonly used terms:

- Artificial intelligence
- Machine learning
- Deep learning

As seen in Fig. 6.1, both machine learning and deep learning are subsystems of AI. Further, deep learning (a model with multiple layers) is a subsystem of machine learning. So, AI is a broad encompassing term.

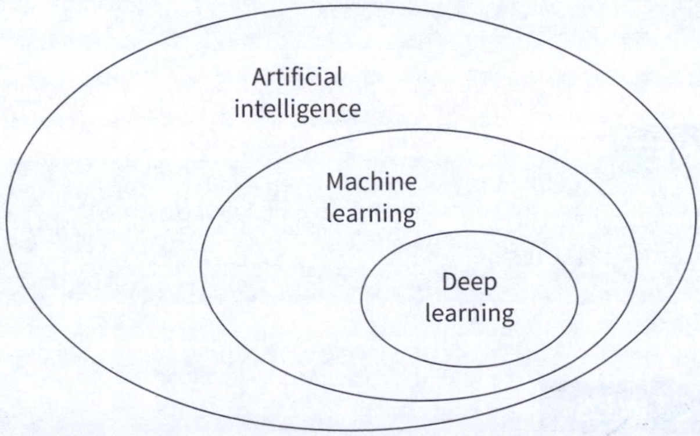

Fig. 6.1 Deep learning and machine learning are constituent parts of AI

So, what exactly do we mean when we say that a machine has AI capabilities. Do we mean that the machine can think and act humanly or do we mean that the machine can think and act rationally? It is not easy to come up with a definitive rule or test to determine if a machine is AI certified. There is one AI test that has been around for some time and is accepted as a reasonable test. It is known as the Turing[2] test, named after Alan Turing (British computer scientist) who described it in a paper written in 1950.

The way the Turing test (also known as the imitation game) is set up is as follows. A human interrogator is made to interact with a human and a computer/machine (shown on top of Fig. 6.2). The interrogator would pose written questions to both the human and the machine. Based on the response, if the machine is able to convince the interrogator that it is a human, then the machine would have passed the Turing test. This may sound and appear trivial, but there are many underlying technologies that have to be in place for a machine to pass this test. Turing test uses pen pal type interaction between human–human and human–machine. To pass the test, the human–machine interaction should be similar to human–human.

Let us put together the capabilities needed by the computer (that is imitating a human) to pass the Turing test.

[1]Timeline of artificial intelligence (AI), https://en.wikipedia.org/wiki/Timeline_of_artificial_intelligence (accessed 17 November 2022).

[2]Alan Turing, Computing machinery and intelligence, 1950, https://academic.oup.com/mind/article/LIX/236/433/986238 (a ccessed 16 November 2022).

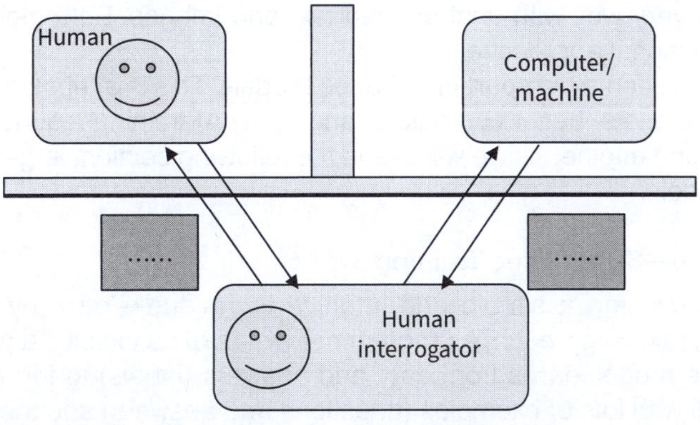

Fig. 6.2 Turing test interaction between human–human and human–machine

Table 6.1 AI model creation

AI Approach	Brief Description
Unsupervised learning	Algorithms make sense of data without any training. Example: clustering of data
Supervised learning	Training data includes answers or labels
Reinforcement learning	The learning system (called an agent) observes the environment, performs actions and gets either a penalty or reward. It updates its policy (learning step) to maximize rewards

- Natural language processing (NLP) to comprehend written text
- Reasoning to answer questions and carry forward the conversation
- Skills to adapt, detect, and extrapolate patterns in conversation

Turing's test did not have direct physical interaction between the human and the computer. A new test proposed by Harnard[3] in 1991 extended the requirements of the computer before we certify it as a human. This test is known as total Turing test and includes a video signal for the human to test the machine's perceptual abilities. It also proposes a window to pass physical objects to the machine. To pass the total Turing Test, the machine now needs to have two more skills.

- Computer vision to classify, detect, and perceive objects
- Robotics to grip and manipulate objects and be mobile

Contemporary state-of-the-art AI technology is working to master these five fundamental AI skills. Generative AI models such at ChatGPT can pass the Turing test quite easily. Technology for passing the total Turing test is work in progress.

AI models are created using three major techniques (mentioned in Table 6.1). The most popular is supervised learning, where examples are presented for learning. Systems which interact with the physical world employ reinforcement learning for training.

6.2 | Computing, Data, and AI Models

This brings us to our next topic of discussion. What kinds of problems is AI useful for and how does it work? AI shines in problems that cannot be solved using classical mathematical or programming

[3]Harnad, Stevan (1991), Other bodies, Other minds: A machine incarnation of an old philosophical problem. Minds and Machines, 1, 43–54, https://eprints.soton.ac.uk/253379/ (accessed 17 November 2022).

approaches. It works very well with unstructured text and images. Both these problems were not tractable using conventional approaches.

The last decade has seen a big spurt in AI-based models. This is attributed to three major factors: availability of larger datasets, better computers, and novel AI training algorithms. Datasets are the fodder for the AI learning engine. As we will see in the following section, large labeled datasets help in creating robust models.

Teaching by Example—Supervised Training

AI models are trained using a simple and intuitive technique—learn by example. Top half of Fig. 6.3 shows the classical approach. A programmer writes rules to solve a problem. In supervised machine learning, the model learns from data and answers (labels) to form the rules. Effectively, we present the model with lots of examples (questions and answers) and the model is able to form connections between them. A well-trained model works well not only for data on which it trained on, but also for novel data.

Let us relate this technique to conventional learning. It is equivalent to looking at thousands of solved problems to understand the underlying theory. As mentioned in the previous paragraph, models have to learn to generalize. Some students do well on examples or solved problems (by memorizing them), but fail miserably on tests where novel problems are asked.

Image classification problem using supervised learning If a model needs to recognize different kinds of fruits, it is trained using hundreds of images of each variety of fruit it needs to classify. An image of each fruit is presented along with its name (label). The model learns to correlate features of a fruit with its name. It may use the shape or color as learnt features to associate fruits.

The idea of supervised learning is not limited to images. It spans across several domains. Figure 6.4 shows three examples of supervised learning. In supervised training, inputs and outputs (questions and answers) are provided. The model is trained to learn the relationship between the two. The first consists of sentiment analysis. Paragraphs of text are provided to an AI model along with a sentiment. The model learns to associate words, such as *happy, cheerful, made my day* with positive sentiment and words such as *bad, gloomy, cheated, angry* with negative sentiment. Similarly, an object detection model is trained by providing images with bounding boxes drawn around objects of interest.

To summarize the concept of supervised learning or learning by example, we need to consider three things

- Input data—If the task is bird sound recognition the training data is sound files of bird calls. On the other hand, if the task is image classification, the training data consists of pictures that need to be classified.

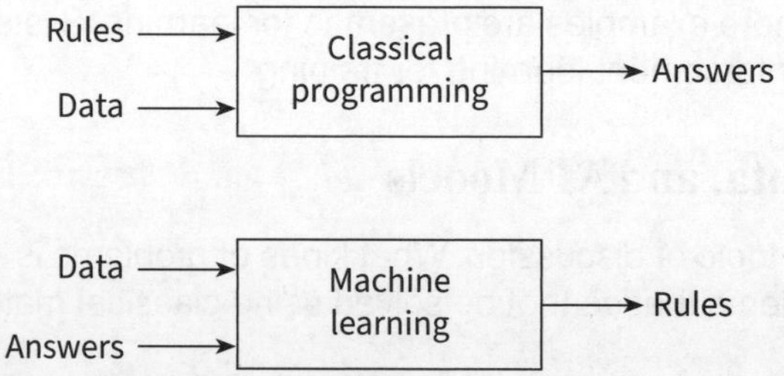

Fig. 6.3 Paradigm shift in creating code using machine learning

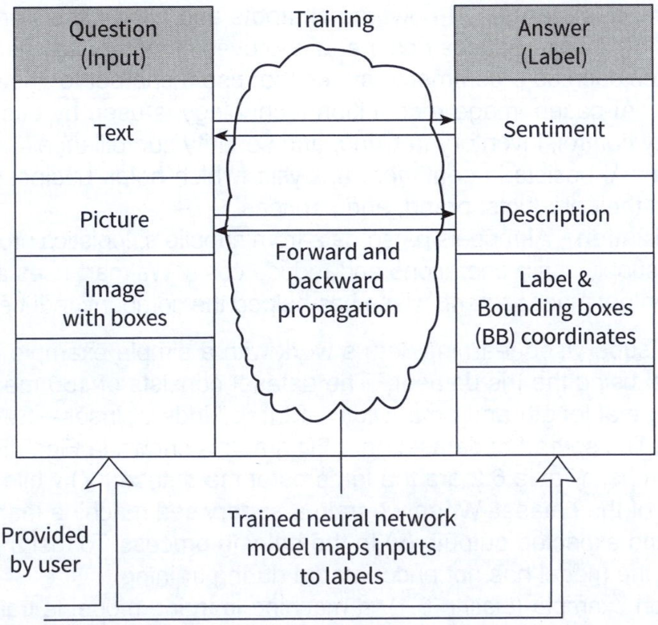

Fig. 6.4 Supervised training setup and process

- Examples of the expected output—In a bird sound recognition task, these could be labels of bird names. In a fruit image task, expected outputs could be labels, such as "apple," "orange," and so on.
- A metric to measure whether the algorithm is doing a good job. In Fig. 6.4, you see that the model makes several forward and backward passes through the dataset. In each backward pass, it fine-tunes its programmable variables to better correlate the input with the output. The process is called learning.

6.3 | AI and Business Applications

Businesses have tons of unstructured data that needs to be analyzed using AI models. These models work with a variety of data—text, images, and video. As most models are open source, businesses do not have to reinvent the wheel for AI model creation. Businesses can use pre-trained AI models to improve their operations and decision-making processes. Few applications where businesses apply AI include:

Personalized marketing Analyze customer data and behavior to provide personalized marketing messages and recommendations. AI model improves customer engagement and loyalty. For example, Netflix uses AI algorithms to recommend movies and TV shows based on each user's viewing history.

Predictive maintenance Train AI model using data from sensors and equipment to predict when maintenance is needed. This reduces downtime and improve productivity. General Electric uses AI to monitor and predict the performance of its jet engines, which helps airlines save millions of dollars in maintenance costs.

Fraud detection AI models analyze financial transactions and detect fraudulent activity, which reduces the risk of financial losses. Mastercard and Visa use AI to monitor credit card transactions and identify suspicious activity in real-time.

Chatbots and virtual assistants AI-powered chatbots and virtual assistants provide customer service and support 24/7. This reduces costs and improves customer satisfaction. You must have come across Websites such as e-commerce stores that use a chatbot to answer basic questions.
Image recognition AI-based image recognition technology is used by businesses to automate tasks, such as quality control, inventory tracking, and security surveillance.
Sentiment analysis AI assists in sentiment analysis, which helps businesses understand how customers feel about their products, brand, and services.
Supply chain optimization AI models parse data from suppliers, logistics providers, and inventory systems to optimize supply chain operations and reduce costs. Walmart uses a floor scrubber[4] and AI to optimize its inventory management, which has helped the company reduce out-of-stock items.

Using the idea of supervised learning, let us work with a simple example of creating a logistic (classification) model using the Iris dataset.[5] The dataset consists of 150 measurements of sepal length, sepal width, petal length and petal width of three kinds of irises—Setosa, Versicolor, and Virginica (Table 6.2). The spread of dataset on a 2D graph is shown in Fig. 6.5.

The first four columns in Table 6.2 are the features of the dataset (X) while the last column (Iris type) is the label (y) of the dataset. When we train a supervised machine learning model, we provide the inputs (X) and expected outputs (y) to the training process. To test the model, we provide values of inputs that the model has not encountered during training.

In this classification example (Listing 6.1), a machine learning model is trained to map features of three species to their names. Take a look at the comments (lines with # prefix) in the code to understand the steps followed for model training and test. The trained model is tested on 45 values (30 percent of dataset) of novel data (line 9). Logistic regression model uses linear lines to divide the space into three areas. Each area represents one species of the Iris dataset. Model training is carried out using the .fit method by passing training data (X) and label (y) as arguments (line 13). The trained model is tested using the .predict method by using test data (line 15), which was not used during training. The evaluate_model function on line 17 determines the model's accuracy by using 45 test values. It compares the predicted value with y_test to validate the model's answer. The arguments to the evaluate_model function are predictions and y_test. As output, the function returns the model's accuracy as a percentage value. The calculated value of accuracy is printed by line 21 of the code.

Please try out the code in Listing 6.1 and print intermediate values, such as X, y, X_train, X_test, y_train, and y_test to get more insight into the idea of supervised learning.

Table 6.2 Input features and output label of Iris dataset—The output label is mentioned in the last column

Sepal Length	Sepal Width	Petal Length	Petal Width	Iris Type
				Setosa
				Versicolor
				Virginica

[4]How Walmart is using A.I. to make shopping better for its millions of customers, CNBC, https://www.cnbc.com/2023/03/27/how-walmart-is-using-ai-to-make-shopping-better.html (accessed 3 April 2023).
[5]Iris dataset, https://scikit-learn.org/stable/auto_examples/datasets/plot_iris_dataset.html (accessed 8 June 2023).

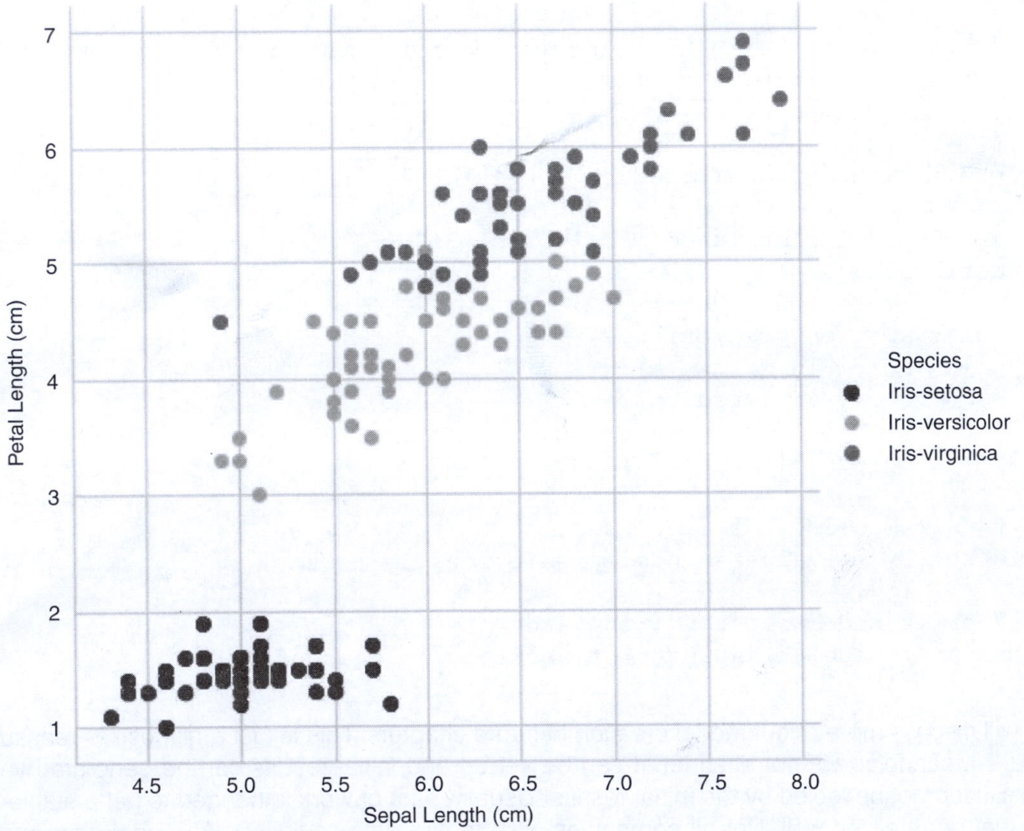

Fig. 6.5 Distribution of features representing three species of Iris dataset

Listing 6.1 Logistic regression based classification model using supervised learning

```
from sklearn.datasets import load_iris
from sklearn.model_selection import train_test_split
from sklearn.linear_model import LogisticRegression

# load iris dataset
iris= load_iris()

# split dataset into input features (X) and labels (y)
X,y = iris.data[:,:], iris.target[:]

# further split dataset into training (70%) and testing (30%)
X_train,X_test,y_train,y_test= train_test_split(X,y,test_size=0.3)

# use classical machine learning logistic regression model
model = LogisticRegression()
```

(Continued)

Listing 6.1 (*Continued*)

```
# train model using fit method and point to inputs and output
model.fit(X_train, y_train)

# test the model on inputs not seen during training
predictions = model.predict(X_test)

# function to evaluate model predictions
def evaluate_model (predictions, y_test):
      correct=0
      a = len(predictions)
      for i in range (a):
            if (predictions[i] == y_test[i]):
                  correct = correct + 1
      return ((correct/a)*100)

# call model prediction function
accuracy = evaluate_model(predictions, y_test)

# print model classification accuracy
print ('Model classification accuracy is', accuracy)
```

We will discuss more about model creation in future chapters. This is just a glimpse to reassure you that AI technology is not abstract. It can be set up and initial results can be generated very quickly. But do not be fooled by the initial results! Usually, a lot of work is needed to get a stable AI model that generalizes well. Not all companies wish to hire data scientists, AI model developers and training hardware at the outset. They may like to find out if AI is worthwhile for their company. To cater to such customer requirements, cloud service providers have access to a vast library of customizable open-source models that can be used. Some tools use a graphical approach to avoid code. An example of such a tool is seen in Fig. 6.6. The following steps are needed to create an AI model using a structured dataset.

- Import relevant datasets and merge into one
- Identify the input features (columns) and the output (target column)

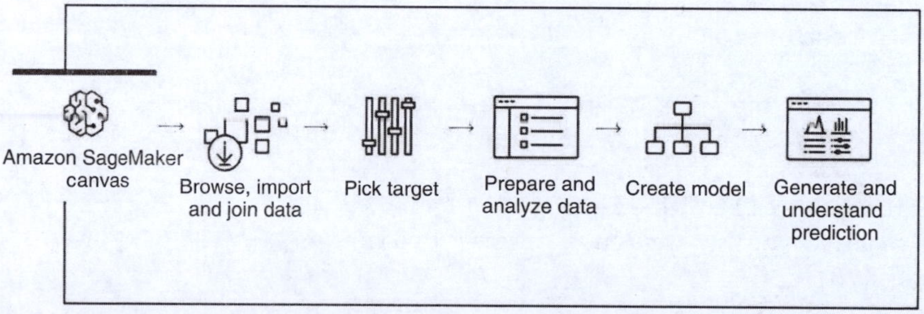

Fig. 6.6 Graphical tool from AWS[6] to create AI model using dataset

[6]Amazon Sagemaker Canvas, https://aws.amazon.com/sagemaker/canvas/ (accessed 17 November 2022).

- Parse input to detect missing rows, out-of-bound values, etc.
- Partition dataset into training and test data
- Use cloud service create a model using training data
- Exercise the newly created model by having it make predictions on test data

6.4 | Conclusion

The idea of AI has been around for about 75 years. In this time, AI has seen a few cycles of winter and spring. Contemporary AI systems have the ability to pass the Turing test which was created in 1950. AI models created using supervised learning have made big strides in computer vision and NLP.

Exercises

A. State True/False

1. Development of AI started in the 1990s.
2. Supervised learning involves the use of questions and labels (or answers) for training.
3. Turing test checks to see if a machine (or computer) can provide human-like response.
4. Reinforcement requires training data (questions and labels (or answers)).
5. Total Turing test checks for human-like vision and motion capability.

B. Short-answer Questions

1. In Listing 6.1, which function is used to split dataset into training and test sections.
2. How many features and data samples (rows) make up the Iris dataset.
3. Using Listing 6.1, mention the name of the methods to train and test the model.
4. From Listing 6.1, find out the name of the function used to determine the accuracy of the model.
5. Considering the Iris dataset, if the train_test_split (test_size) is 0.2, how many samples are used to train the model.

C. Long-answer Questions

1. Enumerate some present-day applications that use AI capabilities.
   (Hint: Think about NLP and computer vision applications.)
2. Mention an application that would be suitable for each learning technique, (1) Unsupervised training, (2) Supervised training, and (3) Reinforcement learning.
3. Create an Iris like dataset suitable for supervised learning using data to classify 5 different cars. The dataset should comprise of at least 10 samples per car (based on different car variants). You can pick the features that are most suitable and the labels should be the name of the car.
4. Train a classifier model using the data generated and check the model's accuracy using the test portion of the dataset.

D. Explore and Experiment

1. Work with the diabetes dataset[7] to identify input features (data) and label (answers) to create a dataset suitable for supervised learning. Then use the logistic regression algorithm to build a binary classification model. Test the model on the test dataset.

[7]Diabetes dataset, https://archive.ics.uci.edu/ml/datasets/diabetes (accessed 2 June 2023).

2. Supervised or learning by example is a powerful tool. In Fig. 6.7, we ask Generative AI to come up with AI applications that are based on supervised learning.

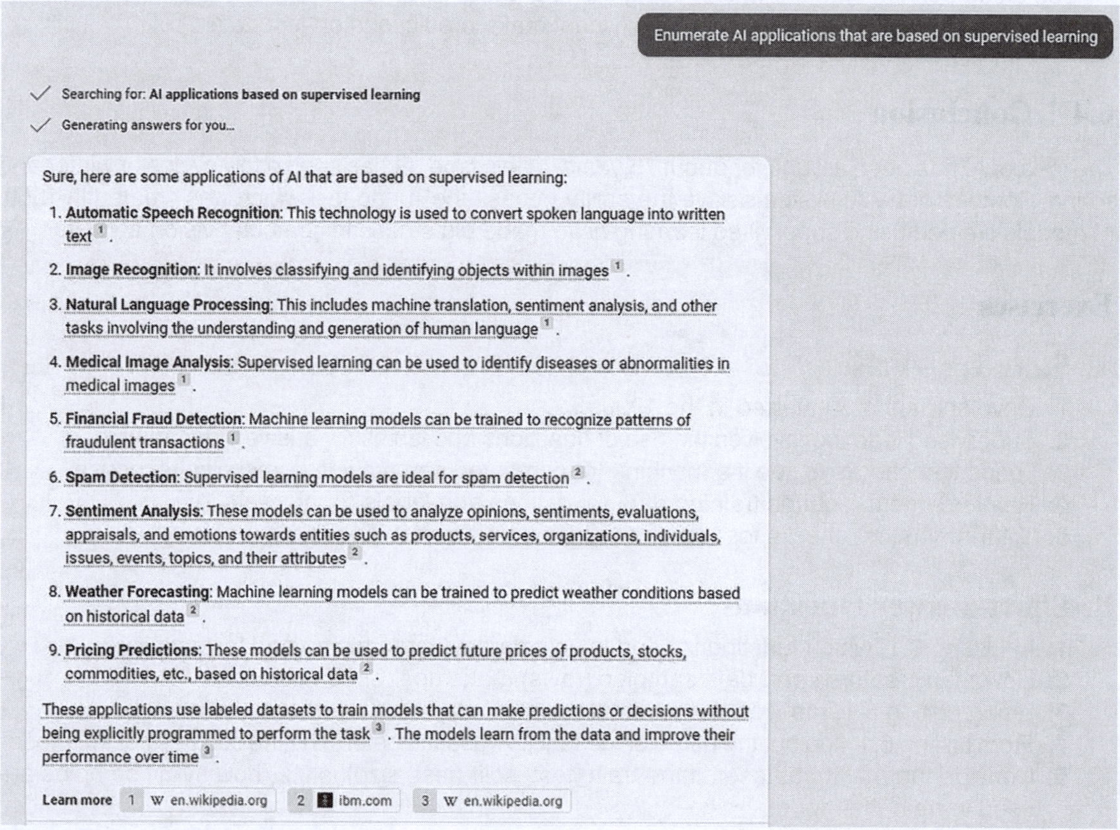
Enumerate AI applications that are based on supervised learning

✓ Searching for: **AI applications based on supervised learning**

✓ Generating answers for you...

Sure, here are some applications of AI that are based on supervised learning:

1. **Automatic Speech Recognition**: This technology is used to convert spoken language into written text [1].
2. **Image Recognition**: It involves classifying and identifying objects within images [1].
3. **Natural Language Processing**: This includes machine translation, sentiment analysis, and other tasks involving the understanding and generation of human language [1].
4. **Medical Image Analysis**: Supervised learning can be used to identify diseases or abnormalities in medical images [1].
5. **Financial Fraud Detection**: Machine learning models can be trained to recognize patterns of fraudulent transactions [1].
6. **Spam Detection**: Supervised learning models are ideal for spam detection [2].
7. **Sentiment Analysis**: These models can be used to analyze opinions, sentiments, evaluations, appraisals, and emotions towards entities such as products, services, organizations, individuals, issues, events, topics, and their attributes [2].
8. **Weather Forecasting**: Machine learning models can be trained to predict weather conditions based on historical data [2].
9. **Pricing Predictions**: These models can be used to predict future prices of products, stocks, commodities, etc., based on historical data [2].

These applications use labeled datasets to train models that can make predictions or decisions without being explicitly programmed to perform the task [3]. The models learn from the data and improve their performance over time [3].

Learn more 1 W en.wikipedia.org 2 ibm.com 3 W en.wikipedia.org

Fig. 6.7 Some useful AI models based on supervised learning

E. Generate Use Case on AI

Use Case: E-mail Spam Filters

Brief description: Most of us receive a few unsolicited e-mails every day. These unwanted e-mails get caught by the spam filter and do not reach our inbox. For Gmail users, Google looks at various features of e-mails to classify them as spam and not spam.

Study the blog to understand the features of an e-mail that Google trains its AI model. Create a use case on e-mail spam filter using the template given below.

Resources

Google Blog, Understanding Gmail's spam filters, Neil Kumaran https://workspace.google.com/blog/identity-and-security/an-overview-of-gmails-spam-filters

Template for Creating Use Case on E-mail Spam Filter

Define goal and purpose	Goal statement
	Identify stakeholders
	Define scope
Details to include in use case	Capture how technology helps business process
	Keep use case findings description textual, with a few simple flowcharts if needed
	Focus on describing how technology benefits the use case
Future applications	Mention any new applications that can leverage the technology used

Suggested Reading

1. Aurélien Géron, Hands-On Machine Learning with Scikit-Learn, Keras, and TensorFlow: Concepts, Tools, and Techniques to Build Intelligent Systems 2nd Edition, O'Reilly.

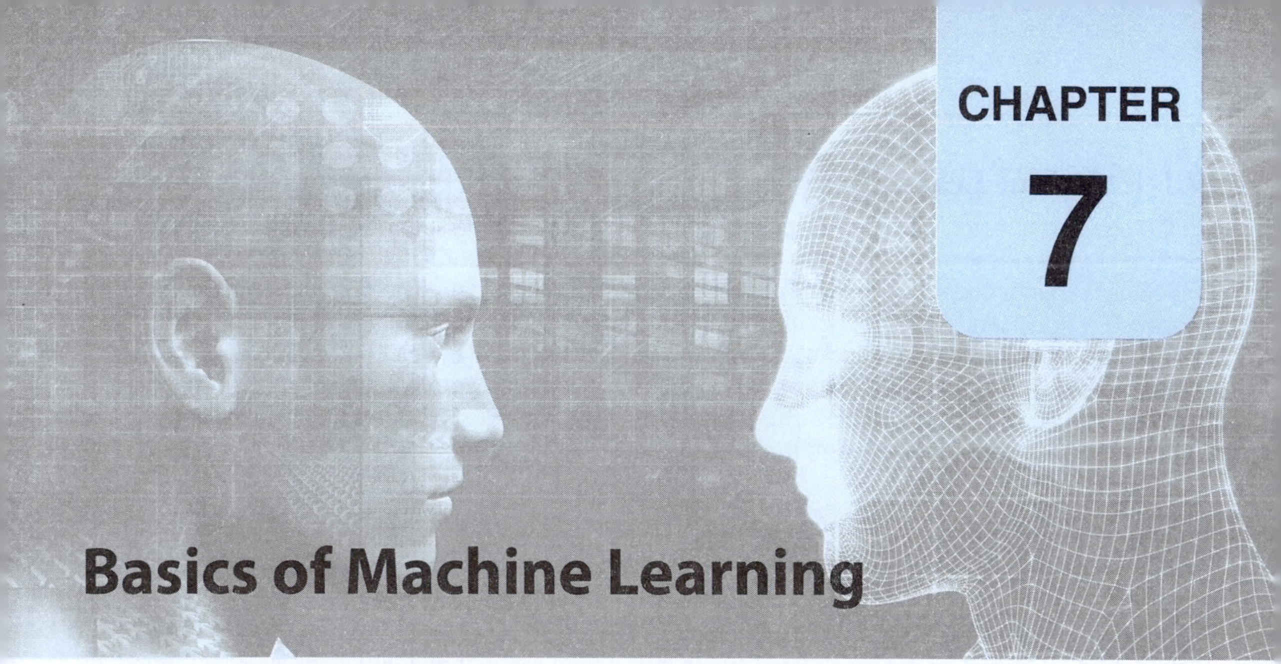

CHAPTER 7

Basics of Machine Learning

CHAPTER OUTLINE

7.1 Machine Learning
7.2 Clustering
7.3 Decision Trees, Random Forests, and Gradient Boosting
7.4 Metrics to Measure Model Quality

LEARNING OBJECTIVES

After reading this chapter, you will be able to:

- understand machine learning algorithms for structured data
- use clustering—an example of unsupervised learning
- use decision trees—an example of supervised learning

Effective Management Using Classification, Regression, and Clustering

A large amount of business data is stored as tables. These tables relate to product sales, demographics of consumers, and other similar details. To find linkages between different parameters and connect them to a particular outcome is very difficult. Like finding a needle in a haystack! This is where decision trees are useful. They help correlate huge tables of data to an output and provide surprising insights into customer behavior. If you get a chance read this article[1] about how companies use data analytics to deduce many details about their customers.

[1]How companies learn your secrets, The New York Times Magazine, https://www.nytimes.com/2012/02/19/magazine/shopping-habits.html (accessed 20 November 2022).

7.1 | Machine Learning

In the previous chapter, we briefly discussed the idea of artificial intelligence (AI). AI is a broad domain and comprises classical machine learning algorithms and deep neural network models. Conventional machine learning models work very well with structured (tabular) data. These models are of great help because a significant portion of business data is tabular and stored in relational database systems.

Classical machine learning consists of techniques mentioned in scikit-learn.[2] These techniques help to classify, predict, and cluster data contained in tables. We talked about a cloud-based tool to create AI models without code in Section 6.3. Now, we will dive deeper and understand how machine learning models help and the kind of problems they can solve.

7.2 | Clustering

The idea of clustering is to find and group similar data within a dataset. K-means is a popular "clustering" algorithm. K-means stores ***k*** centroids to define ***k*** clusters. A point is considered to be in a particular cluster if it is closer to that cluster's centroid than any other centroid. K-means works with a dataset where each sample(row) has a set of features, but no labels. Labels are needed for supervised learning algorithms.

The working of K-means is understood using Fig. 7.1 and following steps:

1. Select "k-means" (3 in our case) from random locations in a dataset
2. K clusters are created by associating every observation with the nearest mean
3. The centroid of each of the k clusters becomes the new mean
4. Steps 2 and 3 are repeated until convergence is reached

Clustering is used by businesses to group similar items or entities together based on their characteristics or attributes. Clustering is used for the following applications:

- **Customer segmentation** Segment customers into groups based on similar attributes, such as age, income, location, or purchase history. This allows businesses to target specific groups with tailored marketing campaigns and improve customer experiences.
- **Fraud detection** Identify groups of transactions that are anomalous or suspicious, helping businesses detect fraudulent activity and take action to prevent financial losses.
- **Product categorization** Group products together based on similar attributes, such as size, color, or price. This helps businesses optimize inventory management and improve product recommendations.
- **Anomaly detection** Clustering can be used to identify anomalies or outliers in data sets, such as abnormal behavior in financial transactions or sensor data. Using this, businesses can identify potential problems and take corrective action.

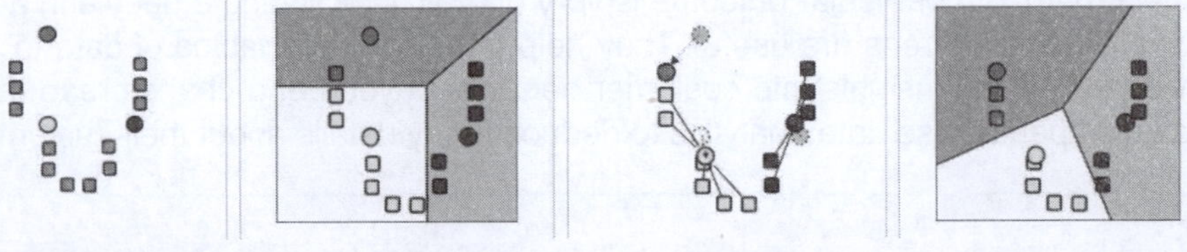

Fig. 7.1 Working of K-means algorithm[3]

[2]Classical machine learning, https://scikit-learn.org/stable/ (accessed 19 November 2022).

[3]K-means clustering https://en.wikipedia.org/wiki/K-means_clustering (accessed 20 November 2022).

Table 7.1 Tabular data from customer survey for a similar product

Household Income	Household Size	Household Location (urban, rural, suburban)

Listing 7.1 Features and label of California housing dataset (first two rows)

```
    MedInc HouseAge  AveRooms  AveBedrms  Population AveOccup  Latitude \
0  8.3252     41.0  6.984127    1.02381       322.0 2.555556     37.88
1  8.3014     21.0  6.238137    0.97188      2401.0 2.109842     37.86

   Longitude   MedHouseVal
0    -122.23         4.526
1    -122.22         3.585
```

In a retail marketing scenario, companies use clustering to identify households, spending, and household size. The input data is the tabulated consumer data survey results which includes features mentioned in Table 7.1. A clustering algorithm (without supervised training) segregates this tabular data into different clusters. The clusters may represent

- small urban family, high spenders, high income
- large rural family, high spender, low income
- and so on

Based on the information determined from cluster size, the company can then target households and locations which are likely to buy their product.

To solidify our understanding of clustering, let us try it on the California housing dataset.[4] The dataset consists of 8 features and one label (house value). The features and label are enumerated in Listing 7.1. We will use clustering to understand the distribution of income in the state of California. To perform clustering, we consider three features of the dataset—median income, latitude, and longitude. Five rows of the three features are seen in Table 7.2.

Table 7.2 First five rows of median income, latitude and longitude of California dataset

	Median Income	Latitude	Longitude
0	8.3252	37.88	−122.23
1	8.3014	37.86	−122.22
2	7.2574	37.85	−122.24
3	5.6431	37.85	−122.25
4	3.8462	37.85	−122.25

[4]California housing dataset, https://scikit-learn.org/stable/datasets/real_world.html#california-housing-dataset (accessed 10 June 2023).

Listing 7.2 Code for creating six income clusters for the state of California

```
01. import matplotlib.pyplot as plt
02. import pandas as pd
03. import seaborn as sns
04. from sklearn.cluster import KMeans
05. from sklearn.datasets import fetch_california_housing

06. # load California dataset as Pandas frame
07. cal = fetch_california_housing(as_frame=True)

08. # Concatenate features and label columns. Clustering is
    unsupervised
09. df = pd.concat([cal.data, cal.target], axis=1)
10. print (df.head(2)) # use for printing listing 7-1

11. # isolate three features to use for clustering
12. X = df.loc[:, ["MedInc", "Latitude", "Longitude"]]
13. X.head() # Used to print Table 7.2

14. # setup up kmeans for creating 6 clusters
15. kmeans = KMeans(n_clusters=6)

16. # perform clustering using fit method
17. X["Cluster"] = kmeans.fit_predict(X)
18. X["Cluster"] = X["Cluster"].astype("category")

19. X.head()

20. # visualize clusters created by k-means
21. sns.relplot(
22. x="Longitude", y="Latitude", hue="Cluster", data=X, height=6,
23. )
```

Please experiment with the code presented in Listing 7.2 and play around with the number of clusters. The number of clusters is currently defined as 6 in line 15. Try and identity the high-income clusters (Fig. 7.2) and correlate it with the major industry in that area. To see the clusters distinctly, you will have to run the code and visualize the clusters represented by six different colours on the computer screen. The Python code of Listing 7.2 is part of Digital App.

7.3 | Decision Trees, Random Forests, and Gradient Boosting

Let us discuss about two important data analytics techniques that learn from data: classification and regression.

Classification correlates data characteristics/features to a certain class. An e-mail classifier checks whether an e-mail is spam or not. A credit card transaction classifier checks to see if the transaction is fraudulent or genuine. Tabular data from the past credit card transactions are used to create a classifier. A fully populated Table 7.3 serves as a starting point for creating a classifier.

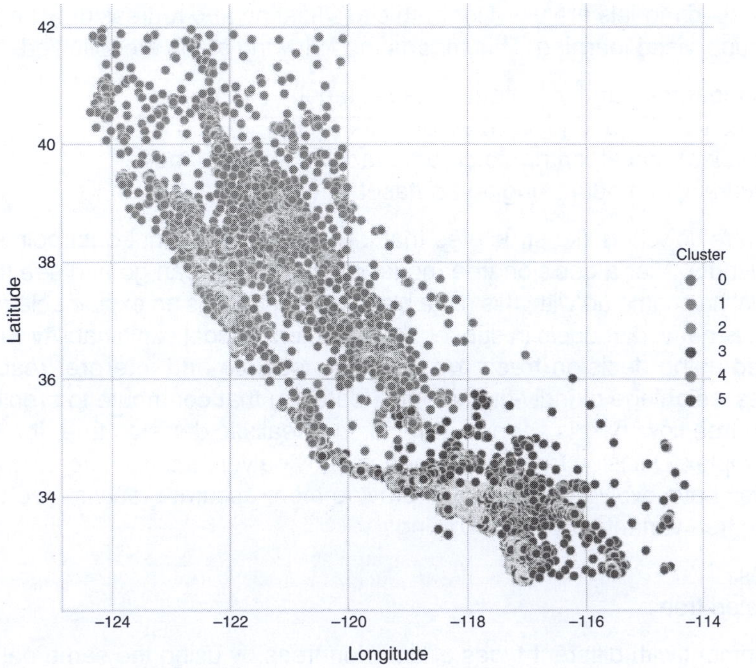

Fig. 7.2 Income cluster created using k-means algorithm and three features—median income, latitude, and longitude for the state of California, USA

Table 7.3 Classification of credit card transaction

Feature 1	Feature 2	Feature 3	Label (Fraudulent)
Location	Last Transaction	Amount	Yes/No

Regression estimates the relationships between an output variable (label) and one or more input variables (features). Housing datasets provide good examples for understanding regression. A housing dataset from Taiwan[5] has the following features:

1. Transaction date (for example, 2013.250 = 2013 March, 2013.500 = 2013 June, etc.)
2. House age (unit: year)
3. Distance to the nearest mass rapid transit station (MRT) (unit: meter)
4. Number of convenience stores in the living circle on foot (integer)
5. Geographic coordinate, latitude (unit: degree)
6. Geographic coordinate, longitude (unit: degree)

The output variable (label) is the house price of unit area (10,000 New Taiwan Dollar/Ping, where Ping is a local unit, 1 Ping = 3.3 meter squared). Regression will help establish the relationship between features (house age, location, and distance to mass transit) and the cost of a house.

[5]Taiwan housing dataset, https://archive.ics.uci.edu/ml/datasets/Real+estate+valuation+data+set (accessed 20 November 2022).

Decision tree-based models are used for both classification and regression. These models learn from data using supervised learning. This means the following steps are followed.

- Define **X** (input features) and **y** (output variable, label)
- Split dataset into training and test (70/30 or other ratio)
- Run supervised learning algorithm to create machine learning model
- Determine accuracy of model using test dataset

Decision trees are flowchart-like structures that let you correlate input data points or predict output values given inputs. After a decision tree model is trained, one can go and see the decision tree structure the model has come up with. It is not a black box; rather it is an explainable model. When we discuss deep neural network models in subsequent chapters, model explainability will surface again.

Models created using decision trees are easy to visualize and interpret results. The model summary provides weightage of individual inputs (features) that contribute to predicting an output. A simple decision tree flowchart is seen in Fig. 7 3. In a realistic decision tree, the structure would be much more complex. Decision tree-based models provide very intuitive means to relate inputs to output. These trees have evolved over time to provide more accurate results. Two commonly used (popular) decision tree variants are the following:

- Random Forest
- Gradient boosted trees

One can experiment with different types of decision trees by using the same dataset and swapping out different decision tree models. If you are conversant with the Python programming language (if not, invest some time and learn basics), check out these code snippets.[6]

Table 7.3 enumerates different types of decision tree-based models and provides a brief description of their approach. The best way to learn more about decision trees (or for that matter anything) is to try it out and get your hands dirty. This Jupyter notebook[7] shows decision tree-based classification of penguins using features, such as bill length, flipper length, and body mass. After training, the model summary provides the following details:

- **Type of Model** The learning algorithm used to train the model (Random Forest in our case).
- **Task** The problem solved by the model (Classification in our case).

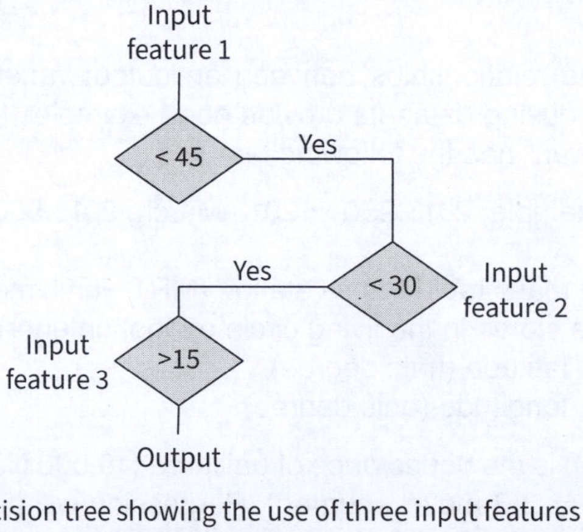

Fig. 7.3 Trivial (hypothetical) decision tree showing the use of three input features to determine the output

[6]Decision tree classifier, https://scikit-learn.org/stable/modules/tree.html#classification (accessed 20 November 2022).
[7]Decision Forests notebook, TensorFlow, https://www.tensorflow.org/decision_forests/tutorials/beginner_colab (accessed 20 November 2022).

Table 7.3 Decision tree-based models

Decision Tree Type	Brief Description
Decision tree	A decision tree is a model composed of a collection of "questions" organized in the shape of a tree
Random forest	A random forest is an ensemble of decision trees which use random input features to create an uncorrelated forest of decision trees. A conventional decision tree considers all the possible feature splits; random forest works with randomly selected subsets of input features
Bagging	Bagging is a technique in which each decision tree in the random forest is trained on a different subset of input data
Gradient boosted trees	A gradient boosting tree (like a random forest) uses an ensemble of weak prediction models, generally from decision trees. It uses gradient boosting as a way to improve by iteratively training new models that address the weak points of the previous models

- **Input Features** The input features of the model.
- **Variable Importance** Different measures of the importance of each feature for the model.
- **Number of {trees, nodes} and Other Metrics** Statistics about the structure of the decision forest

These details help in understanding the basis (or explainability) of the generated model. Like clustering, decision trees are commonly used in various business applications where decision-making is required based on certain criteria. Some examples of business applications of decision trees are:

Risk management Decision trees are used to assess risks associated with different business decisions. For example, they can be used to evaluate the risk associated with investments or to determine the likelihood of default on a loan.
Marketing campaign optimization Optimize marketing campaigns by identifying the most effective channels, messages, and target audience.
Fraud detection Identify patterns in data that indicate fraud or other irregularities. This can be useful for detecting credit card fraud or other types of financial fraud.
Supply chain management Use existing data to train a model that optimizes a supply chain management by identifying the most efficient transportation routes, warehouse locations, and inventory management strategies.

We will use a familiar dataset (the Iris dataset) to grok decision trees. You may wonder how the logistic regression approach (from Chapter 6) is different from that of decision trees. Logistic regression uses straight lines to classify or differentiate classes. Decision trees on the other hand, bisect the space into smaller and smaller regions for classification.

In this example, the Iris dataset from scikit-learn is loaded and split into training and testing datasets using train_test_split (line 11) function of Listing 7.3. An instance of DecisionTreeClassifier is created (line 13), trained on the training dataset (line 15). A plot of the decision tree (Fig. 7.4) is created by line 17. The trained model is used to predict the target values for the testing dataset (line 19). The accuracy score of the model is then calculated using accuracy_score. This example is for a classification problem, but decision trees can also be used for regression problems. The decision tree plot in Fig. 7.4 mentions feature index x[i] and a Gini index. Gini index represents measure of impurity or disorder within a set of data points.

The next example uses the California dataset to exercise the decision tree regression model. Here, the model is trained to correlate 8 features to the value of the house. Since it is a regression model, the loss function is mean square error (MSE). The code in Listing 7.4 follows the same approach as the decision tree classifier.

Listing 7.3 Use of decision trees to classify Iris species

```
from sklearn.datasets import load_iris
from sklearn.tree import DecisionTreeClassifier
from sklearn.model_selection import train_test_split
from sklearn.metrics import accuracy_score
from sklearn import tree

# load the dataset
iris = load_iris()
X = iris.data
y = iris.target

# split the dataset into training and testing datasets
X_train, X_test, y_train, y_test = train_test_split(X, y,
                                   test_size=0.1, random_state=42)

# create an instance of Decision Tree Classifier
dt_classifier = DecisionTreeClassifier()

# train the model on the training dataset
dt_classifier.fit(X_train, y_train)

# Plot decision tree
tree.plot_tree(dt_classifier)

# predict the target values for the testing dataset
y_pred = dt_classifier.predict(X_test)

# calculate the accuracy score of the model
accuracy = accuracy_score(y_test, y_pred)
print('Accuracy:', accuracy)
```

Before we move on to the next topic, let us talk about the max_depth parameter mentioned in line 10 (Listing 7.4) of the decision tree regressor model. The model predicts house prices in California. Changing max_depth affects the model's ability to generalize. A small value of max_depth produces a model that underfits, while a large value of max_depth creates a model that overfits. A model that overfits has excessive resources and ends up memorizing training data; while a model that underfits does not have enough resources to understand and capture the pattern of the training data. This is clearly seen in Fig. 7.5. To reiterate our earlier recommendation—make friends with the code by playing with it. Try out new datasets and values of max_depth to see its effects on MSE.

7.4 | Metrics to Measure Model Quality

Let us continue our discussion with the Iris dataset we talked about earlier. So far, we have created two kinds of classifier for the Iris dataset. The first classifier we created was the logistic regression classifier, while the second one was a decision tree classifier. How do we go about assessing the

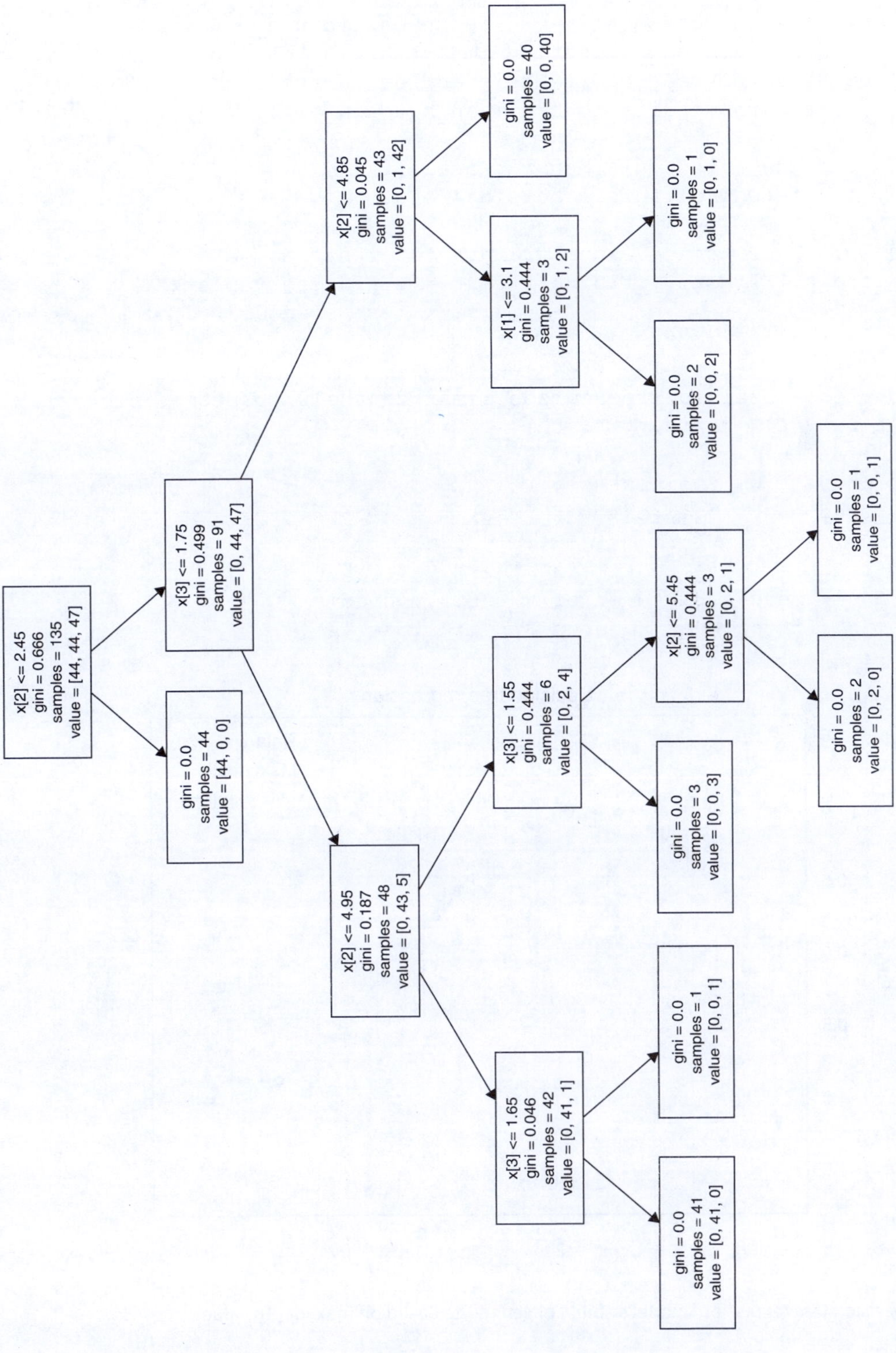

Fig. 7.4 Decision tree created using decision tree classifier algorithm on Iris dataset

Listing 7.4 Decision tree regression on California housing dataset

```
from sklearn.datasets import fetch_california_housing
from sklearn.model_selection import train_test_split
from sklearn.tree import DecisionTreeRegressor
from sklearn.metrics import mean_squared_error

# load the California Housing dataset
X, y = fetch_california_housing(return_X_y=True, as_frame=True)

# split the dataset into training and testing sets
X_train, X_test, y_train, y_test = train_test_split(X, y,
                                   test_size=0.2, random_state=42)

# train the decision tree regressor
dt_reg = DecisionTreeRegressor(max_depth=10, random_state=42)
dt_reg.fit(X_train, y_train)

# predict on the test set
y_pred = dt_reg.predict(X_test)

# calculate the root mean squared error
rmse = mean_squared_error(y_test, y_pred)
print(f'Root Mean Squared Error: {rmse:.2f}')
```

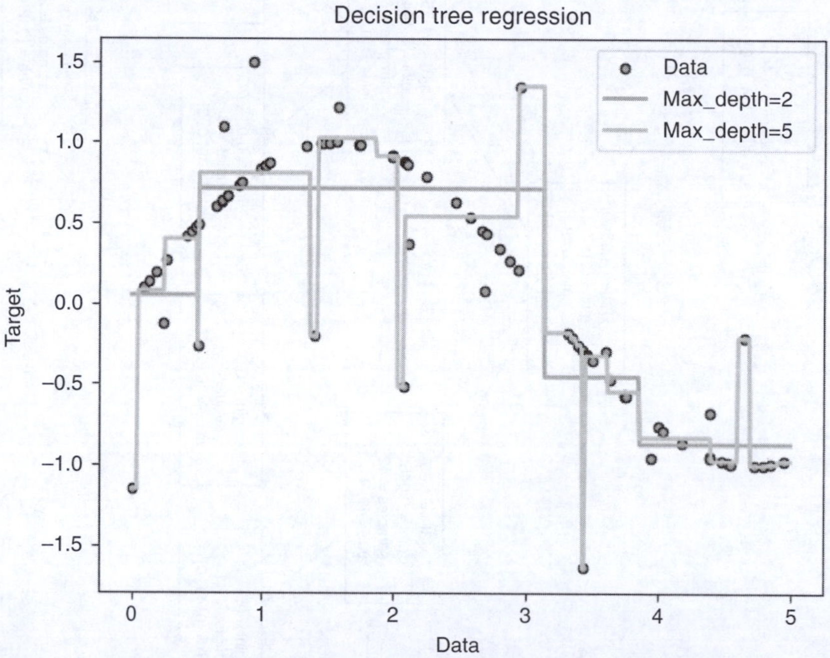

Fig. 7.5 Decision tree regression[8] model's ability of generalize based on max_depth value

[8]Decision tree regression, Scikit learn, https://scikit-learn.org/stable/auto_examples/tree/plot_tree_regression.html (accessed 4 June 2023).

Table 7.4 Confusion matrix for a binary classifier

		Predicted	
		Has Cancer	**Does Not Have Cancer**
Ground Truth	**Has Cancer**	TP	FN
	Does Not Have Cancer	FP	TN

True-positive (TP): Positive class samples the model predicted correctly.
True-negative (TN): Negative class samples the model predicted correctly.
A good model would have high values for both TP and TN.

False-positive (FP): Negative class samples the model predicted incorrectly.
False-negative (FN): Positive class samples your model predicted incorrectly.
Both FP and FN indicate weaknesses of the model.

quality of a given classifier? This is where metrics become useful. The most popular metrics are the following:

- Accuracy
- Confusion matrix
- Precision and recall
- F1-score

The following examples on model metrics are based on the blog on Metrics in machine-learning complete guide.[9] Let us consider a binary classifier to detect whether a person has cancer or not. We start with the confusion matrix to check the robustness of the classifier. As seen in Table 7.4, a confusion matrix is a tabular visualization of the ground-truth labels versus model predictions. The rows of the confusion matrix represent ground truth, while the columns represent predicted values from the model. Let us first start with accuracy. Accuracy is the ratio of correct predictions (both TP and TN) calculated over all possible scenarios (TP, TN, FP and FN). Accuracy is applicable to both binary and multi-class data classification.

This leads us to the precision metric. Precision is defined by the ratio given below.

$$\text{Precision} = \frac{\text{TP}}{\text{TP} + \text{FP}}$$

A precision score closer to 1 signifies that the model does very well in detecting true-positives. Precision does not determine the model's performance on false-negatives—cases where a person having cancer is classified as not having cancer.

The recall metric is able to factor in the performance of the model with respect to false–negatives.

$$\text{Recall} = \frac{\text{TP}}{\text{TP} + \text{FN}}$$

Both precision and recall metrics have some level of similarity; this makes it difficult to understand the first time. Figure 7.6 provides a good visual to distinguish between precision and recall. Precision tells you how many retrieved items are relevant; while recall tells you how many relevant items are retrieved.

[9]Metrics in machine learning, complete guide, https://neptune.ai/blog/performance-metrics-in-machine-learning-complete-guide (accessed 13 May 2023).

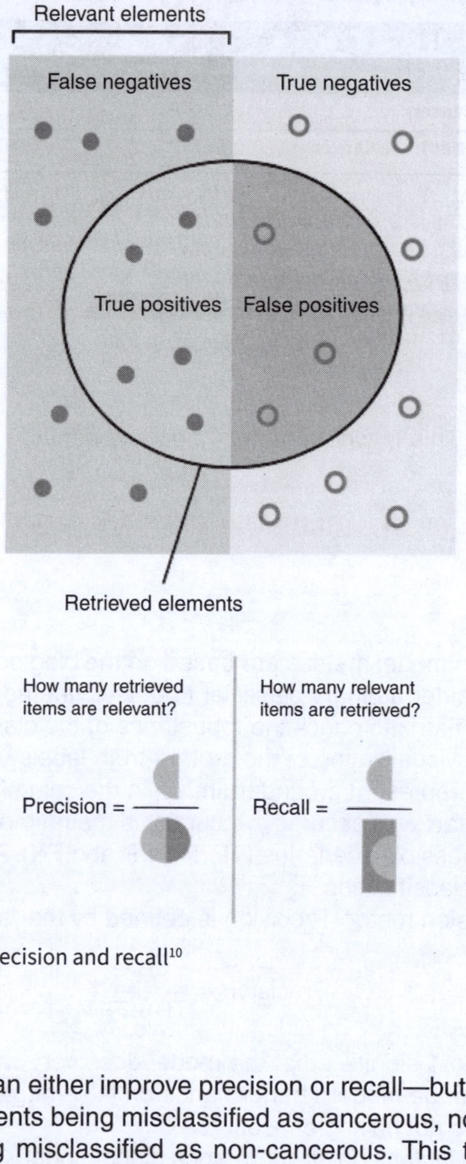

Fig. 7.6 A good visualization of precision and recall[10]

Precision-Recall Trade-off

To improve the model, one can either improve precision or recall—but not both! If we try to reduce cases of non-cancerous patients being misclassified as cancerous, no direct effect will take place on cancerous patients being misclassified as non-cancerous. This trade-off impacts real-world scenarios. As a result, precision and recall are not used as independent metrics.

A new metric (F1-score) uses a combination of precision and recall. It is the harmonic mean of the two. The formula for the F1-score is

$$\text{F1-score} = \frac{2}{\frac{1}{\text{Recall}} + \frac{1}{\text{Precision}}} = 2\,\frac{\text{Recall} \times \text{Precision}}{\text{Recall} + \text{Precision}}$$

F1-score is a metric of choice and is used in corporate reports and online competitions.

Before we end the chapter, it is worthwhile to reiterate that a machine learning model is as good as the data that is used to generate it. Instead of frantically trying out different models to achieve

[10] F-score, Wikipedia, https://en.wikipedia.org/wiki/F-score (accessed 10 June 2023).

higher accuracy, it may be a smart idea to review the dataset. Adding new features (columns) may improve model accuracy. Think top down. Spend more time assimilating meaningful data about your use case. Talk with subject matter experts and people on the ground. Model training is usually a matter of minutes or at most hours if the right data is available.

7.5 | Conclusion

Data classification, regression, and clustering are important tools to visualize, classify and predict data. Clustering represents an example of unsupervised learning. Use of decision tree-based models (that learn from data), makes the task of data classification and regression straight forward. This chapter includes Python code to get started with clustering and decision trees algorithms. It also discusses metrics such as precision, recall and F1 score in the context of a binary classifier.

Exercises

A. State True/False

1. Decision trees work on unstructured data such as images.
2. Decision tree is an explainable machine learning algorithm.
3. Clustering is performed by decision trees.
4. K-means is an example of unsupervised learning.
5. Classification is used to predict future values.

B. Short-answer Questions

1. Which line in Listing 7.2 is used to define the number of clusters for the dataset?
2. Line 13 of the Python code in Listing 7.3 is used to select the Decision tree classifier. What changes are needed in Listing 7.3 to choose and use a different classifier.
3. Explain the use of the max_depth argument, while configuring the Decision tree regressor.
4. In the Python code Listing 7.5, use the confusion matrix output to determine accuracy, precision, recall and f1. Check your answer by executing the code.

Listing 7.5 Python classification code for breast cancer dataset

```
#Import the necessary libraries

from sklearn.datasets import load_breast_cancer
from sklearn.model_selection import train_test_split
from sklearn.ensemble import RandomForestClassifier
from sklearn.metrics import confusion_matrix
import seaborn as sns
import matplotlib.pyplot as plt
from sklearn.metrics import accuracy_score, precision_score, recall_
    score, f1_score

# Load the breast cancer dataset
X, y= load_breast_cancer(return_X_y=True)
X_train, X_test, y_train, y_test = train_test_split(X, y,test_
    size=0.25)
```

(Continued)

Listing 7.5 *(Continued)*

```
# Train the classifier model
clf = RandomForestClassifier(random_state=23)
clf.fit(X_train, y_train)

# preduction
y_pred = clf.predict(X_test)

# compute the confusion matrix
cm = confusion_matrix(y_test,y_pred)

#Plot the confusion matrix.
sns.heatmap(cm, fmt='d', annot=True, square=True,
            cmap='gray_r', vmin=0, vmax=0,  # set all to white
            linewidths=0.5, linecolor='k',  # draw black grid lines
            cbar=False)                     # disable colorbar

# Re-enable outer spines
sns.despine(left=False, right=False, top=False, bottom=False)

plt.ylabel('Prediction',fontsize=13)
plt.xlabel('Actual',fontsize=13)
plt.title('Confusion Matrix',fontsize=17)
plt.show()

# Finding accuracy, precision, recall and f1 score
accuracy = accuracy_score(y_test, y_pred)
print("Accuracy :", accuracy)

precision = precision_score(y_test, y_pred)
print("Precision :", precision)

recall = recall_score(y_test, y_pred)
print("Recall :", recall)

f1 = f1_score(y_test, y_pred)
print("f1 :", f1)
```

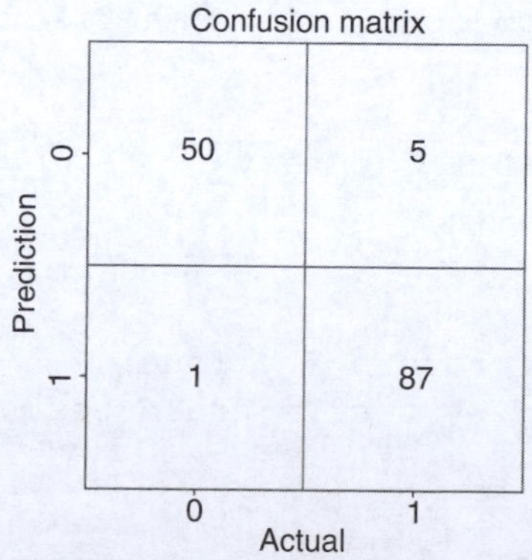

5. In the above code, if the train/test split of the dataset is changed; are the metrics evaluated earlier also going to change? Explain your answer.

C. Long-answer Questions

1. A real-estate company has each prospective house buyer fill out a form containing different questions. Using collected data, they create a decision tree model to predict whether a customer will purchase a house or not. Is this a classification or regression model? Suggest features to include for training the model.
2. A company offers a service to different cities across a country. The charges of the service vary based on the demographics of the city. The company wishes to expand their business to a new city and wish to use their existing tabular data to predict the right price for the service. Is this a classification or regression model? Think of a service and populate five rows of a table to train a decision tree.
3. Compare accuracy of a decision tree classifier, and a logistic regression on the same dataset with similar train/test split ratio. Explain why the decision tree classifier is likely to give higher accuracy.
4. Change the max_depth of the decision tree regression model (line 10 of Listing 7.4) and comment on how the model performs.

D. Explore and Experiment

1. Identify a clustering, classification, and regression business dataset from the UCI machine learning repository. Try out the k-means, decision tree classification, and decision tree regression models on the datasets.
2. Install Simple ML add-on for Google Sheets (https://workspace.google.com/marketplace/app/simple_ml_for_sheets/685936641092) and try the tasks mentioned in the screen shot below.

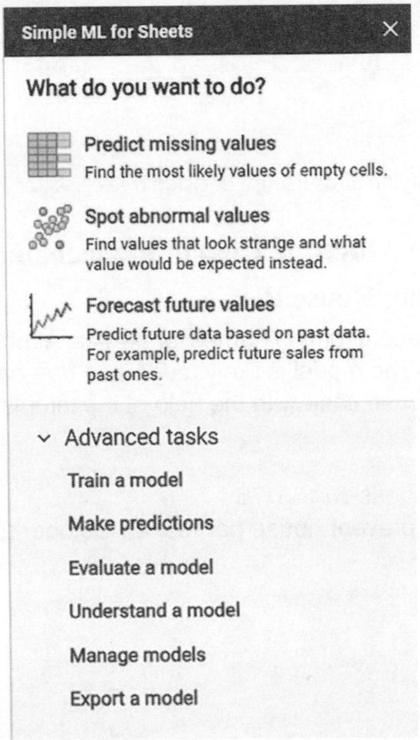

3. Generative AI generated Python code in Fig. 7.7 is used for classifying birds using decision trees. I encourage you to check if the generated code works right away or needs modifications.

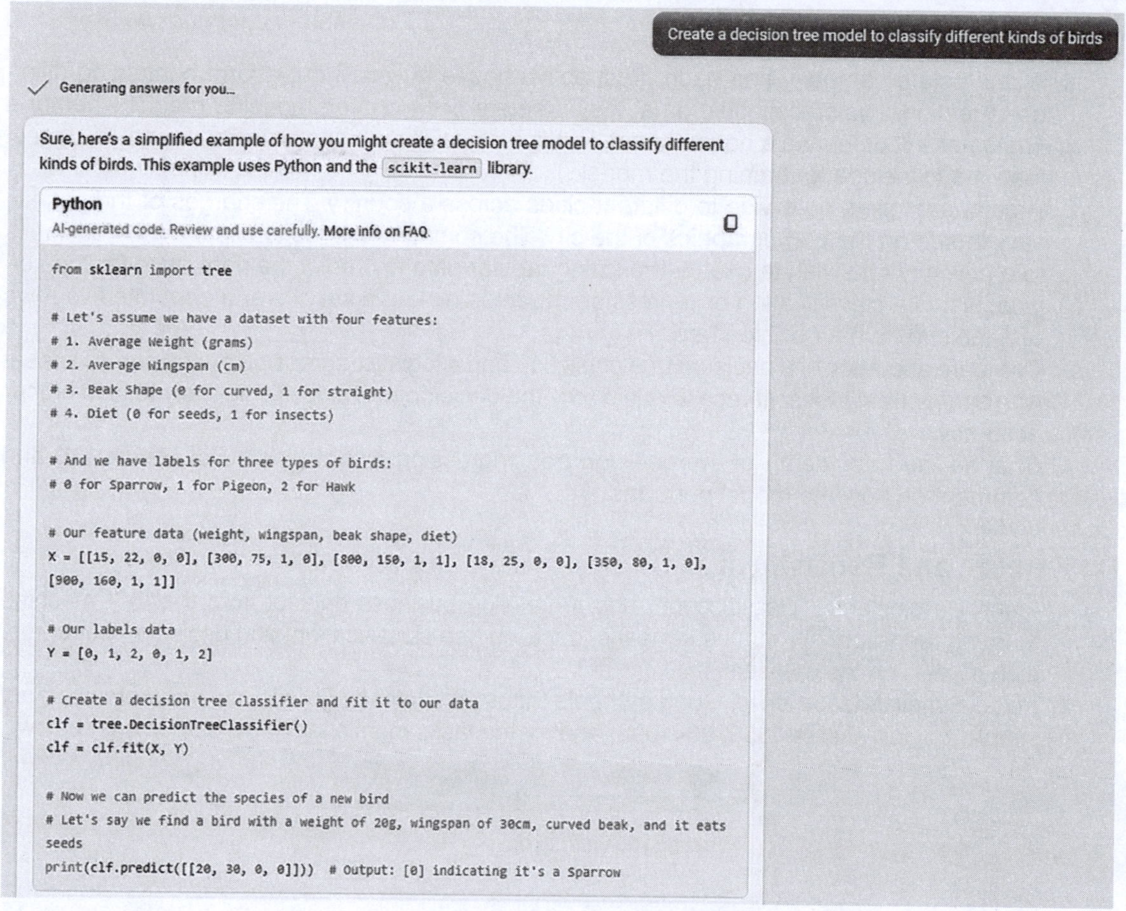


```
from sklearn import tree

# Let's assume we have a dataset with four features:
# 1. Average Weight (grams)
# 2. Average Wingspan (cm)
# 3. Beak Shape (0 for curved, 1 for straight)
# 4. Diet (0 for seeds, 1 for insects)

# And we have labels for three types of birds:
# 0 for Sparrow, 1 for Pigeon, 2 for Hawk

# Our feature data (weight, wingspan, beak shape, diet)
X = [[15, 22, 0, 0], [300, 75, 1, 0], [800, 150, 1, 1], [18, 25, 0, 0], [350, 80, 1, 0],
[900, 160, 1, 1]]

# Our labels data
Y = [0, 1, 2, 0, 1, 2]

# Create a decision tree classifier and fit it to our data
clf = tree.DecisionTreeClassifier()
clf = clf.fit(X, Y)

# Now we can predict the species of a new bird
# Let's say we find a bird with a weight of 20g, wingspan of 30cm, curved beak, and it eats
seeds
print(clf.predict([[20, 30, 0, 0]]))  # Output: [0] indicating it's a Sparrow
```

Fig. 7.7 AI generated code for classifying birds using a decision tree classifier

E. Generate Use Case on Machine Learning Decision Trees

Use Case: Airbnb Preventing House Parties

Brief description: To prevent people renting homes for parties, Airbnb created an AI model to predict the probability of a house party. The model is likely a decision tree-based classification model. Study the resources note and create a use case with the help of the template below.

Resources

https://www.bbc.com/news/business-67156176
BBC, Airbnb turns to AI to help prevent house parties, 25 October 2023

Template for Creating Use Case on use of Decision Trees

Define goal and purpose	Goal statement
	Identify stakeholders
	Define scope
Details to include in use case	Capture how technology helps business process
	Keep use case findings description textual, with a few simple flowcharts if needed
	Focus on describing how technology benefits the use case
Future applications	Mention any new applications that can leverage the technology used

Suggested Readings

1. Aurélien Géron, Hands-On Machine Learning with Scikit-Learn, Keras, and TensorFlow: Concepts, Tools, and Techniques to Build Intelligent Systems 2nd Edition, O'Reilly.
2. Andriy Burkov, The Hundred-Page Machine Learning Book.

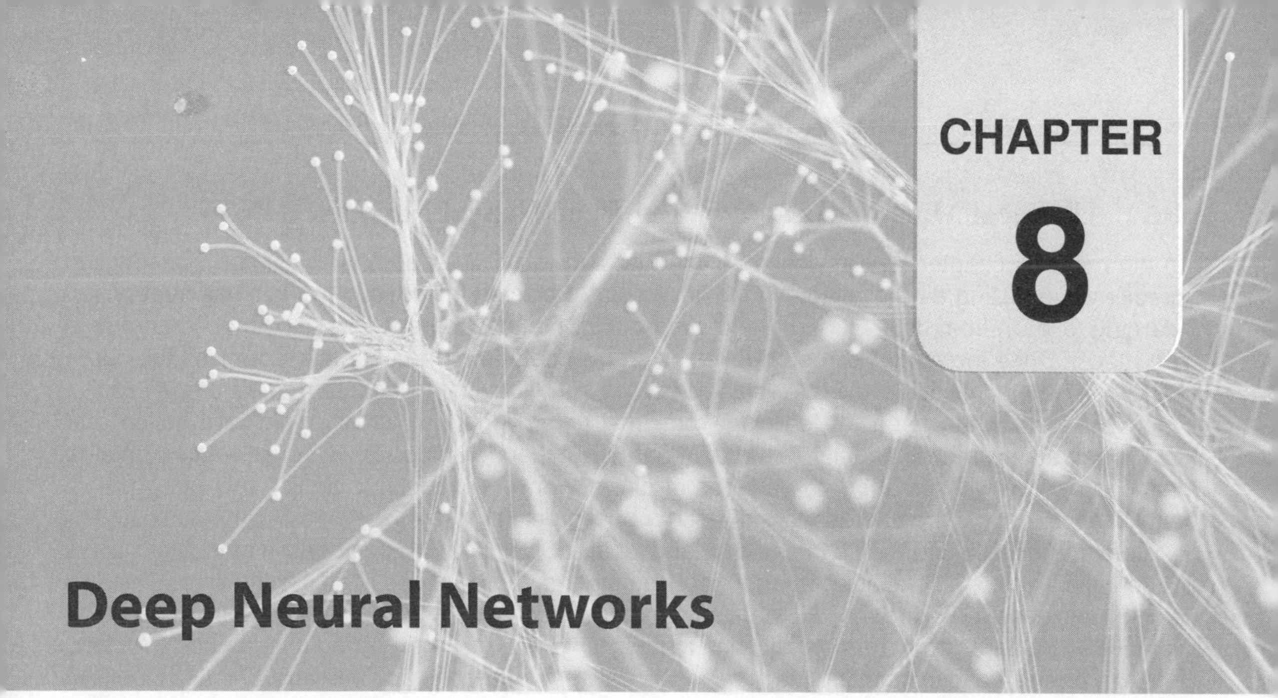

CHAPTER 8

Deep Neural Networks

CHAPTER OUTLINE

LEARNING OBJECTIVES

After reading this chapter, you will be able to:

- understand the limitations of classical machine learning models
- grasp steps required to train a deep neural network model
- know different types of deep neural networks
- map neural network models to use cases

Effective Management Using Deep Neural Network (DNN)

Good amount of business data is stored in the form of unstructured data such as images and text. Examples of text data include customer feedback, internal reports, and much more. While conventional techniques have worked well with tabular structured data, deep neural networks can help unlock value from unstructured data.

8.1 | Classical Machine Learning and Deep Neural Network (DNN)

In the previous chapter on classical machine learning, we discussed how to cluster, classify, and predict values using data available in tabular format. Decision tree-based models use supervised learning to learn from data. During model generation, the test dataset determines the accuracy of the model. Once the model is in production, it is novel data from the user that exercises the capabilities of the model. Figure 8.1 shows a representation of how decision tree models are utilized.

DNNs excel when used for learning from unstructured data. It is important to mention that DNNs can also work with tabular (structured data), but their main use is with unstructured data. In this chapter, we will talk about three types of neural network models. Table 8.1 lists out possible applications that can be addressed with each model type.

Before progressing further, let us understand what a DNN is. A DNN comprises of multiple layers of neurons. These neurons adjust their weights during the training process. Recall the time when you studied lots of solved exercises to understand underlying concepts. A DNN does something very similar to learn. It learns from examples. During training, DNNs look at train_x (input) and train_y (output, answer, label) data to understand the relationship between questions and answers. The DNN looks at the training data thousands of times to identify the features that relate inputs to the outputs. It is important to bear in mind that the DNN model training are usually not successful the first time. AI researchers who create these models, have to tweak the model architecture, the number of layers/neurons and the training dataset. That being said, the methodology to train a model is fairly mature and is listed below.

- Start with a labeled dataset (containing examples and labels)
- Normalize each feature to a value between 0,1 or –1 and 1
- Split dataset into training and test data fractions
- Create a multilayered neural network model (each layer contains multiple neurons)
- Feed batches of training data (example and label) to the model
    - Model compares its predicted output with ground truth using a loss function
    - Based on the value of loss, the model updates weights and biases of each neuron
    - Training data is used multiple times in the training process
    - Once loss reaches a small value (or completes a fixed number of training cycles), the training stops

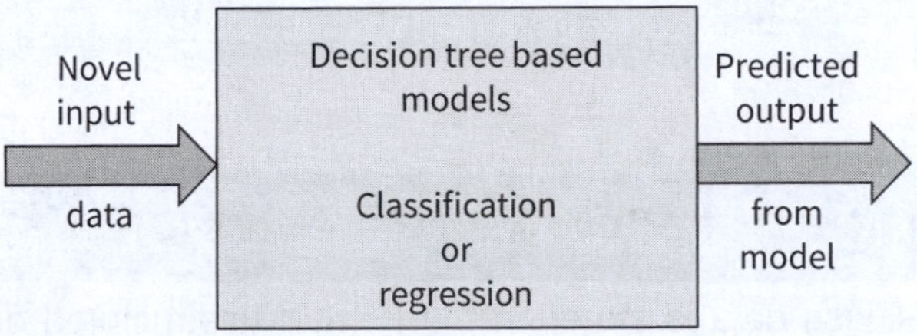

Fig. 8.1 Deployment of classical machine learning models such as decision trees

Table 8.1 Types of deep neural networks

Model Type	Application Area
Fully connected or dense	General purpose
Convolutional neural network (CNN)	Works well with images
Recurrent neural network	Sequences such as audio (sentences) and video (image frames)

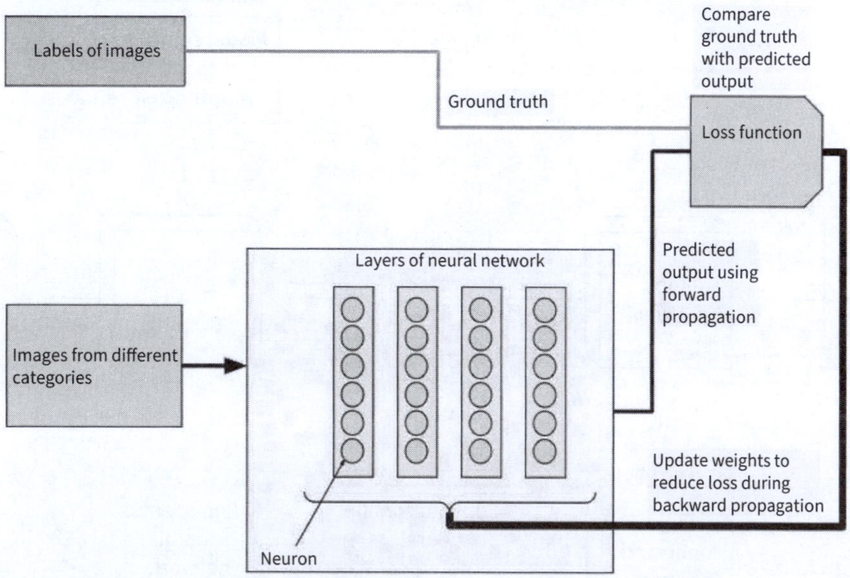

Fig. 8.2 Process of training a deep neural network

- Evaluate the trained neural network model on the test data, which was initially kept aside
- If the model performs well on the data, it may be suitable for production/deployment
- In case the loss value does not decrease with training, choose a different model architecture (number of layers) or improve the dataset

Let us talk about the model training process shown in Fig. 8.2. In the figure, we see that the images we wish to classify are fed to the model along with the labels. If an image is of a cat, the label would be a cat. Using the neural network, the model makes a prediction on the image. This prediction is compared with the true (ground truth) value by the loss function. Based on the output of the loss function, the model updates the weights during backpropagation. When a model is being trained for the first time, it is difficult to estimate the number of neurons/layers needed for the model. Many times, a model has an excessive number of neurons, leading to overfitting, while at other times it may have less than the required number of neurons, leading to underfitting. Let us learn more about these two terms.

Model overfitting A model that performs very well on the training dataset (by memorizing it) and fares poorly on the test dataset is a model that overfits. This kind of model cannot be generalized. The condition of overfitting is resolved by using hyperparameters such as dropout (removing random neurons during training) and regularization (removing neurons with outlier weights).

Model underfitting A model with fewer resources (number of neurons/layers) is not able to do well even on training data. The loss value during training continues to remain high. This is resolved by adding extra layers to the model.

The model training flow for a DNN model is illustrated as building blocks in Fig. 8.3(a). Each model type (fully, CNN, recurrent) has a different kind of layer. Other than that, all DNN models follow a similar training flow.

The Simplest Neural Network

Let us create the simplest possible neural network. A network with one neuron. Each neuron in a neural network consists of two computation elements—linear and nonlinear. The linear element

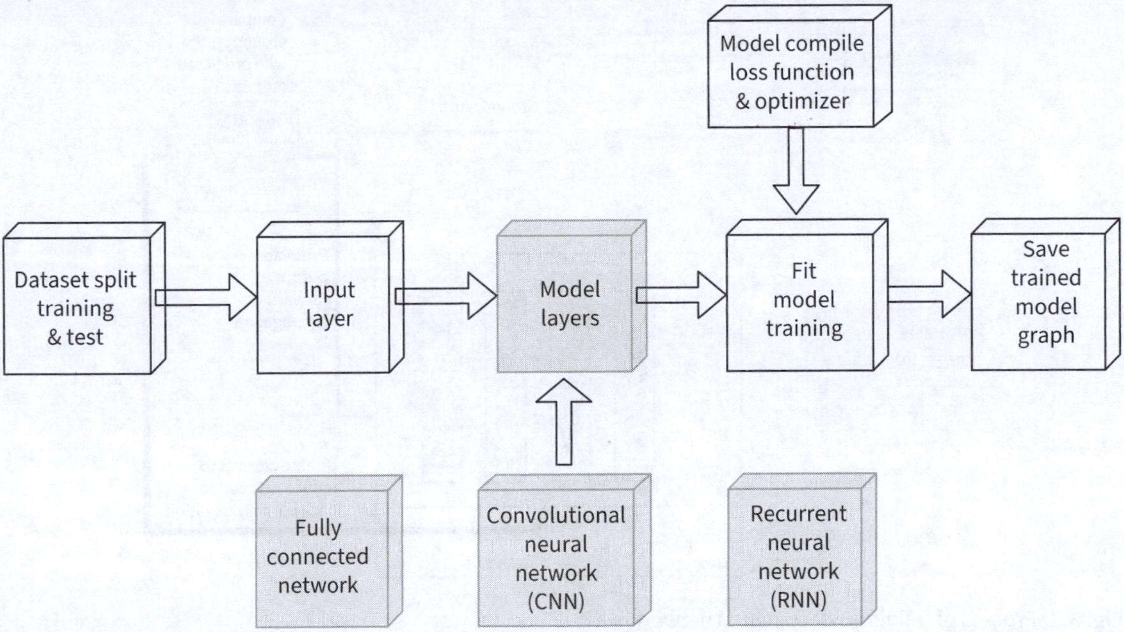

Fig. 8.3 (a) Steps needed to train a deep neural network model

```
import tensorflow as tf
# Create a simple Keras model. Expected output is 2x-1
X = [-1, 0, 1, 2, 3, 4, 5, 6, 7, 8]
y = [-3, -1, 1, 3, 5, 7, 9, 11, 13,15]
model = tf.keras.models.Sequential(
[tf.keras.layers.Dense(units=1, input_shape=(1,))])
model.compile(optimizer='sgd', loss='mean_squared_error')
model.fit(X, y, epochs=200)
model.summary()
weights = model.get_weights()
print (weights)
Model: "sequential"
```

Fig. 8.3 (b) Keras API for training DNN model

represents the equation of a line: mx + b. During training, the model determines the value of the slope (m) and the bias (b). The output of the linear unit is fed to a nonlinear unit—known as the activation function. The rectified linear unit (ReLU) is an example of a frequently used activation function.

Our simple neural network will model the equation of a line by using its linear computation unit. We give it two lists. The input list X, and the output or labels list y. In our example, we expect the model to determine the slope of the line and the bias. The neuron consists of a trainable weight, which is

```
 Layer (type)                Output Shape              Param #
=================================================================
 dense (Dense)               (None, 1)                 2
=================================================================
Total params: 2
Trainable params: 2
Non-trainable params: 0
_________________________________________________________________
[array([[1.9581021]], dtype=float32), array([-0.7592758], dtype=float32)]
```

Fig. 8.3 (c) Model summary of single neuron model

multiplied by the input and a trainable bias. If you take a look at the code below you will see the following methods to train the neuron. These methods are presented as steps in Fig. 8.3(b).

- (layers.dense) to setup one layer of a fully connected network with one neuron
- (model.compile) to setup the loss function for training, and specify the optimizer
- (model.fit) to train the model using X (training) and y (label) dataset
- (model.summary()) to print out model architecture
- (model.get_weights()) to know the value of weight and bias of our neuron

Returning back to lists X and y, you will see the equation of line is $y = 2x - 1$. Our model has computed the slope (weight) to be 1.96 and the bias to be (–0.76). This is mentioned along with the model summary shown in Fig. 8.3(c). If you rerun the training process multiple times, you will get different values of weight and bias. This happens because model training is a stochastic process. Also note in this example, we are only using the linear part of the neuron. The activation function is unused.

Try out this code in Google Colab and experiment with different equations of a line. Modify lists X and y to represent your own line and check if the model can figure out its slope and bias. Congratulations! You have successfully trained your first deep neural network AI model.

8.2 | Fully Connected Network

A fully connected or densely connected network consists of multiple layers of neurons. They are general-purpose neural network architectures that work with multiple domains—structured (tabular data), images or simple text classification. Figure 8.2 provides a good representation of how neurons and layers are arranged.

To demonstrate the power of a fully connected network, we will use it to predict a sequence. For this example, we train the model to predict future values of a Fibonacci sequence. We provide the model with training data and have it figure out how the sequence works. To train the model, we provide three values of the sequence and the corresponding output (next value in the sequence). The training dataset (X,y) is seen in Listing 8.2. As seen in line 15 of the code (Listing 8.1), 100 neurons[1] are used in the model. Since this is a regression problem, mean square error (MSE) is used as the loss function. Keras timeseries_dataset_from_array is used to create a dataset suitable for supervised learning. To test our model we provide three inputs that the model has not encountered during training (line 20 of Listing 8.1). When the novel input sequence of 34,55,89 is presented to the model, it provides 143.8 as its predicted value. This value is very close to the right value of 144. Experiment with different input values in line 20 of the code in Listing 8.1.

[1]The number of neurons needed for a given problem is determined experimentally. To start with, the model is made to overfit by starting with a large number of layers/neurons. Then by tuning hyperparameters and regularization techniques, the model is made to generalize. Feel free to experiment with different number of neurons.

Listing 8.1 Fully connected network for Fibonacci sequence

```
from tensorflow import keras
from keras.utils import timeseries_dataset_from_array
from numpy import array
from keras.models import Sequential
from keras.layers import Dense

input_seq = array([0,1,1,2,3,5,8,13,21,34,55,89])

seq_length = 3

training_dataset = keras.utils.timeseries_dataset_from_array(
data=input_seq[:],
targets=input_seq[3:],
sequence_length=3,
batch_size=1,
)

model = Sequential()
model.add(Input(shape=(seq_length,)))
model.add(Dense(100, activation='relu'))
model.add(Dense(1))
model.compile(optimizer='adam', loss='mse')
model.fit(training_dataset, epochs=200, verbose=0)
#Test trained model using new input
x_input = array([34, 55,89]).reshape((1, seq_length))
y_output = model.predict(x_input, verbose=0)
print(y_output)
```

Listing 8.2 Training data for Fibonacci series and output generated by model

```
Training data:
Inputs(X)           Label (y)
[0, 1, 1]           2
[1, 1, 2]           3
[1, 2, 3]           5
[2, 3, 5]           8
[3, 5, 8]           13
[5, 8, 13]          21
[8, 13, 21]         34
[13, 21, 34]        55
[21, 34, 55]        89

Output of the model when presented sequence 34, 55,89
[[143.804]]
```

Parsing Datasets and Prepping for Supervised Learning

Let us revisit the publicly available real-estate valuation dataset.[2] The features of this dataset are as follows:

X1 = the transaction date (for example, 2013.250 = 2013 March, 2013.500 = 2013 June, etc.)
X2 = the house age (unit: year)
X3 = the distance to the nearest mass rapid transit (MRT) station (unit: meter)
X4 = the number of convenience stores in the living circle on foot (integer)
X5 = the geographic coordinate, latitude (unit: degree)
X6 = the geographic coordinate, longitude (unit: degree)

The output or label is as follows:
Y = house price of unit area (10,000 New Taiwan Dollar/Ping, where Ping is a local unit, 1 Ping = 3.3 meter squared)

The input features (X1..X6) and output (y) are mentioned in Table 8.2. For the sake of brevity and clarity, we just list the first 11 rows of the dataset. The total number of rows in the dataset is 414. To correlate house features to their price is a regression problem that we will solve using a fully connected neural network. We start by converting the dataset from Microsoft Excel into a comma separated values (CSV) format. Columns X1–X6 are input features, and the last column Y is the output or label.

The code to train and test the regression model on the housing dataset is presented in Listing 8.3. Once you study the code, you will observe the following:

- We use a function called train_test_split to split our dataset for training and testing
- We specify the columns that are input features (X) and the column that is the label(y)

Table 8.2 Snapshot of real-estate dataset

No.	X1 Transaction Date	X2 House Age	X3 Distance to the Nearest MRT Station	X4 No. of Convenience Stores	X5 Latitude	X6 Longitude	Y House Price of Unit Area
1	2012.917	32.0	84.87882	10	24.98298	121.54024	37.9
2	2012.917	19.5	306.5947	9	24.98034	121.53951	42.2
3	2013.583	13.3	561.9845	5	24.98746	121.54391	47.3
4	2013.500	13.3	561.9845	5	24.98746	121.54391	54.8
5	2012.833	5.0	390.5684	5	24.97937	121.54245	43.1
6	2012.667	7.1	2175.03	3	24.96305	121.51254	32.1
7	2012.667	34.5	623.4731	7	24.97933	121.53642	40.3
8	2013.417	20.3	287.6025	6	24.98042	121.54228	46.7
9	2013.500	31.7	5512.038	1	24.95095	121.48458	18.8
10	2013.417	17.9	1783.18	3	24.96731	121.51486	22.1
11	2013.083	34.8	405.2134	1	24.97349	121.53372	41.4

Columns X1–X6 are the feature columns (training) while Y is the output (labels) column.)

[2]Real-estate valuation data set Data Set, https://archive.ics.uci.edu/ml/datasets/Real+estate+valuation+data+set# (accessed 6 December 2022).

Listing 8.3 Training a real-estate valuation dataset using fully connected network

```
# Modules from Sklearn and Keras/TensorFlow
from sklearn.preprocessing import StandardScaler
from sklearn.model_selection import train_test_split
import numpy as np
import keras
from numpy import loadtxt
from keras.models import Sequential
from keras.layers import Dense

# load the dataset
dataset = np.genfromtxt('housing-dataset.csv', delimiter=',')

# split into input (X) and output (y) variables
X = dataset[:,2:5]  # Three features for model training - X2,X3,X4
y = dataset[:,7]

X_train, X_test, y_train, y_test = train_test_split(X, y,
                                    test_size=0.30, random_state=42)

#print (X_train, y_train)

print ('Length of Training data', len(X_train))
print ('Length of Test data', len(X_test))

scaler = StandardScaler()
scaler.fit(X)

Train_X = scaler.transform(X_train)
Test_X = scaler.transform(X_test)

# define the keras model
model = Sequential()
model.add(Dense(16, activation='relu', input_shape = (3,)))
model.add(Dense(16, activation='relu'))
model.add(Dense(16, activation='relu'))
model.add(Dense(16, activation='relu'))
model.add(Dense(1))

# compile the keras model
model.compile(loss='mean_squared_error', optimizer='adam')

# fit the keras model on the dataset
model.fit(Train_X, y_train, epochs=200, batch_size=16)

predictions = model.predict(Test_X)
for i in range (len(predictions)):
print (predictions[i], y_test[i])
```

Listing 8.4 Output of regression AI mode, on prediction of housing price

```
Length of Training data 289
Length of Test data 125

[55.013714] 45.1
[41.64347] 42.3
[43.070034] 52.2
[50.894684] 37.3
[21.555698] 22.8
```

- We normalize data for input features using the StandardScaler function from Sklearn.
- Our model consists of three layers and a total of 65 neurons.

The methods to setup the loss function, optimizer and training remain the same are our earlier single neuron example. The code in Listing 8.3 uses the Keras library to define and train a fully connected model for predicting real-estate prices based on three input features—house age, proximity to MRT, and a number of nearby convenience stores. The dataset is loaded from a CSV file (line 10), split into training and testing sets (lines 14,15), and normalized to improve model performance. A fully connected AI model architecture consisting of four hidden layers with ReLU activation functions and a linear output layer is experimentally created. While creating the model input layer, input_shape is set to 3 as three features of the dataset are used.

The model is compiled with the mean squared error loss function and the Adam optimizer (line 31). Subsequently, the model is trained for 200 epochs (line 33), with 70% of the data (X_train). The trained model is evaluated using 30% of unseen test data (lines 34–36). First five values of the model's predicted versus actual output values are seen in Listing 8.4. Experiment and see if the error changes if you allocate more data samples for training. This is done by changing the test_size argument in line 14 of the code in Listing 8.3.

8.3 | Convolutional Neural Network

The year 2012 was a watershed moment for neural networks. This was the year, when a CNN-based AI model—AlexNet[3] won the ImageNet challenge by a huge margin. The ImageNet challenge required the classification of images into 1000 categories. Today, CNNs play a big role in most successful applications of deep learning such as self-driving cars, speech recognition systems, and optical character recognition.

As seen in Fig. 8.4, convolutional filters in a CNN model learn spatial patterns, while sliding across an image. Filters identify and extract features from an image. All extracted features are combined together. The classifier determines the object that matches the identified features. These filters detect simple patterns like horizontal or vertical lines, changes in color, or grid patterns. When stacked in layers, they recognize more complex patterns, building upon the simpler convolutions from the preceding layers.

A simple analogy from a folk story may help understand CNNs better. This story is about six visually challenged people who are tasked to identify an elephant. Five touch different parts of the

[3]Alex K. et al, ImageNet Classification with Deep Convolutional Neural Networks, 2012, https://proceedings.neurips.cc/paper/2012/file/c399862d3b9d6b76c8436e924a68c45b-Paper.pdf (accessed 21 November 2022).

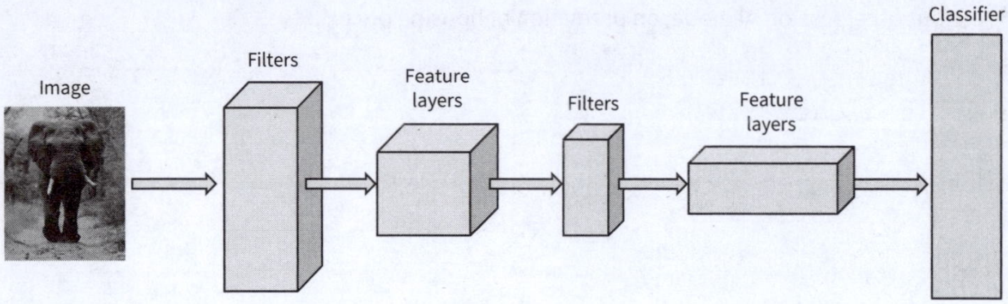

Fig. 8.4 Working of a CNN

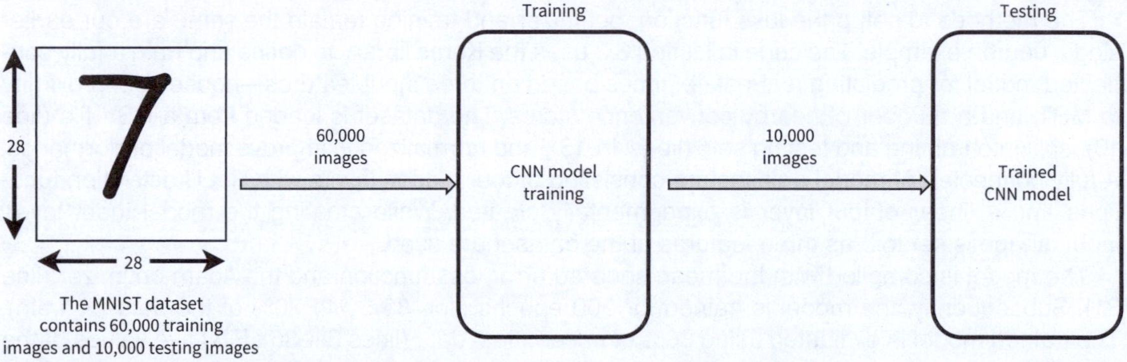

Fig. 8.5 Details of the MNIST dataset

elephant and report the following: it is a wall (touching stomach), tree trunk (legs), rope (tail), snake (trunk), and spear (tooth). They bring their findings to the sixth person who is sitting at a distance.

Each of the five people who touch the elephant acts as a filter. They discover a certain feature of the elephant. The sixth person acts as the classifier. He combines the features and determines the object is an elephant. This is how CNN models are trained to recognize objects in images. The feature layers extract features, which are then correlated by the classifier.

Let us now turn our attention to the dataset that was used to train the first CNN model, the Modified National Institute of Standards and Technology (MNIST) dataset. The MNIST dataset is a large collection of handwritten digits. It consists of 60,000 (28 × 28 pixel) grayscale images of handwritten digits 0–9, along with a test set of 10,000 images. Each image has pixel values in the range from 0 to 255. Pictorially, Fig. 8.5 shows the details and use of the MNIST dataset.

The MNIST CNN model was trained using images shown in Fig. 8.6. Among the first reported uses of a CNN model was to determine amounts mentioned on bank checks.[4] It was also used to read handwritten zip codes on letters to assist sorting in a post office. Contemporary CNN models are able to achieve high accuracy (>99%) on the MNIST dataset with few simple APIs.

[4]Yann Lecun et. al, Gradient-based learning applied to document recognition, http://yann.lecun.com/exdb/publis/pdf/lecun-01a.pdf (accessed 8 June 2023).

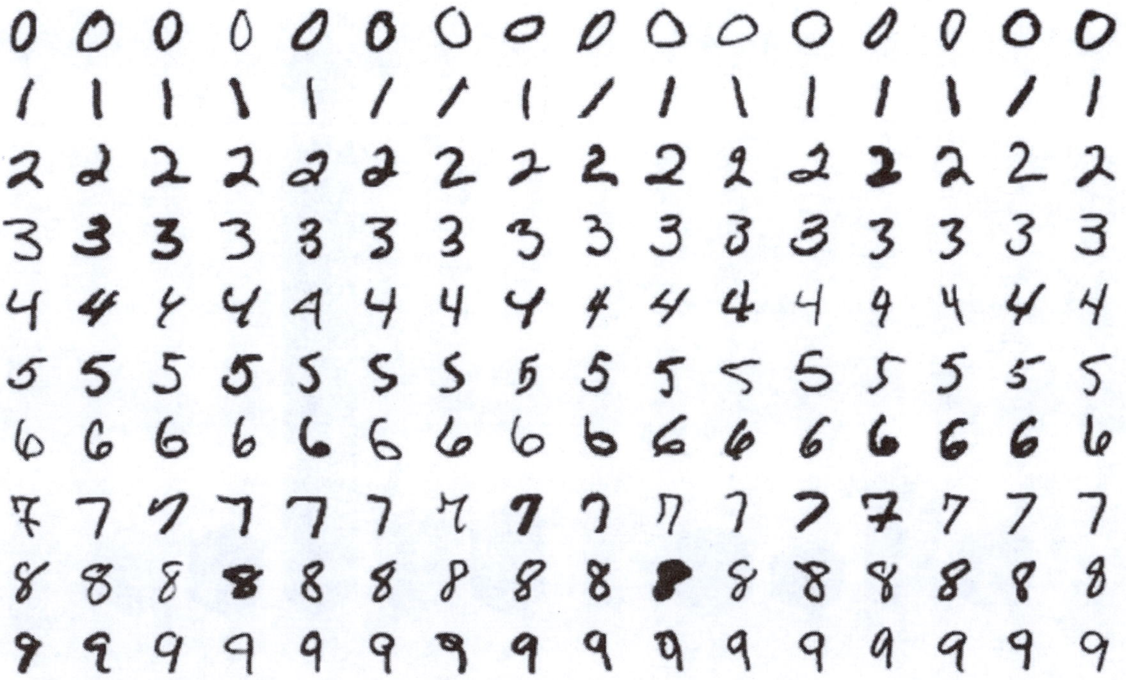

Fig. 8.6 Sample images from the MNIST dataset[5]

To reiterate, CNN models are a type of neural network that are designed to work with image data. They are composed of layers of interconnected neurons that apply mathematical operations to the input data, such as convolution and pooling, to extract features that are relevant for classification. The basic operation of a CNN is described as follows:

Input layer The first layer of the CNN takes the raw input image and passes it through a set of convolutional filters to create feature maps. These filters are learned during training and represent patterns that are relevant to the task at hand.

Convolutional layer Each convolutional filter is applied to the input image to create a feature map that highlights the presence of a particular feature in the image. The filters slide over the entire image, pixel by pixel, and perform a dot product between their weights and the corresponding pixels in the input image.

ReLU layer Output from the convolutional layer is then passed through a Rectified Linear Unit (ReLU) activation function, which applies a threshold function to the output of each neuron. This introduces nonlinearity into the model, allowing it to capture more complex relationships between the input and output.

Pooling layer The output of the ReLU layer is downsampled using a pooling operation, which reduces the dimensionality of the feature map while retaining the most important features.

Fully connected layer The output of the pooling layer is then flattened and passed through one or more fully connected layers, which perform a linear transformation on the data to generate the final output.

[5]Sample images from MNIST test dataset, MNIST dataset, https://en.wikipedia.org/wiki/MNIST_database (accessed 12 April 2023).

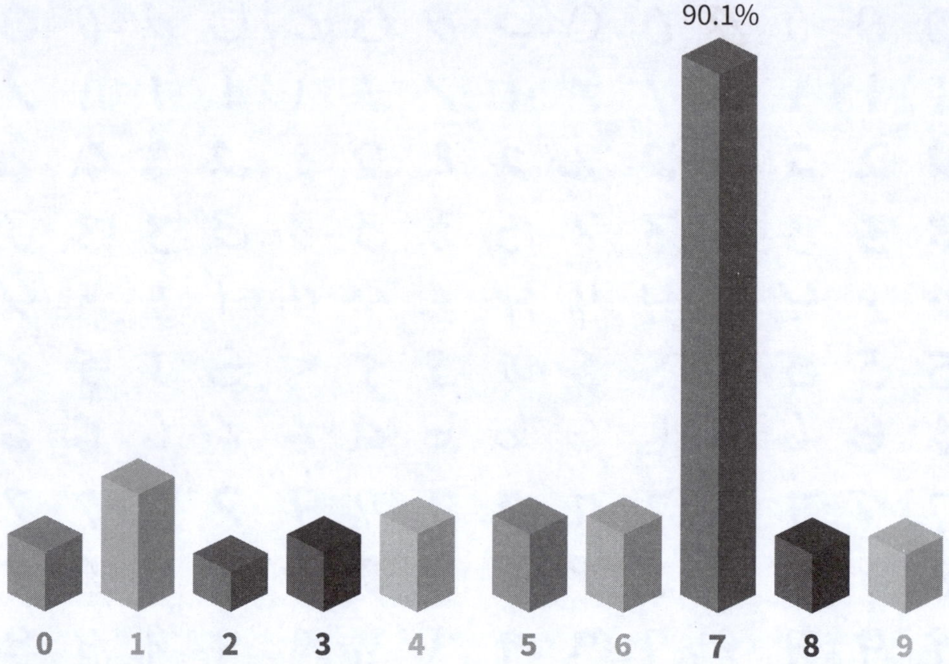

Fig. 8.7 MNIST classification model output

Output layer In the case of MNIST classification, the final layer of the CNN produces the output of the model, which is a classification label probability. As seen in Fig. 8.7, digit 7 has the highest probability since it was the digit the model was given to classify. Digit 7 is followed by digit 1, second highest.

The code in Listing 8.5 uses convolution layers in place of fully connected layers. These layers detect features in the input images and map them to the output labels. Two convolution layers of 32 and 64 filters are used to extract features from the MNIST dataset images. The accuracy of the CNN model on 10,000 test images from the MNIST dataset is an impressive value of 99.14%.

Listing 8.5 Training and evaluating a MNIST model using CNN layers

```
import numpy as np
import tensorflow as tf
from tensorflow import keras
from tensorflow.keras import layers

# Define the model architecture
model = keras.Sequential()
model.add(layers.Conv2D(filters=32, kernel_size=(3, 3),
          activation='relu', input_shape=(28, 28, 1)))
model.add(layers.MaxPooling2D(pool_size=(2, 2)))
model.add(layers.Conv2D(filters=64, kernel_size=(3, 3),
          activation='relu'))
model.add(layers.MaxPooling2D(pool_size=(2, 2)))
model.add(layers.Flatten())
model.add(layers.Dense(units=128, activation='relu'))
```

Listing 8.5 *(Continued)*

```
model.add(layers.Dense(units=10, activation='softmax'))
# Compile the model
model.compile(optimizer='adam', loss='categorical_crossentropy',
              metrics=['accuracy'])
# Load the data and preprocess it
(x_train, y_train), (x_test, y_test) =
                       keras.datasets.mnist.load_data()
x_train = np.expand_dims(x_train, axis=-1) / 255.0
x_test = np.expand_dims(x_test, axis=-1) / 255.0
y_train = keras.utils.to_categorical(y_train, 10)
y_test = keras.utils.to_categorical(y_test, 10)

# Train the model
model.fit(x_train, y_train, epochs=10, batch_size=128,
                          validation_data=(x_test, y_test))

## Evaluate the trained model

score = model.evaluate(x_test, y_test, verbose=0)
print("Test loss:", score[0])
print("Test accuracy:", score[1])
```

```
Test loss: 0.031228240579366684
Test accuracy: 0.9914000034332275
```

8.4 | Recurrent Neural Network

Recurrent neural networks (RNNs) are good with applications where an ordered sequence needs to be detected. The most intuitive example of an ordered sequence is words as part of a sentence. Most digital assistants (Alexa, Hey Google or Siri) use RNNs under the hood. RNNs can handle inputs with different sequence lengths. This works well with sentences that have a varying number of words. Applications that utilize RNNs include weather prediction, natural language processing (NLP), predictive maintenance, and many more. The basic idea behind RNNs is to introduce a feedback loop that allows the network to maintain an internal state or "memory" of the past inputs it has seen. This internal state is updated at each time step based on the current input and the previous internal state, and is then used to produce the output at the current time step.

RNNs are trained in a similar way as other DNNs. But they use a unique building block (which also consists of trainable neurons). These blocks are known as long short-term memory (LSTM)[6] and Transformer.[7] The code snippet of Listing 8.6 shows an LSTM-based model to predict values of a harmonic series sequence. The methods for model compilation, training and prediction are the ones we used for fully connected and CNN-based neural networks. You can view the complete LSTM-based model on Google Colab.

[6]Understand LSTM networks, Colah's Blog, https://colah.github.io/posts/2015-08-Understanding-LSTMs/ (accessed 21 November 2022).

[7]What is a Transformer model, Nvidia blog, https://blogs.nvidia.com/blog/2022/03/25/what-is-a-transformer-model (accessed 21 November 2022).

Listing 8.6 Training a LSTM model to predict values of harmonic sequence

```
# define model
model = Sequential()
model.add(LSTM(20, activation='relu', input_shape=(n_steps,
n_features)))
model.add(Dense(1))

model.compile(optimizer='adam', loss='mse')
model.summary()

# fit model
model.fit(X, y, epochs=2000, verbose=0)


# Input for experimentation on Harmonic sequence
x_input = array ([0.14, 0.125, 0.11])

x_input = x_input.reshape((1, n_steps, n_features))

y_output = model.predict(x_input, verbose=0)

print(f'predicted output from RNN-LSTM for Harmonic sequence
{y_output}')
```

```
predicted output from RNN-LSTM for Harmonic sequence [[0.10280988]]
```

8.5 | Conclusion

DNNs are an important tool for analyzing unstructured data. In this chapter, we discussed the training process of DNNs and the concept of model overfitting and underfitting. We also talked about three DNN architectures—fully connected, CNN and RNN and their specific characteristics. Code examples using TensorFlow Keras APIs were presented to explain the steps needed for training a DNN model.

Exercises

A. State True/False

1. Deep neural networks (DNNs) can handle unstructured data and use supervised training.
2. Fully connected neural networks are recommended for images.
3. Applications that require sequence detection (such as words in a sentence) use RNN.
4. Features of a dataset are normalized before using it for DNN training.
5. DNN always provides good accuracy on the test dataset.

B. Short-answer Questions

1. How many training/test images are included in the MNIST handwritten digits dataset?
2. During training, model weights are updated during forward or backward propagation?
3. How many neurons are needed for a model to determine slope and offset parameters for a straight line represented by y = mx + b.

4. Mention the Keras method used for training a model, when train_X and train_y values are available.
5. Name the cost function to train a regression model and to train a classification model.

C. Long-answer Questions

1. Enumerate applications that could use CNN models.
   (Hint: Think of applications that use some kind of computer vision.)
2. Comment on the role of data in training a DNN. Which of the following do you think is best for training a DNN—(a) poorly labeled low quantity of data, (b) poorly labeled large quantity of data, (c) accurately labeled large quantity of data, or (d) large quantity of data with reasonable accuracy. In a real-world scenario, which of the above-mentioned data categories you are likely to encounter.
3. Download the CIFAR 10 dataset and find out the following details:
   Number of classes:
   Training images:
   Test images:
4. Epochs represent the number of times a training dataset is completely parsed during model training. Experiment by changing the training epochs for the listings given in the chapter and comment on its effects on model accuracy. (line 18 of Listing 8.1, line 33 of Listing 8.3).

D. Explore and Experiment

1. Create a CNN model using a Web-based GUI tool (Teachable Machine[8]). This tool helps in creating models that can classify pictures, sounds, and poses. For creating a model, the user needs to provide training data either using files, a webcam or a microphone (Figure (a)).

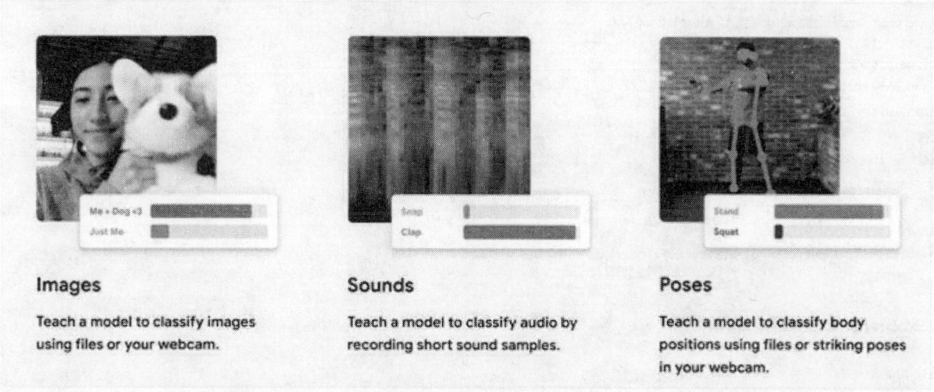

(a) Different types of data the model can work with

2. Upload or create different training classes for model training. Once the data is in place, go ahead and train the model; using step 2 in figure (b) below. The tool splits the data into two parts—training and testing. The test data are used to check robustness of the model by metrics such as confusion matrix. Watch this video,[9] if you wish to get a tutorial on the tool. The trained model can be used on a computer or a mobile device.

[8] Teachable Machine, https://teachablemachine.withgoogle.com/ (accessed 13 May 2023).
[9] Teachable Machine video, https://www.youtube.com/watch?v=T2qQGqZxkD0 (accessed 9 June 2023).

I recommend that you try out all three categories—image, sound, and pose.

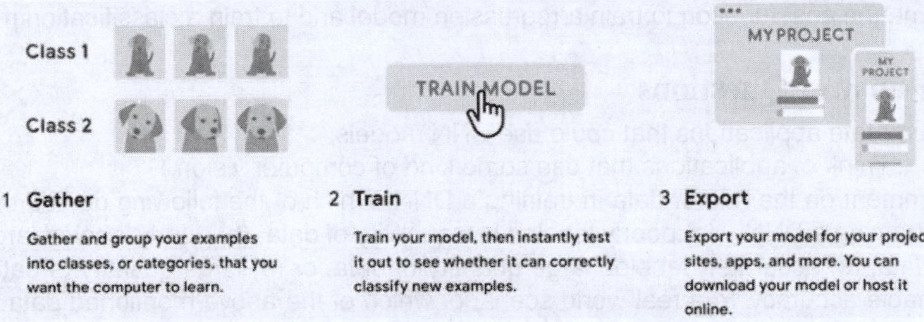

(b) Steps for model training using GUI tool

3. In Fig. 8.8, we use Generative AI to create an underfitting AI model code. This model has a single hidden layer with only 5 neurons, which might be too simple to capture complex patterns in the data, leading to underfitting. Here only 5 neurons are used for an AI model, where input tensor is of 10-dimensions.

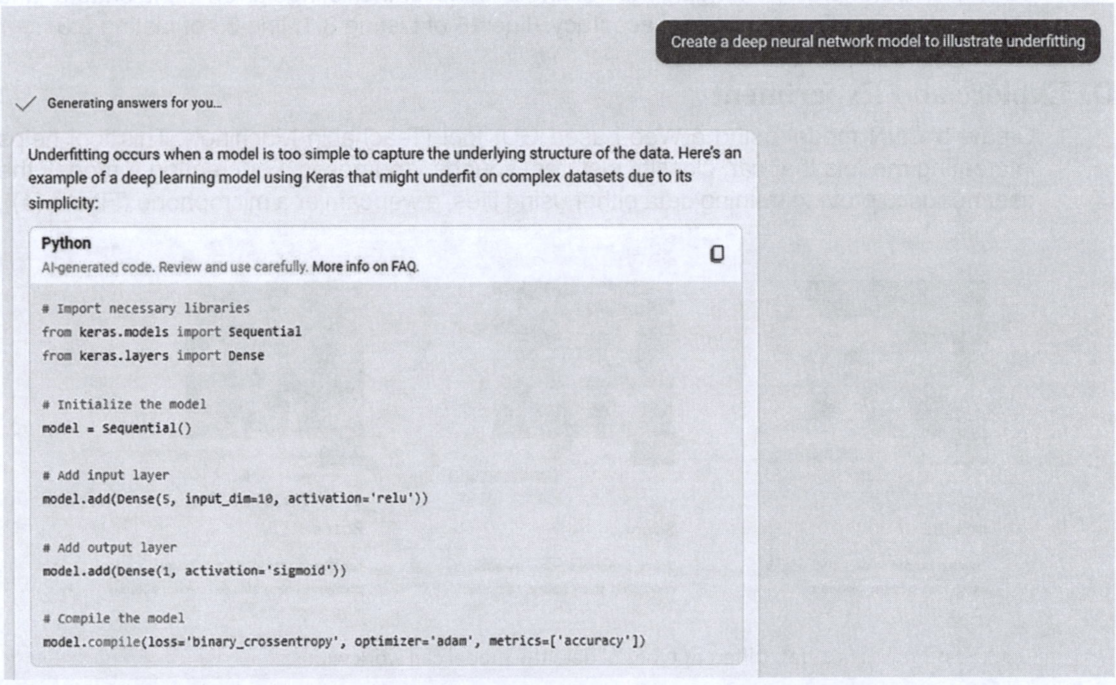

Create a deep neural network model to illustrate underfitting

Generating answers for you...

Underfitting occurs when a model is too simple to capture the underlying structure of the data. Here's an example of a deep learning model using Keras that might underfit on complex datasets due to its simplicity:

Python

AI-generated code. Review and use carefully. More info on FAQ.

```
# Import necessary libraries
from keras.models import Sequential
from keras.layers import Dense

# Initialize the model
model = Sequential()

# Add input layer
model.add(Dense(5, input_dim=10, activation='relu'))

# Add output layer
model.add(Dense(1, activation='sigmoid'))

# Compile the model
model.compile(loss='binary_crossentropy', optimizer='adam', metrics=['accuracy'])
```

Fig. 8.8 AI code to demonstrate underfitting

E. Generate Use Case on Deep Learning Neural Network for Saving Forests

Use Case: Saving Forests Using CNN Models on Low Cost Phones

Brief description: Human demand for wood is growing. This has lead to illegal logging in many parts of the world. Deep neural network models can identify specific sounds that correlates to logging activity. In this use case, a network of listening nodes is setup in the forest to monitor logging activity. The neural network model run on an old smartphone and relays logging activity information to forest rangers. Study the resources mentioned below and create a use case using the template given below.

Resource

Google stories: Is it possible to save a rainforest by listening to it? A tribe in the Brazilian state of Pará is exploring ways to use old cell phones and machine learning to fight deforestation.
https://about.google/intl/ALL_us/stories/rainforest/

Template to Generate Use Case on Deep Neural Network

Define goal and purpose	Goal statement
	Identify stakeholders
	Define scope
Details to include in use case	Capture how technology helps business process
	Keep use case findings description textual, with a few simple flowcharts if needed
	Focus on describing how technology benefits the use case
Future applications	Mention any new applications that can leverage the technology used

Suggested Reading

1. François Chollet, *Deep Learning with Python*, Manning Publications, 2021, Second Edition.

Resources

Define goal and purpose	[illegible]
	[illegible]
	[illegible]
Details to include	[illegible]
	[illegible]
	[illegible]
Future applications	[illegible]

Suggested Read

CHAPTER

9

Text Analytics Using AI

CHAPTER OUTLINE

LEARNING OBJECTIVES

After reading this chapter, you will be able to:

- acknowledge the prevalence of text and untapped insights
- know the available techniques to parse and make sense of text
- understand real life applications such as sentiment analysis, real-time chatbot agents, and Generative AI-based dialogue models

Effective Management Using Text Analytics

Though most business data is captured in the form of tables; a lot of valuable data exists as unstructured text. Techniques to ingest relevant information from unstructured text can provide useful insights for business operations. A tool that can make this happen, will unlock lot of value.

9.1 | Unstructured Text

In our hypothetical business scenario (Fig. 9.1), text serves as the eyes and ears of the business. Data from multiple sources is aggregated in cloud computers; a central repository. There is data from customer support services, e-mails, video conferencing meetings, reports from different business

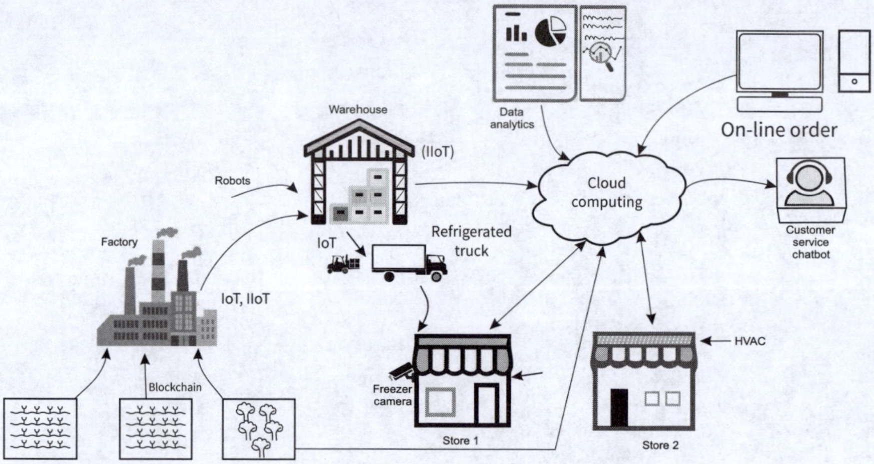

Fig. 9.1 Role of text analytics in contemporary business environment

Table 9.1 Creation of text and audio data

Business Function	Text/Audio Data Generation
Customer interaction	E-mails, voice calls
Internal communication with different business units	E-mails, Zoom meetings
Documentation related to various operations in a business	Reports containing findings, recommendations, concerns, opportunities, and threats

units and other sources. Until now, all this data was not utilized to yield something useful, as most of the text data is siloed in different departments of a business/organization. Now, with the help of natural language processing (NLP) and deep neural network (DNN)-based Generative AI models, it is possible to extract meaningful insights from this data. Text and audio data flow into a business environment through several channels. Some of these are enumerated in Table 9.1.

9.2 | How AI Helps with Text Analytics

Natural languages (both spoken and written) have evolved over time. Even though natural languages have a set of linguistic rules, it has not been easy to create handcrafted rules to comprehend language. DNN-based models have the ability to directly learn from data samples without the need for rules. An AI model is trained by presenting sample data along with a corresponding label. The process of training discovers the mapping with data samples and labels.

Numerous datasets have been used to train NLP models. These include datasets for sentiment analysis, text classification, translation, question and answer (Q&A), content filtering and language inference. With rapid strides in language models (such as BERT[1] for Q&A and language inference), text analytics has addressed multiple domains dealing with text. Some popular subdomains of text analytics are seen in Table 9.2.

[1] Jacob D. et al, BERT: Pre-training of Deep Bidirectional Transformers for Language Understanding, 2019, https://arxiv.org/abs/1810.04805 (accessed 22 November 2022).

Table 9.2 Different uses of text analytics

Usage Example	Text Analytics Subdomain
Determine topic of chapter	Text classification
Check if text contains abuse	Content filtering
Find out if this customer feedback sounds "positive or negative"	Sentiment analysis
Sentence autocomplete	Language modeling
Translate this sentence to French	Translation
Summarize this article in one paragraph	Summarization
Engage in dialogue across different topics	Generative AI—ChatGPT

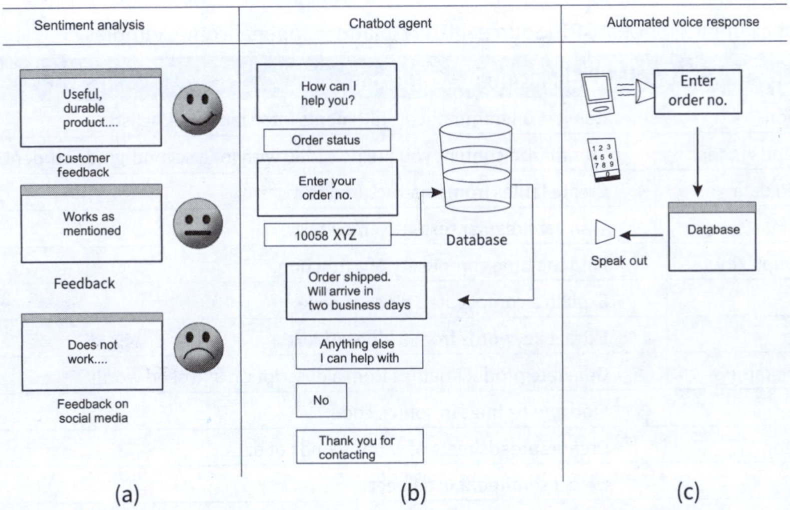

Fig. 9.2 Three different applications that utilize text analytics using AI. (a) Sentiment analysis. (b) Chatbot agent, and (c) Automated voice response system

Some intuitive applications of text-based analytics are pictorially seen in Fig. 9.2. These include sentiment analysis from customer feedback, a chatbot interacting with a customer who wishes to get details on order status and an automated voice response system that converts information retrieved from a database into voice with the help of text to speech software.[2]

Even though language models have made big progress in the last decade, text-processing models recently seem to have attained a human-like understanding of the language with the Generative AI model—ChatGPT. Earlier models latched on to statistical regularities in input data, which was good enough for simple tasks. NLP models are trained to understand patterns in words, sentences and paragraphs. Commonly used applications of text analytics include (along the lines of Fig. 9.2):

- **Sentiment analysis** Analyze customer feedback, social media posts, and other sources of unstructured data to determine the overall sentiment about a product, brand, or service. This can improve marketing strategies, customer service, and product development.

[2]AWS text to speech software, https://aws.amazon.com/polly/ (accessed 22 November 2022).

- **Customer service** Text analytics can be used to analyze customer service interactions, including e-mails, chat logs, and call recordings. Using this, businesses identify common issues, improve response times, and personalize the customer experience.
- **Competitive analysis** Monitor and analyze competitor activity, including product launches, marketing campaigns, and customer feedback. Help businesses identify areas for improvement and develop competitive strategies.
- **Fraud detection** Identify fraudulent activity, including phishing scams, social engineering attacks, and other types of cybercrime.

On 30th November 2022, the ChatGPT (Chat Generative Pre-trained Transformer) model was launched, and it became a giant step in the area of text-based Generative AI. It used a pre-trained large language model (LLM), which allowed it to present information as coherent sentences, in response to query prompts. A list of some prompts is collated in Table 9.3.

Table 9.3 Prompt examples for ChatGPT (Source: https://platform.openai.com/examples)

Prompt Type	Application Area of Prompt
Grammar correction	Convert ungrammatical statements into standard English.
Summarize for a 2nd grader	Summarize content you are provided with for a second-grade student.
Parse unstructured data	Create tables from unstructured text
Emoji Translation	Translate regular text into emoji text.
Calculate time complexity	Find the time complexity of a function.
Explain code	Explain a complicated piece of code.
Keywords	Extract keywords from a block of text.
Product name generator	Generate product names from a description and seed words.
Python bug fixer	Find and fix bugs in source code.
Spreadsheet creator	Create spreadsheets of various kinds of data.
Tweet classifier	Detect sentiment in a tweet.
Airport code extractor	Extract airport codes from text.
Mood to color	Turn a text description into a color.
VR fitness idea generator	Generate ideas for fitness promoting virtual reality games.
Marv the sarcastic chat bot	Marv is a factual chatbot that is also sarcastic.
Turn by turn directions	Convert natural language to turn-by-turn directions.
Interview questions	Create interview questions.
Function from specification	Create a Python function from a specification.
Improve code efficiency	Provide ideas for efficiency improvements to Python code.
Single page website creator	Create a single page website.
Rap battle writer	Generate a rap battle between two characters.
Memo writer	Generate a company memo based on provided points.
Emoji chatbot	Generate conversational replies using emojis only.
Translation	Translate natural language text.
Socratic tutor	Generate responses as a Socratic tutor.
Natural language to SQL	Convert natural language into SQL queries.
Meeting notes summarizer	Summarize meeting notes including overall discussion, action items, and future topics.

Table 9.3 *(Continued)*

Prompt Type	Application Area of Prompt
Review classifier	Classify user reviews based on a set of tags.
Pro and con discusser	Analyze the pros and cons of a given topic.
Lesson plan writer	Generate a lesson plan for a specific topic.

Training Preparation of NLP Models

NLP models are designed to process and understand human language. The general approach of an NLP model is to take raw text input, preprocess it, and then use various techniques to analyze the text and extract useful information. With the help of Fig. 9.3, let us get a basic overview of how text data for the NLP model is preprocessed.

Preprocessing Text is preprocessed to remove unnecessary characters, punctuation, and special characters. It is then converted to lowercase to standardize the text.

Tokenization The text is split into individual words, called tokens. This allows the model to analyze the text at a more granular level.

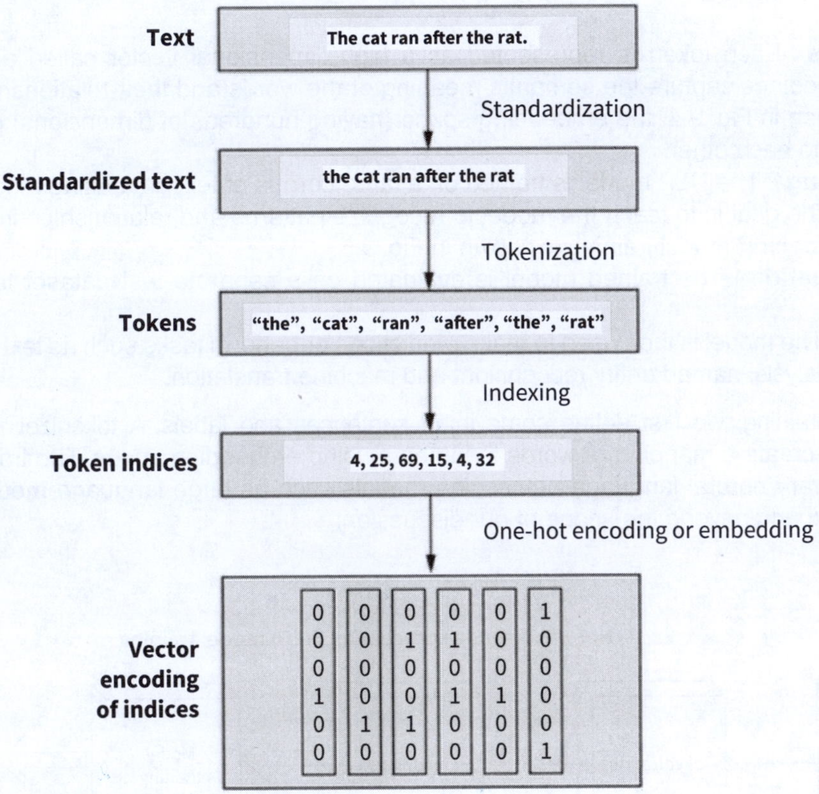

Fig. 9.3 Steps for preprocessing raw text for NLP training

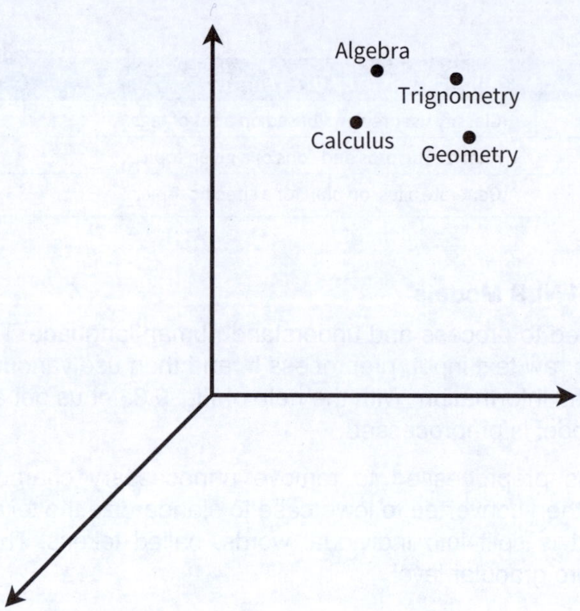

Fig. 9.4 Representative embedding space with math topics clustered together

Embeddings Each token is represented as a high-dimensional vector called an embedding. These embeddings capture the semantic meaning of the words and their relationships with other words. As seen in Fig. 9.4, the embedding space (having hundreds of dimensions) places related words close to each other.

Model training The NLP model is trained on a large corpus of text data using machine learning algorithms. The goal is to teach the model to recognize patterns and relationships in the text data. Basic steps for NLP model training is shown in Fig. 9.5.

Model evaluation The trained model is evaluated on a separate test dataset to measure its performance.

Inference The model is then used to make predictions or perform tasks such as text classification, sentiment analysis, named entity recognition, and machine translation.

For NLP training, we first define some input sentences and labels. A tokenizer processes the sentences to create a mapping of words to integers using embedding space. The training process of contemporary natural language processing models such as large language models (LLMs) is quite complex and beyond the scope of our discussion.

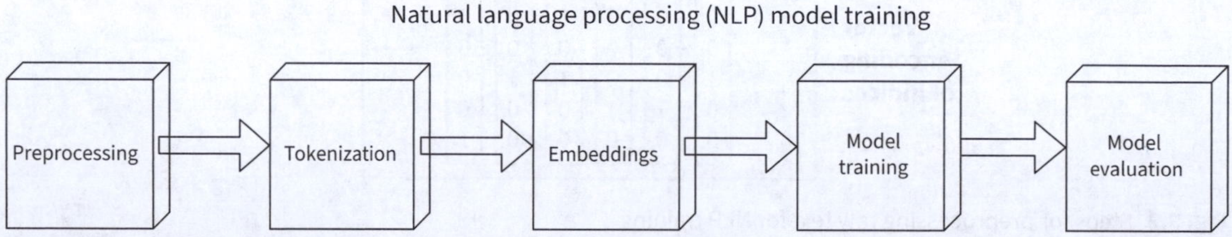

Fig. 9.5 NLP model training steps

9.3 | Idea of Self-Attention and Generative AI Based Dialogue Models

As you read this chapter, you may pay more attention to some sections, while others you may gloss over. The sections you read carefully are aligned with your personal learning outcome. AI models also leverage the idea of self-attention. Based on the desired outcome, models pay more attention to some features and pay less attention to other features. If you remember our discussion on CNN, you may recall that filter layers are tasked with detecting features, while the max pooling selects just one feature to keep from the pool of detected features. This is an example of an all-or-nothing form of attention. The max pooling retains the most important feature and discards the rest.

A continuous form of attention is used in NLP. It assigns scores to tokens based on how the information each token is likely to carry. Important tokens get higher scores, while irrelevant tokens are given a low score. This attention mechanism allows the model to capture long-range dependencies and relationships between different parts of the input, making it particularly effective for NLP tasks.

Generative AI refers to a class of AI models capable of generating new content that did not exist before. The new content is based on existing fragmented content from the training data that is cohesively and coherently put together by the Generative AI model. New content generated is based on the user prompt.

In addition to generating convincing text, Generative AI has a wide range of applications in fields, such as art, music, and literature. Again, the model creates new works using existing examples. It can also be used in fields, such as product design, where it can generate new designs based on existing examples or user input. One of the key challenges with Generative AI is making sure that the generated output is useful and accurate. Generative AI models are known to hallucinate and come up with content that may be incorrect or impractical.

While Generative AI algorithms are rapidly evolving to produce high-quality outputs; users of Generative AI need to put in place guard rails (common sense or detailed checks) before consuming the output produced by the model. Let us briefly discuss the working of a popular Generative AI model—ChatGPT from OpenAI. ChatGPT is a large language model (LLM) trained by OpenAI-based on the GPT (generative pre-trained transformer) architecture. The model was trained on a large corpus of text from the internet and other sources, which allows it to generate human-like responses to a wide range of queries and prompts. When a user enters a text prompt or question, ChatGPT first tokenizes the text into smaller units called tokens. These tokens are then fed into the model, which uses its pre-trained knowledge to generate a response. The response is generated by predicting the most probable next token based on the input prompt, and repeating this process until a stopping criterion is met (e.g., reaching a maximum length or generating an end-of-sentence token).

Businesses can use this dialogue producing generative ChatGPT model in different ways:

Customer support ChatGPT is trained on customer support data and used to provide automated responses to customer queries. This reduces the burden on customer support teams and provides faster responses to customers.

Personalized recommendations ChatGPT uses search history, purchase history, and preferences to provide personalized recommendations to users.

Marketing and sales Generative models engage with potential customers and provide them with information about products and services. This can help generate leads and increase sales.

HR management ChatGPT can be used to automate the process of screening resumes and conducting initial interviews.

Virtual assistants When used as a virtual assistant, ChatGPT can perform tasks, such as scheduling appointments, setting reminders, and generating short reports. It does this by gleaning information from e-mails, chats, calendars, and contacts (Microsoft 365 Copilot).

Though the generative model is capable of accomplishing all of the functionality mentioned above, many companies are adopting a cautious approach to using ChatGPT. The major concern is data leaks from within the organization to ChatGPT. Many Generative AI models such as Llama from Meta or Gemma from Google can be hosted on local machines where the possibility of data leaks is very low.

The ability of Generative AI models to deduce information from data and present it in a meaningful manner is not limited to data on the internet. It can also be trained to look at data from documents, spreadsheets, e-mail, and meetings on an individual's workstation. Microsoft 365 Copilot is an example of such a tool. The functionality of Copilot includes[3]:

- Summarizing discussion points of a meeting
- Creating PowerPoint presentations
- Drafting e-mails
- Analyzing e-mail threads and documents
- Creating summaries and graphs of data on an Excel spreadsheet

Figure 9.6 shows the steps used to train a custom generative model using the Microsoft 365 Copilot. Let us briefly discuss this. Microsoft 365 Copilot continuously accesses content and context in the Microsoft Graph. This enables it to generate answers in the context of your work by accessing your documents, e-mails, calendar, chats, meetings, contacts, and other business data. It combines information, both old and new from e-mail exchanges, chat conversations, reports received by you or created by you. The steps are illustrated in Fig. 9.6(a)–(c). In the first step of pre-processing, the Copilot parses information from user account or files and stores it in a graph (graph is created). During the post-processing step, the collected data is connected with a large language model (LLM) that contains embeddings to provide coherent output, thus enriched. When a user prompt is presented to the Copilot, data is searched and collated from the graph, transformed into meaningful sentences using the LLM, and presented to the user.

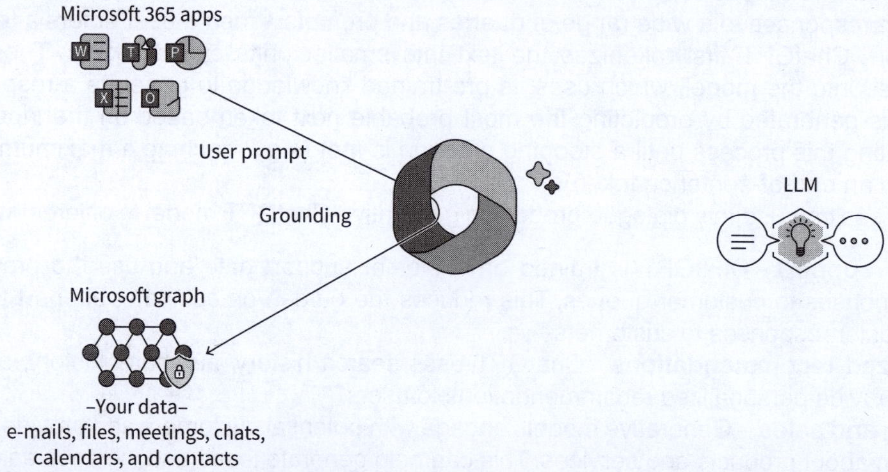

Fig. 9.6 (a) Example of Microsoft 365 Copilot pre-processing

[3]ChatGPT-style tech brought to Microsoft 365, BBC News, https://www.bbc.com/news/technology-64970062 (accessed 14 April 2023).

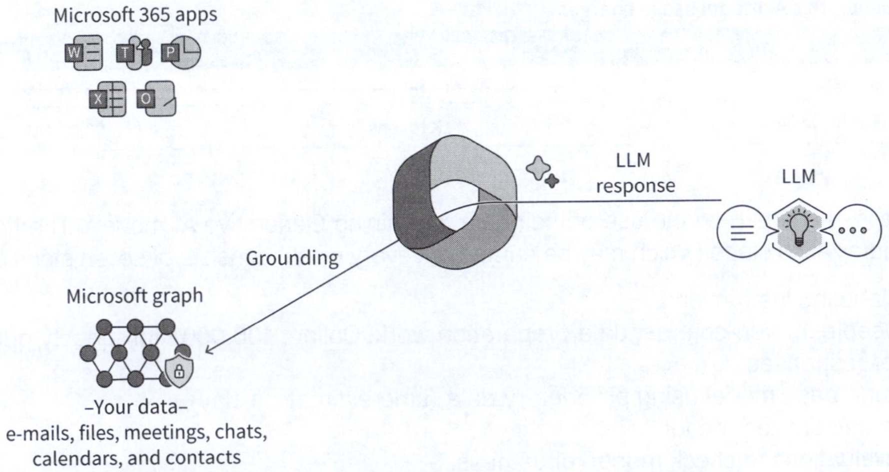

Fig. 9.6 (b) Microsoft 365 Copilot post-processing

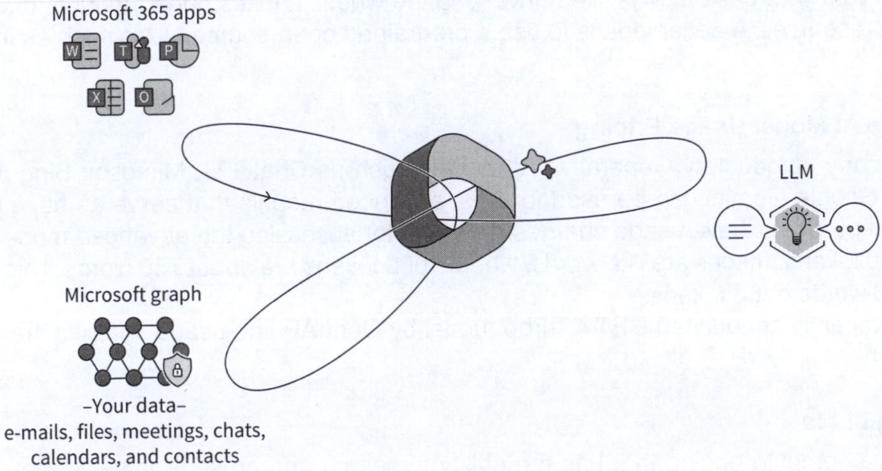

Fig. 9.6 (c) Microsoft 365 Copilot final step

Source: Explaining the Microsoft 365 Copilot System. https://www.youtube.com/watch?v=E5g20qmeKpg (accessed 23 Mar 2023)

Creating an LLM[4]

The process of obtaining a customized LLM is divided into two stages: pretraining and fine-tuning. The pretraining stage; which is usually performed once a year, consists of four steps as follows:

1. Assimilate text—approximately 10 TB of text (mostly from the Internet)
2. Provision a cluster of about 6000 GPUs
3. Prepare the text for a neural network and train (approximate cost and time: $2 million, 12 days)
4. Obtain base model

Intellectual Property (IP) concerns have emerged for the data used in training a large language model. Several prominent content creating organizations such as script writers association and newspapers

[4]Andrej Karpathy, Intro to Large Language Models, YouTube: https://www.youtube.com/watch?v=zjkBMFhNj_g.

Table 9.4 Generative AI model usage charges

Model	Input	Output
gpt-4-1106-preview	$0.01 / 1K tokens	$0.03 / 1K tokens
gpt-4-1106-vision-preview	$0.01 / 1K tokens	$0.03 / 1K tokens

have expressed concern on the use of their data for training Generative AI models. The finetuning or model customization stage (which may be carried out every week) consists of seven steps as follows:

1. Write labeling instructions.
2. Hire people, or sub-contract data preparation work. Collect 100,000 high-quality question and answer responses.
3. Fine-tune base model using proprietary data (time estimate: 1 day).
4. Obtain customized model.
5. Run evaluations to check model robustness.
6. Deploy model.
7. Monitor and collect incorrect answers and revisit the step to correct it.

Training your own base LLM is like reinventing the wheel. It takes huge amounts of energy and computing resources. A better idea is to use a pre-trained open-source LLMs such as the Llama-3 from Meta.

Generative AI Model Usage Pricing

Although many introductory Generative AI models such as ChatGPT, Microsoft Bing AI-powered Copilot or Google Gemini can be used for free; advanced models that serve as base models for commercial purposes have usage charges. The cost for accessing the advanced models is based on per 1000 tokens. Tokens are like words, where 1000 tokens are about 750 words. This paragraph is about 66 words or 88 tokens.

For the recently announced GPT-4 Turbo model by OpenAI[5], the usage charges are mentioned in Table 9.4.

Extending LLMs

An LLM is a compute engine that has the ability to search and present new information from its training data in a coherent manner. The model can be useful for different tasks. It could be made a doctor's assistant by further training it with medical data or a lawyer's assistant by fine-tuning it with information about laws and cases.

For several tasks, the LLM may not have access to up-to-date information. The first ChatGPT model had a training data cut-off date of September 2021. If you queried for facts after September 2021, it did not have an answer. Recent models are more up-to-date. To assist the LLM model to obtain information it does not have, agents are used. The idea behind agents is to allow a language model to choose a sequence of actions to take. If needed, agents can explore sources such as Google Search, Wikidata or a math tool for carrying out a calculation, as seen in Fig. 9.6(d). These agents can also connect to proprietary data of a company to create customized LLM dialogue models. Many companies such as Salesforce have created agents that use LLMs to interact with data stored in customer relation management software.

[5]OpenAI, new models and developer products announced at DevDay (6 Nov 2023) GPT-4 Turbo with 128K context and lower prices, the new Assistants API, GPT-4 Turbo with Vision, DALL·E 3 API, and more. https://openai.com/blog/new-models-and-developer-products-announced-at-devday.

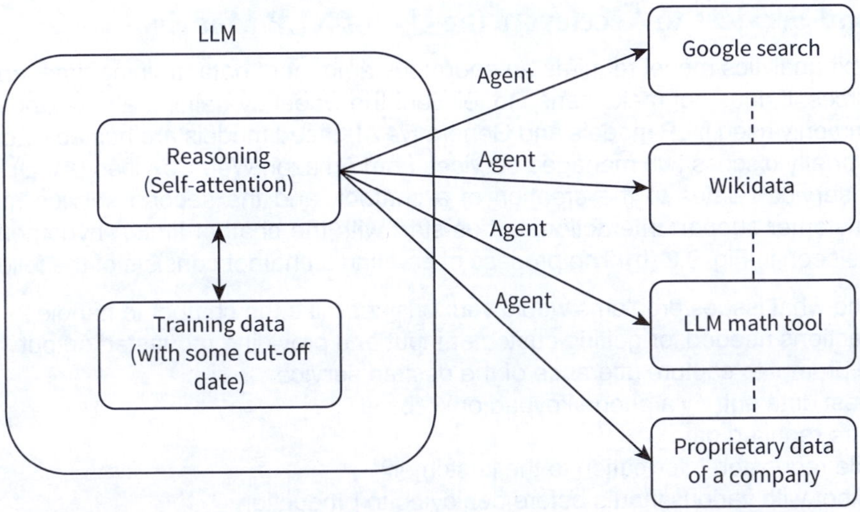

Fig. 9.6 (d) Use of agents to extend LLM model functionality

Retrieval-Augmented Generation (RAG)

RAG is a technique used to enhance the capabilities of Large Language Models (LLMs) by allowing them to access and incorporate information from external knowledge sources. Figure 9.6(e) shows its working. Information from a new data source is broken down into chunks and converted to vectors using an embedding space. These vectors are saved to a Vector Database (DB) for easy retrieval. The next diagram (fig. 9.6(f)) shows how a LLM uses retrieved data from the Vector DB to provide an augmented response to a query using LLM.

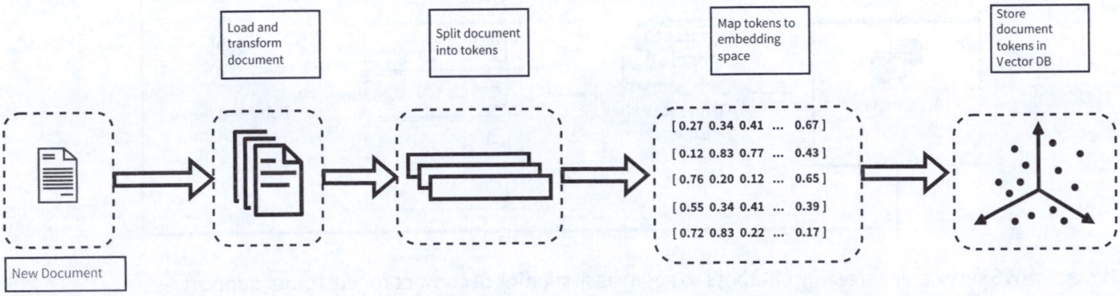

Fig. 9.6 (e) Using Retrieval Augmented Generation (RAG) to include a new document or data source to work with a LLM

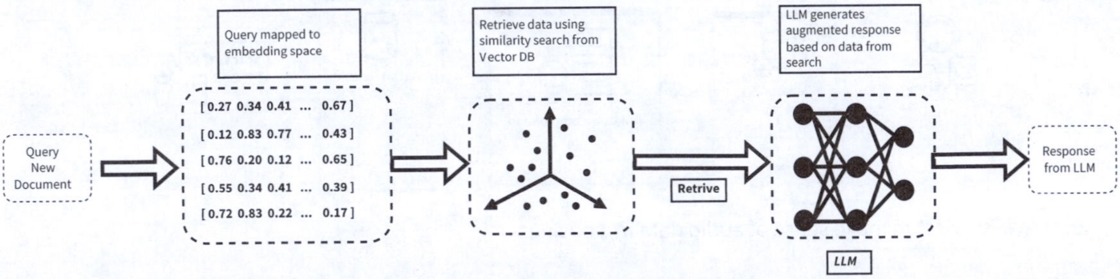

Fig. 9.6 (f) Interacting with new document added using RAG with help of LLM based query and augmented response

9.4 | Cloud Services to Accelerate the Use of NLP Models

Training a text analytics model requires an enormous amount of data, training time, and computational resources. It does not make sense to reinvent the wheel by training a new language model. Several commonly used NLP models and Generative AI-based models are hosted by cloud providers. We will briefly discuss two managed services from Amazon Web Services (AWS).[6]

The first service relates to the creation of a chatbot, and the second service monitors and manages customer support interaction. Let us start with the chatbot first. A hypothetical chatbot interaction is seen in Fig. 9.2 (b). The process of creating a chatbot consists of the following steps.

- Determine what issues/problems would your business like the chatbot to handle
- Identify actions needed for getting customer input and providing requested output
  - Voice prompt to capture utterance of the desired service
  - Request data entry via phone keypad or Website
  - Capture required data
  - Provide requested information to the customer
- Test chatbot with various inputs before deploying to production

These steps are depicted in Fig. 9.7.

Creating a cloud service to collect insights from customer support data—e-mail, chat, social media, and voice calls. This is shown in Fig. 9.8.

- Store text data and transcribed audio from customer support to a database
- Process stored text to look for key phrases to carry out further analysis
- Identify actions that led to positive results
- Create a feedback loop to reinforce these actions in future customer support staff training

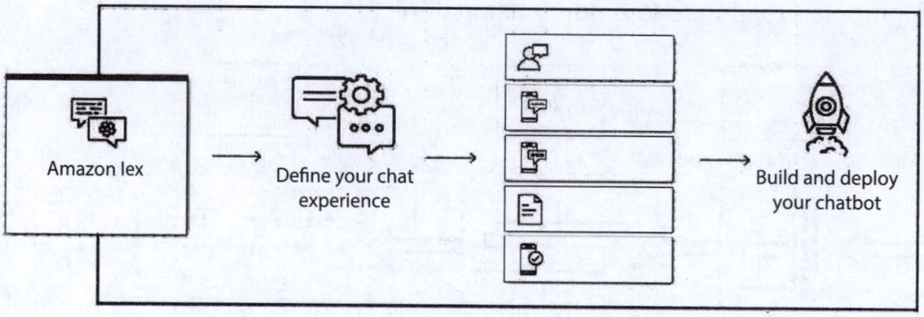

Fig. 9.7 AWS service[7] for creating chatbots to serve as first point of contact for customer support

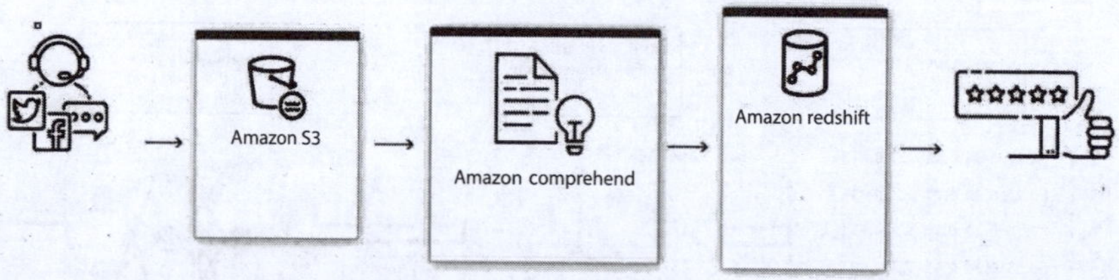

Fig. 9.8 AWS service[8] to make sense of audio data in a business

[6]We use AWS as an example; comparable services are available from other cloud providers.

With the explosion of the Internet and social media, there are numerous datasets to train NLP models. Let us enumerate some commonly used datasets for training sentiment analysis models.

IMDB reviews This dataset contains 50,000 movie reviews with sentiment labels, which can be used to train a binary classifier to predict positive or negative sentiment.
Yelp reviews Over 5 million reviews of businesses from Yelp, useful for training sentiment analysis models for different business domains.
Amazon reviews 130 million reviews of products sold on Amazon, used to train sentiment analysis models for e-commerce applications.
Twitter sentiment analysis 1.6 million tweets with sentiment labels; dataset for training sentiment analysis models for social media applications.

Just like sentiment analysis, there are datasets to train chatbots, translation models, and so forth.

9.5 | Conclusion

NLP based on text analytics is a valuable business tool. It enables a wide variety of applications, such as sentiment analysis, chatbots, text classification and content filtering. LLMs require huge datasets and considerable training time. The best way to make use of pre-trained language models is to use them with the help of cloud services. Recent introduction of Generative AI models has contributed to NLP's widespread usage.

Exercises

A. State True/False

1. Large Language models have human-like understanding of language.
2. Language models can perform sentiment analysis.
3. Training a language translation model requires a small amount of data.
4. Language model-based services is offered by cloud providers.
5. To analyze spoken language, it is first transcribed and then fed to NLP model.

B. Short-answer Questions

1. What are the challenges faced when training an LLM?
2. Name the idea that led to the creation of generative AI-based dialogue model.
3. Name applications of generative AI that could be of use to a student.
4. Enumerate concerns relating to the use of generative AI.
5. Explain the usage cost for a paid generative AI model.

C. Long-answer Questions

1. With the help of the paper "Deep learning-based text classification,[9]" identify datasets for training sentiment analysis models.

[7]AWS Lex, https://aws.amazon.com/lex/ (accessed 22 November 2022).
[8]AWS Comprehend, https://aws.amazon.com/comprehend/ (accessed 22 November 2022).
[9]Deep learning based text classification, Shervin M. et. al, 2021, https://arxiv.org/pdf/2004.03705.pdf (accessed 21 November 2022).

2. A CEO of a company wishes to determine the motivation level of employees in the company. Design a system based on text analytics and recorded Zoom meeting conversations to help the CEO find out sentiments of employees.
3. Document the possible applications with the following generative AI-based models:
   (a) Claude
   (https://www.anthropic.com/index/claude-2-1)
   (b) Llama-3
   (https://ai.meta.com/llama/)
   (https://www.llama.com/)
   (c) Stable diffusion
   (https://stability.ai/stable-diffusion/)
   (d) DALL-E3
   (https://openai.com/dall-e-3)
4. A company (having 100 employees) uses a commercial version of Generative AI Model (based on pricing mentioned in Table 9.2). Estimate the annual cost of using Generative AI if each employee submits 20 prompts (30 words) each day and the reply from the model is of 80 words. Assume 260 working days in a year.

D. Explore and Experiment

1. Explore the free version of Microsoft AI-powered Copilot[10] and have it generate Python code for different purposes.

   A sample prompt for creating a spreadsheet is shown as an example in Fig. 9.9.

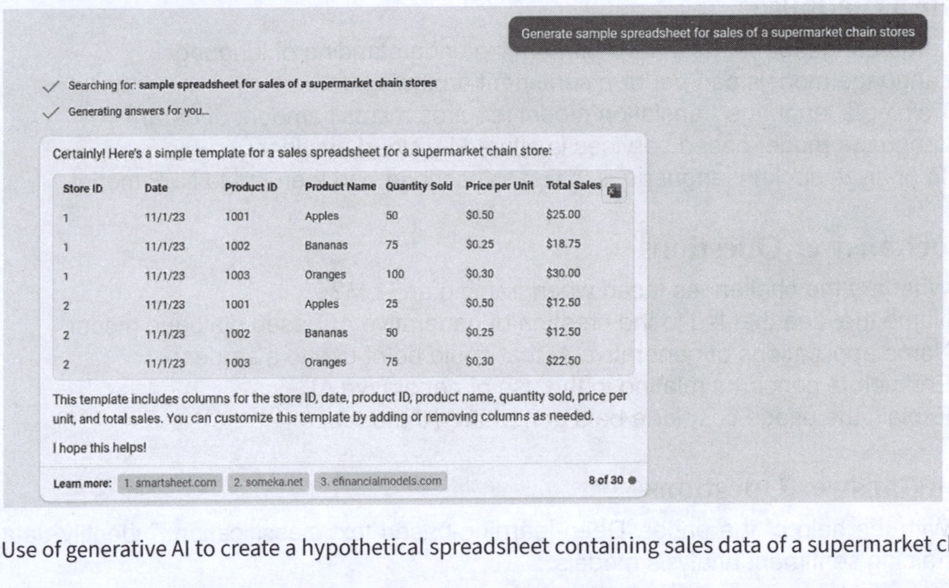

Fig. 9.9 Use of generative AI to create a hypothetical spreadsheet containing sales data of a supermarket chain

2. Visit https://gemini.google.com/extensions and allow Google to access information from documents, e-mails and other sources to provide customized personal feedback based on your prompt. Gemini is a Generative AI tool created by Google, based on an LLM. Sample screenshot to configure Google Gemini extensions is shown in Fig. 9.10.

[10]GitHub Copilot, https://github.com/features/copilot (accessed 10 June 2023).

By allowing Google Gemini to access Google Workspace (Gmail, Drive, and Docs), functionality similar to Microsoft 365 Copilot is obtained.

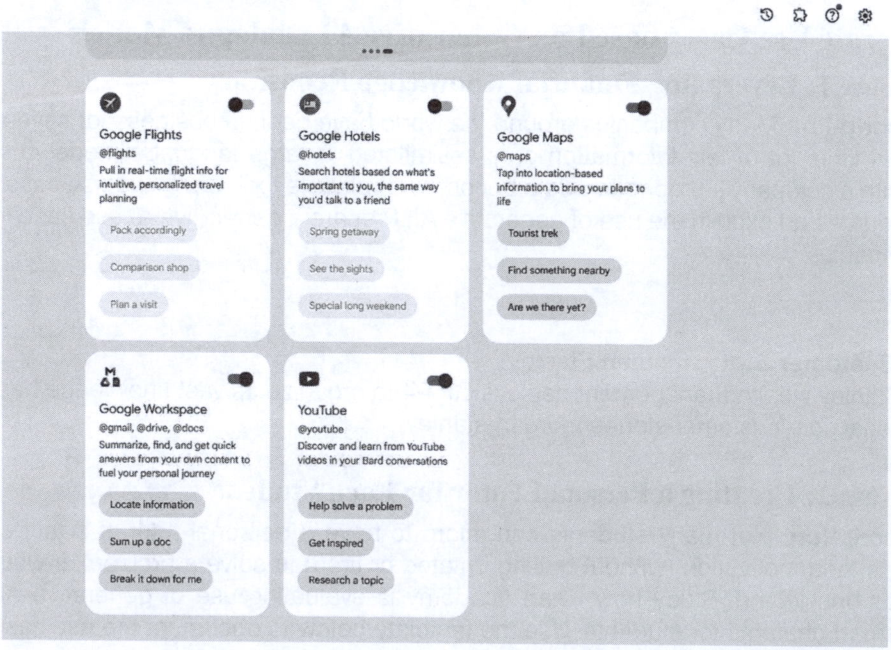

Fig. 9.10 Configuring Google Gemini extensions

3. In Fig. 9.11, we ask generative AI model to provide examples of real-world applications powered by text analytics.

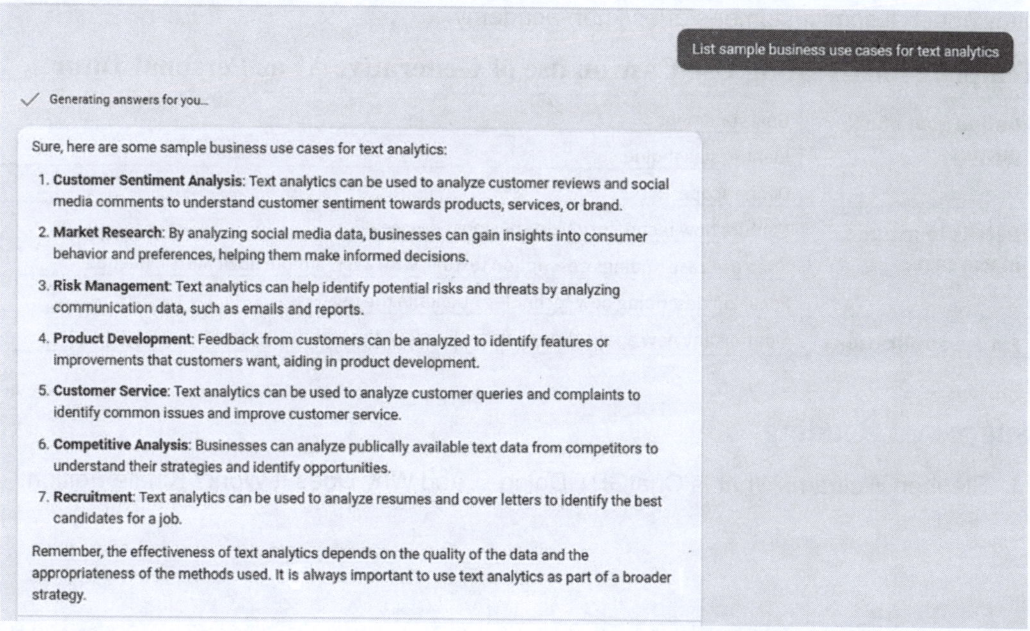

Fig. 9.11 Generative AI enumerating wide-ranging applications that use text analytics

4. Check out Google NotebookLM (https://notebooklm.google/) that allows you to upload documents in different formats, generate insights, and also create an audio overview of the material.

E. Generate Use Cases based on Generative AI Dialogue Models

1. Use Case 1: Leveraging Financial Knowledge Repository

Brief description: Many companies around the world have been in business for several decades. During this time, lot of text information gets assimilated. A large language model customized to interact with a company's proprietary data becomes a valuable tool. Study the use case mentioned in the resource and explain the use of generative AI. Prepare a generative AI use case template for other companies.

Resource

OpenAI Customer Story: Morgan Stanley
Morgan Stanley wealth management deploys GPT-4 to organize its vast knowledge base.
https://openai.com/customer-stories/morgan-stanley

2. Use Case 2: Creating a Personal Tutor for Each Student

Brief description: Not many students can afford to have a personal tutor. If a tool can provide hints, steps, and motivation (without getting irritated or tired) to solve a problem, it would become a student's best friend. Study how Khan Academy is evaluating use of generative AI model for creating smart chatbots for students. Use the template below to document the use case and think of other ways to use this idea.

Resource

OpenAI Customer Story: Khan Academy
Khan Academy explores the potential for GPT-4 in a limited pilot program.
https://openai.com/customer-stories/khan-academy

Template for Creating Use Case on use of Generative AI as Personal Tutor

Define goal and purpose	Goal statement
	Identify stakeholders
	Define scope
Details to include in use case	Capture how technology helps business process.
	Keep use case findings description textual, with a few simple flowcharts if needed.
	Focus on describing how technology benefits the use case.
Future applications	Mention any new application that can leverage the technology used.

Suggested Reading

1. Stephen Wolfram, What Is ChatGPT Doing ... and Why Does It Work? Kindle Edition.

CHAPTER

10

AI Learning Techniques

CHAPTER OUTLINE

LEARNING OBJECTIVES

After reading this chapter, you will be able to:

- understand the importance of HITL to accelerate training
- appreciate how reinforcement learning works

Effective Management Using Human-in-the-Loop and Reinforcement Learning

Conventional approach of using examples and labels to train a deep neural network (DNN) has certain limitations. In several cases, it is difficult to provide training data for corner cases. It is here that the human-in-the-loop (HITL) approach assists the model in identifying and strengthening its weak areas. Similarly, for systems that do not have a readily available training dataset, the model learns by trying out new actions and learning from those actions. This is the idea behind reinforcement learning, and many systems and reasoning models stand to benefit from it.

10.1 | Learning Using Human-in-the-Loop Approach

So far, the learning mechanism we have discussed involved presenting data examples and labels from different classes. Humans are tasked to carry out annotations of data for the model to train on. The job of the human does not end here. After a model gets trained, it is tested using various metrics before it is deployed or used in production. Most models do not perform exactly the way one would expect them to. They usually require some tweaking and adjustments (retraining). This is where the HITL is useful. The operator or user of the model finds out the model's weak spots and lets the model developer know about it. The developer may decide to gather additional data or add an extra feature to improve model performance. Annotation and active learning are two important features of HITL machine learning. Table 10.1 presents some applications that use HITL for model retraining.

Let us take the case seen in Fig. 10.1 to understand the workings of HITL. In this hypothetical setup, an autonomous tractor encounters a scarecrow in the field and stops. The computer vision system on the tractor has low confidence in classifying the scarecrow. Using a secure communications channel, the tractor computer contacts a team of humans for support. The human team classifies the scarecrow as an object the tractor can drive around. This way, the HITL support helps in the continued operation of the tractor and also updates the AI model for other autonomous tractors in the world.

Table 10.1 Examples of HITL-based training for model update

Application	Role of Human	Action
Robotic pick and place	Determine which object or objects gets erroneously picked up.	Retrain computer vision model for specified object.
Automated voice response	Establish that order number details not clearly specified.	Retrain on phrases requesting complete order details.
Chatbot	Find out if the chatbot misses commonly used terms for requests.	Expand and map vocabulary of requests to actions.
Humanoid Robot	Teach movements for performing a factory task that is usually performed by humans.	Learn the sequence, speed and accuracy of movements needed for a particular task.

Fig. 10.1 Autonomous tractor using HITL for uninterrupted operation

This example shows how training of an HITL-based AI system can be broken down into several steps listed as follows. For the most part, it follows the conventional supervised learning approach we have discussed so far.

1. **Data collection** The first step in building a HITL-based AI system is to collect and label data. This can be done either manually or using an automated system. The data should be comprehensive and representative of the problem domain.
2. **Model training** Once the data has been collected, it is used to train the machine learning model. The model is trained using a variety of techniques, including supervised learning, unsupervised learning, and reinforcement learning.
3. **Human review** After the model has been trained, a human reviews the results to ensure they are accurate and reliable. This step is critical to ensure the model is making correct predictions.
4. **Model adjustment** If the model is not making correct predictions during deployment, the human can make changes to the model in real-time to improve it. This can be done by retraining the model using additional data, changing the model's parameters, or modifying the model's architecture.
5. **Repeat** The entire process is repeated until the model is accurate and reliable.

The biggest differentiator is the human involvement during model deployment. Take a look at this company's[1] Website that provides HITL as a service.

The pseudocode in Listing 10.1 provides the sequence of steps to implement HITL learning. It assumes that the data is already labeled and that the model is trained using supervised learning. The key is to ensure that the human is involved in the decision-making process to improve the accuracy and reliability of the model. If an AI model is used to command a robotic arm to unload or load a truck, the job of the human operator is to closely monitor the robot and see if it is following the right sequence of steps. In Listing 10.1, line 9 mentions the role of human review. Based on human review, the model may require retraining (lines 12,13).

Listing 10.1 Pseudocode for HITL training

```
01.  # Data collection
02.  data = collect_data()

03.  # Model training
04.  model = train_model(data)

05.  # Human review
06.  results = []
07.  for image in test_set:
08.     prediction = model.predict(image)
09.     review_result = human_review(prediction, image)
10.     results.append(review_result)

11.  # Model adjustment
12.  if results.contains(errors):
13.    model = retrain_model(data)

14.  # Repeat
15.  if model_accuracy < target_accuracy:
16.     data = collect_more_data()
17.     model = train_model(data)
```

[1]Resolve AI edge cases in real-time, https://www.spark.ai/ (accessed 10 June 2023).

10.2 | Reinforcement Learning

So far we have discussed two forms of learning. Unsupervised learning (used for data clustering) and supervised learning (used for training decision tree-based models and DNNs). Reinforcement learning takes a slightly different approach to training. A neural network is used to develop policy in the reinforcement learning setup. The policy decides the action the agent should use in a given situation. In reinforcement learning, an agent (physical or simulated learning system), which is capable of interacting with the environment is used. It performs actions and gets either rewards or penalties (negative rewards) for it. Based on the feedback on its actions, it creates a strategy or policy to get the most rewards over time.

This is intuitive and relatable to human behavior and learning. Humans understand and know what kind of behavior leads to rewards or reprimands. The goal of reinforcement learning is to learn the optimal policy (behavior) in a given environment. Learning follows an iterative process of trial and error. The agent starts with an initial random action and analyses its outcome. Each action and outcome is stored as a state (Fig. 10.2). Then the agent takes a new step and stores its state. Over time, the agent figures out the actions that lead to long-term rewards. A complete cycle from the initial to the final state is an episode. To further understand reinforcement learning, think back to the time when you were learning to ride a bicycle. Each time, you fell down or could ride for a few meters, your brain was capturing the data about your actions, environment and feeding it to your brain to understand how to balance. After a few trail and error (episodes), the brain figured out (by training its neurons) how to balance and as a result, you learned how to ride a bicycle.

Table 10.2 depicts some applications and their use of reinforcement-based training. Figure 10.3 shows the setup of the video game for identifying the role of agent, environment, policy, and action.

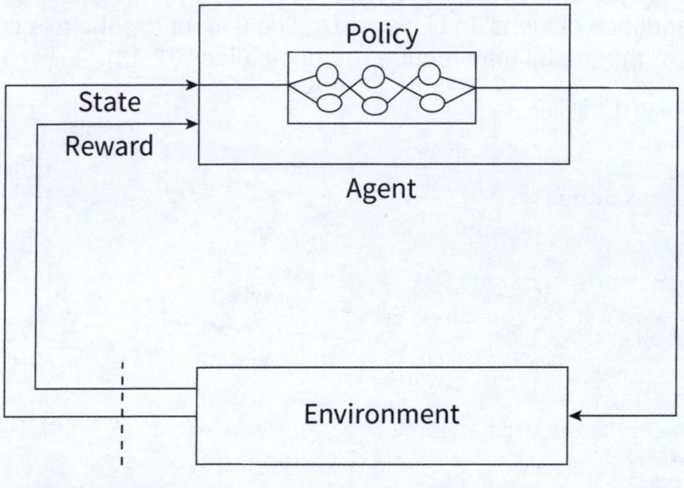

Fig. 10.2 Reinforcement learning setup

Table 10.2 Role of agents in reinforcement learning scenario

Application	Role of Agent
Control of robot	Agent observes the environment using sensors. Takes action by actuating its motors. Gets rewarded for following a path and penalized for straying from the path
Video game	Agent takes action by using a joystick. It uses computer vision to see the environment. Game points relate to rewards
Placing ads on a Web page	Agent places ads on the webpage. Gets rewarded if the user clicks on the ads
AI Reasoning models	Reasoning models use reinforcement learning agents to improve problem-solving strategies. Agents are rewarded for generating correct and logical solutions.

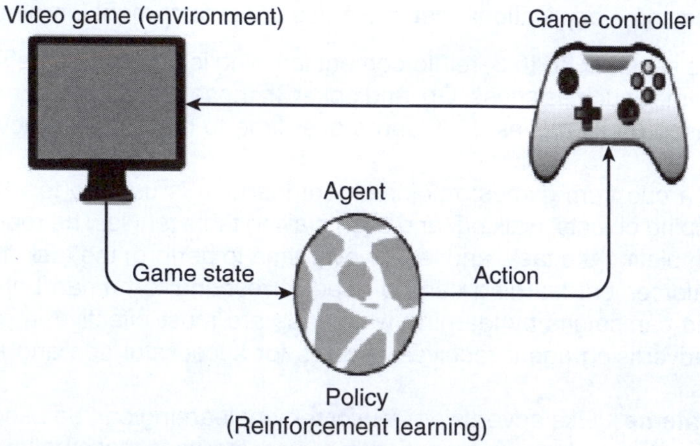

Fig. 10.3 Setup to apply reinforcement learning to a video game

Table 10.3 Comparison of learning methodologies

	Supervised Learning	Unsupervised Learning	Reinforcement Learning
Training data	Labeled data	Unlabeled data	Real-world or simulated data gathered by agent, while interacting with the environment
Use of training data	Create a mapping of example data to labels	Identify clusters of data with similar characteristics	Determine optimum actions to maximize rewards over the entire cycle of operation
Model adaptability	Retraining required to improve model accuracy	Retraining needed if data changes	Model adapts to changes by generalizing its learning

The video game is a good example to demonstrate reinforcement learning. For any video game, the goal usually is to maximize points. Every time you do something stupid, you lose points and vice versa. Over time, you learn the rules of the game and end up winning or becoming a higher scorer.

To summarize, we compare reinforcement learning with supervised and unsupervised learning approaches. Table 10.3 captures training data requirements, motivation, and adaptability of models trained using different learning approaches. Reinforcement learning has several business applications. These applications range from advanced electronics and semiconductors to transport and logistics. A McKinsey report[2] provides a table of applications that stand to benefit from reinforcement learning and categorizes potential advantages as,

- Optimization of product development cycle
- Optimization of complex operations
- Information on the next best action

[2]Jacomo C. et al, It's time for businesses to chart a course for reinforcement learning, QuantamBlack, AI by McKinsey, 2021, https://www.mckinsey.com/capabilities/quantumblack/our-insights/its-time-for-businesses-to-chart-a-course-for-reinforcement-learning (accessed 23 November 2022).

Let us enumerate some applications that make use of reinforcement learning:

Game playing As seen in Fig. 10.3, reinforcement learning is used to create AI systems that can learn how to play games such as chess, Go, and poker. In these games, the agent receives rewards or punishments based on its moves, and learns over time to make better moves to maximize its reward.

Robotics Taking a cue from games, reinforcement learning is used to teach robots to perform tasks, such as grasping objects, walking, and even playing table tennis. The robot receives rewards for successfully completing the task, and learns over time to perform the task more effectively.

Advertising Reinforcement learning can be used to respond to human behavior. It is used to optimize advertising campaigns by learning which ads are most effective in generating clicks or conversions. The advertising agent receives rewards for successful ads and learns over time to generate better ads.

Recommender systems Like advertising, reinforcement learning can be used to build personalized recommender systems. The recommendation system learns to make better recommendations, by factoring in past successes and failures.

Traffic control Reinforcement learning can be used to optimize traffic flow in cities by learning how to control traffic lights. Traffic controller receives rewards for reducing congestion and learns over time to create more efficient traffic flow.

Use of Reinforcement Learning for Dialogue AI Models

The most talked about dialogue model ChatGPT also uses reinforcement learning under the hood. It is trained using *reinforcement learning from human feedback* (RLHF). The model is initially trained using supervised learning. Human AI trainers provide conversations in which they play both roles—the user and an AI assistant.

To create a reward model for reinforcement learning, trainers collect comparison data, which consists of two or more model responses ranked by quality. To collect this data, conversations that AI trainers have with the chatbot is collated. Randomly, a model-written message is selected, along with several alternative completions. Three AI trainers rank the completions. Using the reward models and several iterations, the final model is fine-tuned using Proximal Policy Optimization (PPO). PPO is a popular reinforcement learning algorithm that helps AI agents learn to make better decisions over time.

Let us now walk though the process explained in Fig. 10.4, from the OpenAI blog. The training process starts with a simple prompt—*Explain reinforcement learning to a 6-year-old child.* It starts with the conventional supervised learning approach (column on the left). A labeler nudges the model towards the best output using reinforcement learning (treats or punishment). This data is then used to fine-tune the model by way of supervised learning.

In the centre column of Fig. 10.4, the model is given the same prompt—*Explain reinforcement learning to a 6-year-old child*. The model generates four possible outputs, which are ranked by the labeler from best to worst. This ranking data is subsequently used to train the rewards model.

The last column on the right of Fig. 10.4 uses the PPO[3] reinforcement learning model that is simpler to implement and tune. There is a feedback loop from the reward policy to the PPO network. Every time the PPO generates an output, the rewards model evaluates it and uses it to update the PPO network. This virtuous cycle nudges the model to produce the content the user is looking for.

[3]PPO, https://openai.com/research/openai-baselines-ppo (accessed 10 June 2023).

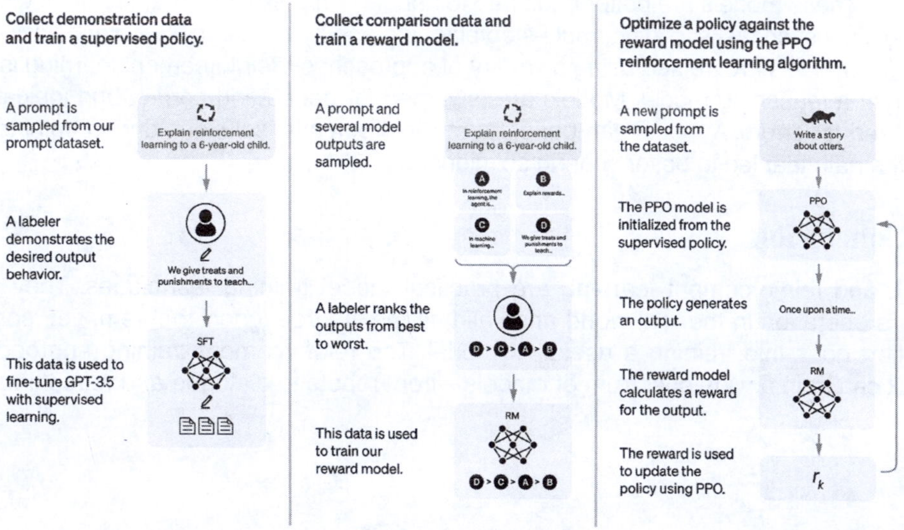

Fig. 10.4 Training steps used to train a dialogue model[4]

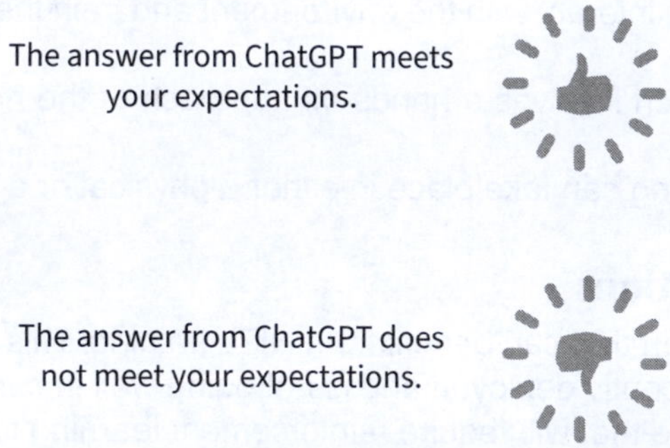

Fig. 10.5 User feedback for reinforcement learning

The reinforcement training process continues during deployment. User feedback is solicited every time the model produces an output. The feedback is usually in the form of a simple emoji—a thumbs-up or thumbs-down gesture (Fig. 10.5). The model also accepts written feedback from the user, in addition to the emoji feedback.

Reasoning Models

Reasoning AI models represent a significant advancement in the direction of complex problem solving. These models share their internal chain of thought that led them to the solution. Models that provide reasoning-based response include DeepSeek-R1, Google Gemini 2.5, GPT-4 variants and

---

[4]ChatGPT blog, https://openai.com/blog/chatgpt (accessed 24 May 2023).

many others. These models are better equipped to handle complex tasks that require logical reasoning. Examples of such tasks: coding, multi-step planning and mathematical problem solving.

Reasoning models are trained using a variety of approaches. Reinforcement learning is one technique to train a reasoning model. Models are rewarded for generating correct and logical solutions and penalized for errors. A model can generate multiple potential solutions during training and then reinforce the path that led to better scoring solutions.

10.3 | Conclusion

Both HITL and reinforcement learning are practical model training techniques. They pertain to the model's operation in the real world and validate the 'no free lunch' theorem; i.e., considerable human effort goes into training a useful AI model. The reinforcement training approach is quite versatile; it can train a wide spectrum of models—from robots to dialogue and reasoning models.

Exercises

A. State True/False

1. An AI model's accuracy is based on the accuracy of examples presented for training.
2. In reinforcement learning, examples and labels are presented to the model for training in an offline mode.
3. An AI agent's job is to interact with the environment and train the model using either rewards or penalty.
4. HITL training approach involves a hands-off approach of the human operator working with AI-enabled machine.
5. Reinforcement learning can take place in either a physical or a simulated environment.

B. Long-answer Questions

1. Think of an application that can benefit from HITL training. This application should involve a new model that is recently deployed and is not doing well in certain scenarios.
2. Document a use case that will require reinforcement learning to train the model. The learning can take place using a physical or simulated environment.

C. Explore and Experiment

1. Execute tutorial examples from Gymnasium[5]—provides an API for single-agent reinforcement learning environments.
2. We use generative AI in Fig. 10.6 for sample code to train a reinforcement learning model. The objective is to balance a pole on a moving platform. In the training process, the model records actions that are successful in balancing the pole and stores them as rewards. Refer to Fig. 10.2 to understand the terminology of the code mentioned in Fig. 10.6.

[5]Gymnasium documentation, https://gymnasium.farama.org/content/basic_usage/# (accessed 10 June 2023).

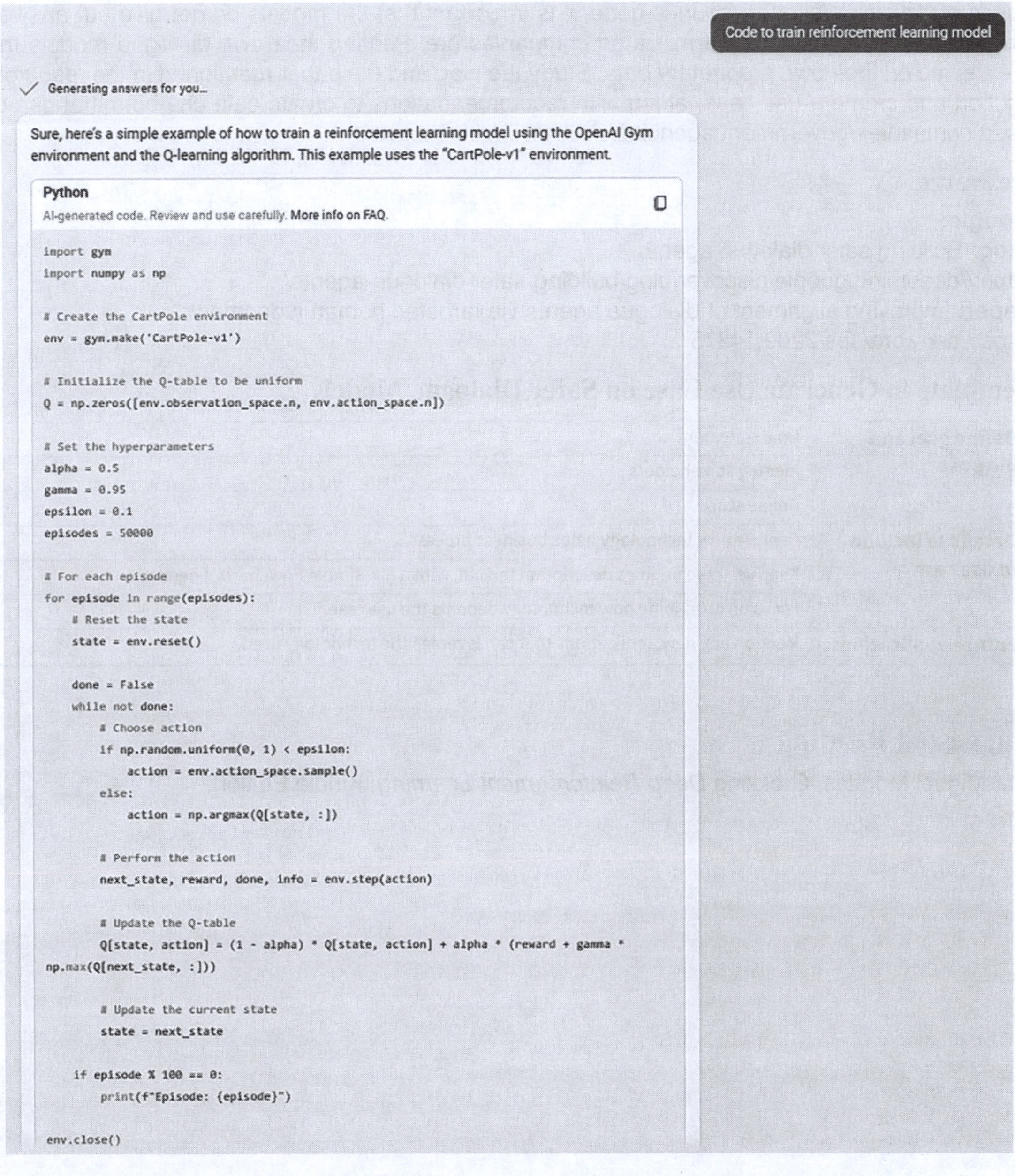

Code to train reinforcement learning model

Generating answers for you...

Sure, here's a simple example of how to train a reinforcement learning model using the OpenAI Gym environment and the Q-learning algorithm. This example uses the "CartPole-v1" environment.

Python

AI-generated code. Review and use carefully. More info on FAQ.

```
import gym
import numpy as np

# Create the CartPole environment
env = gym.make('CartPole-v1')

# Initialize the Q-table to be uniform
Q = np.zeros([env.observation_space.n, env.action_space.n])

# Set the hyperparameters
alpha = 0.5
gamma = 0.95
epsilon = 0.1
episodes = 50000

# For each episode
for episode in range(episodes):
    # Reset the state
    state = env.reset()

    done = False
    while not done:
        # Choose action
        if np.random.uniform(0, 1) < epsilon:
            action = env.action_space.sample()
        else:
            action = np.argmax(Q[state, :])

        # Perform the action
        next_state, reward, done, info = env.step(action)

        # Update the Q-table
        Q[state, action] = (1 - alpha) * Q[state, action] + alpha * (reward + gamma *
np.max(Q[next_state, :]))

        # Update the current state
        state = next_state

    if episode % 100 == 0:
        print(f"Episode: {episode}")

env.close()
```

Fig. 10.6 Generated AI code to understand training steps used for reinforcement learning

D. Generate Use Case on Reinforcement Learning for Building Safer Dialogue Chatbots

Use Case: Building Safer Dialogue Models

Brief description: Dialogue models (such as ChatGPT) have captured the world's attention. These models have learnt to generalize data available on the internet and provide plausible answers to user's questions. While this sounds good, it is important that the models do not give out answers that can cause any kind of harm. Large companies are creating their own dialogue models that are trained on their own proprietary data. Study the blog and the paper mentioned in the resources section and create a use case, along with recommendations to create safe chatbots that can be used companies/government agencies.

Resource

Google:
Blog: Building safer dialogue agents
https://deepmind.google/discover/blog/building-safer-dialogue-agents/
Paper: Improving alignment of dialogue agents via targeted human judgements
https://arxiv.org/abs/2209.14375

Template to Generate Use Case on Safer Dialogue Models

Define goal and purpose	Goal statement
	Identify stakeholders
	Define scope
Details to include in use case	Capture how technology helps business process.
	Keep use case findings description textual, with a few simple flowcharts if needed.
	Focus on describing how technology benefits the use case.
Future applications	Mention any new applications that can leverage the technology used.

Suggested Reading

1. Miguel Morales, Grokking *Deep Reinforcement Learning*, Kindle Edition.

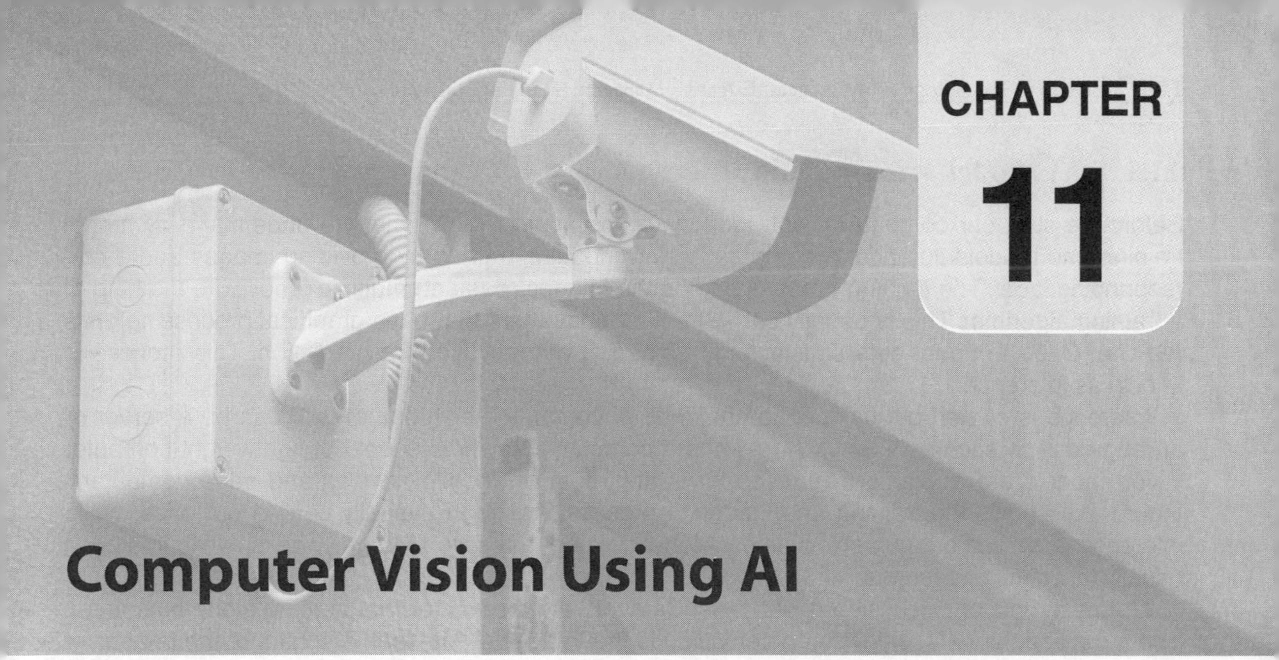

CHAPTER
11

Computer Vision Using AI

CHAPTER OUTLINE

LEARNING OBJECTIVES

After reading this chapter, you will be able to:

- distinguish between computer vision model training and inference
- get to know the role of transfer learning in computer vision
- understand image classification, object detection, and segmentation
- explain the use of video analytics

Effective Management Using Computer Vision

Computer vision makes a picture worth a lot more than thousand words. It has the ability to classify objects in an image, draw bounding boxes around objects, or highlight pixels of a certain object with a specific color for easy visualization. All these operations can be performed on a still image or with image frames changing very quickly (video). With the right application, many business processes stand to benefit from computer vision.

11.1 | AI Model Training and Inference

Before we start our computer vision journey, let us again review what we understand by model training and model inference. A computer vision model is trained by providing images and a corresponding label. The training process parses the images (dataset) multiple times with the help of a training algorithm. This is usually carried out on computers that have graphical processing units (GPUs). Once a model gets satisfactorily trained, it can be used for prediction. This process is known as inference.

Inference is carried out using different kinds of computing environments. It can be a server or an edge device such as a Linux single-board computer.[1] A whole subset of lightweight computer vision models are available to run (perform inference) on mobile devices and edge computers. Figure 11.1 shows the training and inference process. Training is usually carried out once, while inference is carried out numerous times. Model training may take hours or weeks, while inference usually takes ms or seconds.

Our next topic of discussion is datasets. Datasets are the fodder that training algorithms need. The most popular dataset for computer vision is the ImageNet[2] dataset. A subset of the ImageNet is the ImageNet Large Scale Visual Recognition Challenge (ILSVRC)[3] 2012–2017 image classification and localization dataset. This dataset has 1000 object classes and contains 1,281,167 training images, 50,000 validation images and 100,000 test images. Most image classification models are trained on the ImageNet dataset.

To better understand this, let us consider an example. If we choose an image of an object belonging to one of the 1000 categories of the dataset and present it to the trained model, it will correctly determine its label as its predicted output. You can check out all the 1000 categories of ImageNet.[4] We present the first 5 and last 5 class IDs of the dataset in Table 11.1.

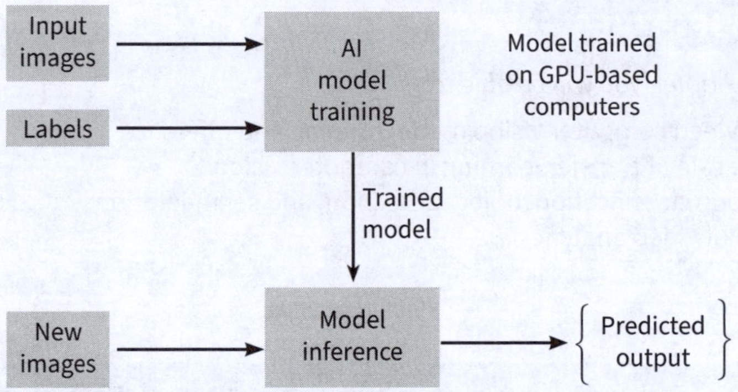

Fig. 11.1 Distinction between model training and model inference

[1] Raspberry Pi Compute Module, https://www.raspberrypi.com/products/compute-module-4/?variant=raspberry-pi-cm4001000 (accessed 8 December 2022).

[2] ImageNet, https://www.image-net.org/about.php (accessed 8 December 2022).

[3] ImageNet Large Scale Visual Recognition Challenge (ILSVRC), https://www.image-net.org/challenges/LSVRC/index.php (accessed 8 December 2022).

[4] ImageNet 1000 class list, https://deeplearning.cms.waikato.ac.nz/user-guide/class-maps/IMAGENET/ (accessed 8 December 2022).

Table 11.1 Snippet from 1000 ImageNet categories

Class ID	Class Name
0	tench, *Tinca tinca*
1	goldfish, *Carassius auratus*
2	great white shark, white shark, man-eater, man-eating shark, *Carcharodon caharias*
3	tiger shark, *Galeocerdo cuvieri*
4	hammerhead, hammerhead shark
995	earthstar
996	hen-of-the-woods, hen of the woods, *Polyporus frondosus*, *Grifola frondosa*
997	bolete
998	ear, spike, capitulum
999	toilet tissue, toilet paper, bathroom tissue

The other popular computer vision dataset is the Common Objects in Context (COCO)[5] dataset. It is a large-scale labeled image datasets available for public use and is used to train applications, such as object detection, segmentation, and captioning.

Contemporary computer vision AI models are used in industry for a wide range of applications, such as quality control, inspection, robotics, automation, security and surveillance, and autonomous systems. Let us briefly enumerate some applications of computer vision.

Quality control Inspect products on the production line to ensure they meet certain quality standards. As an example, in the automotive industry, computer vision systems can inspect car parts for defects such as cracks or dents.

Robotics Assist robots to navigate their environment and identify objects. Robots in warehouses use computer vision to identify items on shelves and move them around.

Security and surveillance Monitor video feeds from security cameras and identify potential threats. Detect unattended bags in an airport or identify individuals on a watchlist.

Autonomous systems Computer vision is a key technology for autonomous vehicles and drones. It allows autonomous systems to "see" and understand their environment and make decisions based on that information.

Transfer learning for computer vision

Image classification and object detection models make use of the feature detection capability of AI models. Features detected by the initial and middle layers of the model are simple features that are universally used by all objects. Instead of training a new model from scratch and investing lots of time relearning simple features, contemporary model training approach takes a pre-trained model and reuses the initial and middle layers. Only the last feature layers and the classifier of a custom model need to be retrained. In fact, one can even get by without retraining any feature layers if the datasets are similar. This process of reusing feature detection layers in an image model is known as transfer learning. It is widely used in industry to create new computer vision models using custom datasets. Transfer learning based training takes a fraction of the time as compared to training a model from scratch. It is used for creating custom models for image classification, object detection, image segmentation, and pose detection.

[5]COCO dataset, https://cocodataset.org/#home (accessed 8 December 2022).

11.2 | Object Classification

Image classification is an intuitive idea. If a pre-trained model on the ImageNet dataset is presented with images from the 1000 categories it has been trained on; it responds with a prediction in the form of a label or class ID. This is illustrated in Fig. 11.2 showing use of Image-classification model. If an image of a Doberman is presented to the model, its prediction will be Class ID 236; corresponding to description of a Doberman.

Some examples of pre-trained image-classification models are seen in Table 11.2. One can choose any one of these publicly available models based on model size (MB) or its Top-1 and Top-5 accuracy. You might be curious about Top-1 and Top-5 accuracy. In Top-1, the model's accuracy is determined by considering only one prediction while in Top-5, the model's accuracy is determined by considering 5 predictions. As you can guess, chances of getting the right answer are much higher when you get to make 5 predictions. That is the reason Top-5 accuracy numbers are higher than Top-1 accuracy.

If a user wishes to incorporate a pre-trained image-classification model in their code, they can go and select a model from a model zoo. One example of a repository hosting pre-trained model is TensorFlow Hub (TF Hub).[6] It contains all kinds of models in different categories. Two examples of pre-trained image-classification[7] models are seen in Fig. 11.3. The MobileNet V2 base model is trained on different datasets. Both models are TensorFlow Lite (TFLite) models that can run on mobile devices. The first model is trained to identify different plants using a dataset from iNaturalist, while the second model is trained on the ImageNet dataset.

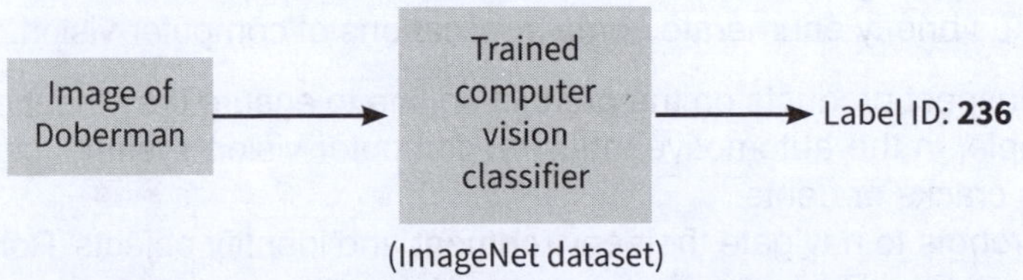

Fig. 11.2 Image-classification model

Table 11.2 Partial list of image-classification models—trained on ImageNet dataset

Model	Size (MB)	Top-1 accuracy (%)	Top-5 accuracy (%)	Parameters (M)
Xception	88	79.0	94.5	22.9
VGG16	528	71.3	90.1	138.4
VGG19	549	71.3	90.0	143.7
ResNet50	98	74.9	92.1	25.6
ResNet50V2	98	76.0	93.0	25.6
ResNet101	171	76.4	92.8	44.7
ResNet101V2	171	77.2	93.8	44.7
ResNet152	232	76.6	93.1	60.4
ResNet152V2	232	78.0	94.2	60.4
InceptionV3	92	77.9	93.7	23.9
InceptionResNetV2	215	80.3	95.3	55.9
MobileNet	16	70.4	89.5	4.3
MobileNetV2	14	71.3	90.1	3.5

[6]TensorFlow Hub, https://tfhub.dev/ (accessed 8 December 2022).

[7]Image classification, TF Hub, https://tfhub.dev/s?deployment-format=lite&module-type=image-classification (accessed 8 December 2022).

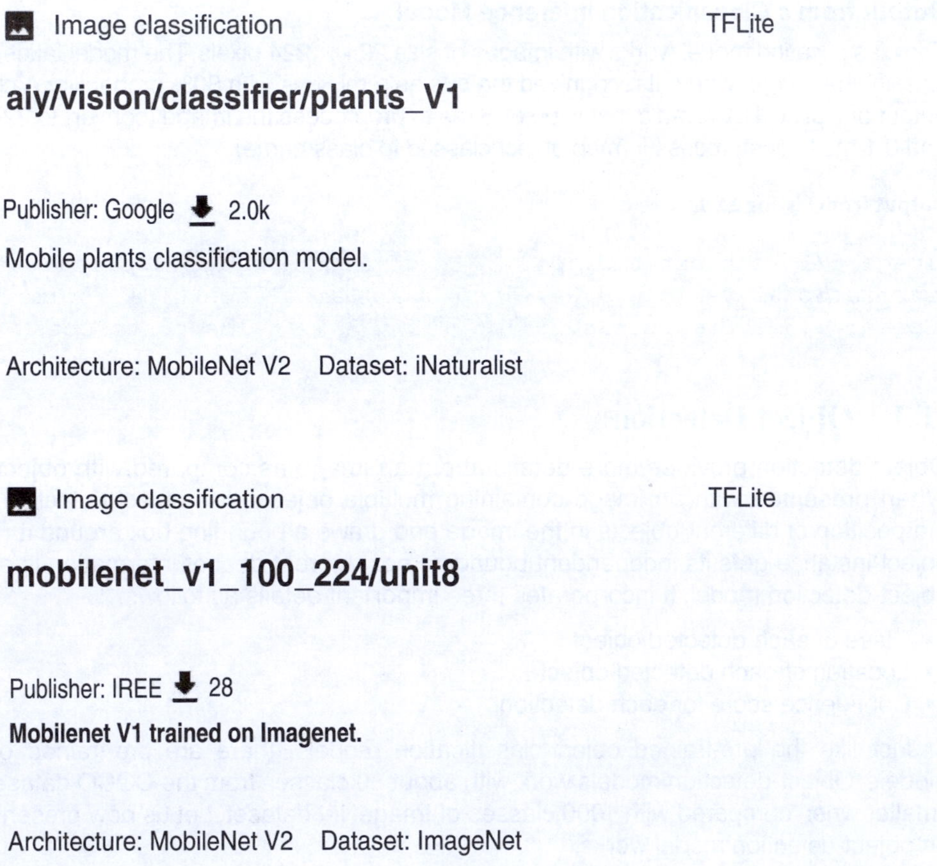

Fig. 11.3 Two representative image-classification models from TF Hub

A new object-classifier model is trained by collating hundreds of images of each class. Each class of images is stored in a separate folder. During training, the model considers the name of the folder as the class of the image. Once you have a trained image classification model, you can use it to make predictions. The code in Listing 11.1 loads a classification model trained on the ImageNet dataset and makes predictions on an image of a bus. The image of the bus can be substituted by an image of your choice.

Listing 11.1 Image classification using pre-trained YOLOv8 model[8]

```
from ultralytics import YOLO

# Load a model
model = YOLO('yolov8s-cls.pt') # load an official model

# Predict with the model
results = model('https://ultralytics.com/images/bus.jpg')
# predict on an image
```

[8]Image classification using YOLOv8, https://docs.ultralytics.com/tasks/classify/#predict (accessed 10 June 2023).

Output from a Classification Inference Model

The classification model works with images of size 224 × 224 pixels. The model takes about 5.1 ms to classify the image, where it recognized the bus as a minibus with 80% probability. A closer look at the output of Listing 11.1 reveals that it took 1.5 ms to preprocess the image (convert to 224 × 224 pixels), and 0.1 ms to postprocess it (map object class id to class name).

Output from Listing 11.1

```
image 1/1 /content/bus.jpg: 224×224 minibus 0.80, police_van 0.11,
recreational_vehicle 0.04, jeep 0.02, ambulance 0.01, 5.1ms
Speed: 1.5ms preprocess, 5.1ms inference, 0.1ms postprocess
```

11.3 | Object Detection

Object detection provides more details about an image as compared with object classification. When presented with an image containing multiple objects, the object-detection model locates the position of different objects in the image and draws a bounding box around it (Fig. 11.4). Each object instance gets its independent bounding box. A great deal of information is extracted by the object-detection model. It incorporates three important details as follows:

- Class of each detected object
- Location of each detected object
- Confidence score for each detection

Just like the pre-trained object-classification models, there are pre-trained object-detection models. Object-detection models work with about 80 classes from the COCO dataset. This is much smaller when compared with 1000 classes of ImageNet dataset. Let us now present details of how an object-detection model works.

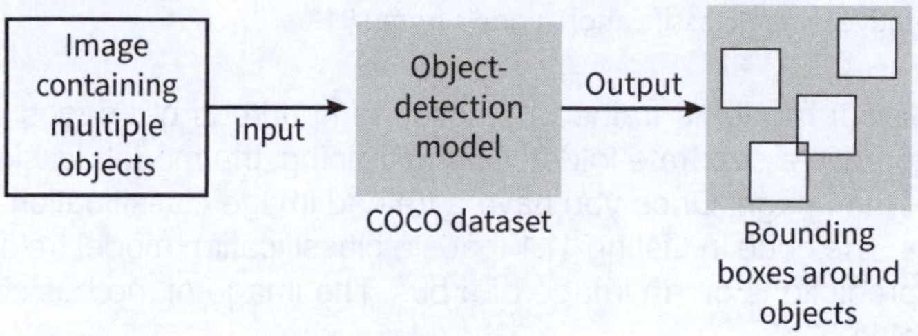

Fig. 11.4 An object-detection model

The model expects the image to be of a particular size. A typical size is 300 × 300 pixels. The size of a colored image is around 270,000 bytes. This is because each pixel consists of three channels (red, blue, and green) of 1 byte each.

When an image is provided to the model, it outputs a list of the objects it detects, the location of a bounding box that contains each object, and a score that indicates the confidence that detection was correct.

The model outputs four arrays, mapped to the indices 0–3. As enumerated in Table 11.3, arrays 0, 1, and 2 describe N detected objects, with one element in each array corresponding to each object.[9]

[9]TensorFlow Object Detection Overview, https://www.tensorflow.org/lite/examples/object_detection/overview (accessed 8 December 2022).

Table 11.3 Output details of object-detection model

Index	Name	Description
0	Locations	Multidimensional array of [N][4] floating point values between 0 and 1, the inner arrays representing bounding boxes in the form [top, left, bottom, right]
1	Classes	Array of N integers (output as floating point values) each indicating the index of a class label from the labels file
2	Scores	Array of N floating point values between 0 and 1 representing probability that a class was detected
3	Number of detections	Integer value of N

For example, when a model trained to detect apples, bananas, and strawberries is presented an image of a fruit basket, it will output a set number of detection results as seen in Table 11.4. The bounding box coordinates of the first banana in table is plotted in Fig. 11.5.

Table 11.4 Sample output of object-detection model containing class id, confidence score, and location [top, left, bottom, right]

Class	Score	Location
Apple	0.93	[18, 21, 57, 63]
Banana	0.82	[100, 30, 180, 150]
Strawberry	0.86	[7, 82, 89, 163]
Banana	0.22	[42, 66, 57, 83]
Apple	0.09	[6, 42, 31, 58]

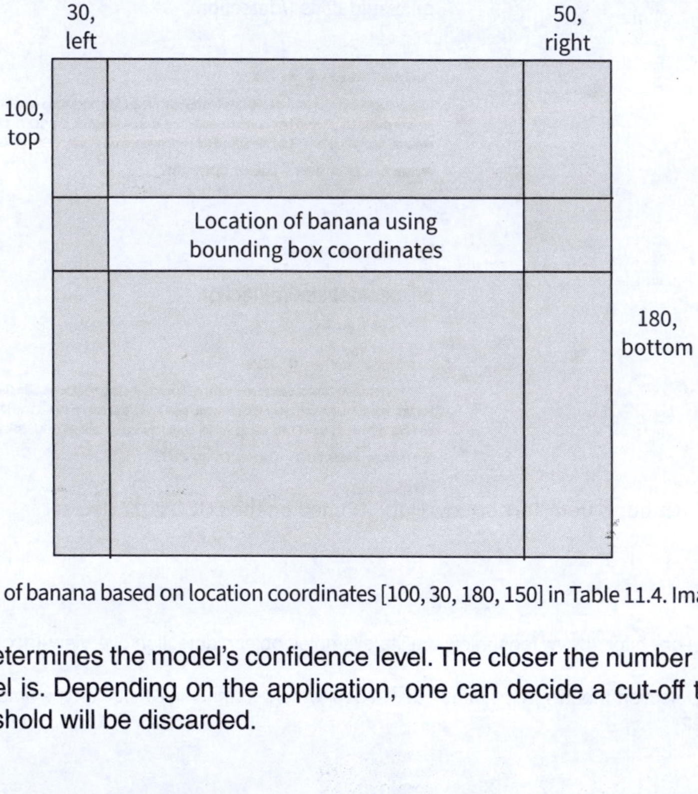

Fig. 11.5 Location of banana based on location coordinates [100, 30, 180, 150] in Table 11.4. Image size is 300 × 300 pixels

The score determines the model's confidence level. The closer the number is to 1, the more confident the model is. Depending on the application, one can decide a cut-off threshold. Detections below this threshold will be discarded.

Just like pre-trained image-classification models, there are pre-trained object-detection models. Figure 11.6 shows a partial list of lightweight object-detection models that can run on a mobile or edge device. A complete list of pre-trained object-detection models can be obtained from TensorFlow Hub.[10]

If you have an object-detection application and your object of interest happens to be part of the COCO 2017 (Table 11.5) dataset, you can go ahead and use a pre-trained object-detection model. The COCO dataset consists of 80 objects ranging from a person to a toothbrush.

If your application has a custom object (not part of the COCO 2017 dataset), you will have to create a customized dataset and then train an object-detection model. A customized dataset is created by drawing bounding boxes around the objects that you wish to detect. There are many popular

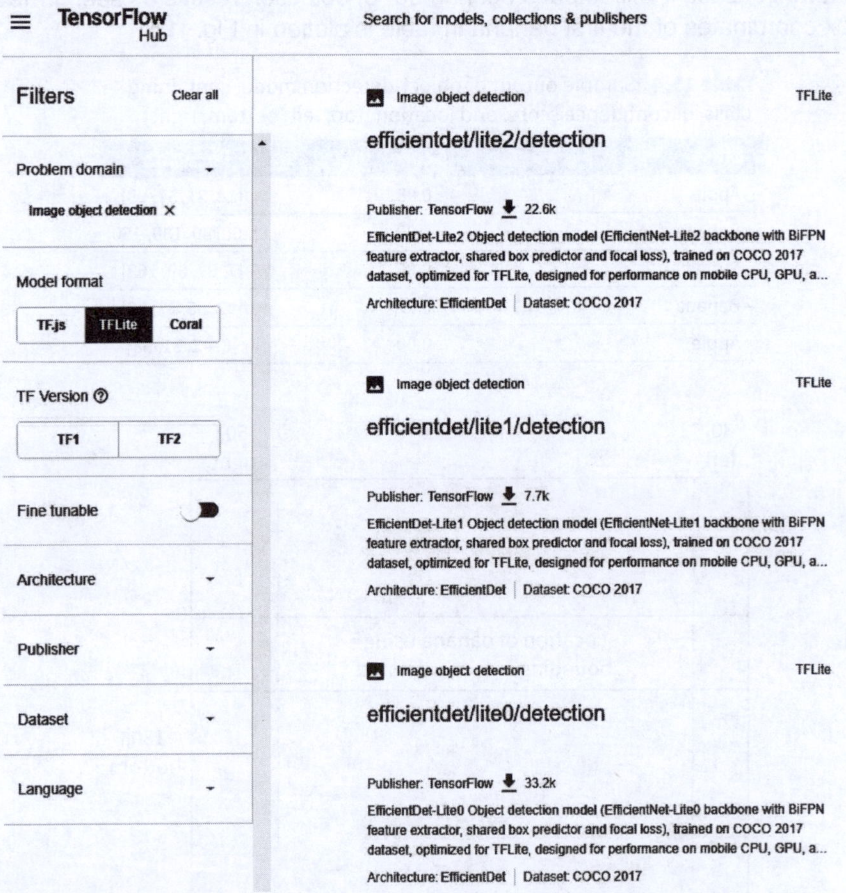

Fig. 11.6 Object-detection models from TensorFlow Hub[11] trained on the COCO 2017 dataset

[10]TensorFlow Object Detection, https://www.tensorflow.org/lite/examples/object_detection/overview (accessed 8 December 2022).

[11]TensorFlow Hub, Object Detection Models, https://tfhub.dev/s?deployment-format=lite&module-type=image-object-detection (accessed 8 December 2022).

Table 11.5 A COCO dataset classes for pre-trained object-detection models

1. person	21. bicycle	41. car	61. motorcycle
2. airplane	22. bus	42. train	62. truck
3. boat	23. traffic light	43. fire hydrant	63. stop sign
4. parking meter	24. bench	44. bird	64. cat
5. dog	25. horse	45. sheep	65. cow
6. elephant	26. bear	46. zebra	66. giraffe
7. backpack	27. umbrella	47. handbag	67. tie
8. suitcase	28. frisbee	48. skis	68. snowboard
9. sports ball	29. kite	49. baseball bat	69. baseball glove
10. skateboard	30. surfboard	50. tennis racket	70. bottle
11. wine glass	31. cup	51. fork	71. knife
12. spoon	32. bowl	52. banana	72. apple
13. sandwich	33. orange	53. broccoli	73. carrot
14. hot dog	34. pizza	54. donut	74. cake
15. chair	35. couch	55. potted plant	75. bed
16. dining table	36. toilet	56. television	76. laptop
17. mouse	37. remote	57. keyboard	77. cell phone
18. microwave	38. oven	58. toaster	78. sink
19. refrigerator	39. book	59. clock	79. vase
20. scissors	40. teddy bear	60. hair drier	80. toothbrush

bounding box labeling[12] tools. To train a custom object-detection model to use You Only Look Once (YOLO) architecture. The bounding box created by the labeling tool is saved in a format represented by four values [x_center, y_center, width, height] as seen in Fig. 11.7. The values x_center and y_center are the normalized coordinates of the center of the bounding box. To normalize coordinates, we take pixel values of x and y, which marks the center of the bounding box on the x- and y-axis. Then we divide the value of x by the width of the image and value of y by the height of the image. Width and height represent the width and the height of the bounding box. They are normalized as well. Fortunately, you do not have to calculate the centers, width and height of the bounding box. It is done by the labeling tool.

The code snippet in Listing 11.2 demonstrates the use of a pre-trained object detection model. We use an image of a bus and people near it, to locate objects the AI model recognizes. When the code in Listing 11.2 is executed, it creates a file by the name of 'object-detected.jpg'. This saved annotated image file contains bounding boxes as seen in Fig. 11.8. The superimposed bounding boxes show accurate detections of persons, a bus, and a stop sign. It also mentions the model's degree of confidence on the detected objects.

[12]Labeling tool, https://sourceforge.net/projects/labelimg.mirror/ (accessed 10 June 2023).

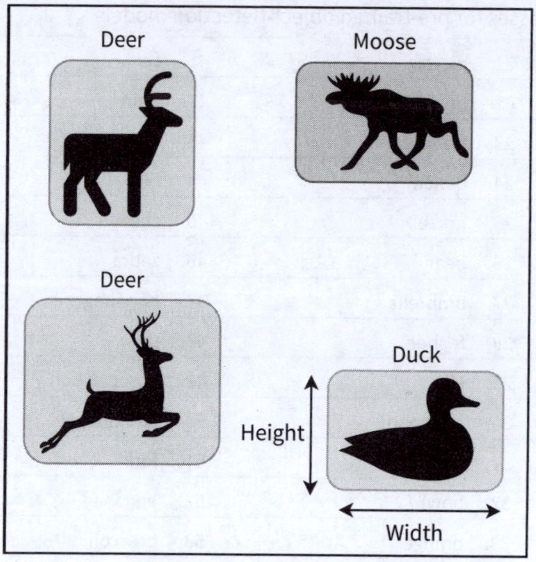

Fig. 11.7 Creating bounding boxes for training an object-detection model

Listing 11.2 Object detection using pre-trained model[13]

```
import cv2
from ultralytics import YOLO

# Load a model
model = YOLO('yolov8n.pt')  # load an official model

# Predict with the model
results = model('https://ultralytics.com/images/bus.jpg')
# predict on an image

# Visualize the results on the frame
annotated_frame = results[0].plot()

filename = 'object-detected.jpg'
# Display the annotated frame
cv2.imwrite(filename, annotated_frame)
```

Let us now break down the details contained in the object detection model inference output. It detected 4 persons, 1 bus and 1 stop sign. The total inference time comprises of preprocessing, inference and postprocessing time. From the output, we can see the total time for performing object detection on one image is 19.6 ms. The output also provides the shape of the image as (1,3,640,640). The first value (1) in the image shape is the number of samples or images presented, the second value (3) is number of channels (3 for color), while the third and the fourth values indicate the size of the processed image—640 × 640 pixels. If the image provided to the model is of higher size, the model preprocessing step will resize it to 640 × 640 pixels. You can experiment more with Listing 11.2.

[13]Object detection using YOLOv8, https://docs.ultralytics.com/tasks/detect/#predict (accessed 10 June 2023).

Fig. 11.8 File created by object-detection model using OpenCV

Provide different images that contain objects from the COCO dataset and check the accuracy of the saved annotated images. This code is available on the Digital App.

Output from Listing 11.2

```
image 1/1 /content/bus.jpg: 640×480 4 persons, 1 bus, 1 stop sign,
14.2ms
Speed: 3.4ms preprocess, 14.2ms inference, 2.0ms postprocess per image
at shape (1, 3, 640, 640)
```

11.4 | Image Segmentation

Image segmentation is slightly different from object detection. Instead of creating a bounding box around an object of interest, image segmentation identifies and highlights each pixel of the object. During training, the model learns to create a mask for the object it is trained on. It then applies this mask, to identify pixels of the object in a new image. Figure 11.9 shows how a trained image segmentation model is used. Pixels of each car in the image are of a specific color.

Image segmentation models are useful in locating defects in industrial products or areas of interest in biomedical images. There are multiple image segmentation models available for different datasets such as COCO and Cityscapes. A list of image segmentation models is available from TensorFlow Hub.[14]

[14]Image segmentation models, TF Hub, https://tfhub.dev/s?module-type=image-segmentation (accessed 8 December 2022).

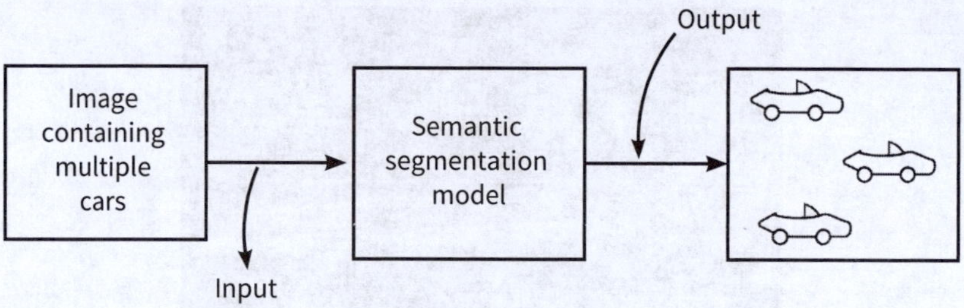

Fig. 11.9 Computer vision analysis using image segmentation

Listing 11.3 Performing image segmentation using a pre-trained model[15]

```
from ultralytics import YOLO

# Load a model
model = YOLO('yolov8n-seg.pt') # load an official model

# Predict with the model
results = model('https://ultralytics.com/images/bus.jpg')
# predict on an image
```

The code in Listing 11.3 demonstrates the use of a computer vision segmentation model. The pixels of each identified object in the image are now highlighted. To view the output of the segmentation model, execute the code using Google Colab.

11.5 | Computer Vision Applications

We now discuss two use cases for computer vision. Once a trained convolutional neural network (CNN) is available for either classification, object detection of semantic segmentation, the following generic steps are needed for most computer vision applications. Here, we assume that the application/model is that of object detection.

1. Load pre-trained CNN model.
2. Load the input image.
3. Preprocess the input image (resize, normalization, etc.).
4. Pass the preprocessed image through the CNN model.
5. Extract the detected objects' bounding boxes and class labels from the output of the CNN model.
6. Draw the bounding boxes around the detected objects in the input image and label them with the corresponding class names.
7. Save the output image with the detected objects and their labels.

The two use cases of a retail self-check-out counter and of object tracking are shown in Fig. 11.10.

[15]Image segmentation prediction, https://docs.ultralytics.com/tasks/segment/#predict (accessed 10 June 2023).

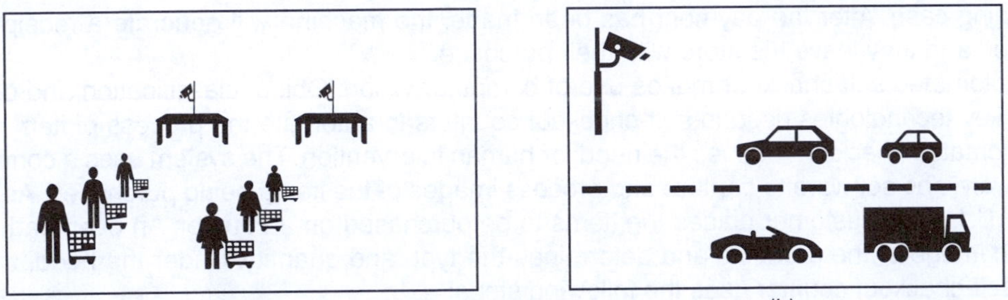

(a) (b)

Fig. 11.10 (a) Retail self-check-out counter (b) Object tracking in a smart city application

11.5.1 Application A: Self-checkout Counter

Checkout counters are used at supermarkets to pay for products. In many countries, labor shortages and the pandemic accelerated the use of self-checkout counters. A conventional self-checkout counter is a machine that allows customers to scan and bag their own purchases without the assistance of a cashier or sales associate. These machines typically consist of a screen monitor, a barcode scanner, a payment terminal, and a bagging area (Fig. 11.11). When a customer arrives at a self-checkout counter, they begin by scanning the barcode on each item they wish to purchase using the built-in scanner. The machine reads the barcode and displays the name and price of the item on the monitor.

Once all items have been scanned and bagged, the customer can then make payment using the payment terminal. This may involve using a debit or credit card, scanning a mobile payment code,

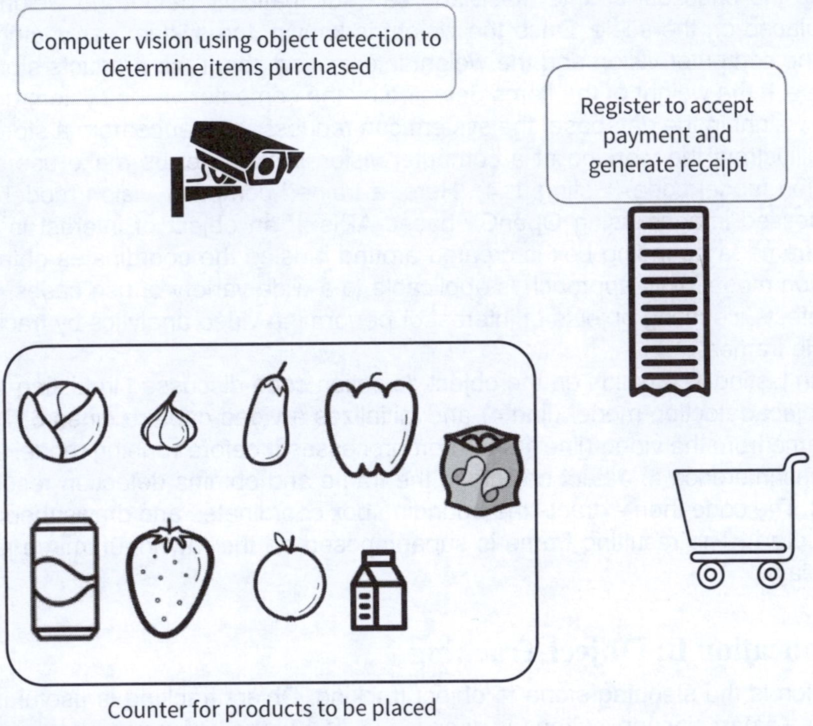

Fig. 11.11 Self-checkout counter automated using computer vision

or inserting cash. After the payment has been made, the machine will generate a receipt for the customer, and they leave the store with their purchase.

An automated self-checkout makes use of computer vision. Object classification and detection are the key technologies used in self-checkout counters to automate the process of item recognition. Automated checkout reduces the need for human intervention. The system uses a combination of hardware and software to capture and process images of the items being purchased. As seen in the Fig. 11.11., the customer places the items to be purchased on a counter. An overhead camera takes an image of the products and determines the type and quantity. Under the hood, the automated self-checkout counter uses the following steps:

(a) **Image capture** An image of the item being scanned is captured using a camera or a series of cameras installed at the self-checkout counter.

(b) **Preprocessing** The image is preprocessed to improve the quality of the image and to remove any noise or distortion that may be present.

(c) **Object detection** The image is analyzed using object detection algorithms to identify the item being scanned. These algorithms use machine learning techniques to identify patterns and features in the image that are associated with the item.

(d) **Item recognition** Once the item is identified, the system uses a database of known items to recognize the item and to retrieve information, such as the item name, price, and description.

(e) **Payment processing** Once all items have been scanned and recognized, the customer can proceed with payment using cash, credit/debit card, or other payment methods.

An automated self-checkout system can use sensor fusion. The computer vision detection is cross-checked by a weighing scale. The use of a weighing scale in a self-checkout counter is to accurately measure the weight of the products that a customer is purchasing. The scale is typically integrated into the checkout counter itself and can automatically detect the weight of the items as they are placed on the scale. Once the weight is known, the system can match the products detected by the computer vision and the weight information about the products stored in the system's database. If the weight of the items detected by the computer vision system does not match the expected weight in the database, the system can request assistance from a store employee.

To further illustrate the working of a computer vision system, let us make use of a simplified object detection model code (Listing 11.4). Here, a trained computer vision model captures and displays processed images using OpenCV-based APIs. If an object of interest is detected in a video image frame, a bounding box is created around it using the coordinates obtained from the computer vision model. This approach is applicable to a wide variety of use cases. One could be looking for defects, counting objects of interest or performing video analytics by tracking an object across multiple frames.

The code in Listing 11.4 builds on the object detection code discussed in Listing 11.2. It loads a pre-trained object detection model (line 4) and initializes a video capture (lines 6, 7). It then captures each frame from the video (line 11) and preprocesses it before running model inference. The model performs inference to detect objects in the frame and obtains detection results as seen in (line 12—run). The code then extracts the bounding box coordinates and draws them on the frame (line 12—visualize). The resulting frame is superimposed on the raw input image and displayed. (line 12—display).

11.5.2 Application B: Object Tracking

Object detection is the stepping stone to object tracking. Object tracking is useful in a variety of scenarios. For a smart city application (as seen in Fig. 11.12), the city may be interested in monitoring traffic count at different times of the day. In a retail setting, counting the number of customers in

Listing 11.4 Object detection using Yolov8 model[16] for a video file. Python packages Opencv-python and Ultralytics need to be installed for this code to run

```
01.  import cv2
02.  from ultralytics import YOLO

03.  # Load the YOLOv8 model
04.  model = YOLO('yolov8n.pt')

05.  # Open the video file
06.  video_path = "path/to/your/video/file.mp4"
07.  cap = cv2.VideoCapture(video_path)

08.  # Loop through the video frames
09.  while cap.isOpened():
10.  # Read a frame from the video
11.  success, frame = cap.read()

12.  if success:
          # Run YOLOv8 inference on the frame
          results = model(frame)

          # Visualize the results on the frame
           annotated_frame = results[0].plot()

          # Display the annotated frame
           cv2.imshow("processed_image", annotated_frame)

13.  else:
          # Break the loop if the end of the video is reached
          break

14.  # Release the video capture object and close the display window
15.  cap.release()
16.  cv2.destroyAllWindows()
```

different sections of a supermarket may provide valuable insights. For both these applications, we use video analytics based on object detection.

An object tracking code uses bounding box detections to track each object across different frames of a video. It factors in the size of the image, speed of the object and inference rate (frames per second) to know how far an object can move between two images. If an object has traveled less than the maximum possible distance (or pixels in the frame), it is the same object from the previous frame. In Fig. 11.12, using the bounding box output, the coordinates of the top left (Xtl,Ytl) and bottom right (Xbr,Ybr) are determined. This is used to calculate the center point of the object (Xn,Yn). The tracker software creates a unique id for each object (car in our case), and tracks it

[16]YOLOv8 for streaming video inference, https://docs.ultralytics.com/modes/predict/#streaming-source-for-loop (accessed 10 June 2023).

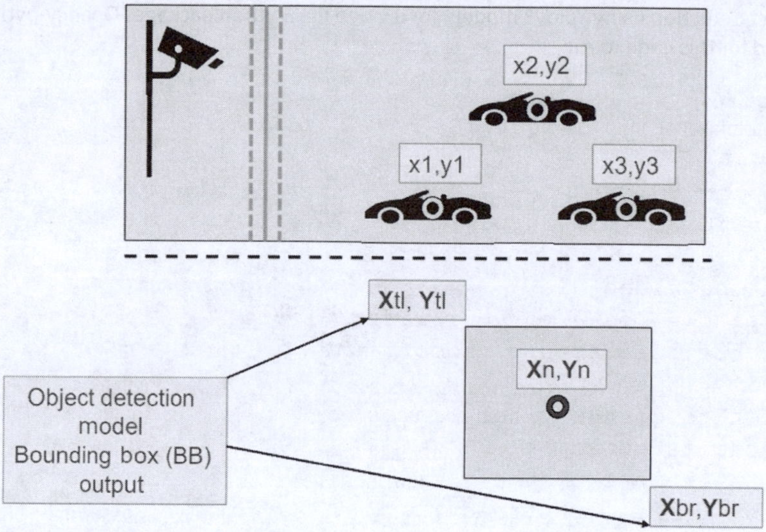

Fig. 11.12 Counting vehicles for a smart city

across subsequent frames by knowing that the object can physically change its position within a certain range.

Object tracking can be used for counting number of individuals entering a certain area. This is done by defining an area in an image frame. Since the camera is fixed, the pixel coordinates of the area are constant. Any time an object of interest appears in the region of interest, a software counter is incremented by one. Figure 11.13 below shows this setup. The idea of object tracking or counting is a powerful one and can be extended to several applications.

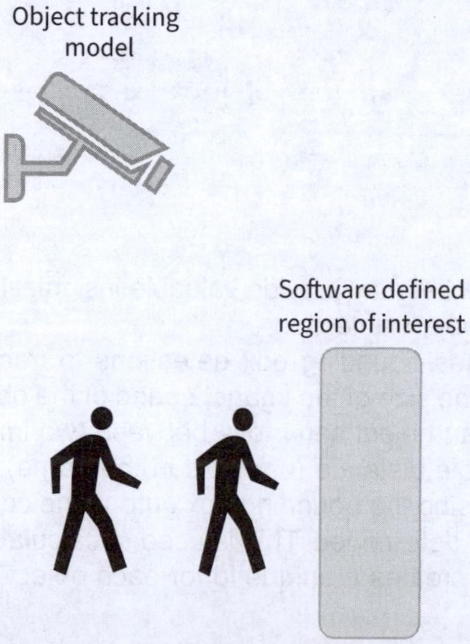

Fig. 11.13 People counting using an object detection model and tracking algorithm

11.6 | Conclusion

We discussed three commonly used computer vision techniques—image classification, object detection and image segmentation. When used correctly for the right application, these techniques unlock a lot of valuable insight from an image. If the application has objects that are part of ImageNet or COCO dataset, an off-the-shelf pre-trained AI model can be used. Otherwise, new computer vision models with custom datasets are created using transfer learning.

Exercises

A. State True/False

1. AI model inference requires more time than model training.
2. ImageNet dataset contains 1000 image categories.
3. Top-1 accuracy means that the model's right answer is part of 5 predictions.
4. An object detection model highlights pixels of recognized objects.
5. Human effort is needed to create a new image dataset for training.

B. Short-answer Questions

1. Estimate the speed (frames per second) at which a computer object detection model can process video by using the details provided by the output of Listing 11.2.
2. Name the dataset used in pre-trained object detection models. Mention the number of classes in the dataset.
3. Enumerate the information provided by an object detection model.
4. Explain why custom computer vision models use transfer learning.
5. Mention one possible application of object segmentation.

C. Long-answer Questions

1. A superstore has an inventory robot. When the store closes, the robot roams the aisles of the store and visually takes inventory of products on the shelves. What kind of computer vision model would you recommend? Do you think the model needs retraining or an existing model can be reused?
2. Specify information expected from video analytics for the following scenarios: (a) crowd control on the day of a big sale, (b) finding number of cars in the parking lot, (c) number of persons in a meeting room, (d) distracted driver monitoring.
3. In the factory automation system seen in Fig. 11.14, explain how a computer vision system can implement quality checks on a bottled product.

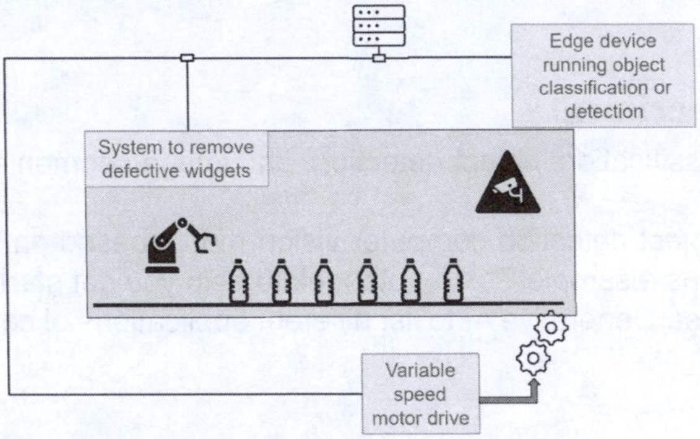

Fig. 11.14 The camera hosts the computer vision model. The classification model checks for any foreign objects in the bottled product

4. Explain how surface water can be estimated using satellite images and object detection. A hypothetical scenario of diminishing the size of water bodies is shown in Fig. 11.15. How do you think this can help monitor the progress of the project mission Amrit Sarovar?[17]

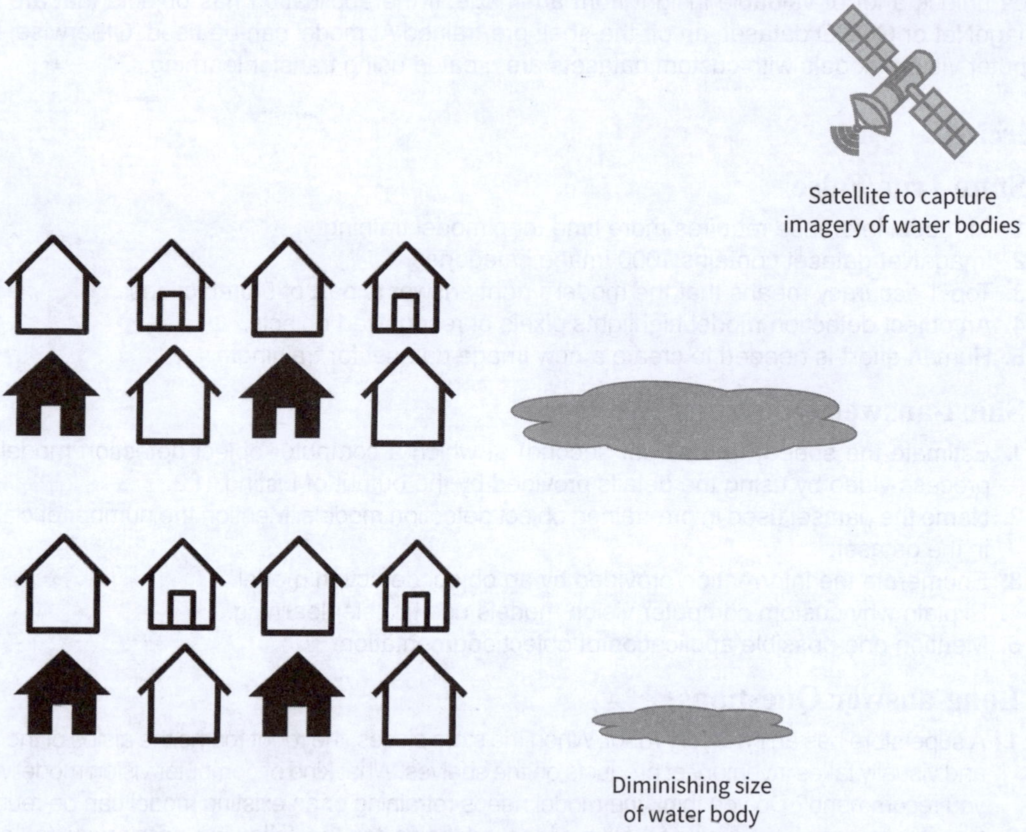

Fig. 11.15 Ascertaining change in water bodies using satellite remote sensing imagery

5. Explain how computer vision can ease road traffic congestion in cities. Devise a plan to effectively manage traffic by use of cameras, object detection models and control of traffic lights. Compare your plan with that envisaged by Google Green Light (https://sites.research.google/greenlight/).

C. Explore and Experiment

1. Try out image classification, object detection, and image segmentation using sample code on Google Colab.
2. Train a custom object detection computer vision model based on YoloV8[18] and test it. The Digital App contains a sample Colab notebook to help you get started.
3. In Fig. 11.16, we use Generative AI to list different applications of computer vision in a smart city context.

[17]Mission Amrit Sarovar, https://amritsarovar.gov.in/ (accessed 26 May 2023).
[18]Train Yolov8 model, https://docs.ultralytics.com/modes/train/ (accessed 10 June 2023).

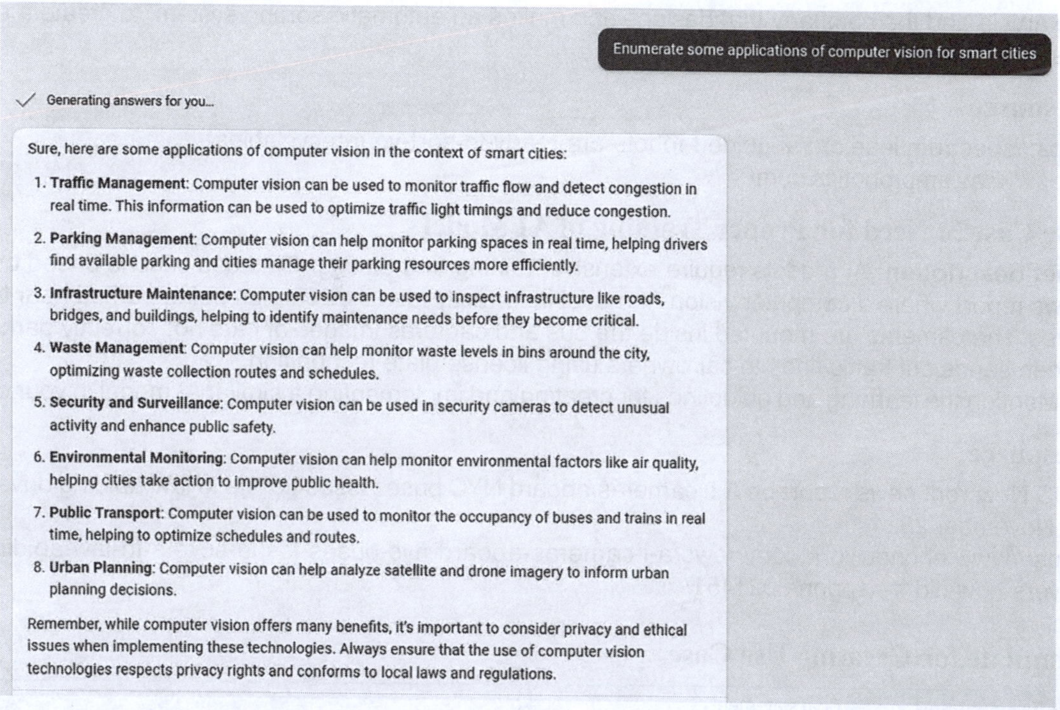

Fig. 11.16 A few of the myriad uses of computer vision listed by Generative AI

4. The ALERTCalifornia website (https://alertcalifornia.org/) provides real-time video information from cameras located at multiple locations across the state. This video feed is analyzed by AI models to detect any incipient incidents such as wildfires. Visit the website and see real-time camera feed from a location of your choice.

D. Generate Use Cases Based on Computer Vision Applications—Learning by Example Approach

Use Case 1: Driver Assistance Technologies for Road Safety

Brief description: Road accidents injure or kill hundreds of people every day across the world. Computer vision technology is very helpful in preventing road accidents, by detecting pedestrians and stopping the motor vehicle if the driver is distracted. The resource mentioned below contains information on use of computer vision for road safety. Study it and then create a use case using the given template.

Resource

National Highway Traffic Safety Administration
https://www.nhtsa.gov/equipment/driver-assistance-technologies

Use Case 2: Sorting Recyclable Materials Using Computer Vision

Brief description: Every day millions of tons of recyclable waste gets produced. If this is not correctly sorted, it is likely to end up in a landfill. Accurate and fast computer vision models using object detection, help a high-speed robotic arm to sort recyclable items traveling on conveyor belts. Study the article and the company that designs and makes an automatic sorting system, to create a use case based on the given template.

Resource

https://spectrum.ieee.org/ai-guided-robots-are-ready-to-sort-your-recyclables
https://www.amprobotics.com/

Use Case 3: Need for Proper Training of AI Model

Brief description: AI models require extensive training and testing. This use case is based on a news report where a computer vision AI model incorrectly identifies cars as being parked near bus lanes. The cameras are mounted inside the bus and captures images of cars not correctly parked. It then sends out traffic fines to car owners using license plate recognition.

Mention the learning and guidelines for creating and implementing a similar AI model in your city.

Resource

NBC New York news report on A.I. cameras aboard NYC buses issue tickets to law-abiding drivers, 27 November 2024
https://www.nbcnewyork.com/news/a-i-cameras-aboard-nyc-buses-issue-tickets-to-law-abiding-drivers-how-did-it-happen/6021451/

Template for Creating Use Case

Define goal and purpose	Goal statement
	Identify stakeholders
	Define scope
Details to include in use case	Capture how technology helps business process
	Keep use case findings description textual, with a few simple flowcharts if needed
	Focus on describing how technology benefits the use case
Future applications	Mention any new applications that can leverage the technology used

Suggested Reading

1. Mohamed Elgendy, Deep Learning for Vision Systems, Manning.

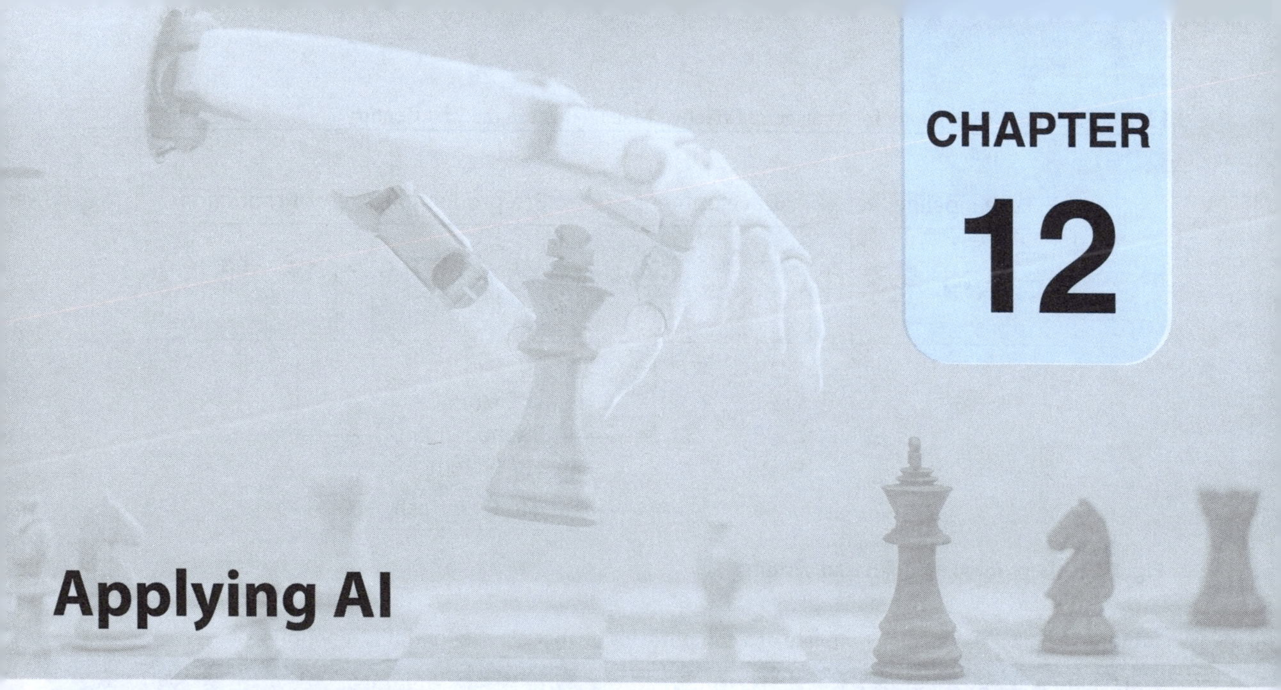

CHAPTER 12

Applying AI

CHAPTER OUTLINE

LEARNING OBJECTIVES

After reading this chapter, you will be able to:

- get acquainted with the steps needed to create an AI model
- accelerate AI model usage by cloud-enabled AI services
- become conversant with the idea of deploying AI models on edge devices

Effective Management Using AI

AI is a great tool. It enables the analysis and use of unstructured data that classical techniques could not do. Like any tool, it is important that we understand its working and derive maximum advantage from it. A systematic approach based on leveraging existing models to develop and deploy AI models increases the probability of success with AI.

12.1 | Machine Learning Operations

Machine learning operations (MLOps) defines a framework to create and deploy models. The process starts by creating a dataset to train a model. Once the model is trained, it is tested for efficacy using real-world metrics. When the model goes in operation, instead of a static dataset, it is fed with real-time

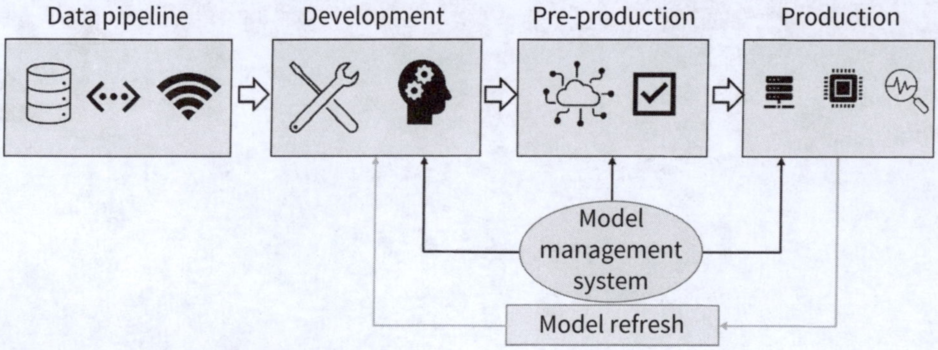

Fig. 12.1 MLOps for AI model-based systems

Table 12.1 Dataset versioning template of a computer vision model used for traffic monitoring

Dataset ID	Date/Time	Comments
ND-CP-Sept-22	10 October 2022	Dataset from New Delhi, Connaught Place, September 2022.

Table 12.2 Model versioning template for a customized generative AI model trained using hospital data

Model ID	Dataset Used	Base Model	Frozen Layers	Hyperparameters
Hospital-A-Jan-23	Hospital-A test records	Llama-3	Not applicable	Not applicable

data from a data pipeline. The data generated by credit card transactions forms the data pipeline of a credit card fraud detection AI model. The model' in production is closely monitored. In case of declining performance, the model is retrained with new or updated data. This is shown in Fig. 12.1.

Data is the key ingredient to train an AI model. It is therefore important that data is carefully versioned. If different datasets are used to train a model, each dataset is likely to give a different model. As a good housekeeping practice, most companies keep a log of different datasets. A simple data versioning control system is seen in Table 12.1. Here each dataset is assigned an ID, date, and time when it was collected or generated along with comments to describe the dataset.

Similarly, when a model is created, it is assigned an ID and the dataset used to create the model is also recorded. If transfer learning is used to customize a model, details of the base model, reused or frozen layers and hyperparameters to tune the model are also logged. Even though no two models are exactly the same[1] (even when trained with the same dataset, hyperparameters), they can be similar for practical purposes. A framework to capture model version details is mentioned in Table 12.2.

12.2 | Developing an AI Model

AI is a versatile tool. It can be applied to a variety of problems. The steps needed to create an AI model are not specific to given problems. They are by and large universal. In a nutshell, trained AI models map any input space to any target space.

The process of developing an AI model starts with putting together a representative dataset about the application. This representative dataset contains data about the input and target space.

[1]Since model training uses a stochastic process, two models are unlikely to have exactly the same values of weights, biases and activation functions.

Table 12.3 Major steps for AI model creation

Step	Process
Problem definition and data availability	Assess if adequate clean data relating to the application is available. If not, additional data may need to be collected and annotated by human labelers.
Metric for success	Discuss with the end-user and come up with a realistic metric for success
Set aside test dataset	Partition dataset into training and test data. The test data is used to check if the model works with novel inputs which it has not seen
Vectorize and pre-process data	Deep learning training frameworks, such as TensorFlow, PyTorch work with data arrays or tensors. Data from an application needs to be pre-processed (e.g., normalized) and converted into tensors
Create baseline model	The first base-line model provides a good estimate of the success of the AI model. If the base-line AI model gives poorer accuracy as compared with classical techniques, maybe an AI-based model is not the best approach.
Check if the model generalizes	Training a model is not a linear process. One of the recommended ways is to start with a model that overfits (has greater neurons/layers than it needs and memorizes training data) and then regularize using techniques such as drop-out. A properly trained model provides similar accuracy on the test data as it does on the training data. If it does, the model generalizes
Deploy model	A trained AI model is stored as a graph. Input from an application is passed to the model as tensors using APIs (application programming interfaces). APIs are available for several programming languages such as JavaScript or C++. A model can be employed on a cloud server or on an embedded device. Embedded constrained devices execute models with a lesser number of parameters. A deployed model is monitored for performance as it works with real-world data. A model may need to be retrained if its performance deteriorates (known as model drift)

The next step is defining what to predict and how to measure success of the model's prediction. These two foundational steps have a big role to play in the development of a robust AI model.

There are several other steps such as vectoring inputs and targets, training a model that generalizes well and then deploying the model for production. These steps are mentioned in Table 12.3, along with a brief explanation.

In Table 12.3 and in the earlier section, we briefly mentioned the need to map input data with target data space. Multiple combinations of data types exist, based on the application. Understanding and correctly preparing input and target data space is a significant pre-processing step. Some of these mappings for commonly used applications are listed in Table 12.4.

Table 12.4 Mapping different types of example data to label data

Mapping Data Types	Applications that Use Mapping Type
Vector to Vector (Structured data)	Map predictor diagnostic variables to an outcome—whether a person has diabetes[2]
Image data to vector	Map pictures of items in a fulfilment centre to description Map pictures of eyes to presence or absence of glaucoma[3]
Time series to vector	Map electromyography (EMG) signal to gesture (as form of human computer interaction)
Text to text data	Map a paragraph in one language to a translated version in another language for machine translation
Images to text	Map images that contain a character or a number (0–9) to the corresponding text string. Useful for reading amount on checks or pin codes on letters

[2]Pima Indians Diabetes Database, https://archive.ics.uci.edu/ml/machine-learning-databases/pima-indians-diabetes/ (accessed 24 November 2022).

[3]S. Gheisari et al., A combined convolutional and recurrent neural network for enhanced glaucoma detection, Nature Scientific Reports, 2021, https://www.nature.com/articles/s41598-021-81554-4 (accessed 24 November 2022).

Table 12.5 Tensor shapes for different types of input data. A tensor is a multidimensional array

Data Type	Tensor Shape	Shape Details	Example
Vector data	2D	Samples, Features	Iris dataset
Time series data	3D	Samples, Timesteps, Features	3-axis accelerometer dataset
Images	4D	Samples, Height, Width, Color channels	MNIST, CIFAR datasets
Videos	5D	Samples, Frames, Height, Width, Color channels	Video sequence of images

A tensor is a multi-dimensional array. A concrete example of tensor shapes is mentioned in Table 12.5. Here we see examples of datasets, such as Iris, Modified National Institute of Standards and Technology (MNIST), and video frames and their corresponding tensor shapes. The dimensions of the input layer of a model have to match the tensor shape of the input data.

Transfer Learning and Model Zoo

There are a large number of open-source pre-trained AI models. These models are listed and hosted on Websites known as *model zoos*. Based on the application, a user can pick a computer vision, or an NLP model and then customize it for their own use. This way, users do not have to reinvent the wheel.

Open Neural Network eXchange (ONNX) is an open format to represent machine learning models. You can visit the ONNX model zoo[4] to view the different types of AI models hosted there. There are many training frameworks for training AI models. Each framework ends up saving the trained model in its own format. ONNX has emerged as a popular format to represent trained model. There are Python-based converter scripts to change different model formats to ONNX (Fig. 12.2).

One way to check that model conversion from one format to another has taken place successfully is to use a tool called Netron. Netron can parse models saved in several formats and display the model graph as seen in Fig. 12.3. The graph shows a model similar to MNIST with 10 classes. A quick check would be to see the dimensions of the input and output tensors of the model.

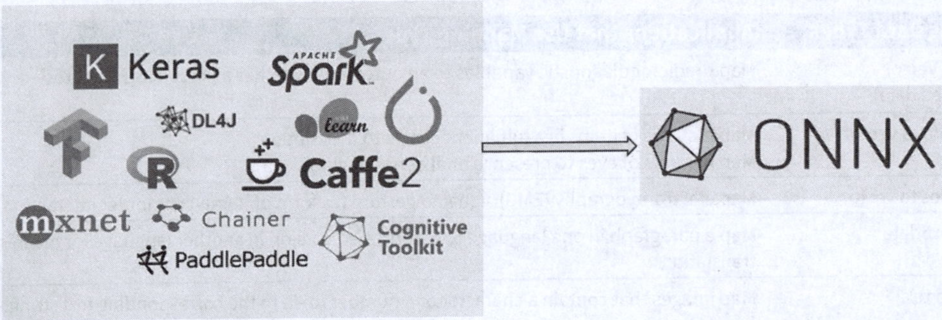

Fig. 12.2 Model formats and conversion to ONNX

[4]ONNX model zoo, https://github.com/onnx/models (accessed 10 June 2023).

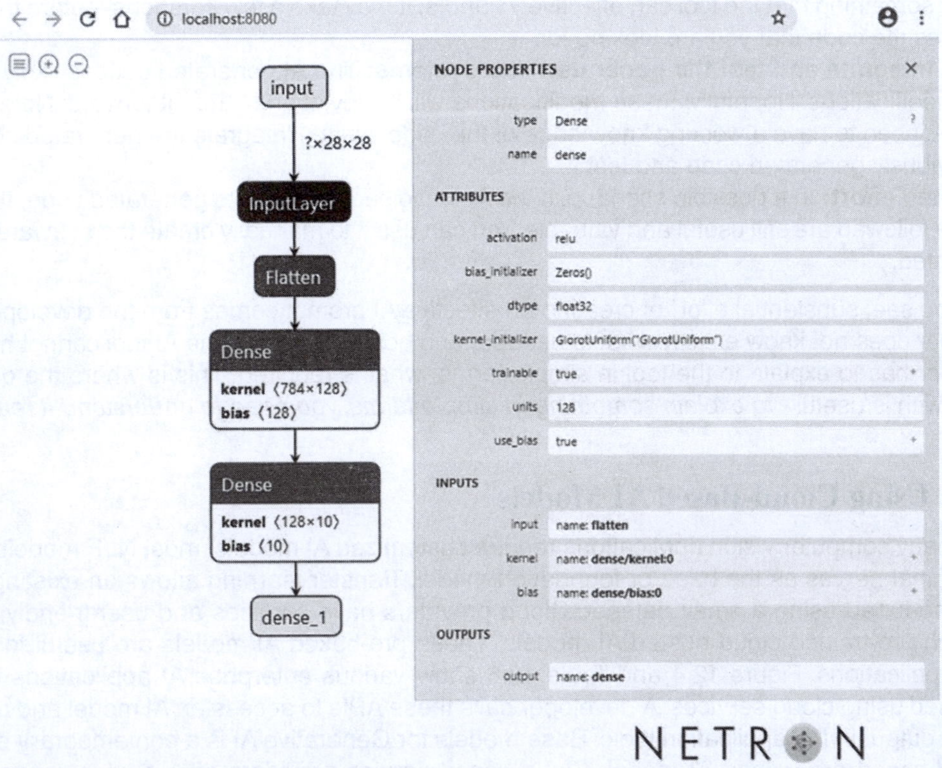

Fig. 12.3 Netron[5] to visualize model graph

AI-Assisted Software Code Generation

There is a quote that is often attributed to Albert Einstein, "If you can't explain it simply, you don't understand it well enough". Around the world, many companies and developers are using AI to accelerate software system implementation using AI. You may think that AI is doing all the heavy lifting, but at the end of this section, we will explain again that there is no really no free lunch. To get AI to do something meaningful, you will have to put in some work. Here is the recommended approach to use AI for software code generation.

Most GenAI tools are similar: Do not waste time evaluating and experimenting with different GenAI tools. Choose the one you like the most and stick with it. This approach should work with most tools.

Know precisely what you want the software system to do: This is where you should invest most of your time. Enumerate the requirements and strategy (algorithms) you wish to use to realize your software system. This is where your understanding of the system becomes useful. Create a system level architecture to get started.

Breakdown the system into several miniature sub-systems: Use the system architecture and requirements to breakdown the system into miniature sub-systems or modules. Try to simplify the modules to the lowest level of abstraction you possibly can.

Write a prompt to realize the miniature sub-system: Now write a prompt to request the GenAI tool to generate code for the simplified miniature sub-system. This request is likely to be simple and

[5]Netron Web app, https://netron.app/ (accessed 10 June 2023).

precise; something that the tool can effectively handle. It may take a few iterations, before the AI tool generates the code that you are looking for.

Modify, integrate and test the generated sub-systems: The AI generated code is likely to need some modifications. Hopefully, these modifications will be trivial and straight forward. Note, for this step, you need to have a working knowledge of the code syntax. Integrate the generated code with the previously generated code and test it.

No wasted effort: In a possible scenario, if the AI tool disappoints by its generated code, the steps we have followed are still useful and valuable. You can use it to manually create the software system you wanted.

As you see, substantial effort of creating an effective AI prompt comes from the developer. If the developer does not know exactly what is needed, and how to render it, the AI tool cannot help. The developer has to explain to the tool in simple terms, what is required. This is where the quote we started with is useful - *to explain something in simple terms, you need to understand it really well*.

12.3 | Using Cloud-Based AI Models

While many computer vision applications require customized AI models, most NLP models rely on an LLM that serves as the base or foundation model. Transfer learning allows an existing model to be fine-tuned using a small dataset. Cloud providers have services and user-friendly APIs to use such pre-trained cloud hosted AI models. These pre-baked AI models are useful for a variety of applications. Figure 12.4 and Table 12.6 show various enterprise AI applications that are addressed using cloud services. A developer calls these APIs to access an AI model and uses the model's output in the application logic. Base models for Generative AI is a contemporary example of cloud-based pre-trained AI model. Cloud-based service providers offer a wide range of pre-trained generative AI based models, that can be customized using user data. To learn more about cloud-based AI services, check out the Website of a cloud provider.[6]

Cloud service companies not only offer access to pre-trained models they also host AI models on their servers. A good example of a cloud-based AI model is a fraud-detection model. In Fig. 12.5(a), we see transactions originating from retail stores using credit card or mobile apps. A cloud-based

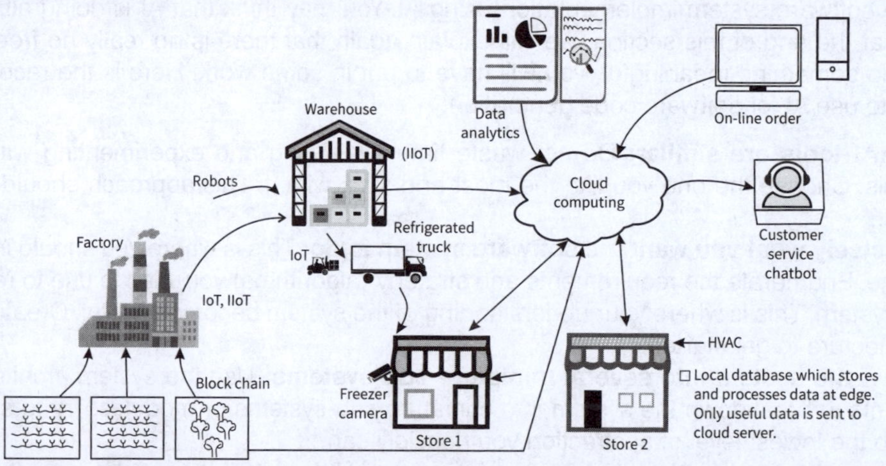

Fig. 12.4 Use of cloud-based AI models in a modern enterprise

[6]AWS AI services, https://aws.amazon.com/machine-learning/ai-services/ (accessed 24 November 2022).

Table 12.6 AI model-based services offered by cloud providers

Application	Description of Service
Computer vision	Analyze images and videos to determine customer footfalls Detect defects using automated inspection
Data extraction and analysis	Extract information from large number of documents Apply NLP on unstructured text data from customer feedback
Chatbots and virtual agents	Build chatbots for Website-based 24×7 customer service Transcribe using automated speech recognition
Business metrics	Analyze time series data to create prediction models for orders Detect fraud on financial transactions
Industrial AI	Detect abnormal machine conditions using vibration and temperature sensors Plan for predictive maintenance
Generative AI	Create customized dialogue models using foundation models such as LLa Meta Llama (LLM Meta AI) –2

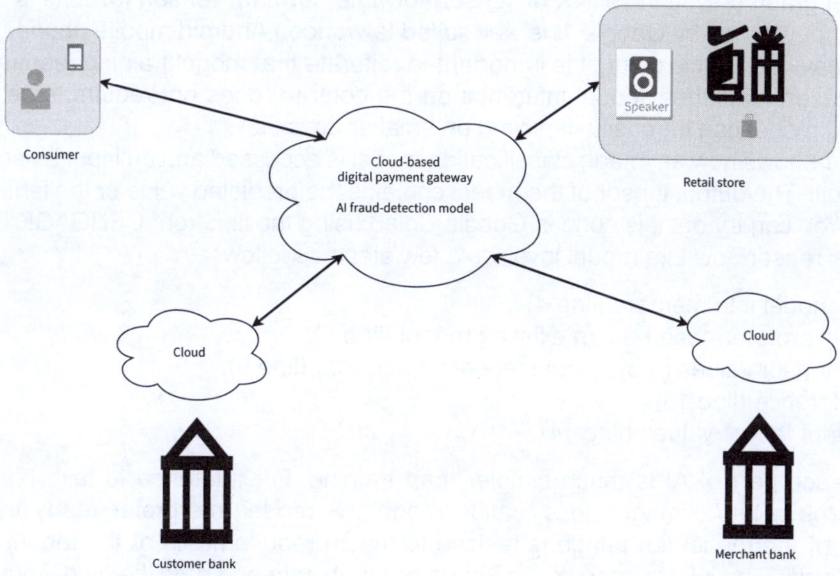

Fig. 12.5 (a) Cloud-based AI fraud-detection model

AI model looks into each transaction's data packet for location, time, and date details. Based on certain features of the transaction, it may classify a transaction to be suspicious and not process it. The model may inform the bank or the consumer of the transaction if it is fraudulent. These models are very similar to e-mail spam filter AI models. They process a large number of transactions every second and need to be continuously updated based on newer data or newer threats.

12.4 | Locally Hosted AI Models

In the earlier section, we talked about cloud-hosted AI models. Applications such as computer vision require the AI model to run at a physical location close to the process. These models run on devices that do not have continuous high-speed connectivity to a cloud computer. Such devices are said to reside at the edge of the network and are called *edge devices*. There are many advantages of running an AI model at the edge. These include the following:

- **Real-time insights** Zero-latency, as data does not travel to cloud
- **Lower operating costs** Cloud server and data transfer charges eliminated
- **Increased privacy** Data does not leave the premises
- **High availability** No dependence on data connectivity and cloud server hardware
- **Persistent improvement** Better monitoring of model performance

Lightweight computer vision AI models work very well on constrained computers at the edge. The APIs for accessing and using an AI model on the edge are very similar to those on the cloud. These edge devices carry out image classification, object detection (find location of objects in an image using bounding box), and semantic segmentation. Language models are usually not hosted on edge devices as they require considerable computational resources. Recent advances in light-weight large language models (LLMs) has opened up the possibility of hosting LLMs on edge devices.

CNN-based computer vision model can be hosted on a single-board computer (like Raspberry Pi[7]) located near a machine or embedded in a machine. A simple runtime is needed to execute the trained model graph (saved in ONNX or TensorFlow Lite[8] format). TensorFlow Lite is a lightweight model format developed by Google. It is well suited to work on Android mobile phones and smaller constrained devices. At this point, it is important to reiterate that model training requires the use of large GPU-based machines. Model inference on the contrary does not require large GPUs. As a result, trained model can be easily deployed on smaller devices.

Listing 12.1 shows how an image classification model is accessed and an input tensor (an image) is assigned to it. The output tensor of the model contains the predicted value or the label of the identified image. You can try out this code in Google Colab using the link from CENGAGE Digital App.

Running a TensorFlow Lite model involves a few steps as follows:

- Load the model into memory (line 4).
- Build an interpreter based on an existing model (line 6).
- Set input tensor values (resize input tensors if needed) (line 8).
- Invoke inference (line 13).
- Read output tensor values (line 14).

The inference part of AI is much simpler than training. For inference to take place, a model is loaded (MobileNetV2 image classification model). A model interpreter reads the input and output ports of the model. An image is resized to match requirements of the model input tensor (224 × 224 pixels). The interpreter sets the image as input_data and runs the model graph by calling interpreter.invoke method. After processing, the model output is available on its output tensor. The final classification involves matching the numeric value from output tensor to a human label text file.

Embedding AI into Existing Business Processes

Let us end this chapter by discussing some intuitive guidelines for incorporating AI models in business processes.

1. **Define the use case** Clearly define the business problem that the AI model will solve, and how it will do so.
2. **Develop a proof of concept** After defining the use case, the next step is to develop a proof of concept. Businesses should create a prototype AI model and evaluate its effectiveness.

[7]Raspberry Pi, https://www.raspberrypi.com/products/raspberry-pi-4-model-b/ (accessed 24 November 2022).
[8]TensorFlow Lite, https://www.tensorflow.org/lite (accessed 10 June 2023).

Listing 12.1 Image Classification Model (MobileNet) inference using TensorFlow Lite runtime

```
import numpy as np
import tensorflow as tf
import tflite_runtime.interpreter as tflite

model = tf.keras.applications.MobileNetV2(
weights="imagenet", input_shape=(224, 224, 3))

converter = tf.lite.TFLiteConverter.from_keras_model(model)
            tflite_model = converter.convert()

interpreter = tflite.Interpreter(model_content=tflite_model)
interpreter.allocate_tensors()

input_details = interpreter.get_input_details()
output_details = interpreter.get_output_details()

input_shape = input_details[0]['shape']
input_data = np.array(image(input_shape),
                      dtype=np.float32)

interpreter.set_tensor(input_details[0]['index'], input_data)

interpreter.invoke()

prediction= interpreter.get_tensor(output_details[0]['index'])
```

3. **Evaluate the results** Once the proof-of-concept AI model has been developed, it is time to measure the effectiveness of the technology and assess its impact on the business.
4. **Develop a deployment plan** If the proof-of-concept is successful, the next step is to develop a deployment plan. A detailed plan is needed to deploy the AI model and integrate it into existing systems.
5. **Monitor and optimize** Once the AI model has been deployed, a plan is put in place to monitor its performance and optimize it so that it continues to address the business challenges effectively.

It is now easy to host and experiment with LLM models locally on a workstation or laptop computer using a tool called as LM Studio (https://lmstudio.ai). LM Studio can be downloaded and installed on a Windows, Linux or Mac computer. Once installed, a welcome screen resembling Fig. 12.5(b) will appear. Users can search for different models from a repository. A sample model list is shown in Fig. 12.5(c). When a model is successfully installed it is possible to query a model using APIs. Fig. 12.5(d) shows model response to a GET /v1/models query.

A business can test and use a customized LLM based AI model by hosting the model on an intranet and then develop APIs to query a model. Multiple users from across the business can query the hosted model to get answers and data by writing query in simple language.

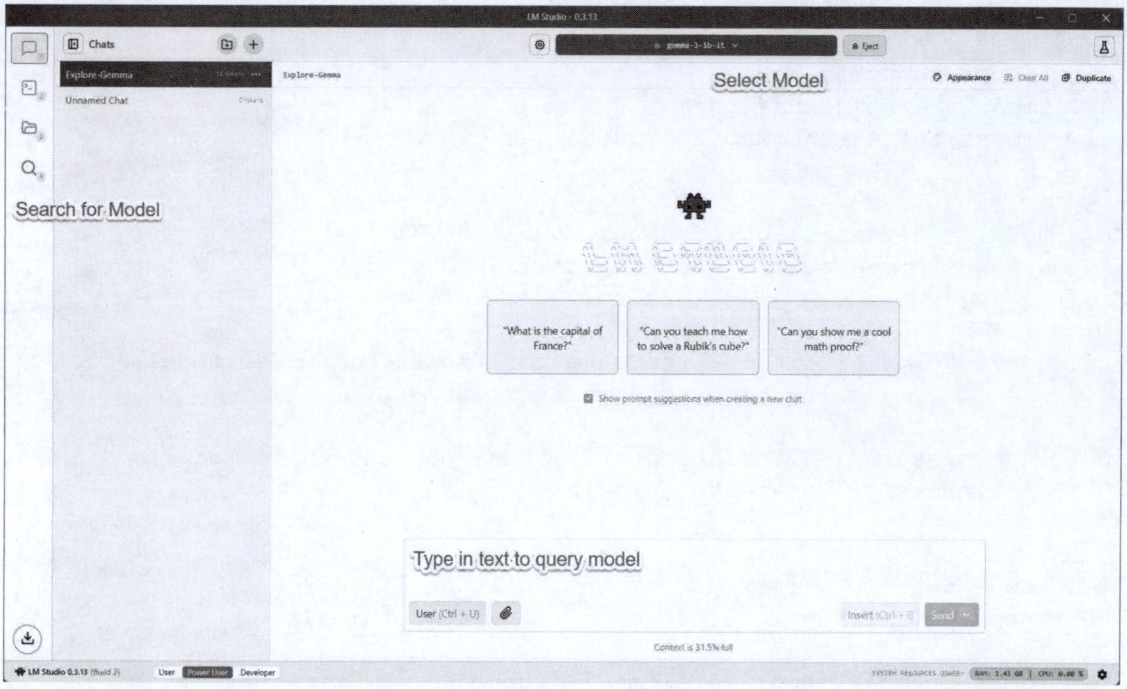

Fig. 12.5 (b) Welcome screen of locally hosted LM Studio

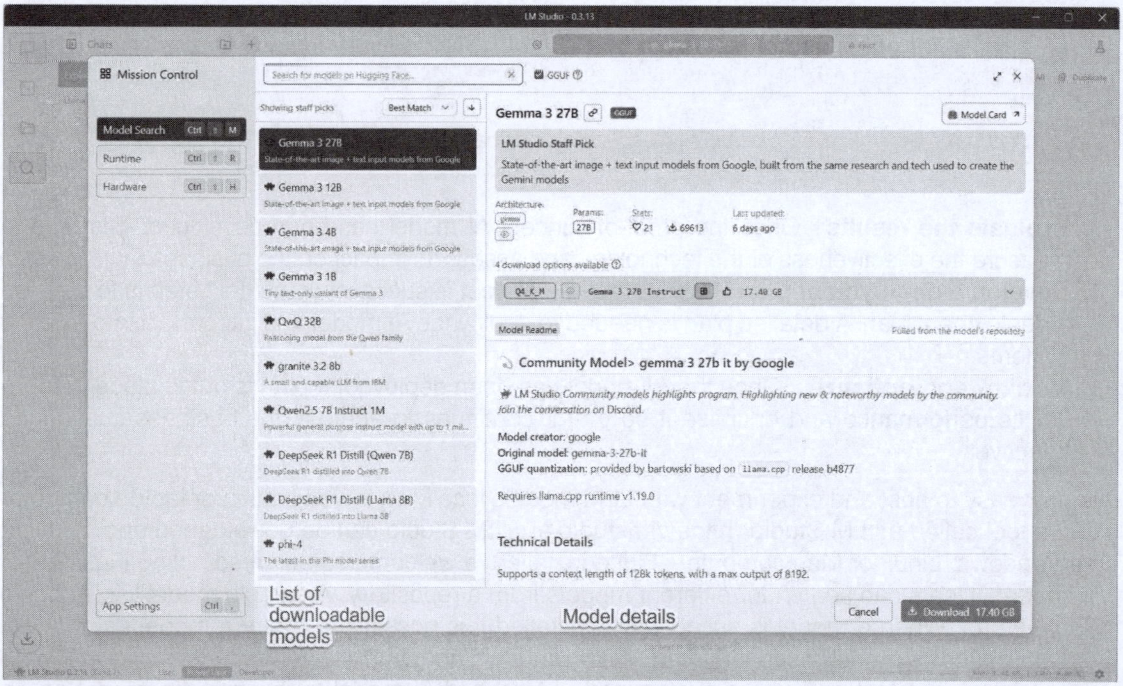

Fig. 12.5 (c) Listing of downloadable models that can be hosted using LM Studio

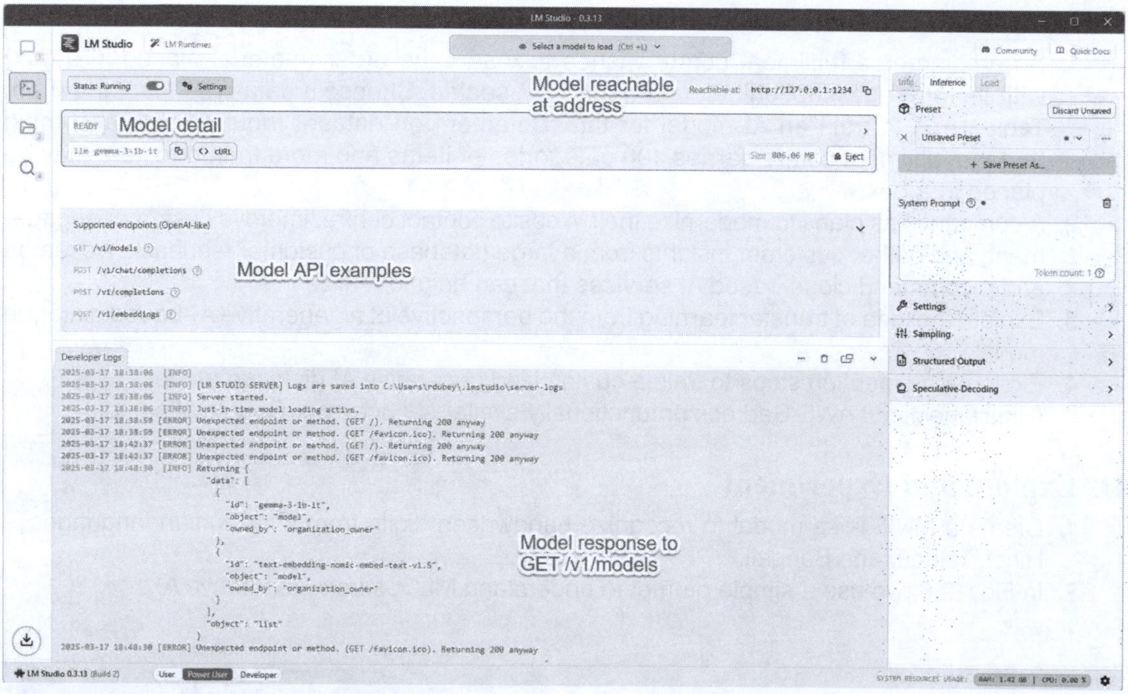

Fig. 12.5 (d) Response from LM Studio to a GET /v1/models details query. It validates that model Gemma-3-1b-it is loaded. The 1b stands for 1 billion parameters

12.5 | Conclusion

AI has emerged from research labs and is now easily accessible and usable. To create an AI model, the first step is to get relevant data from the application. This data is pre-processed and set up for supervised learning. Many applications do not require creation of an AI model from scratch. There are many ready-made models for common business needs hosted by cloud service providers, which can be customized using transfer learning. All AI models need not be deployed on servers. Smaller computer vision models can be hosted on smartphones or on single-board computers.

Exercises

A. State True/False

1. Cloud services offer AI-based products with pre-trained models.
2. A model zoo is a Website to obtain pre-trained AI models.
3. The tensor shape for video data type is 2D—samples, features.
4. Chatbot is an AI service provided by cloud providers.
5. Edge-based AI models need network connectivity to run.

B. Short-answer Questions

1. What is the name of the framework to create and manage AI models?
2. Why is model/data versioning an important part of MLOps?
3. State two foundation/base models used for dialogue-based generative AI applications.
4. Name the tool used to explore the graph of a trained neural network model.
5. Provide the name of a lightweight model format that works on Android smartphones.

C. Long-answer Questions

1. An e-commerce fulfilment centre wishes to match the order (material placed in a box) with the order description before the box gets sealed. Choose a data-type mapping (from Table 12.2) to train an AI model for this. Comment on dataset requirements assuming that the fulfilment centre carries 100 categories of items and more than one item may be placed in a box.
2. A company has plans to modernize their Website contact centre, improve customer engagement, and gather customer insights from a large database of customer feedback. Research and recommend cloud-based AI services that can help to realize this.
3. Explain the idea of transfer learning from the perspective of a generative AI-based dialogue model.
4. Explore and mention steps to train a customized generative AI dialogue model.
   (Hint: Check out AWS Bedrock or functionally similar service from Google/Microsoft)

D. Explore and Experiment

1. Create a MNIST-like model to recognize handwritten digits from three Indian languages—Hindi, Telugu, and Bengali.
2. In Fig. 12.6, we use a simple prompt to understand MLOps from generative AI.

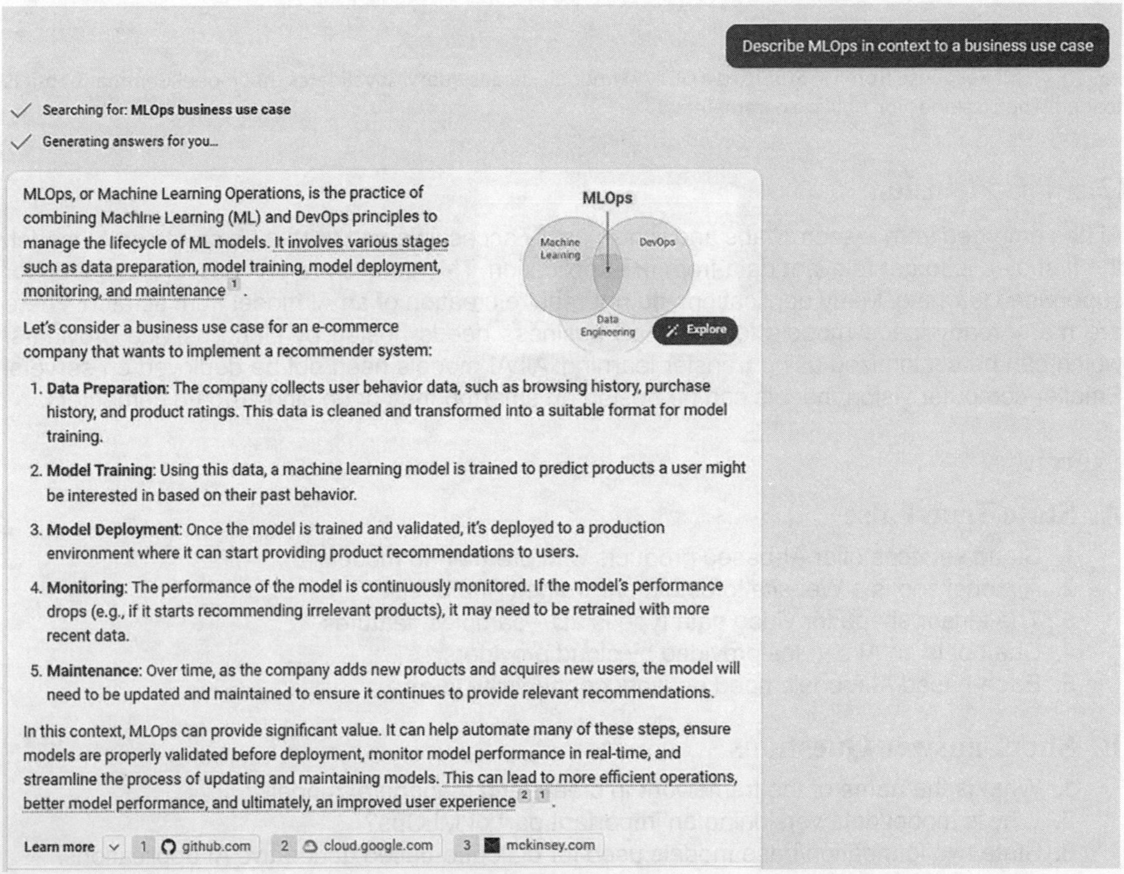

Fig. 12.6 Role of MLOps for managing lifecycle of AI models

E. Generate Use Cases based on Applying AI—Learning by Example Approach

Use Case: Applications of Generative AI in Government

Brief description: Governments across the world are overburdened and short staffed. Generative AI is a tool that can address many citizen queries using information from digital public infrastructure. Study the document mentioned in the resource and come up with a use case of how a state/central document can leverage generative AI.

Resource

Deloitte AI Institute, The Generative AI Dossier (Download 146 page PDF document)
A selection of high-impact use cases across six major industries.
https://www2.deloitte.com/us/en/pages/consulting/articles/gen-ai-use-cases.html
Nandan Nilekani, A.I. Can Be Transformational For India's Digital Public Infrastructure, July 2024, CNBC-TV18 Interview (https://www.youtube.com/watch?v=yvwoDRNuA7Q), Starting time: 5.20

Template for Creating Use Case

Define goal and purpose	Goal statement
	Identify stakeholders
	Define scope
Details to include in use case	Capture how technology helps business process
	Keep use case findings description textual, with a few simple flowcharts if needed
	Focus on describing how technology benefits the use case
Future applications	Mention any new applications that can leverage the technology used

Suggested Readings

1. An executive's guide to AI, QuantumBlack, AI by McKinsey, https://www.mckinsey.com/capabilities/quantumblack/our-insights/an-executives-guide-to-ai (accessed 24 November 2022).
2. Executive's guide to developing AI at scale, QuantumBlack, AI by McKinsey, https://www.mckinsey.com/capabilities/quantumblack/our-insights/executives-guide-to-developing-ai-at-scale#intro (accessed 24 November 2022).
3. The executive's AI playbook, QuantumBlack, AI by McKinsey, https://www.mckinsey.com/capabilities/quantumblack/our-insights/the-executives-ai-playbook (accessed 24 November 2022).

[illegible] Use Cases Based on Applying AI—Learning by Example Approach

Use Cases Applications of Generative AI in Government

Brief description: Governments across the world are [illegible] [illegible] [illegible] [illegible] [illegible] [illegible] [illegible] [illegible] [illegible] how [illegible] generative AI.

Resource:

Deloitte AI Institute. The Generative AI Dossier [illegible] [illegible] [illegible] [illegible] [illegible] [illegible] [illegible] [illegible] [illegible] [illegible] [illegible] July 2024; [illegible] [illegible] [illegible] [illegible]

Template for Capturing Use Case

[illegible]	[illegible]
[illegible]	[illegible]
	[illegible]
[illegible]	[illegible]
[illegible]	[illegible]
	[illegible]
[illegible]	[illegible]

[illegible]

1. [illegible] guide to AI [illegible] [illegible] [illegible] [illegible] [illegible]
2. [illegible] [illegible] [illegible] [illegible] [illegible] [illegible] [illegible] [illegible] 2023).
3. [illegible] [illegible] [illegible] [illegible] [illegible] November 2023.

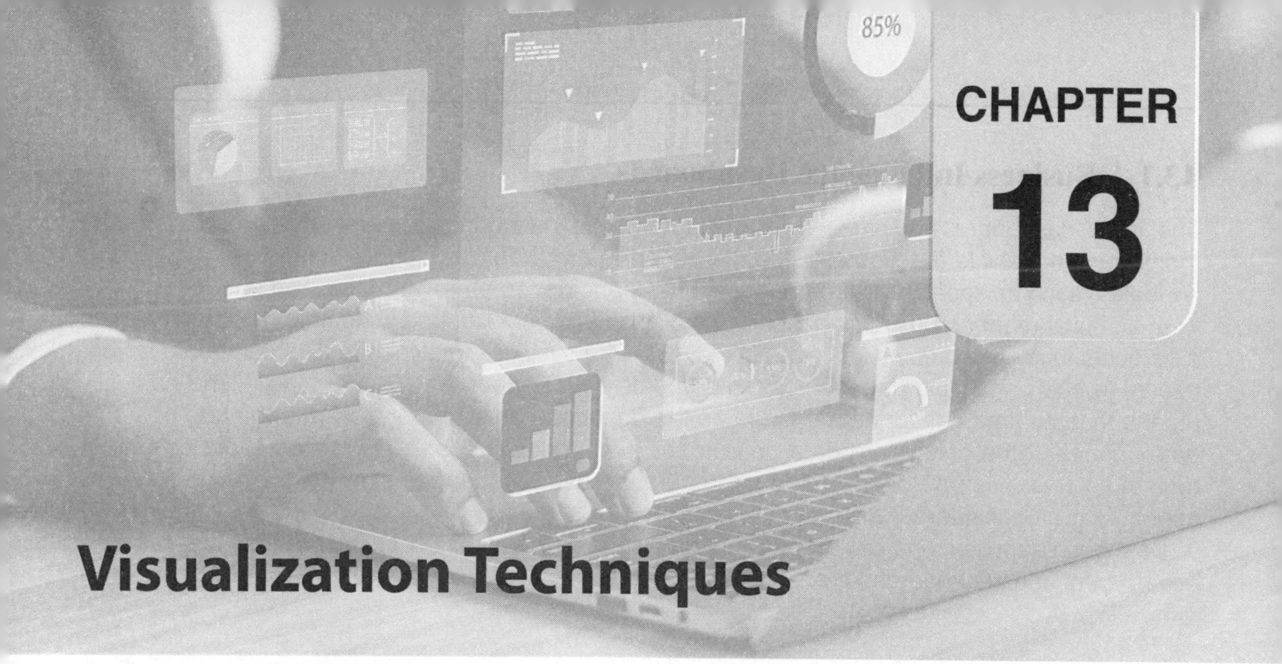

CHAPTER 13

Visualization Techniques

CHAPTER OUTLINE

13.1 Business Intelligence (BI) Dashboards
13.2 Augmented Reality (AR)
13.3 Virtual Reality (VR)

LEARNING OBJECTIVES

After reading this chapter, you will be able to:

- understand the use of dashboards to visualize key performance indicators of a business
- distinguish between augmented reality (AR) and virtual reality (VR)
- understand the use and benefits of AR and VR

Effective Management Using Visualization Techniques

They say, a picture is worth a thousand words! In business, a dynamic picture consisting of key metrics may be worth millions of dollars. It therefore makes sense to assimilate the right set of metrics for different hierarchies in a company and present it using an easy-to-understand graphical interface. There are many situations where one needs a hypothetical perspective. How would the house look if it was painted in a certain color? Or, how would the employees look if we had them wear a uniform of a particular style? A third example, can we virtually open up an equipment and demonstrate it to a technician during training? An early insight into these scenarios would help in better decision-making and learning.

13.1 | Business Intelligence Dashboards

The term 'dashboard' originates from the automobile dashboard, where drivers can view and monitor major vehicle functions via the instrument panel. Vehicle dashboards display a myriad of attributes, such as speed, low tire pressure, check engine, emergency brake, and odometer.

In a similar manner, business dashboards display key performance indicators (KPIs) relevant to a particular business process. As seen in Fig. 13.1, the business intelligence (BI) dashboard is connected to one or multiple data sources that update data periodically. The term 'real-time' basically means that the time unit for data change on the dashboard is synchronized with the rate of actual data change. If the dashboard data on outdoor temperature update 1000 times every second, it does not serve much purpose. Outdoor temperature usually changes slowly. So, an update every minute may be considered real-time.

Dashboard applications are many and diverse. Let us take a look at how businesses and government use dashboards for analysis of real-time data.

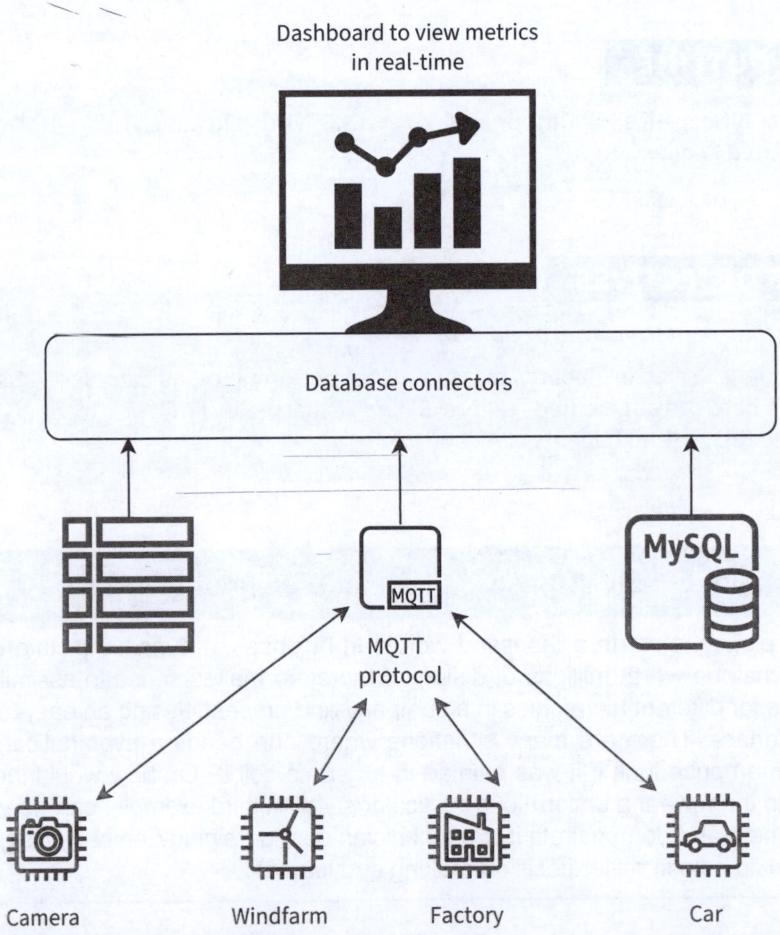

Fig. 13.1 Different data sources populating metrics of a BI dashboard

Sales and revenue The BI dashboards provide real-time insights into sales and revenue data. These dashboards can help businesses to track revenue, identify top-performing products, and monitor sales trends.

Financial These dashboards provide detailed financial analysis to help businesses make strategic decisions. Regular monitoring of expenses, cash flow, and profitability keeps businesses on track.

Marketing Thoughtfully designed dashboards provide insights into marketing campaigns, such as the number of leads generated, conversion rates, and return of investment (ROI). Periodic review of information from dashboard helps businesses optimize their marketing strategies and campaigns.

Operations Managing diverse business activities requires real-time insights into operational metrics, such as production levels, inventory management, and logistics. Insights from a dashboard help businesses to optimize their operations and improve efficiency.

13.1.1 Data Analytics for Business Dashboards

As shown in Fig. 13.1, the data used in business dashboards is often collected from multiple sources, such as internal systems, external partners, and public databases. To use databases effectively in business dashboards, the data needs to be cleaned, transformed, and modeled to make it usable for analysis. This is typically done through a process called ETL (extract, transform, and load), which extracts data from various sources, applies transformations to make it compatible with the target system, and loads it into a database. Once the data is in the database, business dashboard tools query it to generate reports, visualizations, and other analytics that help organizations to make data-driven decisions. These reports and visualizations can be customized to fit the specific needs of the organization, and can be updated in real-time to reflect changes in the underlying data.

AI models can also be used in business dashboards to provide deeper insights and automate certain aspects of the analysis. For example, machine learning algorithms can be used to detect patterns in the data, predict, and provide recommendations based on the findings. NLP is also used to enable users to ask questions in natural language and receive automated responses.

Creating a business dashboard

The process of creating a business dashboard is iterative and involves several steps. This includes defining requirements, selecting the right data sources, designing the dashboard layout, and integrating it with the data sources. Here is a general outline of the process:

Define requirements Determine what data is important for the business and what metrics or KPIs will be tracked on the dashboard. Also, consider the intended audience of the dashboard and their level of technical expertise. A dashboard meant for the VP sales may be different from the dashboard of a production supervisor.

Select data sources Identify the data sources that will be used to populate the dashboard. This may include databases, spreadsheets, APIs, or other sources of data.

Connect to data sources Connect the dashboard to the selected data sources using appropriate data connectors or APIs.

Design the dashboard Determine the layout of the dashboard, including the types of charts, graphs, and tables that will be used to display the data. Consider the colors and fonts that will be used to make the dashboard easy to read and visually appealing.

Develop the dashboard Develop the dashboard using a BI platform or dashboard builder tool. Use the chosen data sources to create the charts, graphs, and tables that will display the data.

Test the dashboard Test the dashboard to ensure that it is functioning correctly and that the data is being displayed accurately.

Deploy the dashboard Deploy the dashboard to the intended users through either a Web-based application or mobile application.

Maintain and update the dashboard Maintain and update the dashboard as needed to ensure that it continues to meet the business needs and displays relevant data.

A useful dashboard does not require constant viewing. It can also be configured to respond to specific events in the data. For example, a dashboard monitoring the temperature of a building can send out an e-mail or text alert if the temperature starts to rise or fall.

13.1.2 Visualization Tools and Databases for Creating Dashboards

There are many visualization tools to create a business dashboard. Bear in mind, it is not the tool that creates a useful dashboard. It is the KPI and right data to support the KPI that makes a useful dashboard. The bells and whistles a tool provides may not be of much use, if the underlying data and KPI are not identified correctly. Most dashboard tools enumerated below have a free evaluation version. If dashboards interest you, go ahead and try out some of these tools.

Tableau It is a widely used data visualization and business intelligence tool. The tool allows users to connect to various data sources and create interactive dashboards with drag-and-drop functionality.

Power BI A popular analytics service by Microsoft. It provides interactive visualizations and business intelligence capabilities with an interface simple enough for end users to create their own reports and dashboards.

SAP BusinessObjects Suite of BI and reporting tools that enables users to create interactive dashboards, reports, and analytics.

Domo A cloud-based BI and data visualization platform that allows users to create real-time dashboards, reports, and data visualizations.

This is not a comprehensive list of BI tools. There are several other notable BI tools, such as Grafana from GrafanaLabs and Quicksight from AWS. Most tools have many common features (such as database access and visualization), along with some features that make them different.

Another important component (besides the visualization tool) of the business dashboard is the database. There are several popular databases used for BI dashboards. Here are a few examples:

MySQL (briefly discussed in Chapter 2) It is an open-source relational database management system that is widely used for BI dashboards.

PostgreSQL It is another open-source relational database management system that is popular for BI dashboards.

Microsoft SQL Server A relational database management system developed by Microsoft. It is widely used for BI dashboards because of its integration with other Microsoft tools such as Excel and Power BI.

Oracle Database A relational database management system developed by Oracle Corporation.

Amazon Redshift AWS developed cloud-based data warehousing solution that is popular for BI dashboards.

Again, this is not a comprehensive list of popular databases used for BI dashboards. The choice of database depends on various factors, such as the size of data, the complexity of the analysis, and the budget available.

Listing 13.1 Pseudocode to connect BI visualization tool to a database

```
// Establish a connection to the database
conn = openDatabaseConnection(dbName, dbUser, dbPassword);

// Retrieve data from the database
query = "SELECT * FROM sales_data WHERE date BETWEEN :startDate
         AND :endDate";

params = {
"startDate": "2022-01-01",
"endDate": "2022-01-31"
};

results = executeQuery(conn, query, params);

// Transform the data into a format suitable for the dashboard
dashboardData = transformData(results);

// Render the dashboard using the transformed data
renderDashboard(dashboardData);

// Close the database connection
closeDatabaseConnection(conn);
```

So far, we have discussed theoretically the use of databases for creating business dashboards. Let us understand this by the help of a high-level pseudocode.

In the example pseudocode mentioned in Listing 13.1, the openDatabaseConnection function is used to establish a connection to a database with a specified name, username, and password. The executeQuery function is used to retrieve data from the database using an SQL query with specified parameters. The transformData function is used to transform the raw data into a format suitable for display on the dashboard, such as aggregating sales data by month. Finally, the renderDashboard function is used to render the dashboard using the transformed data, while the closeDatabaseConnection function is used to close the database connection once all data has been retrieved.

A working dashboard code is presented in Listing 13.2. In this script, a Pandas DataFrame is created with some sample data. Python's Dash package is used to create html page layout, dropdown menu, and a graph. When executed, a drop down menu is presented to choose the data to be plotted. The dropdown menu contains the unique city names from the DataFrame. When a city is selected from the dropdown menu, the graph updates to display the amount of each type of fruit purchased in the selected city. The Web browser is a universal option to host dashboards. Using dropdown menus the dashboard is customized for viewing specific information. You can try out this code using CENGAGE Digital App.

Listing 13.2 Web browser-based dashboard code using Python

```
import dash
import dash_core_components as dcc
import dash_html_components as html
from dash.dependencies import Input, Output
import pandas as pd

# Create a pandas DataFrame for illustration
df = pd.DataFrame({
   'Fruit': ['Apples', 'Oranges', 'Bananas', 'Apples', 'Oranges', 'Bananas'],
    'Amount': [400, 111, 277, 234, 489, 555],
    'City': ['Mumbai', 'Delhi', 'Mumbai', 'Mumbai', 'Mumbai', 'Delhi']
})

# Initialize the Dash app
app = dash.Dash(__name__)

# Define the layout of the app
app.layout = html.Div([
    dcc.Dropdown(
        id='city-dropdown',
        options=[{'label': i, 'value': i} for i in df['City'].unique()],
        value='Mumbai'
    ),
    dcc.Graph(id='graph')
])

# Define the callback to update the graph
@app.callback(
    Output('graph', 'figure'),
    [Input('city-dropdown', 'value')])
def update_graph(selected_city):
    filtered_df = df[df['City'] == selected_city]
    figure = {
        'data': [{
            'x': filtered_df['Fruit'],
            'y': filtered_df['Amount'],
            'type': 'bar'
        }],
        'layout': {
           'title': 'Amount of Fruit purchased in {}'.format(selected_city)
        }
    }
    return figure

# Run the app
if __name__ == '__main__':
    app.run_server(debug=True)
```

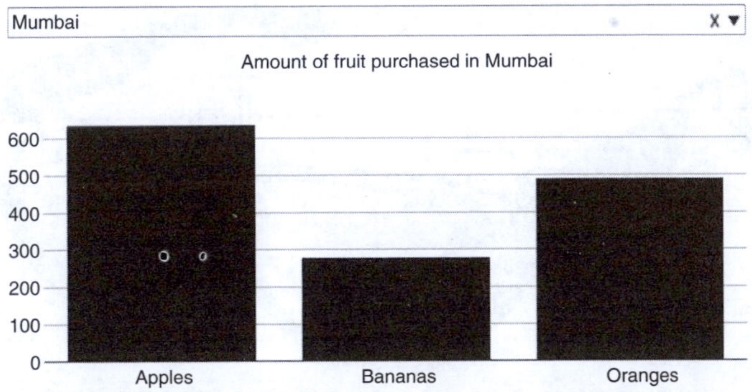

13.2 | Augmented Reality

Merriam Webster[1] defines *augmented* as 'made greater, larger, or more complete'. This is very close to what we accomplish by augmented reality (AR). AR overlays virtual elements on top of the real world to experiment with different ideas. This could be taking a picture of a real house and showing how it would look when painted in different colors.

AR owes a lot of its success to AI. An AI image segmentation algorithm identifies the pixels of the house in the picture and then the AR algorithm only recolors those pixels for visualizing the house in different colors. This may be a trivial example, but it shows the possibility of how AR is used to answer many what-if questions. AR combines the digital world with real-world elements. It works on both mobile devices and desktops.

Let us now consider a case, where a technician is troubleshooting a machine at a remote location. They use the camera on their smartphone to livestream what they see to a service helpdesk of the equipment manufacturer. The service helpdesk annotates or augments their livestream image with suggestions of what action needs to be taken. Again, this does not sound very high-tech but it saves a trip of a specialized technician to the site to rectify it. This is a cost-effective AR application, which does not need any specialized devices.

Google Glass[2] was among the first AR devices that caught the world's attention. It is able to gather information from the Internet or relevant servers and displays it on a prism projector, using an image size of 640×360 pixels. Besides this, Google Glass has other features. It has wireless connectivity, inertial sensors, among others,[3] and also includes a camera, a touchpad, a microphone, a speaker, and a battery. The camera takes pictures and records video, and the touchpad allows users to control the device by swiping and tapping. The microphone and speaker are used for voice command and feedback. Google has halted software updates for Google Glass enterprise edition from 30 September 2023.[4] Even though Google glasses have been discontinued, similar devices from Meta and other companies are available.

The wearer of Google Glass accesses different resources (using data connectivity) needed to perform a task. It also frees up both hands of the wearer to carry out work. Using Google Glass, a technician has access to relevant datasheets, video, and manuals for carrying out repairs. Figure 13.2 shows and lists different features of Google Glass.

---

[1]Definition of augmented, https://www.merriam-webster.com/dictionary/augmented (accessed 25 November 2022).

[2]Google Glass, https://www.google.com/glass/start/ (accessed 25 November 2022).

[3]Google Glass technical specifications, https://www.google.com/glass/tech-specs/ (accessed 25 November 2022).

[4]Google Glass enterprise edition FAQ, https://support.google.com/glass-enterprise/customer/answer/13417888?hl=en&ref_topic=13418584&sjid=6010667465124470930-NA (accessed 10 June 2023).

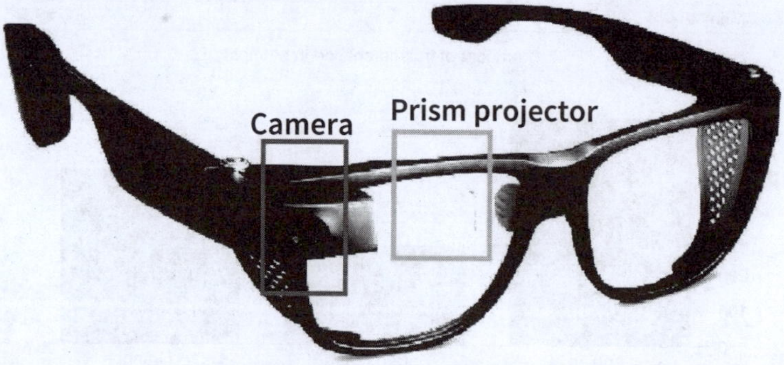

Fig. 13.2 Google Glass

Along these lines, several applications have benefitted from AR.[5] These include the following:

- Construction and logistics to quickly log and get meaningful information
- Field service technicians to access remote datasheet or resources
- Doctors to enable fast access of patient records

13.3 | Virtual Reality

Virtual reality (VR) is complete immersion in a new, virtual world by use of a computer-generated simulation. This is quite different from AR, which has elements of the real physical world that get augmented with additional data.

To enter a VR world, it is necessary to use a specialized headset device. The device covers both eyes to project a simulated image. Some devices allow a see-through feature, which accesses cameras mounted on the hardware to perceive the external real world. This hybrid combination (virtual reality along with real world) is known as *mixed reality* (MR). Microsoft HoloLens[6] projects holograms to enable interaction with the virtual world. It uses the real-world user input, such as hand and eye tracking, along with spatial mapping to correctly project the hologram at the right location.

The uses and advantages of VR include the following:

- Immersive learning using computer-simulated environment
- Enable trainee doctors to train on surgical techniques
- Allow technicians to train on complex machine repair and understand inner working of a machine

Considerable software effort is needed to create a convincing VR or MR environment. Several new entrants in the marketspace of AR, VR, and MR devices include Meta and Apple. Companies that make hardware for VR, AR, and MR devices also provide developer tools to create custom environments.

[5]Google Glass, case studies, https://www.google.com/glass/case-studies/ (accessed 25 November 2022).
[6]Microsoft HoloLens, https://www.microsoft.com/en-us/hololens (accessed 25 November 2022).

13.4 | Conclusion

In this chapter, we discussed business data visualization using dashboards. There are multiple software tools available to get data from different sources such as databases and spreadsheets. Designing the layout and content of a dashboard with the right KPIs is an important aspect of visualization. Augmented, virtual, and mixed realities are visualization techniques that hold a lot of promise. AR overlays virtual elements on top of the real world, while VR is completely computer created. Customization of visualization techniques for a particular application (e.g., explaining the working of an aircraft engine) requires significant domain knowledge along with simulation expertise.

Exercises

A. State True/False

1. VR is based completely on the real world.
2. Google Glass is an example of a VR device.
3. Creating realistic customized VR environments is a trivial job.
4. Google Glass has data connectivity for fetching relevant information.
5. AR applications may or may not require special hardware.

B. Short-answer Questions

1. List a few data sources that feed BI dashboards.
2. What are the two commonly used deployment platforms for dashboards?
3. Provide examples of how businesses use dashboards.
4. Name the dashboard (data visualization) tool offered by Microsoft.
5. Come up with an application that uses a time-series database for a dashboard.

C. Long-answer Questions

1. Identify a use case and explain how AR can improve the functioning or efficiency of an existing business process.
2. Study and make a report of case studies mentioned for Google Glass and Microsoft HoloLens.
3. Create an event-based dashboard using Openweather (https://openweathermap.org/weather-dashboard). Configure the dashboard to send an e-mail when it is likely to rain in a city of your choice. You will have to register on the Website to create an event.
4. Mention ways how a factory maintenance manager can use event-based dashboards.
5. Come up with a business application for Ray-Ban Meta smart glasses. You can learn about the Ray-Ban Meta smart glasses here—https://www.meta.com/smart-glasses/.

D. Explore and Experiment

1. Download a business dashboard[7] tool and install it on your desktop computer. Connect and display values from different data sources (Excel sheets, databases) on graphical widgets of the dashboard.
2. Create a dashboard for the production supervisor, sales manager, and the CEO of a widget-making company. The dashboard should display relevant KPI's for each individual.

[7]Microsoft Power BI, https://powerbi.microsoft.com/en-us/ (accessed 5 June 2023).

3. In Fig. 13.3, we ask generative AI to create a dashboard by querying data from a database. Here, the SQL query obtains total revenue data by product category. Use the generated code along with the code in Listing 13.2 to display bar charts using SQL-queried data.

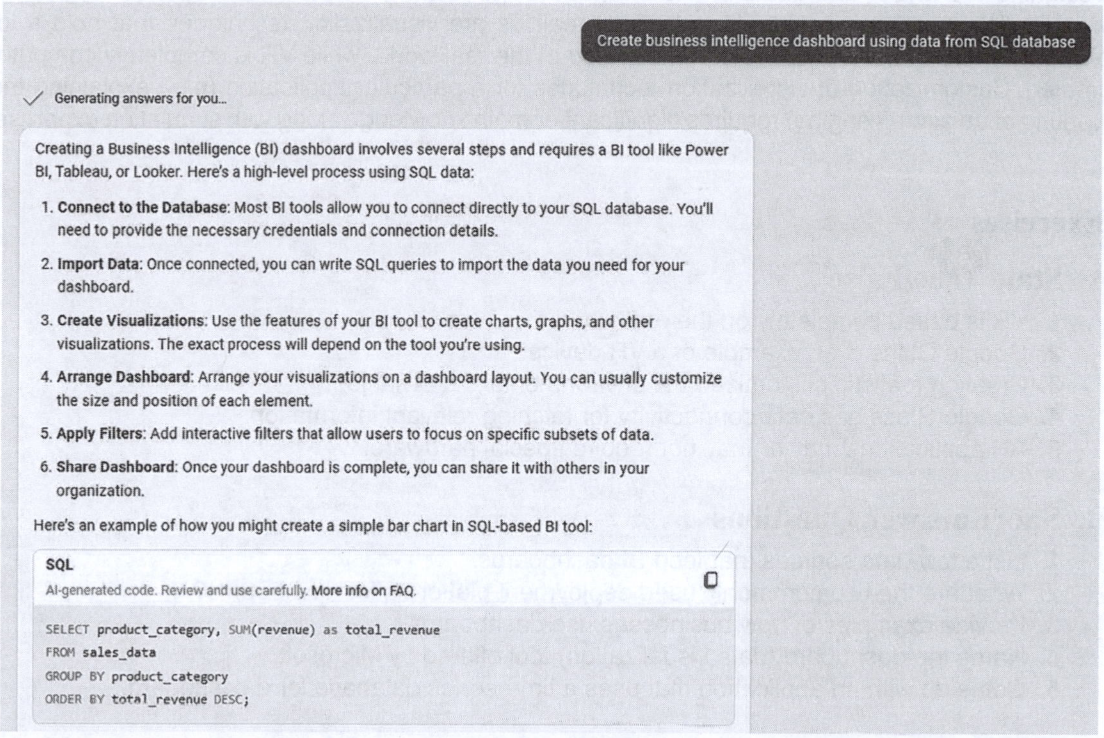

Fig. 13.3 Basic steps from generative AI on creating a BI dashboard

4. Retail supermarkets have lots of items on their shelfs. It is difficult for a store to update price labels of large number of items. Stores such as Walmart now use digital labels that look like paper labels, but can be updated electronically using connection such as Bluetooth. Get to know more about these labels by viewing this resource—https://www.pbs.org/newshour/show/as-more-retailers-embrace-digital-price-tags-on-shelves-how-will-they-be-used

E. Generate Use Case for BI Dashboard

Use Case: Viewing Air Pollution on a Dashboard

Brief description: Due to rising industrialization, air pollution has become a cause of concern in many parts of the world. Environmentalists across the world keep an eye on how various pollution parameters are changing hourly. The website mentioned in the resource provides an example of air pollution dashboard. Try out and study the dashboard and then create a use case using the points mentioned in the table below. Use your best judgement to fill in details about the use case.

Resource

Air quality index dashboard, https://www.aqi.in/dashboard/india.

Template for Creating Use Case on Air Pollution Dashboard

Define goal and purpose	Goal statement
	Identify stakeholders
	Define scope
Details to include in use case	Capture how technology helps business process
	Keep use case findings description textual, with a few simple flowcharts if needed
	Focus on describing how technology benefits the use case
Future applications	Mention any new applications that can leverage the technology used

Suggested Reading

1. Cole Nussbaumer Knaflic, *Storytelling with Data*: *A Data Visualization Guide for Business Professionals*, 1e, Wiley.

CHAPTER 14

Edge Computing

CHAPTER OUTLINE

14.1 Advantages of Edge Computing
14.2 Synergy Between Edge and Cloud
14.3 Edge-Based Gateways and Servers
14.4 Gateway Types and Configurations
14.5 Use Cases of Edge Computing

LEARNING OBJECTIVES

After reading this chapter, you will be able to:

- understand the need for edge computing
- distinguish between edge servers and edge IoT gateways
- realize the need for IoT gateway standards
- apply edge computing and IoT to (two) case studies

Effective Management Using Edge Computing

Many applications, such as retail stores, factory floors, and healthcare providers require low-latency, local data processing. Cloud computing does not meet these requirements and on-premise solutions may be overkill. These applications stand to benefit from edge computing. Contemporary applications of edge computing leverage AI models at the edge. AI at the edge refers to the deployment of artificial intelligence algorithms or models on devices that are close to the data source. The data processing and analysis are performed on the edge devices themselves, without the need to transfer the data to a centralized server for processing. This allows for faster analysis, lower latency, and reduced bandwidth requirements.

14.1 | Advantages of Edge Computing

Edge computing is carried out close to the point where data is generated. This results in data privacy, low-latency time for data processing, and less need to ferry large volumes of data to a cloud computer. You may be tempted to equate edge computing with on-premise computing. But edge computing is different. Edge computing can be carried out on a mobile device[1] for continuous glucose monitoring (CGM) of diabetes patients (Fig. 14.1). The device provides an alert when the glucose level crosses the predefined threshold limits. The CGM device gives feedback to inject insulin[2] as and when needed. All this is performed at the edge without the need for internet connectivity.

To get a greater understanding of the usefulness of edge computing, let us continue our discussion about its use in healthcare.[3] In a healthcare environment, edge computing provides multiple advantages as enumerated below:

- Use of real-time imaging and analytics to improve triaging and clinician support.
- Decentralize internal data to reduce vulnerability to external cyberattacks.
- Comply with data locality and privacy requirements of patient data.
- Use low-latency edge devices to optimize collection and transfer of data.
- Accelerate data analytics and intelligence by bringing it closer to the source.

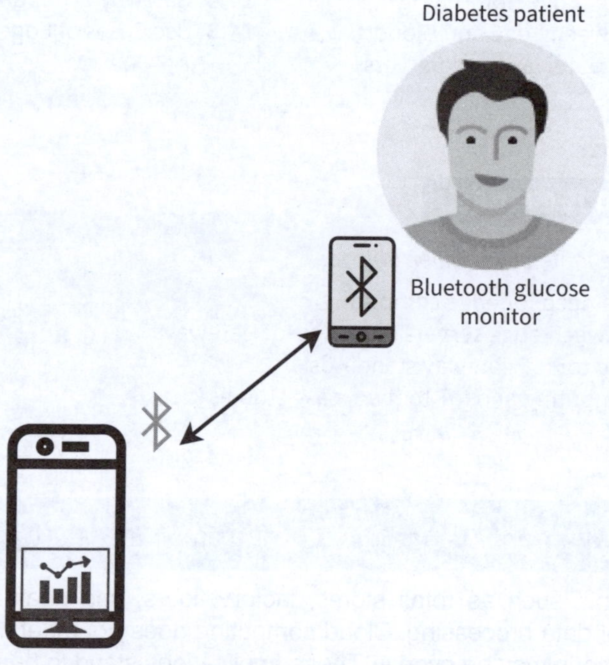

Fig. 14.1 Edge monitoring of glucose level and automated insulin delivery

[1]Dexcom CGM, https://www.dexcom.com/en-us/g7/how-it-works (accessed 9 June 2023).
[2]Omnipod, https://www.omnipod.com/what-is-omnipod/what-is-pod-therapy (accessed 10 June 2023).
[3]PwC, Edge computing in healthcare, https://www.pwc.in/assets/pdfs/emerging-tech/edge-computing-in-healthcare.pdf (accessed 9 June 2023).

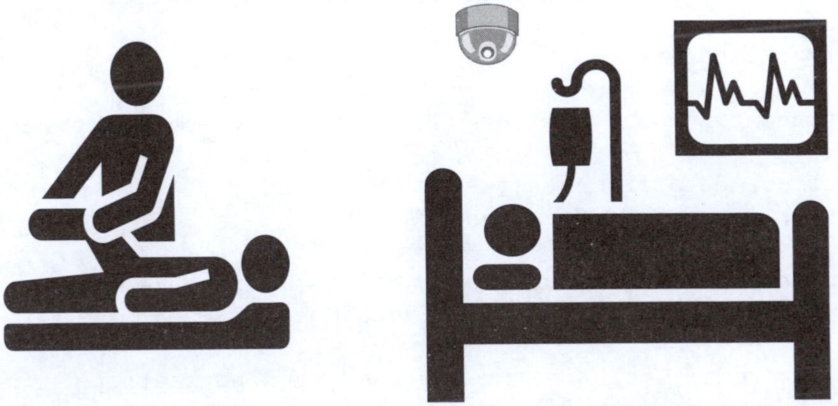

Fig. 14.2 Monitoring patient movement and position using edge computing

To further illustrate the advantages of edge computing, let us consider a large hospital setup, where it is difficult to individually monitor the movements of convalescing patients. Sending live camera feed to a remote data center comes with challenges such as patient confidentiality, network bandwidth constraints and higher latency. Edge-based analytics at the patient's bedside (Fig. 14.2) using camera data addresses the concerns mentioned above and also issues timely alerts. A pretrained Human pose detection AI model (https://docs.ultralytics.com/tasks/pose/) helps detect the movement of patients.

14.2 | Synergy Between Edge and Cloud

Even though edge-based systems do not require internet connectivity to function, most edge-based systems have some kind of connectivity to a cloud-based computer. This connectivity is used to relay information from the edge that may be useful for data analytics. In context to our earlier discussion of the glucose monitoring system, a doctor may get information from a patient's edge device (smartphone) if the glucose level continues to stay low for long periods of time. The important point to understand here is that the edge device does not send large volumes of continuous data to the cloud. It sends filtered data indicating outlier conditions or periodic status updates. If the smartphone were to be in the airplane mode, the glucose monitoring system continues to work. The pseudocode for an edge device to connect with cloud services is mentioned in Listing 14.1. It reads data from sensors, makes a prediction using a pretrained model (to determine if a patient's changing glucose levels need attention) and communicates it to the cloud. The cloud computer can subsequently disseminate this information to concerned users.

This type of edge device-to-cloud interaction is used in various business scenarios, such as predictive maintenance for industrial equipment or real-time monitoring of perishable goods in transit.

14.3 | Edge-Based Gateways and Servers

Edge-based servers and gateways form the first line of computing close to where the data is generated or needed. The software running in the servers at the edge may either be standalone or a

Listing 14.1 Pseudocode for communicating filtered data from edge to cloud

```
// Initialize edge device and connect to cloud services
initialize_edge_device()
connect_to_cloud_services()

// Loop to continuously collect data and make predictions
while true:
    // Collect data from sensors at the edge
    data = collect_data_from_sensors()

    // Preprocess data before feeding into machine learning model
    preprocessed_data = preprocess_data(data)

    // Make prediction using pre-trained machine learning model
    prediction = make_prediction(preprocessed_data)

    // Send prediction to cloud services for further processing and
    // analysis
    send_prediction_to_cloud(prediction)

    // Check for any updates from cloud services
    check_for_cloud_updates()
```

version of the software running on the cloud.[4] Most edge compute devices do have some form of internet connectivity, but they would continue to function even if the connectivity was lost.

We start our discussion with an edge sensor mounted on a farm. This edge device is likely to be solar powered, have rudimentary processing power, and limited data acquisition and communicating abilities. These edge devices serve as useful data gatherers when spread across an area. Local wireless networks that connect these distributed devices together represent a wireless sensor network (WSN).

The WSNs are the base of IoT. They form a network of devices to which IoT system can connect to. The purpose of an IoT gateway module is to extend the reach of the WSNs to the internet. Contemporary IoT gateways are expected to perform several functions. These include the following:

1. Protocol translation: Zigbee, Bluetooth low energy (BLE), Thread, Message Queuing Telemetry Transport (MQTT), Constrained Application Protocol (CoAP), Hypertext Transfer Protocol (HTTP).
2. Storage: Store data values of WSN nodes.
3. Local controller: Respond to the local network events in real-time.
4. Operate offline: Continue operation in the absence of cloud connectivity.
5. Reduce the cost of transporting data: Local processing or filtering of data.
6. Provide secure communication with the cloud computer.

Figure 14.3 illustrates data flow in an IoT setup. Gateways are the first point of contact for the edge devices.

[4] AWS Outposts, https://aws.amazon.com/outposts/ (accessed 7 December 2022).

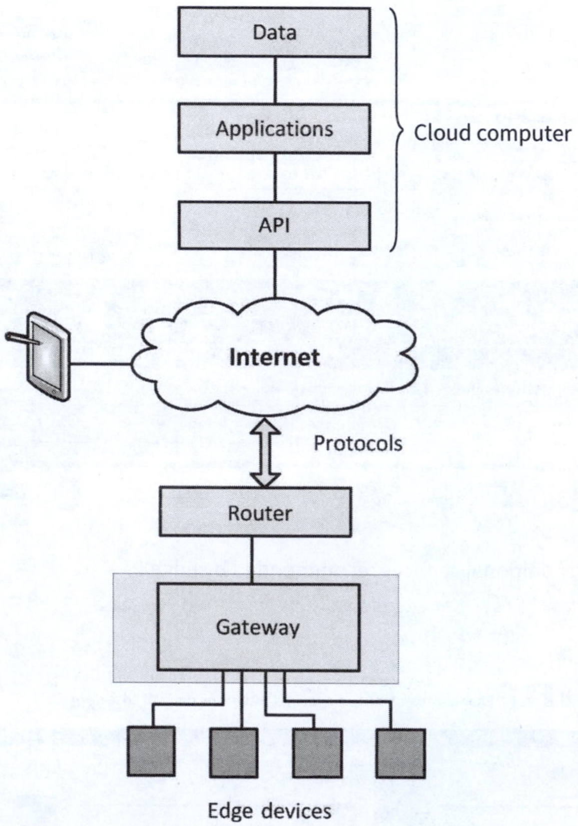

Fig. 14.3 Role of the gateway in the IoT. The gateway communicates with edge devices and can act as a local controller before sending the data to the cloud

14.4 | Gateway Types and Configurations

IoT and edge computing work together. For many applications, the computing ability of the gateway is adequate. Most real-world IoT gateways use Linux OS. Linux provides the necessary communication drivers and also the possibility to program the gateway to perform local control actions. Gateways can be programmed for control action using different programming languages, such as Python, Node JS, and C/C++. The EdgeXFoundry™project is a vendor-neutral open-source project hosted by The Linux Foundation. It builds a common open framework for IoT edge computing. That allows connectivity for existing and upcoming standards.

Gateway Services as Envisaged by EdgeX

Devices or things at the bottom of the IoT pyramid need to support different edge protocols. Taking a cue from the computer motherboard—where slower I/O devices form the south side of the processor chipset and faster memory devices form the north side of the chipset—EdgeX has categorized *things/devices* as *southbound* and *infrastructure connectivity* as *northbound.* As shown in Fig. 14.4, EdgeX requires certain core services, such as storage of core and metadata. It also lists supporting services, such as rules engine, scheduling, and logging. Many of these features are usually part of a cloud platform-based IoT service.

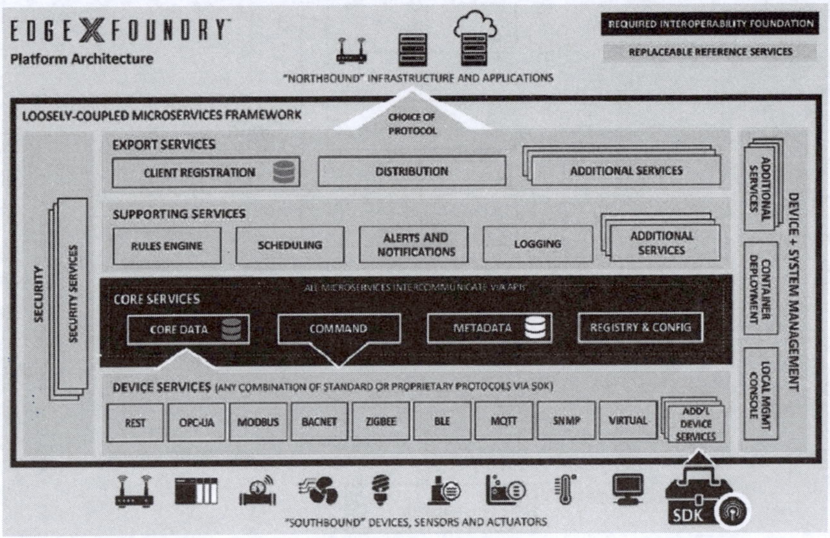

Fig. 14.4 Gateway core and additional services recommended by EdgeX

Source: EdgeX Foundry, available at https://www.edgexfoundry.org/ (accessed 7 December 2022).

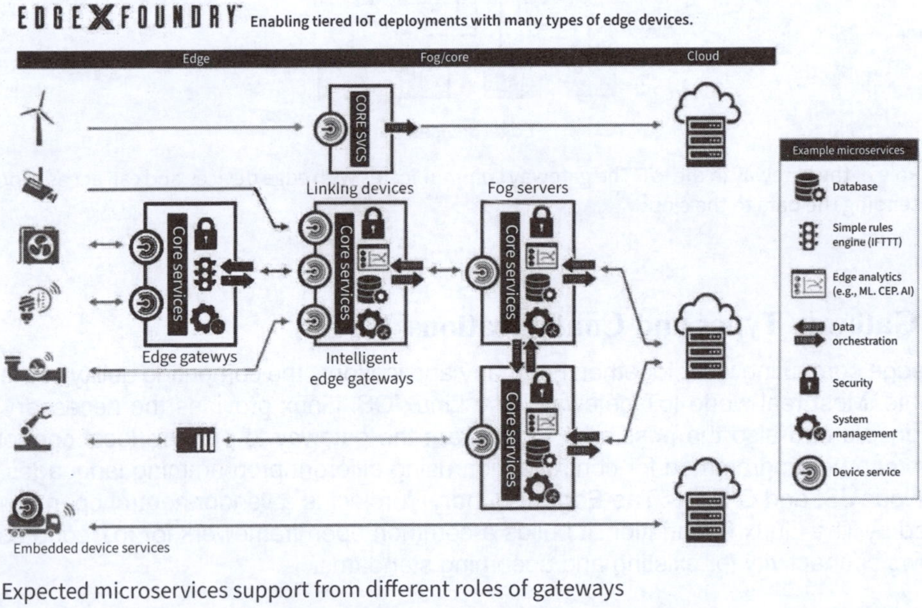

Fig. 14.5 Expected microservices support from different roles of gateways

Source: EdgeX Foundry, available at https://www.edgexfoundry.org/ (accessed 31 August 2018).

Gateways offer different configurations when connecting a thing/device to the cloud server. EdgeX provides recommendations on gateways' microservices for various connectivities. Some of these are shown in Fig. 14.5 and are as follows:

1. Edge gateway (core services, security, simple rules engine, system management).
2. Linking devices (core services).

3. Intelligent edge gateways (core services, security, database, edge analytics, and system management).
4. Fog servers: More than one connected to each other (same functionality as the intelligent edge gateway but with connectivity to the cloud server).

Fog servers (as seen in Fig. 14.5) are at times also referred to as edge servers. The core services of these edge servers include edge analytics using machine learning and AI algorithms, local data storage, system management, and secure data connectivity (if needed to communicate with cloud or external systems). These servers may contain multiple CPUs and GPUs. Most machine learning and computer vision-based AI algorithms are locally hosted on edge servers.

In contrast, edge gateways are lightweight in terms of their functionality and onboard computing resources. Their main job is to act as a messenger for data or perform very simple computing. Since they have a smaller form factor, gateways can be positioned very close to the data source or process. Recent advances in edge-based computer vision AI models have made it possible to host these models on resource-constrained gateways.

14.5 | Use Cases of Edge Computing

Applications are a good way to explain the utility of technology. We will discuss three examples where edge computing is useful.

- Monitoring pollution level of water bodies
- Assisting in public safety
- Tracking traffic violations

14.5.1 Monitoring Pollution Level of Water Bodies

Our first use case is river pollution monitoring. Figure 14.6 shows the IoT water quality monitoring stations along the length of a river. A close-up of one monitoring station is shown in Fig. 14.7. If multiple edge-sensing devices along a certain stretch of the river indicate an increase of pollution levels; this information is shared with local law enforcement. On the other hand, if an increase in water turbidity is seen during rainy season, an alert will not be generated. The edge device generates alerts in real-time by analyzing water quality patterns and outliers. A requirements table for river quality monitoring edge device, mentioning data analytics, communications and sensor interfacing is shown in (Table 14.1).

Fig. 14.6 Several edge devices communicating water quality data to central and regional computers

Fig. 14.7 Actionable real-time data provided by the internet of things to deter industries from polluting rivers

Table 14.1 Edge computing requirements for river water monitoring

	Water Quality Monitoring Solution
Data Analytics	Storage—Save time-series information of water parameters Analyze—Changes in water parameters in different stretches of the river Actionable items—Intimate authorities if water quality deteriorates drastically in a certain section of the river
Gateway/Communication	Cellular/LoraWAN—Outdoor location and the large distance between two edge devices
Edge Device	Sensors—pH, Dissolved Oxygen (DO), temperature, Biochemical Oxygen Demand (BOD) Edge processing—Check sensor connectivity Actuator—Sound local alarm if water quality deteriorates

Each edge device is programmed to operate as per local water quality code. In case of India, the recommended water thresholds for different usage of water is categorized by the Central Pollution Control Board (CPCB) and are given as follows:[5]

1. Fit for irrigation (when meeting criteria limits of pH 6 to 8.5 and electrical conductivity $< 2000\ \mu$m/cm).
2. Fit for the propagation of wildlife and fisheries (when meeting criteria limits of dissolved oxygen DO $\geq$ 4 mg/l, pH 6.5–8.5, and free ammonia $\leq$ 1.2 mg/l).
3. Fit for drinking water (raw) sourcing for conventional treatment [when meeting criteria limits of biological oxygen demand, biochemical oxygen demand (BOD) $\leq$ 3 mg/l, DO $\geq$ 4 mg/l, and pH 6–9].
4. Fit for bathing (when meeting criteria limits of BOD $\leq$ 3 mg/l, DO $\geq$ 5 mg/l, and pH 6.5–8.5).

River water is used for one or more purposes along its path. For a given stretch of the path, water quality edge device can sound a local alarm, if the water is unsuitable for its intended use.

14.5.2 Smart Streetlights for Public Safety

The second edge computing example is from the city of San Deigo (California, USA). In 2017, the city of San Diego installed and tested a smart streetlight platform with several sensors (see Fig. 14.8). The streetlight enclosure includes Bluetooth and WiFi radios; two high definition (HD) cameras; two acoustic sensors; and environment sensors—temperature, pressure, humidity, vibration, and magnetic field. An LTE cellular network is used to transport the collected data to the cloud.[6] As seen in Fig. 14.8, this edge computing setup is capable of:

- Detecting seismic activity
- Monitoring weather conditions
- Crowd and traffic monitoring and parking assistance
- Gunshot detection

Most edge computing systems are reconfigurable using over-the-air updates (OTA). An acoustic sensor used for gunshot detection can be repurposed for detecting events, such as car crashes,

[5]Central Pollution Control Board, Water Quality Criteria, available at https://cpcb.nic.in/wqm/Designated_Best_Use_Water_Quality_Criteria.pdf (accessed 7 December 2022).

[6]Tekla S. Perry, 'San Diego Installs Smart Streetlights to Monitor the Metropolis,' *IEEE Spectrum*,1 January 2018, available at https://spectrum.ieee.org/computing/it/san-diego-installs-smart-streetlights-to-monitor-the-metropolis (accessed 7 December 2022).

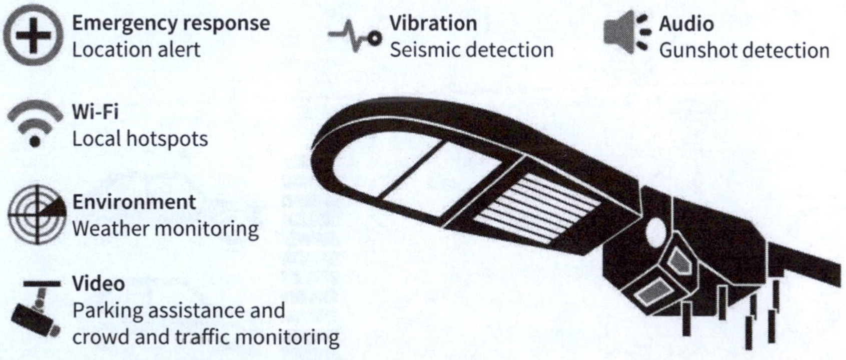

Fig. 14.8 Smart city solution by GE CityIQ

Source: Intel, *Improve Quality of Life and Enable Cities to Thrive with Current by GE City IQ*, available at https://www.intel.com/content/dam/www/public/us/en/documents/brief/ge-cityiq-business-brief.pdf, accessed on December 7, 2022.

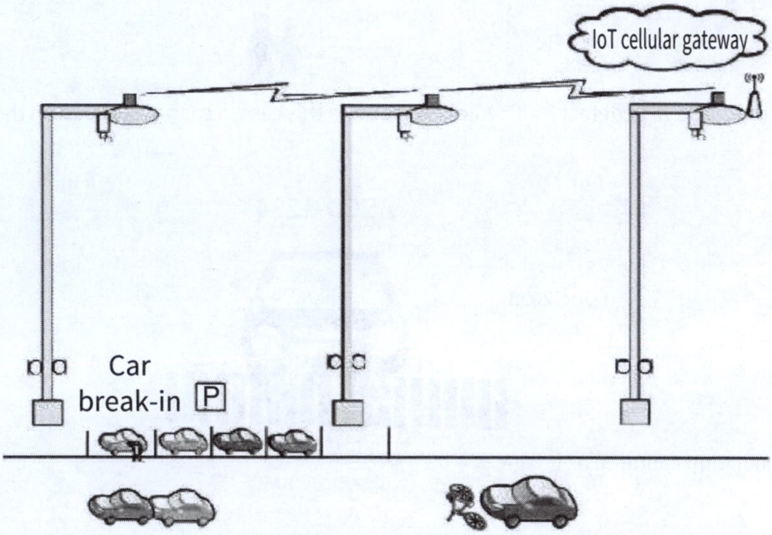

Fig. 14.9 Street scene with smart street lights for monitoring crashes and car break-ins

car vandalism, and hit-and-run occur on the streets (Fig. 14.9). It is often difficult for the police to catch the wrongdoers as the culprits flee the scene. A camera mounted on different street poles can capture the street view from multiple angles for the authorities to analyze. A trigger signal, such as an audio sensor, alerts the authorities and also communicates to the neighboring street poles to save and time-stamp the video data. Data from numerous streetlights is communicated to the cloud for centralized analysis. If for any reason, data connectivity is unavailable, the data is stored locally at the edge and transferred when connectivity is restored.

14.5.3 Edge Computing for Traffic Violations

Many countries across the world are using edge technology to detect and act on traffic violations. Figure 14.10 shows a scenario where a car stops on the pedestrian zebra crossing. An edge

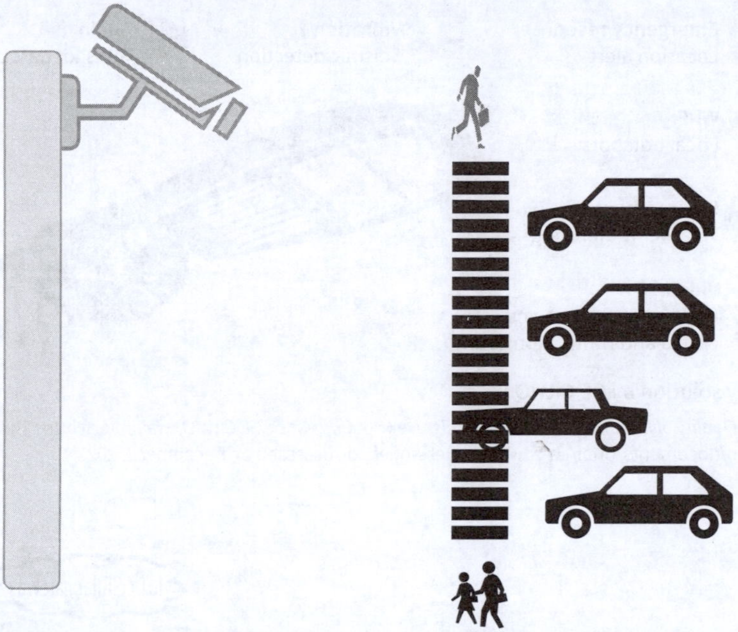

Fig. 14.10 Edge-based system to detect traffic rule violations. In this case, a car has stopped on the pedestrian zebra crossing

Fig. 14.11 Traffic violation captured as image

camera with a license plate reader captures a picture of the car along with a date and time-stamp (Fig. 14.11). It sends the picture of the violation to a cloud computer (remember edge-cloud synergy), which looks up the address through the car's registration details and issues a fine notice to the person who owns the car.

You may ask, what is the role of edge computing in this application. There are three important ways edge computing is contributing:

- **Less network bandwidth usage** No need to stream video data from multiple cameras to a cloud computer.
- **Detection of traffic violation done locally** An operator is not required to manually parse hours of video data to look for a violation.
- **Privacy of traffic camera data** Video stream from cameras cannot be hacked, as video is not transferred.

These examples show the use of edge computing.

14.6 | Conclusion

In this chapter, we discussed edge computing devices for applications that need low-latency and local data processing. These edge devices could either be a server or a gateway. For retail shops, hospitals and factory floors, a server is more suitable. The Linux Foundation EdgeX project provides a template for gateways which is useful for remote locations (such as river water quality monitoring, smart street lights and acting on traffic violations) with power and space constraints.

Exercises

A. State True/False

1. Edge servers require internet connectivity to function.
2. An edge Gateway has fewer computational resources than an edge server.
3. Computer vision AI models can be hosted on an edge gateway device.
4. River water monitoring has edge computing to alert locals if water is unfit for bathing or drinking.
5. Smart city edge computers can store unlimited amounts of video data.

B. Short-answer Questions

1. Explain why streetlight poles are preferred for mounting edge computing devices in a smart city application.
2. Give an example of how edge computing can be used for citizen safety on public transport.
3. Explain why edge computing was used for Chandrayaan-3's lander and rover.
4. How does edge computing reduce the workload of operators who are tasked to look for traffic violations?
5. Find out the specifications and cost of an edge gateway device using Google search.

C. Long-answer Questions

1. Enumerate services that need edge computing (based on low-latency and local processing of data requirement) for a retail store and a hospital.
2. For river water monitoring and street light use case, enumerate what data analytics needs to be shared with cloud (and city authorities), based on conditions determined by edge compute.

D. Explore and Experiment

1. Read about the precision farming application[7] where herbicide is only sprayed on weeds and not crop (Fig. 14.12). Comment on use of edge computing for this application.
2. Step up a Raspberry Pi single-board computer to perform edge computing. Connect a webcam (such as a Logitech C270) to the USB port of the Raspberry Pi and run a computer vision classification model. Write a Python code to send an e-mail whenever a certain object of interest is detected. See the Digital App for sample code to get you started.

[7] John Deere See and Spray, https://www.deere.com/en/sprayers/see-spray-ultimate/ (accessed 10 June 2023).

Fig. 14.12 Use of computer vision at the edge to distinguish weeds from crop

3. Generative AI creates a pseudo code to explain the role and use of Edge Gateways in an edge computing application in Fig. 14.13.
4. Fast food chains are implementing edge computing at many of their stores. Read this news report on how edge computing is used by these stores - https://www.wsj.com/articles/mcdonalds-gives-its-restaurants-an-ai-makeover-2134f01e

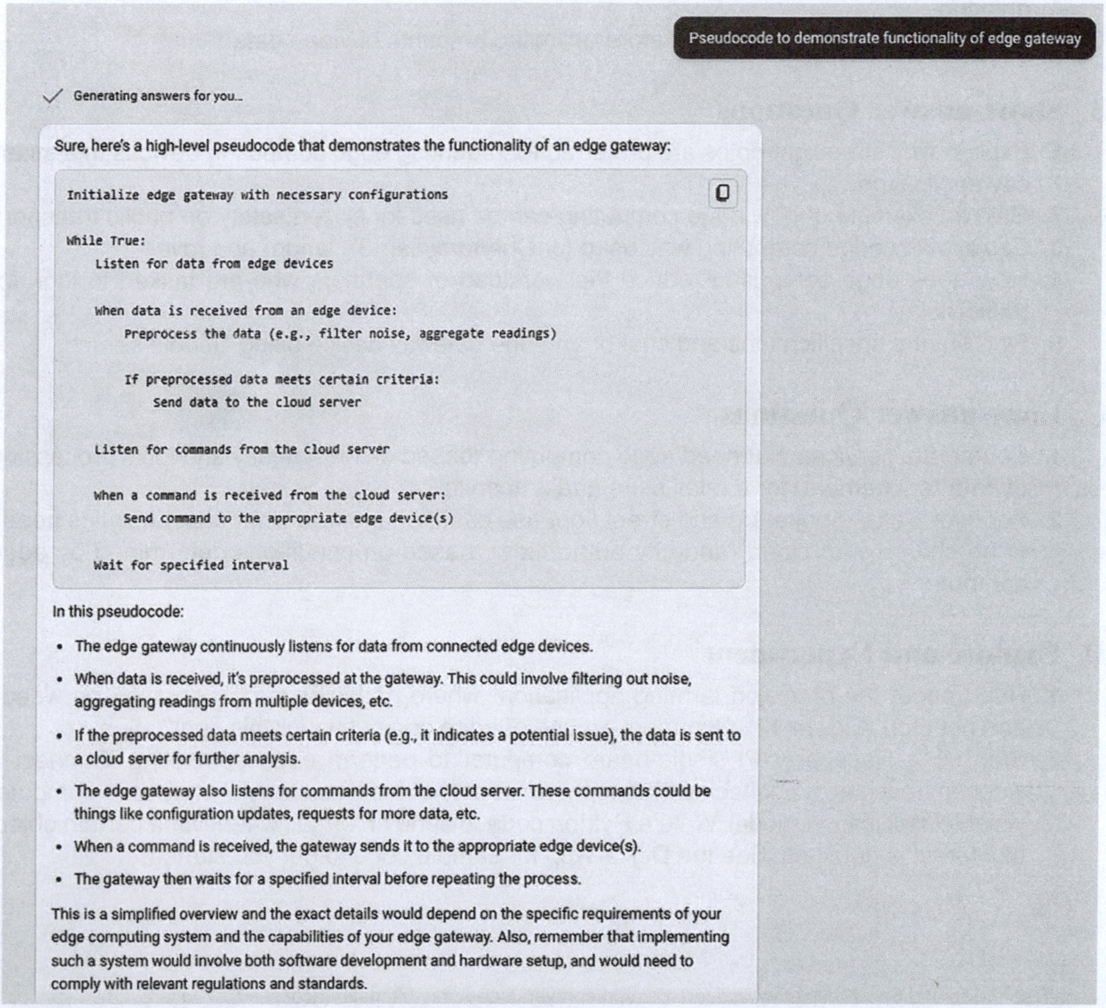

Pseudocode to demonstrate functionality of edge gateway

✓ Generating answers for you...

Sure, here's a high-level pseudocode that demonstrates the functionality of an edge gateway:

```
Initialize edge gateway with necessary configurations

While True:
    Listen for data from edge devices

    When data is received from an edge device:
        Preprocess the data (e.g., filter noise, aggregate readings)

        If preprocessed data meets certain criteria:
            Send data to the cloud server

    Listen for commands from the cloud server

    When a command is received from the cloud server:
        Send command to the appropriate edge device(s)

    Wait for specified interval
```

In this pseudocode:

- The edge gateway continuously listens for data from connected edge devices.
- When data is received, it's preprocessed at the gateway. This could involve filtering out noise, aggregating readings from multiple devices, etc.
- If the preprocessed data meets certain criteria (e.g., it indicates a potential issue), the data is sent to a cloud server for further analysis.
- The edge gateway also listens for commands from the cloud server. These commands could be things like configuration updates, requests for more data, etc.
- When a command is received, the gateway sends it to the appropriate edge device(s).
- The gateway then waits for a specified interval before repeating the process.

This is a simplified overview and the exact details would depend on the specific requirements of your edge computing system and the capabilities of your edge gateway. Also, remember that implementing such a system would involve both software development and hardware setup, and would need to comply with relevant regulations and standards.

Fig. 14.13 Functionality inside an edge gateway (such as EdgeX) for supporting an edge application

E. Generate Use Case for Edge Computing—Learning-by-Example Approach

Use Case 1: Edge Computing for Detecting Weeds and Targeted Spray of Herbicide

Brief description: Many agronomists around the world have expressed concern over excessive use of herbicides. With the help of edge computing, precision agriculture is now a reality. The See and Spray Machine from John Deere uses multiple cameras to detect weeds and then produces a directed spray of herbicide on the weed. The edge computing setup is part of a boom, carried by a tractor. Read about the precision farming application (from the resource) where herbicide is only sprayed on weeds and not crops (Fig. 14.12). Generate a use case of edge computing for this application using the template below.

Resource

John Deere, See & Spray Ultimate: Targeted In-crop Spraying Technology
https://www.deere.com/en/sprayers/see-spray-ultimate/

Use Case 2: Solar-powered edge monitoring of public spaces

Brief description: Public safety is an important part of any smart city. If any untoward incident is detected in a public area such as a park, parking lot or a tourist location, the incident is detected and video evidence is captured. Stampedes can be avoided if cameras can detect and report large crowd formations. Take a look at the products and services described in the two websites below and put together a use case for enforcing public safety using solar-powered edge devices.

Resources

https://www.lvt.com/
https://www.pelco.com/cameras/lpr (for license plate reader)

Template for Creating Use Case

Define goal and purpose	Goal statement
	Identify stakeholders
	Define scope
Details to include in use case	Capture how technology helps business process
	Keep use case findings description textual, with a few simple flowcharts if needed
	Focus on describing how technology benefits the use case
Future applications	Mention any new applications that can leverage the technology used

Suggested Reading

1. Colin Dow, Hands-On Edge Analytics with Azure IoT: Design and develop IoT applications with edge analytical solutions including Azure IoT Edge, Packt Publishing.

[illegible]

Keywords

[illegible]

[illegible]

[illegible]	[illegible]
[illegible]	[illegible]
[illegible]	[illegible]
[illegible]	[illegible]
[illegible]	[illegible]

Suggested Reading

1. [illegible]

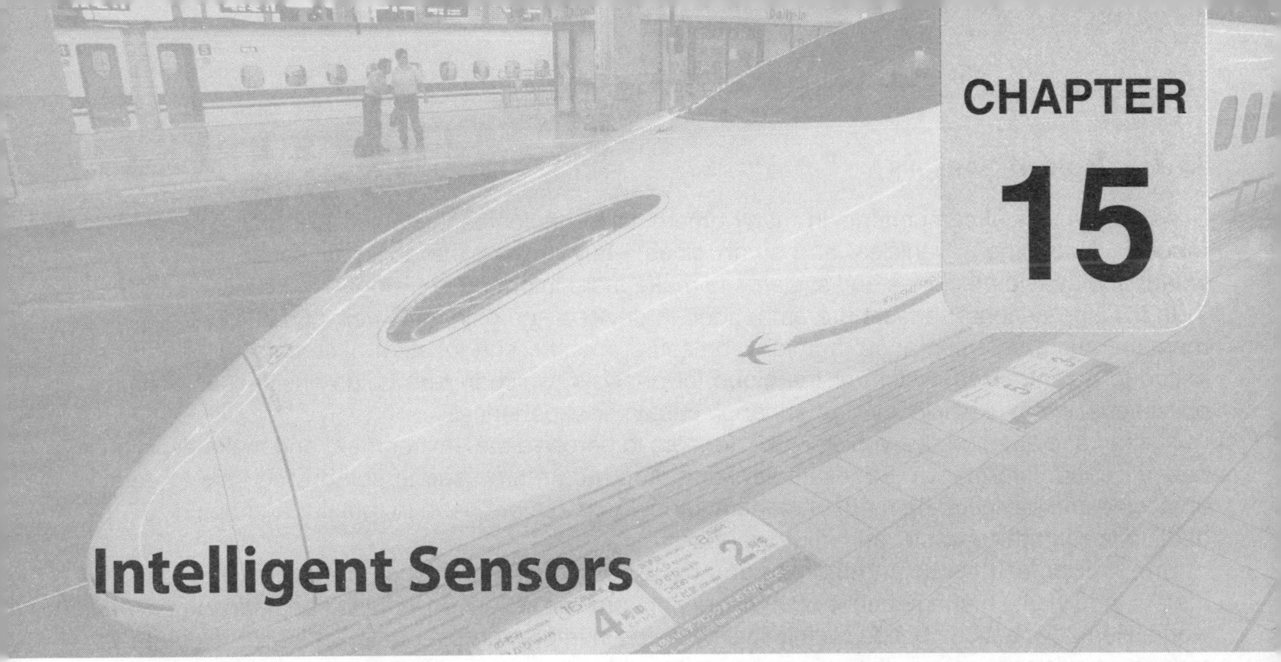

CHAPTER 15

Intelligent Sensors

CHAPTER OUTLINE

LEARNING OBJECTIVES

After reading this chapter, you will be able to:

- be conversant with different kinds of available sensors
- understand how applications use sensors
- develop an intuitive idea of using sensors in different scenarios

Effective Management Using Intelligent Sensors

Sensors are the eyes and ears of any process. They assist in monitoring and capturing information and events. The quick response (QR) code presents information about a vendor's bank details, which expedites digital transactions. Similarly, cameras and microphones are two ubiquitous sensors that help in several business processes. AI-enabled intelligent sensors are able to extract more insights from data provided by traditional sensors. Basic knowledge about sensors opens up possibilities for their use in new applications.

15.1 | Role of Sensors

Sensors are critical components in many emerging technologies, including IoT, digital payments, robotics, autonomous vehicles, and smart cities. They provide the ability to sense the physical world, and enable machines and systems to make more informed decisions.

In IoT applications, sensors are embedded in devices and objects to collect data on their environment, such as temperature, humidity, pressure, motion, and location. This data is then transmitted to a centralized system or the cloud for analysis, which in turn helps businesses optimize operations, improve efficiency, and enhance customer experiences.

Robots and autonomous vehicles use sensors to perceive the environment and make decisions based on that information. For example, lidars and radars are used in self-driving cars to detect obstacles and navigate the road. In manufacturing, sensors are used to monitor and optimize production lines, reduce waste, and improve quality.

Smart cities use sensors to monitor and manage infrastructure, such as traffic lights, parking meters, and waste management systems. Sensors provide insight on what is happening in the real world. Remedial actions based on this insight helps in improving the quality of life for residents by reducing traffic congestion, improving air quality, and enhancing public safety.

15.2 | Sensor Types

Sensors help us perceive the external world. There are sensors that help us measure and quantify temperature, humidity, acceleration, distance…..and many more parameters. Like most technology discussed in this book; low-cost, microelectromechanical systems (MEMS)-based sensors have become available in the last two decades.

Sensors are largely used in smartphones to measure motion, orientation, and various environmental conditions. The broad category of physical sensors in a mobile phone include[1] motion sensors that measure acceleration forces and rotational forces along three axes. Typical motion sensors are accelerometers and gyroscopes. The next category is position sensors that measure the physical position of a device. This includes proximity, GPS, orientation sensors, and magnetometers.

Besides physical sensors, there are software-defined or synthetic sensors. These sensors use inputs from one or more sensors to get a derived value. Take a look at the list of sensors mentioned in Table 15.1. If you wish to try out any sensor mentioned in the table, download a sensor app on your mobile phone and experiment with it. In addition to the sensors listed in Table 15.1, most contemporary smartphones have GPS for location awareness.

Table 15.1 Sensor types supported by the android platform[1]

Sensor	Type	Description	Common Uses
Accelerometer	Hardware	Measures the acceleration force in m/s^2 that is applied to a device on all three physical axes (x, y, and z), including the force of gravity.	Motion detection (shake, tilt, etc.)
Ambient temperature	Hardware	Measures the ambient room temperature in degrees Celsius (°C). See note below.	Monitoring air temperatures

(Contd)

[1]Android sensors overview, https://developer.android.com/guide/topics/sensors/sensors_overview (accessed 10 December 2022).

Table 15.1 *(Continued)*

Sensor	Type	Description	Common Uses
Gravity	Software or Hardware	Measures the force of gravity in m/s^2 that is applied to a device on all three physical axes (x, y, z)	Motion detection (shake, tilt, etc.)
Gyroscope	Hardware	Measures a device's rate of rotation in rad/s around each of the three physical axes (x, y, and z)	Rotation detection (spin, turn, etc.)
Light	Hardware	Measures the ambient light level (illumination) in lx	Controlling screen brightness
Linear acceleration	Software or Hardware	Measures the acceleration force in m/s^2 that is applied to a device on all three physical axes (x, y, and z), excluding the force of gravity	Monitoring acceleration along a single axis
Magnetic field	Hardware	Measures the ambient geomagnetic field for all three physical axes (x, y, z) in μT (micro Tesla)	Creating a compass
Orientation	Software	Measures degrees of rotation that a device makes around all three physical axes (x, y, z)	Determining device position
Atmospheric Pressure	Hardware	Measures the ambient air pressure in hPa or mbar	Monitoring air pressure changes
Proximity	Hardware	Measures the proximity of an object in cm relative to the view screen of a device. This sensor is typically used to determine whether a handset is being held up to a person's ear	Phone position during a call
Relative humidity	Hardware	Measures the relative ambient humidity in percent (%)	Monitoring dewpoint, absolute, and relative humidity

Sensors mentioned in the above table may vary from one phone to another. Table 15.1 should give you an idea of commonly available sensors.

15.3 | Putting Sensors to Use

As an exercise, try to find out sensors hiding in plain sight around you. There are many sensors around us. Sensors inside our home (temperature sensors inside air conditioners and refrigerators, carbon monoxide sensor in smoke alarms, and so forth), sensors on the street (pollution, air quality...), sensors in the car (speed, fuel level...) and inside buildings. Let us talk about some frequently used sensors along with a few applications.

15.3.1 Quick Response (QR) Code

The most ubiquitous sensor that you are likely to encounter is the Quick Response (QR) code. QR codes are two-dimensional barcodes that can be scanned with a smartphone camera and store information like URLs, contact information, and other data. Scan the QR code in Fig. 15.1 with your smartphone to determine the text message it contains.

Let us briefly enumerate some applications where QR codes are typically used:

Advertising and marketing QR codes are used for advertising and marketing purposes, allowing businesses to promote their products and services with a simple scan.
Payments Used to make mobile payments, allowing customers to pay for goods and services using their smartphones.
Inventory management Manage inventory by tracking the movement of products and ensuring that the right products are in the right place at the right time.

Fig. 15.1 QR code containing a text message

This list of QR code applications is just the tip of the iceberg. These codes can be used for embedding information using an easy to create and read process. Check out the explore and experiment section of this chapter to create your own custom QR codes.

15.3.2 Global Navigation Satellite System (GNSS) Receiver

The next sensor in our list is the global navigation satellite system (GNSS) receiver. It helps with navigation and tracking of goods. The sensor is embedded in cars, phones, ships, airplanes, cellular towers, and drones and is commonly referred to as the global positioning system (GPS) device. If this sensor were to fail, many vehicles would come to a halt. You must have observed that Google Maps relies on the location or GPS sensor. To understand more about the output from a GPS receiver, let us review some definitions from a geography class. The GPS receiver output is in terms of latitude and longitude. The equator divides the Earth into the North and South hemispheres and serves as a reference for determining latitude. The Prime Meridian divides the earth along the east and west directions and passes through Greenwich, England (Fig. 15.2). It serves as a reference

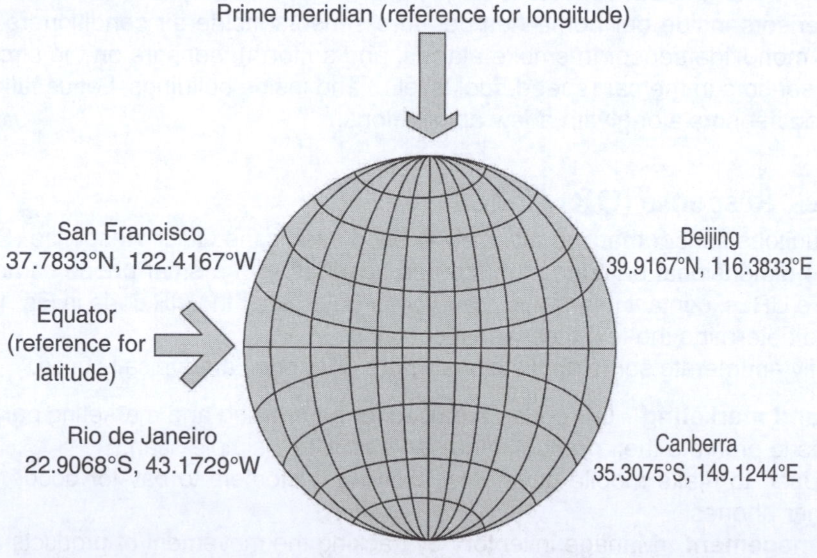

Fig. 15.2 The global positioning system (a) review of latitude and longitude

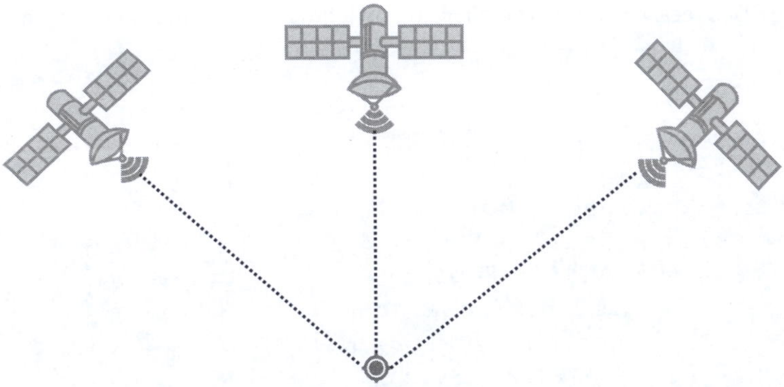

Fig. 15.2 Cont'd (b) Three satellites to determine location

Table 15.2 Data received as part of recommended minimum GPS/Transit data

$GPRMC,	220516,A,5133.82,N,00042.24,W,173.8,231.8,130694, 004.2,W*xx

Table 15.3 Data packets received from GPS

Packet Identity	Value	Explanation
1	220516	Time Stamp in universal time coordinated (UTC)
2	A	Validity—A-ok, V-invalid
3	5133.82	Latitude of fix (DDmm.mm)
4	N	North/South
5	00042.24	Longitude of fix (DDDmm.mm)
6	W	East/West
7	173.8	Speed over ground in knots
8	231.8	True course
9	130694	Universal time (UT) Date Stamp-dd/mm/yy
10	004.2	Magnetic variation degrees
11	W	East/West
12	*70	Checksum

for longitude. To get a intuitive feel of GPS coordinates, check out the latitude and longitude of four major cities in different parts of the globe.

A GPS receiver also obtains information about position, velocity, and time (pvt). This is embedded inside a data frame as shown below. The data frame needs to be parsed to obtain useful information. Table 15.2 describes the significance of each value in the data package. Values in the data packet are separated by a comma, commonly referred to as comma-separated values or CSV. The string GPRMC specifies the data frame uses the recommended minimum specific GPS/Transit data format.

Parsing a GPS data packet is possible using Python string functions. The code below is used to parse the data string (using Table 15.3) and print out values of latitude, longitude, date, and time from the data frame.

Listing 15.1 Parsing a GPS receiver string to obtain values of latitude, longitude, date, and time

```
#!/usr/bin/python3
import serial,time
ser = serial.Serial('/dev/ttyUSB0',9600, timeout=1)
while True:
             x = ser.read(1000)
             pos1 = x.find("$GPRMC")
             pos2 = x.find("/n",pos1)
                     loc = x[pos1:pos2]
                     gps_data = loc.split(',')
             if gps_data[2] == 'V':
                       print ('No location found')
             else:
                       print ("Latitude =" + gps_data[3] +
                       gps_data[4])
                       print ("Longitude =" + gps_data[5] +
                       gps_data[6])
                       print ("UTC Time =" + gps_data[1])
                       print ("UT Date =" + gps_data[9])
             time.sleep(5)
```

Explanation of the Python global positioning system data parsing code

The Python code reads GPS data every 5s, as shown in Listing 15.1. This is carried out using the Python *time.sleep(5)* function within the while True loop. Serial data from the GPS is read into variable **x**–1000 bytes at a time. Variable *pos1* uses the Python string find (*x.find*) method to determine the position of header value $GPRMC from the 1,000 bytes that were read. Similarly, variable *pos2* determines the position of the end-of-line character *(/n)*. The variable *loc* forms a data frame consisting of one valid GPS set of values. Finally, *gps_data* is formed by splitting the data frame using a comma as the separator. Before decoding values from the *gps_data* frame (or Python list), we check to see the validity of the data frame by comparing the value of item 2 in the list with "V." Once we know that the data is valid, we go ahead and print the corresponding items from the *gps_data* list with their descriptions. Appendix A on Python demonstrates two string methods—upper and replace. The code in Listing 15.1 shows the use of two additional methods—find and split.

There are Python libraries that help parse GPS strings, such as the discussed National Marine Electronics Association (NMEA) string. The code in Listing 15.1 serves as an example on use of Python string methods to extract relevant information from text.

15.3.3 Radio Frequency Identification (RFID)

Next on our list of sensors is the radio frequency identification (RFID) sensor. Unlike a GPS receiver that is used outdoors; an RFID tag is affixed to an object and is used to track assets. There are two types of RFID tags: passive and active type. In a passive RFID tag, the RFID scanner or reader provides energy to read the information. While in an active RFID tag, the tag is usually powered by a battery and transmits its data. The data stored on a sensor tag could be information about a library book, details of an asset, or the balance amount to pay toll charges.

Some examples of RFID applications include:

Retail Sewn-in or attached RFID tags to expensive garments or electronic products in a retail store. It prevents shoplifting. If a person walks out with an item containing an activated tag, it sounds an alarm at the exit of the store.

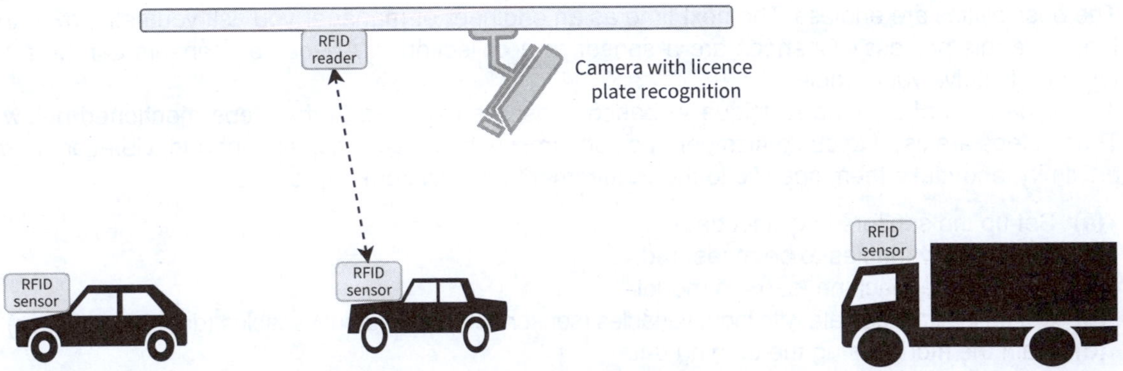

Fig. 15.3 Managing toll collection using RFID and computer vision

Transportation and logistics Permanently attached RFID tags containing information about an asset. In the railroad industry, RFID tags can be mounted on locomotives, rolling stock or any other asset that has been cataloged and needs to be identified later.

Toll charges for bridges, highways In California (specifically San Francisco Bay Area), an active RFID toll tag is used.[2] The lane equipment reads the tag information and the number of axles on your vehicle. This information determines the correct toll and deducts the amount from your account balance. The time, date, and location are collected as well. In India, a passive RFID tag is used to make toll payments.[3] In both cases, these RFID tags allow a customer to drive through toll plazas, without stopping to make toll payments.

We will delve into how FasTrak works in some detail. FasTrak is an electronic toll collection system used on most tolled bridges, lanes, and roads in California. FasTrak uses radio frequency identification (RFID) technology to allow drivers to pay tolls without stopping. Take a look at Fig. 15.3 to understand the setup. A driver purchases a FasTrak transponder from a participating vendor or retail location and registers it, using their vehicle's license plate number. The transponder, which contains a small RFID chip, is attached to the inside of the vehicle's windshield. When the vehicle approaches a toll plaza, sensors mounted above the road read the transponder and automatically deduct the toll amount from the driver's prepaid FasTrak account. If the driver does not have a transponder or their account does not have sufficient funds, cameras capture an image of the vehicle's license plate and a toll invoice is mailed to the owner of the vehicle. In the backend, the system looks up the address of the owner using the license plate and motor vehicle registration records. In this application, we see how FasTrak (and other similar systems) uses RFID and cameras to reduce congestion and save time for drivers by eliminating the need to stop and pay tolls at toll plazas.

15.4 | Artificial Intelligence (AI) Enabled Sensors

Intelligent or smart sensors are traditional sensors with improved functionality. A small camera with a people-sensing artificial intelligence (AI) model becomes a smart sensor, when it is able to turn off a TV when no one is watching or when the person watching it falls asleep. A similar people-sensing algorithm is used to open doors or turn on/off air conditioners in meeting rooms to conserve energy.

[2]What is a toll tag (or transponder?) and how does it work? Fastrak, https://www.bayareafastrak.org/en/support/fastrak-basics-faq2.shtml (accessed 10 December 2022).

[3]National Electronic Toll Collection (NETC) FASTag, https://www.npci.org.in/what-we-do/netc-fastag/product-overview (accessed 10 December 2022).

The possibilities are endless. The next time as an engineer or manager you ask yourself, how can I improve this process? Chances are a sensor or a collection of AI-enabled sensors can be put together to solve your problem.

The process of creating a unique AI-based sensor is captured in the steps mentioned below. These steps are used to customize generic sensors, such as cameras, microphone, vibration, and proximity, and make them specific to the requirements of a system or process.

- **(a)** Set up the sensors to collect data.
- **(b)** Define the variables to be measured.
- **(c)** Initialize the machine learning model.
- **(d)** Set up the training data with input variables (sensor data) and output variables (desired outcomes).
- **(e)** Train the model using the training data.
- **(f)** Test the model using test data to ensure it is accurately predicting outcomes.
- **(g)** Deploy the model to the sensor system to continuously analyze data in real-time.
- **(h)** Implement a feedback loop to refine the model over time.
- **(i)** Use the model's predictions to make decisions or trigger actions based on the analyzed sensor data.

For many applications, multiple sensors are needed to get an accurate understanding of the environment. A good example is the autonomous vehicle. Most cars use cameras, lidars, and ultrasonic sensors to map the surroundings. This multi-sensor approach is known as sensor fusion. The AI-based sensor we discussed uses data from each sensor as a feature and then finds out the right weightage needed from each sensor to create a custom sensor. The pseudocode (Listing 15.2) describes how values from three sensors are read and then processed by the AI model to take action.

Listing 15.2 Pseudocode to illustrate use of sensor fusion in an autonomous vehicle

```
# Initialize sensors
sensor1 = Sensor1()
sensor2 = Sensor2()
sensor3 = Sensor3()

# Initialize fusion algorithm
fusion_algo = FusionAlgorithm()

# Define variables for storing sensor data
sensor1_data = []
sensor2_data = []
sensor3_data = []

# Start sensor data collection
while True:
    # Collect data from Sensor 1
    sensor1_reading = sensor1.read()
    sensor1_data.append(sensor1_reading)

    # Collect data from Sensor 2
    sensor2_reading = sensor2.read()
    sensor2_data.append(sensor2_reading)
```

Listing 15.2 *(Continued)*

```
    # Collect data from Sensor 3
    sensor3_reading = sensor3.read()
    sensor3_data.append(sensor3_reading)

    # Fuse sensor data using the fusion algorithm
    fused_data = fusion_algo.fuse(sensor1_data, sensor2_data,
                                  sensor3_data)

    # Process the fused data using an AI algorithm
    ai_algo = AIAlgorithm()
    result = ai_algo.process(fused_data)

    # Take action based on the AI algorithm's result
    car = Car()
    car.move(result)
```

In this pseudocode, the sensors are initialized and the fusion algorithm is defined. The sensor data is collected continuously and stored in separate lists. Sensor data is fused using the fusion algorithm, and the resulting data is processed using an AI algorithm. The final result is then used to take action, such as moving a car (Fig. 15.4a). An alternative approach would be to train the AI model using sensor data directly (Fig. 15.4b) and have the model assign weights to each sensor to meet the desired outcome. All sensors need to be calibrated prior to use.

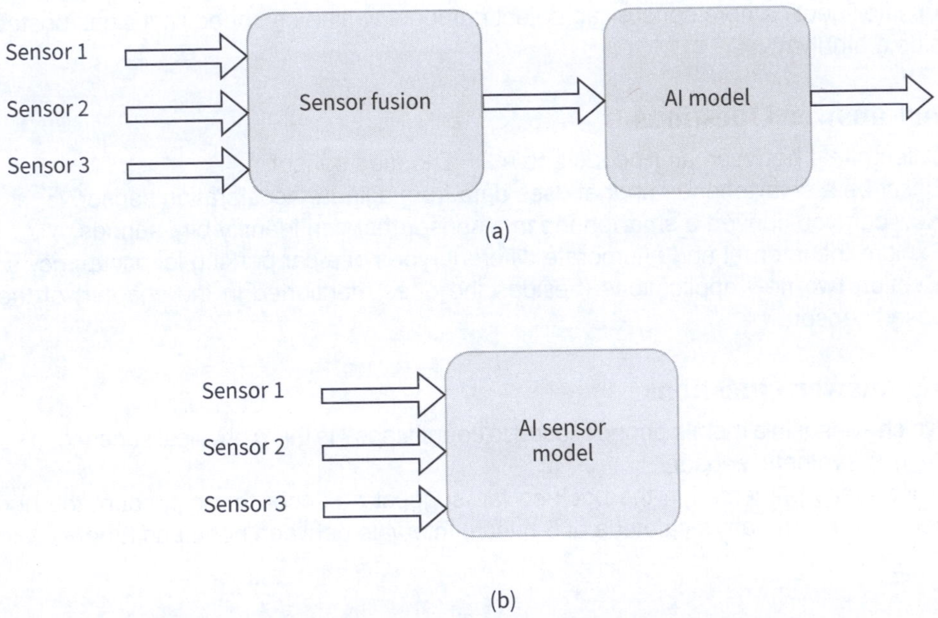

Fig. 15.4 (a) Sensor fusion and AI model as separate entities (Listing 15.2); (b) AI sensor model

Let us end this chapter with an example. There is a logistics company that wishes to rate their package delivery drivers on their safe driving skills. Frequent hard braking is not desirable, but one needs to consider that sometimes traffic or road conditions may force the driver to do so. A time-stamped dashboard camera video superimposed with accelerometer data can quickly determine the cause of hard braking. The data from the road facing camera and the accelerometer sensor when fused together, creates a smart sensor that can tell if the driver was following the vehicle in the front too closely or had to brake to avoid a collision due to a car that abruptly changed lane.

15.5 | Conclusion

We briefly discussed different kinds of sensors available today. One can experiment with these sensors using an app on a mobile phone. RFIDs based sensors are emerging as a popular sensor to track different kinds of physical assets. They are also used for contactless collection of toll charges. On the other hand, QR codes have revolutionized digital payment. More recently, the use of AI has opened up new possibilities for using conventional sensors in novel ways. A traditional vision sensor's usefulness is increased by connecting its output to a post-processing algorithm—such as a computer vision AI model.

Exercises

A. State True/False

1. Most smartphones have an accelerometer sensor.
2. RFID sensor is used only for detecting theft of expensive material in a retail store.
3. AI-enabled sensors can be customized for various applications.
4. An accelerometer is used to determine a crash, hard acceleration, or hard braking.
5. An intelligent camera sensor can detect numbers written on speed limit signs posted alongside a highway.

B. Short-answer Questions

1. Differentiate between a QR code and a RFID-based sensor.
2. Describe a smartphone app that uses data from a linear acceleration sensor.
3. How can you convert a smartphone to a sensor that can identify bird sounds.
4. Explore the internet and enumerate different types of a car parking lot occupancy sensor.
5. Mention two new applications (besides the ones mentioned in the chapter) of the RFID-based sensor.

C. Long-answer Questions

1. Which sensor in a mobile phone is used to count steps? Is this a physical sensor or a software-defined synthetic sensor?
2. Using ideas presented in the book so far, suggest a sensor that can count the number of people in a company's cafeteria at 5-minute intervals between noon and 2 pm.

D. Explore and Experiment

1. Create your own QR codes. Creating a QR code is a straightforward process. Here are the steps to create a basic QR code:
   1. Open a Web browser and go to a QR code generator Website such as https://www.qr-code-generator.com/ or https://www.the-qrcode-generator.com/.
   2. Select the type of content you want to encode, such as a URL, text, e-mail, or phone number.
   3. Customize the design of the QR code, such as changing the colors or adding a logo. Generate the QR code.
   4. Download the QR code image to your computer.
   5. Once you have the QR code image, you can use it in your business in various ways, such as on marketing materials, products, or business cards.
2. Some time back, I took a flight from Ahmedabad to Varanasi. The GPS receiver and compass were active in the flight mode. During my trip, I took a screenshot of my position. Use the screenshot coordinates from Fig. 15.5 to determine my location on the map of India.

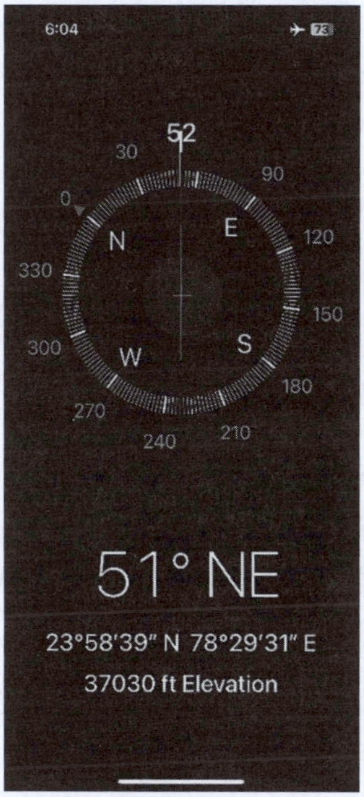

Fig. 15.5 Use of smartphone GPS and altitude sensor to determine location and height during air travel

3. For our Generative AI example, we ask it to generate a Python code to parse GPS data string (Fig. 15.6). Contrast this code with the code given in Listing 15.1. Instead of parsing the GPS string using string methods, the pynmea2 package is used. Try out the code and see if it works!

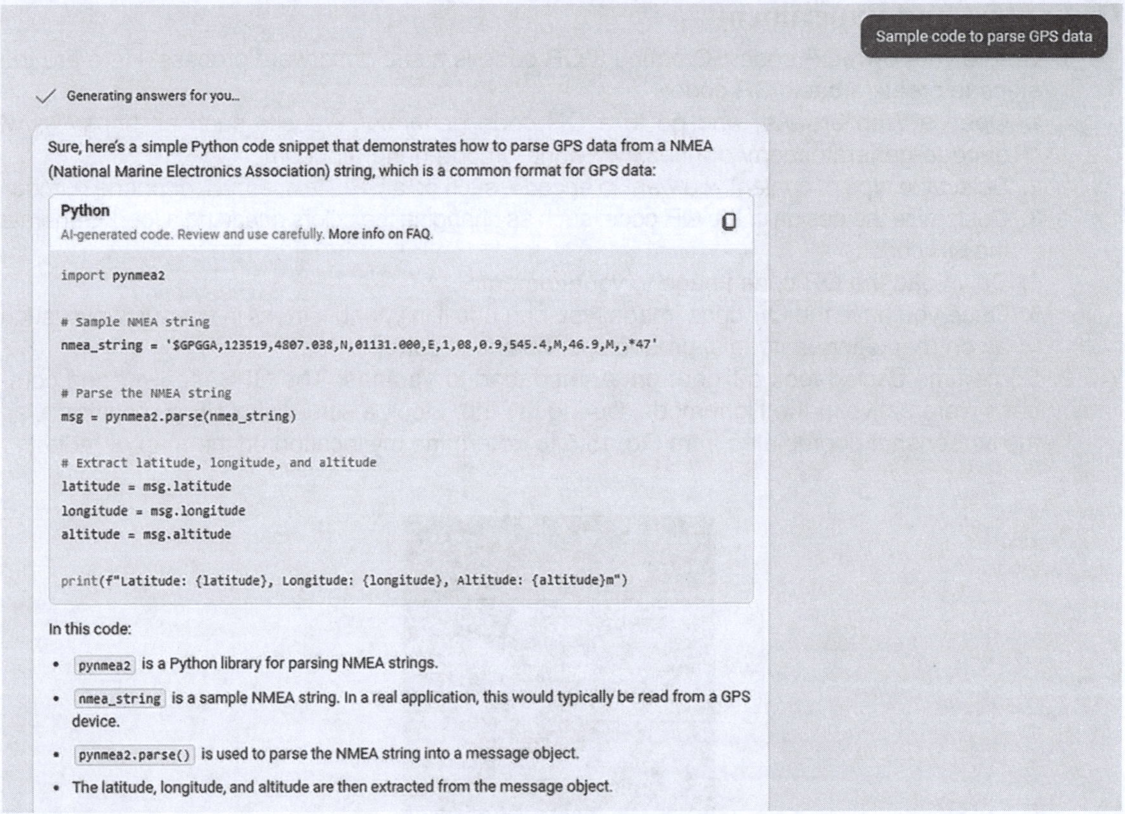

Fig. 15.6 Parsing GPS string using custom Python package

E. Generate Use Case for an AI Powered Smart Sensor

Use Case: Video as a Sensor for Intelligent Transportation

Brief description: With the help of computer vision, the digital camera is now a versatile sensor. The application below demonstrates how a camera mounted on traffic light poles and across different parts of a city can assist with citizen safety and traffic management. Study this application using the YouTube video in the resource, and create a use case on how computer vision is useful for this and other similar problems.

Resources

https://www.youtube.com/watch?v=CVG7_ymt_QQ&t=128s
Bosch Video-as-a-Sensor Solutions for Intelligent Transportation Systems (ITS)

Template Use Case on Intelligent Sensors

Define goal and purpose	Goal statement
	Identify stakeholders
	Define scope
Details to include in use case	Capture how technology helps business process
	Keep use case findings description textual, with a few simple flowcharts if needed
	Focus on describing how technology benefits the use case

Suggested Reading

1. Tero Karvinen, Kimmo Karvinen, Ville Valtokari, Make: Sensors: A Hands-On Primer for Monitoring the Real World with Arduino and Raspberry Pi, 1st Edition, Make Community LLC.

CHAPTER

16

Drones and Robots

CHAPTER OUTLINE

LEARNING OBJECTIVES

After reading this chapter, you will be able to:

- understand capabilities of drones and their use for various applications
- distinguish between industrial and mobile robots
- get to know how robots are used in a warehouse
- appreciate that robots are reconfigurable devices and can be repurposed for different applications

Effective Management Using Drones and Robots

Speed of manufacturing, order processing, and fulfillment go hand in hand. Automation plays a big role in monitoring and executing activities. Recent advances in drones and robots are pivotal in supporting a synchronized manufacturing and fulfillment operation. Outside of manufacturing, monitoring of activities spread across large areas is equally important. These include farms, mines, railroad, and construction sites. Drones make it possible to monitor them using an aerial view. E-commerce and fast delivery times have created a need for automated warehouses. Large number of robots (of different shapes and sizes) help in making sure that the orders are processed quickly.

16.1 | Drone Applications for Industry

Most of the time, we associate drones with hobby activities. Recent applications have demonstrated that drones are an important business tool. They provide a cost-effective and safe way (based on operation) to take aerial pictures and videos. Data contained in these images and videos provide rich analytics for multiple applications. A typical work day of a drone may consist of site pipeline inspection, analyzing crop health, carrying out military reconnaissance and other tasks.[1]

As seen in Fig. 16.1, a typical drone consists of multiple rotors (usually 4), an operator interface to control the drone and also program its flight path, global positioning system (GPS), and ability to carry a payload. In most cases, the payload is a camera, and data from the camera is stored on a memory card onboard the drone.

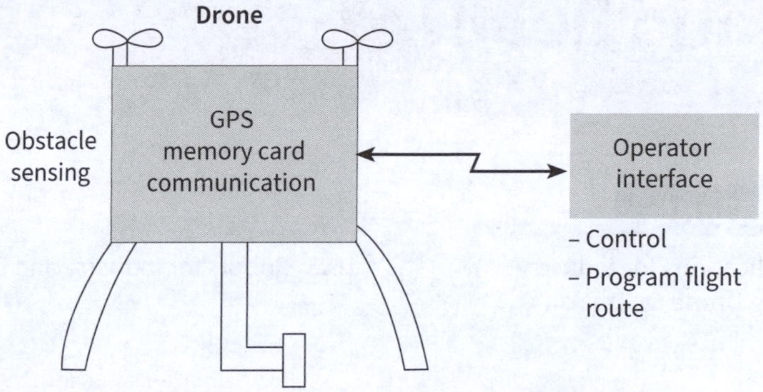

Fig. 16.1 Basic drone components. Contemporary drones offer multiple features[2]

Let us briefly discuss some applications where drones are making a mark.

Drone photography
Drones provide low-cost aerial photography and video for the entertainment and marketing industries. Before drones, it was difficult and expensive to obtain aerial footage. Often it required trained pilots and costly aircraft.

Disaster relief
Drones provide the means to locate missing people on land or in the water. With drones, disaster relief personnel can assess the terrain and plan rescue operations.

Safety inspections
Remote inspections of critical infrastructure is feasible using drones. Drones have the ability to maneuver into hard to reach areas, such as underneath bridges, different parts of buildings, dams, and other construction sites without putting a person at risk.

Drone delivery
Big retail and e-commerce companies are working toward delivering packages using drones. We will have to wait and watch to know if this delivery mechanism is limited to remote locations and small packages or becomes the norm for most deliveries. Figure 16.2 shows safe package delivery by lowering it using a tethered mechanism.

[1]Drones: Reporting for Work, Goldman Sachs, https://www.goldmansachs.com/insights/technology-driving-innovation/drones/ (accessed 8 December 2022).
[2]DJI Drones, https://www.dji.com/ (accessed 8 December 2022).

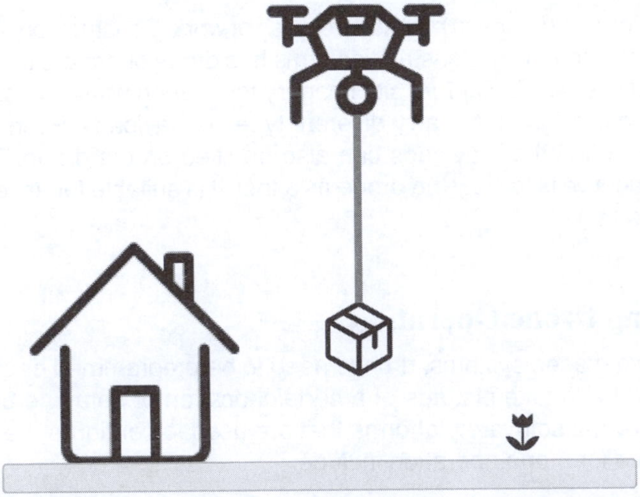

Fig. 16.2 Precise delivery using drone-based tethered package lowering mechanism[3]

16.1.1 Data Gathering, Surveying, Mapping, and Monitoring

Drones are making a big impact on how we survey and map land. It is possible to program drones to fly certain flight paths (using GPS) and gather accurate information from the air. Images and video from the drones can either be transmitted back in real-time or stored in the drone's memory card. Image data gathered from the drones is processed on the ground using AI-based computer vision techniques. Applications, such as object detection, image segmentation, and estimation of crop yields are possible using AI and drone imagery. Figure 16.3 shows applications that could use regular monitoring using drones.

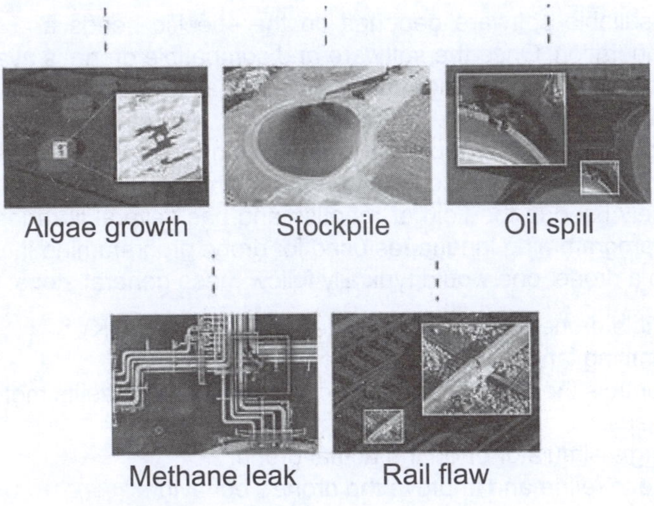

Fig. 16.3 Examples of sites that could be regularly monitored by automated drones[4]

[3]Zipline precise delivery, https://www.flyzipline.com/technology (accessed 5 June 2023).

[4]Automated drones opportunity, American Robotics, https://www.american-robotics.com/post/how-drone-autonomy-unlocks-a-new-era-of-ai-opportunities-1 (accessed 8 December 2022).

16.1.2 Monitoring Construction Progress

Construction companies use drones to monitor progress of work. Construction sites are often massive, and by nature are always changing. Construction firms hire drone operators to visit a construction site at regularly scheduled intervals to capture site imagery for sharing with clients.

Most drones can be configured to carry different types of payloads. Even though the camera is the most common payload other payloads can also be fitted on the drone. The biggest takeaway from a business perspective is to view the drone as a tool. It is suitable for accessing and monitoring difficult to reach areas.

16.2 | Configuring Drone Operation

Just like other computer-based systems, drones need to be programmed or configured to carry out a task. The task could be to take pictures of a certain location or spray herbicide in certain areas of a field. There are several software platforms that are used to configure the operation of a drone. Some popular software for drone operation include:

DJI Assistant 2 Software application developed by DJI, a leading drone manufacturer. It allows users to configure and customize the operation of their DJI drones, as well as update firmware and access flight logs.

Mission Planner An open-source software platform that can be used to program autonomous flights for drones. The software supports various flight modes, including auto, guided, and RTL (return to launch).

QGroundControl Another open-source software platform that can be used to configure and control drones. Works with a wide range of drones, including those that use the MAVLink protocol.

UgCS This is a commercial software platform that is designed for professional drone operations. It allows users to plan and execute complex drone missions, as well as analyze and visualize data collected during flights.

The choice of a suitable software depends on the specific needs and requirements of the drone operator and operation. Once the software and compatible drone is available, one can start the programming process. Programming drones involves using a programming language to write code that can control the drone's flight, sensors, cameras, and other hardware components. The specific programming language and tools used depend on the drone's manufacturer, model, and software development kit (SDK). One common programming language used to program drones is Python; which is widely used in the field of robotics and has several libraries available for drone programming. Other programming languages used for drone programming include C++, Java, and MATLAB. To program a drone, one would typically follow these general steps:

- Acquire a compatible drone and its software development kit (SDK).
- Choose a programming language and development environment.
- Write code that controls the drone's hardware components, such as its motors, sensors, cameras, and other devices.
- Test the code using a simulator or on the actual drone.
- Iterate on the code to refine and improve the drone's behavior.

Programming a drone is not a trivial task. It requires technical expertise and knowledge of the drone's hardware and software. A good way to get started is to use sample code from the manufacturer and adhere to guidelines and best practices for safe drone operation.

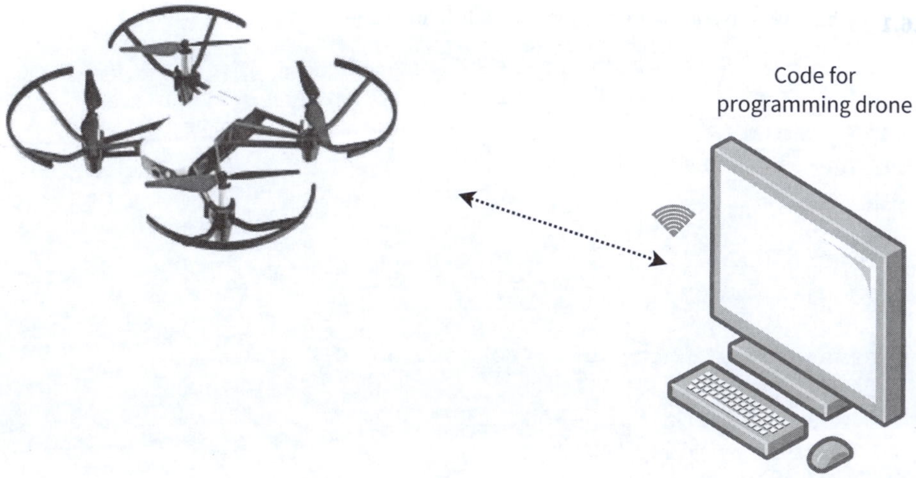

Fig. 16.4 The code written to control the drone is developed on the PC but it runs using the drone's onboard computer

Let us discuss the programming APIs for a simple drone operation. We will see an example code to customize drone operation using Python package[5] and DJI SDK (Software Development Kit) and Tello[6] Drone. All operations are executed using Python or functions from the ***djitellopy*** package. The code assumes you have installed the DJI Tello SDK library using pip and have connected to a DJI Tello drone via Wi-Fi (Fig. 16.4). The example code (Listing 16.1) controls the drone speed, take off (line 20), forward movement (line 22), turns (line 24), altitude (line 26) and landing (line 28). You can customize these operations by changing the values passed to the drone functions, or by adding new functions to the code. Please see the API Reference documentation[7] if you wish to know more about supported functions. Under the hood, the code in Listing 16.1 controls the speed of the drone motors to change speed, make turns or update altitude.

16.2.1 Programming a Drone for Package Delivery

Configuring a drone for package delivery involves various aspects, such as navigation, obstacle avoidance, payload management, etc. In Fig. 16.5, we see a drone programmed to deliver a package to the customer's front or backyard. Depending on the contents of the package, the drone's height can be adjusted before activating the package drop mechanism.

Let us take a look at the pseudocode code (Listing 16.2) that can be used as a starting point for configuring a drone for package delivery:

The APIs discussed in the pseudocode of Listing 16.2 are quite straightforward. The destination's coordinates are fed to the drone, which has an onboard GPS receiver. When the drone reaches its destination, it opens its gripper mechanism to release the package and then returns to its home position (fixed coordinates). A closer look at the code in Listing 16.2 reveals that the delivery location is set in lines 13 and 14. Line 19 commands the drone to fly toward the delivery location coordinates. A while loop (line 21) checks if the drone has reached close to its destination (line 27). Once it is confirmed that the drone is hovering at its delivery location, the drone opens its gripper and

[5]Python Tello Drone library, https://pypi.org/project/djitellopy/ (accessed 6 June 2023).
[6]DJI Tello Drone, https://m.dji.com/product/tello (accessed 6 June 2023).
[7]DJITelloPy API reference, https://djitellopy.readthedocs.io/en/latest/tello/ (accessed 9 June 2023).

Listing 16.1 Python API's to control movement of a DJI Tello Drone

```
# Import necessary libraries
import time
import math
import argparse
import sys

# Import DJI SDK
from djitellopy import Tello

# Define main function to control drone operation
def main():
    # Initialize drone object
    drone = Tello()

    # Connect to drone
    drone.connect()

    # Check if drone is connected
    if not drone.is_connected:
        print("Failed to connect to drone!")
    return

    # Set drone speed and takeoff
    drone.set_speed(30)
    drone.takeoff()

    # Fly forward for 1 meter
    drone.move_forward(100)

    # Turn left by 90 degrees
    drone.rotate_counter_clockwise(90)

    # Fly up for 50 cm
    drone.move_up(50)

    # Land drone
    drone.land()

    # Disconnect from drone
    drone.disconnect()

# Execute main function
if __name__ == '__main__':
    main()
```

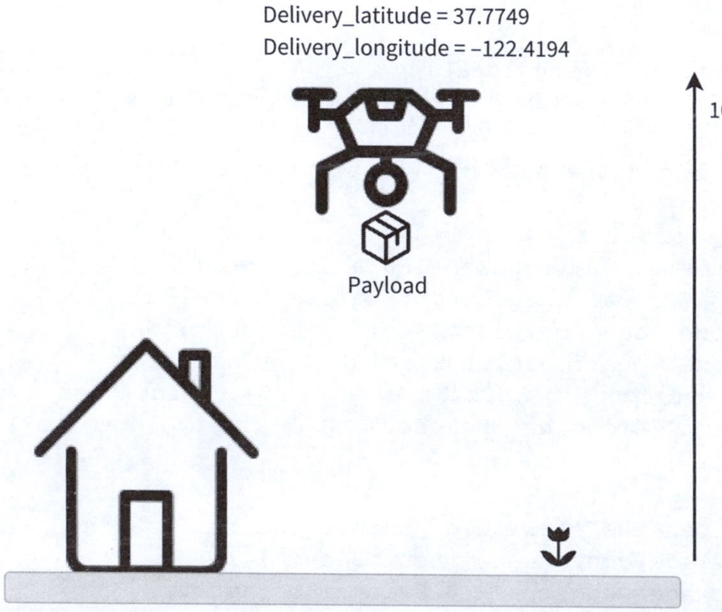

Fig. 16.5 Visual depiction of a package delivery drone

Listing 16.2 Pseudocode for a package delivery drone

```
# Import necessary libraries
import dronekit
from dronekit import VehicleMode
from pymavlink import mavutil

# Connect to drone
connection_string = 'udp:127.0.0.1:14550'
drone = dronekit.connect(connection_string, wait_ready=True)

# Set drone mode
drone.mode = VehicleMode("GUIDED")

# Set the takeoff altitude
drone.commands.takeoff(10)

# Set delivery location
delivery_lat = 37.7749
delivery_lon = -122.4194
delivery_alt = 10
delivery_location = dronekit.LocationGlobal(delivery_lat,
                    delivery_lon, delivery_alt)
```

(Continued)

Listing 16.2 *(Continued)*

```
18. # Navigate to delivery location
19. drone.simple_goto(delivery_location)

20. # Check if the drone has arrived at delivery location
21. while True:
22.     current_location =
23.         dronekit.LocationGlobalRelative
24.         (drone.location.global_relative_frame.lat,
25.          drone.location.global_relative_frame.lon,
26.          drone.location.global_relative_frame.alt)
27.     if current_location.distance_to(delivery_location) < 0.5:
            print("Drone has reached the delivery location")
            break

28.         # Open the package container and release the package
29.         package_container = 'container_1'
30.         package_weight = 2.0 # in kilograms
31.         drone.gripper.open(package_container)
32.         drone.gripper.release(package_weight)

33.  # Return to home location
34.  home_location = drone.location.global_frame
35.  drone.simple_goto(home_location)

36.  # Land the drone
37.  drone.mode = VehicleMode("LAND")
```

releases the package (lines 31,32); and then flies back to its home location (line 35). This pseudocode describes the drone's operations in a simple manner. The actual code is more complex.

16.2.2 Drone Operation Using AI

Drones use AI inference to perform a variety of tasks, such as object detection, tracking, and recognition (discussed in Chapter 13). The basic process involves capturing images or video of a scene with the drone's onboard camera and then using machine learning algorithms to analyze the data and extract information. For example, a drone equipped with an object detection algorithm could fly over a construction site (Fig. 16.6) and identify any safety hazards or potential issues, such as missing safety barriers or equipment that has not been properly secured. Similarly, a drone equipped with an image recognition algorithm could be used to identify different plant species in a field or detect changes in vegetation over time.

The AI inference process involves feeding the captured data into a trained neural network, which then analyzes the data and provides the desired output. This requires significant computational resources, which either can be provided by powerful onboard processors or by cloud-based servers. Overall, AI inference allows drones to perform complex tasks with greater accuracy and efficiency.

Here is an example pseudocode (Listing 16.3) for programming a drone for object detection using the TensorFlow Object Detection API. This pseudocode loads a pre-trained object detection model (line 6)

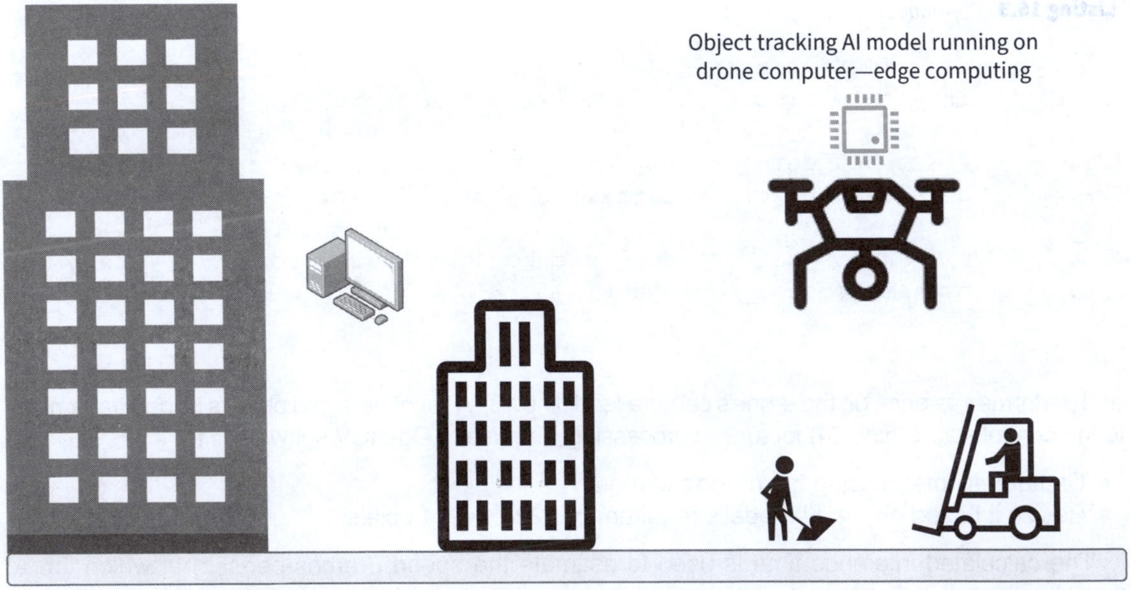

Fig. 16.6 A lightweight AI model runs on the drone. While a more complex AI model runs on a computer server for detailed analysis of imagery captured by the drone

Listing 16.3 Pseudocode for drone-based object detection. Drone camera captures an image and runs AI model for detecting objects of interest

```
import tensorflow as tf
import cv2
import numpy as np
import time

# Load the trained model
model = tf.keras.models.load_model('object-detection.h5')

# Set up video capture from drone camera
cap = cv2.VideoCapture(0)

# Set up communication module to transmit data to ground station

while True:
    # Capture frame from camera
    ret, frame = cap.read()

    # Preprocess frame for inference
    frame = cv2.resize(frame, (224, 224))
    frame = np.expand_dims(frame, axis=0)

    # Perform object detection inference using the model
    start_time = time.time()
    predictions = model.predict(frame)
```

(Continued)

Listing 16.3 *(Continued)*

```
19.        end_time = time.time()
20.        inference_time = end_time - start_time

21.        # Extract detected objects from predictions
22.        detected_objects = extract_objects(predictions)

23.        # Transmit detected objects to control station
24.        transmit(detected_objects)
```

and performs inference on the drone's camera feed (line 18). A list of detected objects is then transmitted to the control station (line 24) for further processing. The use of OpenCV software is to:

- Capture an image using the drone's camera
- Resize it based on the AI model's requirement (224 × 224 pixels)

The calculated inference time is used to estimate the speed (frames-per-sec) at which the AI model runs on the drone computer.

Autonomous drones that use AI based computer vision are used to carry out Intelligence, Surveillance and Reconnaissance (ISR) operations. These rugged drones can be airborne for more than 24 hours at a time and can carry a few hundred kilograms of payload. The payload usually consists of sensor, computation, and communication equipment.

16.3 | Robots for Industry and Business

Robots have been around for quite some time. In the past decade, the population of robots has increased significantly. A new generation of robots are now in homes, warehouses, fast food restaurants, and many more places. Twenty years ago, most robots were stationary industrial robots found in factories for welding, painting, and moving material. Contemporary robots have different set of abilities and applications. Like industrial robots, contemporary robots are used to perform repetitive, time-consuming, labor-intensive and at times hazardous tasks. This saves time and improves safety. Some examples where contemporary robots are used:

Warehousing and logistics In warehouses and logistics centers, robots are used for material handling tasks, such as picking, packing, and shipping. Robots can navigate through narrow aisles, move heavy loads, and operate in different environments, such as cold storage.
Healthcare Robots are used for tasks, such as surgery, rehabilitation, and patient care. Specialized robots execute precise movements and provide consistent care, reducing human error.
Agriculture Here, robots are used for activities such as planting, harvesting, precisely spraying herbicide and monitoring crops. Farm robots work in harsh weather to implement precision agriculture and reduce labor costs.

16.3.1 Industrial Robots

Industrial robots are still the backbone of new applications. If you look closely, you will find that the end effector of a robot is tailored for the task at hand. You may be hearing about an end effector for the first time! An end effector is a device at the end of a robotic arm, designed to help the

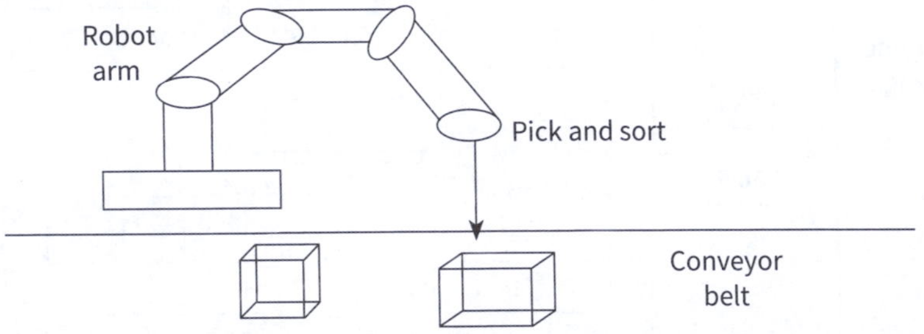

Fig. 16.7 An Industrial robot being used for a pick and sort application. Besides a vacuum-based gripper, the Robot end effector has a camera or barcode reader to distinguish between different packages

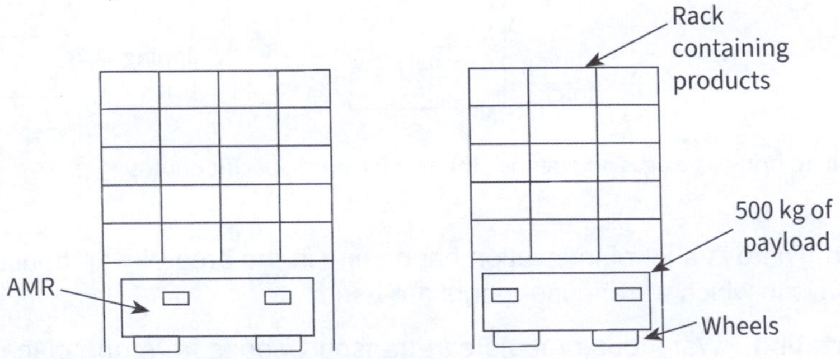

Fig. 16.8 AMRs bring product racks to human operators for packing

robot carry out its task. In a pick-and-place operation of small, fragile objects, the end effector is a vacuum-based gripper (as seen in Fig. 16.7).

16.3.2 Autonomous Mobile Robot (AMR)

An autonomous mobile robot (AMR) is a robot that moves through its environment without being individually controlled by an operator. At an Amazon warehouse,[8] AMRs help move products and improve safety. These robots are equipped with different kinds of sensors to help them navigate safely. Figure 16.8 shows an AMR in action at a warehouse. Based on instructions, the AMR picks up a rack (containing an ordered product) and brings it to a human operator. The human operator selects the right item from the rack.

AMR swarms

AMRs are reconfigurable and can carry out different operations. In Fig. 16.9, we see AMRs bringing fulfilled packages and depositing them in different chutes. Each chute is configured for different locations. Packages collected at the end of the chute are loaded on a truck and shipped to a certain geographical area.

Modern day robots are leveraging advances in computer vision, data, and distributed computing technology. There is a good amount of synergy between robots and above-mentioned technologies. We are at the threshold of a robotics revolution and a big use case (like the warehouse) will determine the next large innovation of robotic technology. A student of technology or management knows what is possible with contemporary technology and knows how and when to apply it for a

[8]Amazon warehouse robots, https://www.aboutamazon.com/news/operations/10-years-of-amazon-robotics-how-robots-help-sort-packages-move-product-and-improve-safety (accessed 8 December 2022).

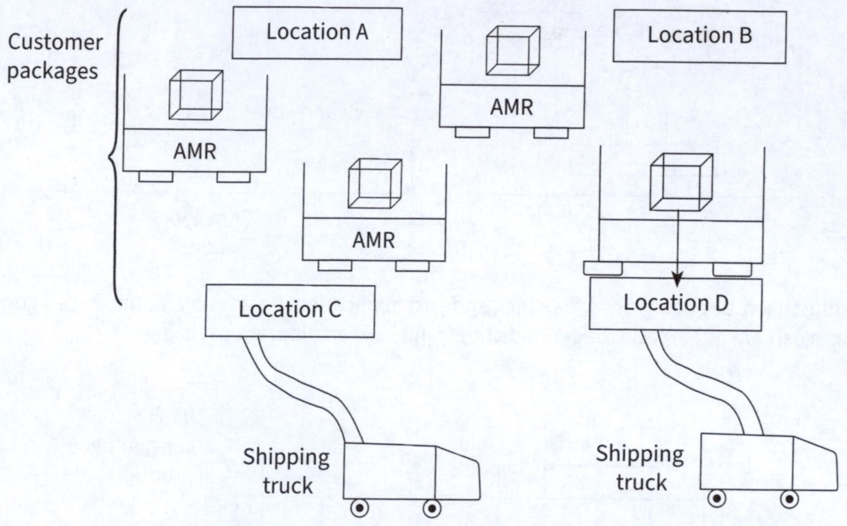

Fig. 16.9 Use of AMR to bring packages and deposit them in location-specific chutes

suitable use case. There is a lot of innovation happening in the area of warehouse robots.[9] Let us enumerate the ways in which warehouse robots are used:

Goods transportation Warehouse robots can transport goods from one place to another in a warehouse or distribution center, reducing the need for human labor and increasing efficiency.
Picking and packing Robots are used for picking and packing of goods in a warehouse. They can pick items from shelves and pack them into boxes or containers for shipping.
Inventory management Warehouse robots can be used for inventory management, including stock counting and tracking of goods in the warehouse.
Sorting and categorizing Robots can sort and categorize items based on different criteria, such as size, weight, and color.

Use of Robotic arm and AMR in fulfillment centers

The most human intensive task in a fulfillment center is to pick and box items for each customer order. Even though AMRs carry racks containing items to the human operator, the human operator has to pick the product from the rack and place it inside a package. Warehouse workers across the world pick items up, sort them, and package them millions of times every day. Now it is possible to employ an industrial robotic arm to carry out this operation. Amazon Sparrow[10] uses suction cups and AI to correctly identify an item and then place it into a customer package. Figure 16.10 shows how multiple cameras assist the robot to correctly identify an object, pick it up and place it. Highly accurate, AI object detection models are used by the robotic arm to carry out this demanding operation. A conveyor belt brings in items for a customer's order. The robot picks up the right item and places it in the customer order box. Multiple robotic arms may work concurrently for fast order fulfillment.

[9]Amazon robotics, https://amazon.jobs/en/teams/amazon-robotics (accessed 9 June 2023).
[10]Amazon Sparrow, https://www.wsj.com/articles/amazon-looks-to-sparrow-to-carry-its-robotics-ambitions-11668797969 (accessed 10 June 2023).

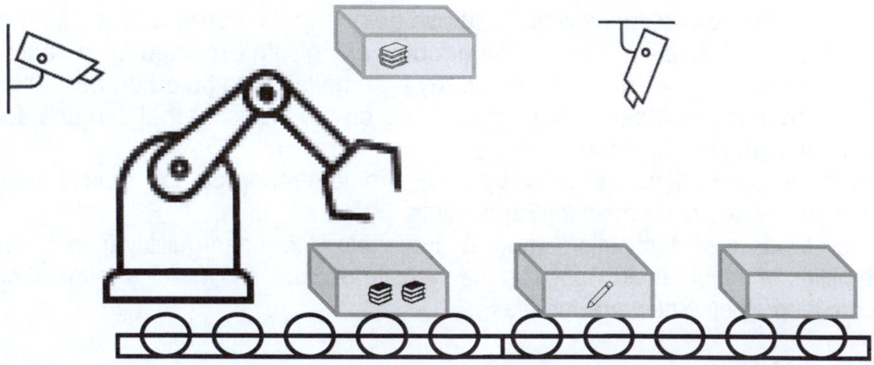

Fig. 16.10 Robotic arm for e-commerce fulfilment center

16.3.3 Humanoid Robots

Multiple countries and companies across the globe are in a race to create Humanoid Robots. These Robots are designed to work in human workspaces for long hours without getting tired. Several technologies- such as computer vision, AI, small and powerful electrical motors, and long lasting batteries are making Humanoid Robots a reality. A Humanoid Robot is programmed to work in different capacities. It has the dexterity to work in a factory for a specific task, or can be at home helping with household chores or giving a senior citizen a helping hand. In the coming decade, it is very likely that these Robots would become part of our workplace and home.

16.4 | Conclusion

Both drones and new age robots are becoming mainstream tools. This chapter discussed several business applications that have benefitted from drones and robots. It is not important to know how these devices operate under the hood. The same goes for the Python code in the chapter. Understand how a drone or robot application can be configured using the high-level APIs/functions presented in the chapter. Use the ideas on capabilities of drones and robots to create new use cases that will benefit businesses and society.

Exercises

A. State True/False

1. Drones capture ground pictures with a better resolution than satellites.
2. Contemporary drones have technology for obstacle avoidance.
3. AMRs assist in moving material in a warehouse or factory.
4. Industrial (stationary) robots are only used for car welding and painting.
5. AMRs are rated for different payload capacities. One such rating is 500 kg.

B. Short-answer Questions

1. Explain why a drone's GPS location sensor is useful for the site monitoring application shown in Fig. 16.3.
2. What kinds of new jobs do you foresee in the fulfilment centers?
3. Explain with a simple diagram, how a robotic arm can be repurposed as a fruit picking robot.
4. Find out from the internet, how robotic arms are used in the kitchens of restaurant chains.
5. List the sensors on a delivery drone, that prevents it from crashing into objects.

C. Long-answer Questions

1. Come up with two use cases which can use autonomous mobile robots (like the ones used in warehouses.[11]) Explain the role of the robots along with expected functionality.
2. Visit and study the Website[12] of a company that makes automated drones. Think of a business application (besides the ones mentioned on the Website) that can use such an automated surveying drone setup.
3. Study drone applications presented by DJI.[13] Create a report on how drones are used for different use cases in enterprise and agriculture.
4. Mention a business application where a Humanoid Robot can quickly fit in. Learn about the capabilities of a Humanoid Robot on the website of Boston Dynamics (https://bostondynamics.com/blog/electric-new-era-for-atlas/).

D. Explore and Experiment

1. Get a programmable drone for your Emerging Technologies class. Learn to program the drone using Python APIs to fly defined trajectories. Use it to create an aerial video of your college/university. You can get help from YouTube videos,[14] for connecting and programming the drone.
2. Use of Generative AI to explore tasks performed by an autonomous mobile robot (AMR) in a warehouse setting (Fig. 16.11). Using Generative AI, find out if an AMR can be helpful in a hospital environment. Also, check to see if Generative AI can create sample code for programming drones.

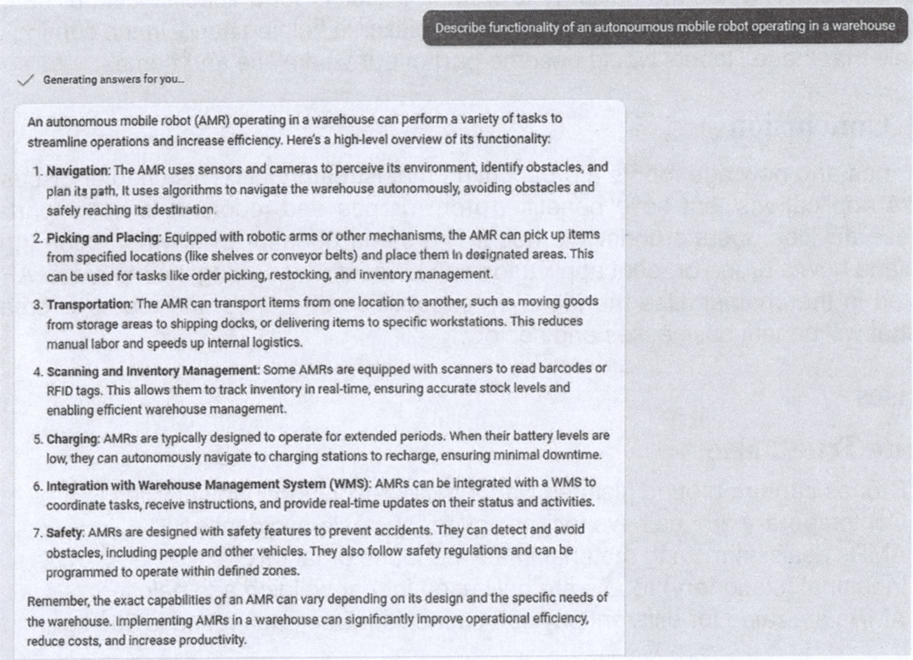

Fig. 16.11 Operation of AMR in a warehouse environment

[11] Amazon science, Robotics, https://www.amazon.science/latest-news/amazon-robotics-autonomous-drive-units-hercules-pegasus-xanthus-xbot (accessed 8 December 2022).
[12] American Robotics, fully automated drones, https://www.american-robotics.com/ (accessed 8 December 2022).
[13] DJI Drones, https://www.dji.com/ (accessed 8 December 2022).
[14] Drone Programming using Python, https://www.youtube.com/watch?v=LmEcyQnfpDA&t=7126s (accessed 9 June 2023).

E. Generate Use Case for Drones and Robots—Learning by Example Approach

Use Case: Drone Delivery

Brief description: Drone delivery has been a topic of conversation for several years now. There are recent announcements (see resources below) that claim that it is finally here! Study the resources below and create a use case on how drones are used for delivering various kinds of items. Use the template below for creating the use case.

Resources

https://www.bbc.com/news/business-67132527

BBC, Amazon pledges parcels in an hour using drone deliveries, 19 October 2023

https://techcrunch.com/2023/03/15/zipline-unveils-cute-little-droid-to-make-drone-delivery-more-accurate/

TechCrunch, Zipline unveils cute little droid to make drone delivery more accurate, 15 March 2023

Template for Creating Use Case for Drone Delivery

Define goal and purpose	Goal statement
	Identify stakeholders
	Define scope
Details to include in use case	Capture how technology helps business process
	Keep use case findings description textual, with a few simple flowcharts if needed
	Focus on describing how technology benefits the use case
Future applications	Mention any new applications that can leverage the technology used

Suggested Reading

1. Ian Cinnamon, Romi Kadri, Fitz Tepper, DIY Drones for the Evil Genius: Design, Build, and Customize Your Own Drones 1st Edition, McGraw-Hill TAB.

CHAPTER 17

Cybersecurity

CHAPTER OUTLINE

LEARNING OBJECTIVES

After reading this chapter, you will be able to:

- become mindful about cybersecurity
- understand how a business can fall victim to cyberattacks
- know ways to prevent cyberattacks in your organization

Effective Management Using Cybersecurity

Technology is a dual edged sword. Interconnectivity of computers around the world makes e-commerce easier, but it comes at a price. The price is being susceptible to cyberattacks. Cyberattacks can freeze business operations by ransomware; or it can drain bank accounts. As a result, protecting against potential cyberattacks is as important as innovation for the survival of a business.

17.1 | Primer on Cybersecurity

The other day, I read a news report on BBC[1] about cyberattacks on small firms. The news mentioned smaller firms are seeing more attacks as most larger organizations have a secure IT infrastructure in place. What really stood out was the fact that as per the National Cybersecurity Alliance, about 60% of small businesses shut down within 6 months of facing an attack. Cybersecurity is no longer something that only large firms have to worry about. It is of universal concern.

In the previous chapters, we talked about various advantages of using internet-based services to speed up business transactions. Many individuals and businesses enroll on payment Websites for autopay. Companies entice you with a discount if you register for autopay. Believe it or not, everyone loves a discount! The autopay is usually linked to a credit card or a bank account.

When a company you have shared payment details with gets hacked, someone out there ends with your credit card or bank account details. This is just one possible scenario of a future cyberattack.

Before we get started with a discussion on how cyberattacks are carried out and ways to avoid them, let us establish common ground with the terminology. A glossary of commonly used cybersecurity and related technology terms[2] from National Institute of Standards and Technology (NIST) is collated below. These terms are listed alphabetically from A–W.

Access control The process of granting or denying specific requests to: (i) obtain and use information or related systems or services or (ii) enter specific physical facilities.

Antivirus/anti-malware Software A program designed to detect many forms of malware (e.g., viruses and spyware) and prevent them from infecting computers. It may also cleanse already-infected computers.

Authentication Verifying the identity of a user, process, or system, often as a prerequisite to allowing access to resources in an information system.

Backups A copy of information, files, and programs to facilitate recovery. Backups may be stored on the same machine that contains the original information, another machine, a storage device, such as a thumb drive, or "in the cloud."

Business E-mail scams A scam that targets businesses by using social engineering or computer intrusion to compromise legitimate business e-mail accounts and conduct unauthorized fund transfers or obtain personal information.

Cybersecurity An approach or series of steps to prevent or manage the risk of damage to, unauthorized use of, exploitation of, and—if needed—to restore electronic information and communications systems, and the information they contain, in order to strengthen the confidentiality, integrity, and availability of these systems.

Data Breach An incident that involves sensitive, protected, or confidential information being copied, transmitted, viewed, stolen, or used by an individual unauthorized to do so. Exposed information may include credit card numbers, personal health information, customer data, company trade secrets, or matters of national security, for example.

Digital forensics The practice of gathering, retaining, and analyzing computer-related data for investigative purposes in a manner that maintains the integrity of the data.

---

[1]Cyber-attacks on small firms: The US economy's 'Achilles heel'?, BBC, https://www.bbc.com/news/business-63260648 (accessed 9 December 2022).

[2]Glossary of Cybersecurity terms, NIST, https://www.nist.gov/itl/smallbusinesscyber/cybersecurity-basics/glossary (accessed 9 December 2022).

Encryption The transformation of data (called "plaintext") into a form (called "ciphertext") that conceals the data's original meaning to prevent it from being known or used. If the transformation is reversible, the corresponding reversal process is called "decryption," which is a transformation that restores encrypted data to its original state.

Firewall A device or program that restricts data communication traffic to or from a network and thus protects that network's system resources against threats from another network.

Hacker Someone who attempts to or gains access to an information system, usually in an unauthorized manner. A "white hat" hacker is a cybersecurity specialist who breaks into systems with a goal of evaluating and ultimately improving the security of an organization's systems.

Identity theft Crime in which someone wrongfully obtains and uses another person's personal data in some way that involves fraud or deception, often for economic gain.

Information security The approach to protect and manage the risk to information and information systems from unauthorized access, use, disclosure, disruption, modification, or destruction in order to provide confidentiality, integrity, and availability.

Intrusion detection system/intrusion prevention system A system or software that monitors and analyses network or system events for the purpose of finding and providing real-time or near real-time warning of attempts to access system resources in an unauthorized manner. In addition, intrusion prevention systems can also attempt to stop the activity, ideally before it reaches its targets.

Malware A computer program that is covertly placed onto a computer or electronic device with the intent to compromise the confidentiality, integrity, or availability of data, applications, or operating systems. Common types of malware include viruses, worms, malicious mobile code, Trojan horses, rootkits, spyware, and some forms of adware.

Multi-factor authentication/two-factor authentication/dual factor authentication Authentication using two or more different factors to provide increased security during log-ins. Factors may include: (i) something you know (e.g., password/PIN); (ii) something you have (e.g., cryptographic identification device, token); or (iii) something you are (e.g., biometric).

Passphrase A secret sequence of words or other text used to authenticate a person's or system's identity. A passphrase is similar to a password but is generally longer for added security.

Personally identifiable information (PII) Information which can be used to distinguish or trace the identity of an individual (e.g., name, social security number, biometric records, etc.) alone, or when combined with other personal or identifying information which is linkable to a specific individual (e.g., date and place of birth, mother's maiden name, etc.).

Phishing A technique for attempting to acquire sensitive data, such as bank account numbers, or access to a larger computerized system through a fraudulent solicitation in e-mail or on a Website. The perpetrator typically masquerades as a legitimate business or reputable person.

Ransomware A type of malware that attempts to deny access to a user's data, usually by encrypting the data with a key known only to the hacker who deployed the malware, until a ransom is paid.

Spam Electronic junk mail or the abuse of electronic messaging systems to indiscriminately send unsolicited bulk messages.

Spear phishing A highly targeted phishing attack, usually to a specific individual or department within an organization.

Spyware Software that is secretly or surreptitiously installed into an information system to gather information on individuals or organizations without their knowledge.

Tech support scams A security exploit in which scammers call, place alarming pop-up messages on a computer, offer free "security" scans, or set up fake Websites to convince someone that his/her computer is infected or has a problem. The scammers then ask to be paid to fix the non-existent problem.

Threat Any circumstance or event with the potential to adversely impact organizational operations (including mission, functions, image, or reputation), organizational assets, individuals, other organizations, or the Nation through an information system via unauthorized access, destruction, disclosure, modification of information, and/or denial of service.
Viruses A computer program that can copy itself and infect a computer without permission or knowledge of the user. A virus might corrupt or delete data on a computer, use e-mail programs to spread itself to other computers, or even erase everything on a hard disk.
Virtual private network (VPN) Virtual network built on top of existing networks that can provide a secure communications mechanism for data and Internet Protocol (IP) information transmitted via the virtual network.
Vulnerability A weakness in a system, application, or network that is subject to exploitation or misuse.
Watering hole attack A security exploit where the attacker infects Websites that are frequently visited by members of the group being attacked, with the goal of infecting a computer used by one of the targeted group when they visit the infected Website.
Whitelist An approved list or register of entities provided a particular privilege, service, mobility, access, or recognition.
Wiping Overwriting media (like a hard drive) or portions of media to hinder reconstruction of the data. In the following sections we will use several terms listed in this terminology to explain cyberattack patterns and ways to prevent it.

17.2 | Cyberattack Patterns

Techniques used for cyberattacks and data breaches keep changing and getting sophisticated. It is a cat and mouse game between hackers and cybersecurity experts. A hacker can launch an attack against a business by targeting its,

Infrastructure security
Network security
Application security
Information security
Cloud Security

Since all computer systems are interconnected, a breach in one can lead to other systems also getting compromised. If you get a chance, read about how hackers got access to a fish tank[3] system and through that accessed data of a casino. Unsecured IoT devices that people forget after connecting to their network, turn out to be the Achilles heel in terms of cybersecurity.

Common techniques used for cyberattacks include

- Phishing e-mails
- Unintended spyware downloads from Websites
- Download links in e-mails that seem genuine
- E-mail forwards to different employees in a company with the same download link

This is just the tip of the iceberg in terms of how cyberattacks can take place. There is no one methodology that will work all the time. The best way is to periodically review all sensitive systems and share best practices among employees.

[3]A smart fish tank left a casino vulnerable to hackers, CNN, July 2017, https://money.cnn.com/2017/07/19/technology/fish-tank-hack-darktrace/index.html (accessed 9 December 2022).

17.3 | Cybersecurity Recommendations

In the last section, we acknowledged that it is not possible to prevent cyberattacks by one single action. It is a series of continuous actions by the entire company that will ensure long-term security. Most large corporations have strong rules and systems that prevent copying and downloading of files from unrecognized or personal computers. Small businesses may not have access to IT teams and resources to implement this. To help small businesses from becoming victims of cyberattacks, the United States Federal Communications Commission FCC[4] has released a cybersecurity tip sheet. It enumerates 10 basic recommendations, mentioned below:

1. **Train employees in security principles**
   Establish basic security practices and policies for employees, such as requiring strong passwords, and establish appropriate Internet use guidelines that detail penalties for violating company cybersecurity policies. Establish rules of behavior describing how to handle and protect customer information and other vital data.
2. **Protect information, computers, and networks from cyberattacks**
   Keep clean machines: Having the latest security software, Web browser, and operating system are the best defenses against viruses, malware, and other online threats. Set antivirus software to run a scan after each update. Install other key software updates as soon as they are available.
3. **Provide firewall security for your Internet connection**
   A firewall is a set of related programs that prevent outsiders from accessing data on a private network. Make sure the operating system's firewall is enabled or install free firewall software available online. If employees work from home, ensure that their home system(s) are protected by a firewall.
4. **Create a mobile device action plan**
   Mobile devices can create significant security and management challenges, especially if they hold confidential information or can access the corporate network. It requires the users to password-protect their devices, encrypt their data, and install security apps to prevent criminals from stealing information while the phone is on public networks. Be sure to set reporting procedures for lost or stolen equipment.
5. **Make backup copies of important business data and information**
   Regularly backup the data on all computers. Critical data includes word processing documents, electronic spreadsheets, databases, financial files, human resources files, and accounts receivable/payable files. Backup data automatically if possible, or at least weekly and store the copies either offsite or in the cloud.
6. **Control physical access to your computers and create user accounts for each employee**
   Prevent access or use of business computers by unauthorized individuals. Laptops can be particularly easy targets for theft or can be lost, so lock them up when unattended. Make sure a separate user account is created for each employee and require strong passwords. Administrative privileges should only be given to trusted IT staff and key personnel.
7. **Secure your Wi-Fi networks**
   If you have a Wi-Fi network for your workplace, make sure it is secure, encrypted, and hidden. To hide your Wi-Fi network, set up your wireless access point or router, so it does not broadcast the network name, known as the Service Set Identifier (SSID). Passwords-protect access to the router.

[4]Cybersecurity for Small Businesses, FCC, https://www.fcc.gov/communications-business-opportunities/cybersecurity-small-businesses (accessed 9 December 2022).

8. **Employ best practices on payment cards**
   Work with banks or processors to ensure the most trusted and validated tools and anti-fraud services are being used. You may also have additional security obligations pursuant to agreements with your bank or processor. Isolate payment systems from other, less secure programs and do not use the same computer to process payments and surf the Internet.
9. **Limit employee access to data and information, limit authority to install software**
   Do not provide any one employee with access to all data systems. Employees should only be given access to the specific data systems that they need for their jobs, and should not be able to install any software without permission.
10. **Passwords and authentication**
    Require employees to use unique passwords and change passwords every 3 months. Consider implementing multifactor authentication that requires additional information beyond a password to gain entry. Check with your vendors that handle sensitive data, especially financial institutions, to see if they offer multifactor authentication for your account.

It is better to be prepared than to be sorry later. Hackers often bring businesses to a grinding halt. Cybersecurity going forward is no longer optional or good to have! It is a necessity. Before we finish our discussion on cybersecurity, let us talk about the use of cryptography for improving cybersecurity. Cryptography involves the use of mathematical algorithms and protocols to secure communication channels and protect sensitive information from unauthorized access, disclosure, and modification. We briefly talked about the hash function in our discussion on blockchain. Hash function is part of cryptographic hash function algorithm, that maps an arbitrary binary string to a binary string with a fixed size of ***n*** bits. In our earlier discussion on blockchain, we had used a size of 256 bits as the hash value or digest in our pseudo code in Listing 5.1. Cryptography helps cybersecurity in multiple ways:

Confidentiality Cryptography makes sure that only authorized users can access sensitive information. This is achieved through encryption, where the information is transformed into an unreadable format that can only be deciphered by the intended recipient.

Integrity Cryptography ensures that the information transmitted over a network is not tampered with or altered in any way. Digital signatures and message authentication codes (MACs), are used to verify the authenticity and integrity of the data.

Authentication Cryptography is used to ensure that users are who they claim to be. This is achieved through various methods, such as digital certificates, public-key cryptography, and multifactor authentication.

Key management Cryptography is used to manage cryptographic keys, which are used to encrypt and decrypt information. Key management involves generating, distributing, storing, and revoking cryptographic keys to ensure the security of the information.

Cloud services by default have secure protocols in place (Fig. 17.1). Identity and access management (IAM) help specify access to different resources on a cloud setup. The process of connecting to a cloud-based virtual machine requires setting up of public and private security keys. Public and private keys are generated using mathematical algorithms, with help of operations with prime numbers. The public key is derived from the private key, and both are generated together as a pair to ensure their mathematical relationship.

Sending and receiving data using public–private keys consists of five basic steps. We describe the steps to securely send data from the developer's workstation to the cloud virtual machine. Similar steps would be needed when sending data from the cloud virtual machine to the developer's workstation.

1. **Key generation** Both developer and cloud virtual machine generate a public and private key.
2. **Key exchange** Cloud virtual machine and developer exchange public keys.

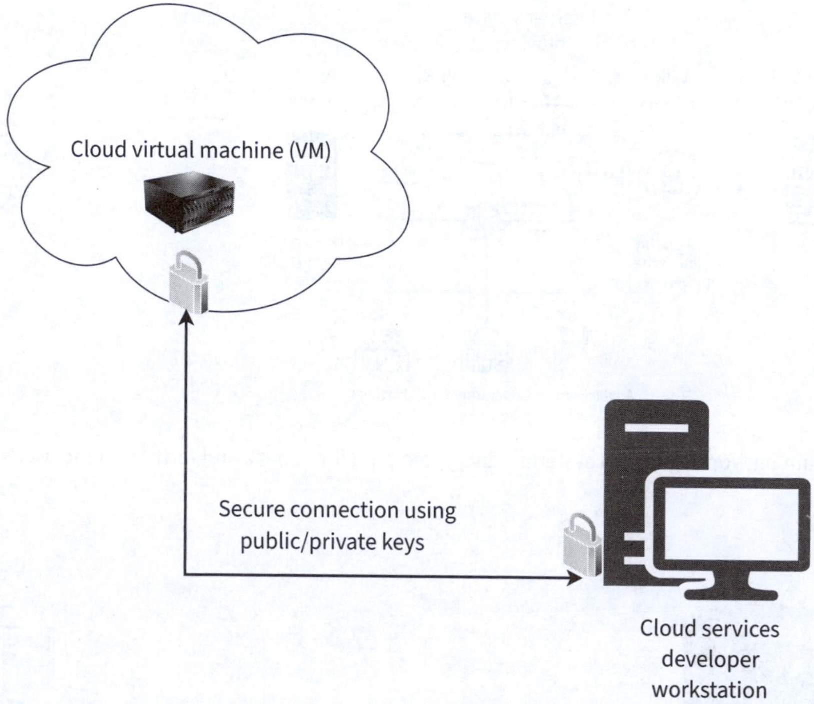

Fig. 17.1 Secure connection for accessing cloud virtual machine using public–private keys

3. **Encryption** Developer data is encrypted using the cloud virtual machine's public key.
4. **Sending encrypted data** The encrypted data is sent to the cloud virtual machine.
5. **Decryption** The cloud virtual machine decrypts the message using its own private key.

Virtual Private Networks for Secure IT Systems

Distributed enterprise computer systems use virtual private networks for data security and privacy. Let us briefly define a virtual private network. A virtual private network (VPN)[5] routes a user's internet traffic using a private data packeting service rather than the regular internet service provider (ISP). More specifically, the VPN creates a private, encrypted tunnel through which a user can access the internet while hiding their personal information, location, and other data. As seen in Fig. 17.2, a VPN client software and a VPN server work together to manage secure data transfer. When the user connects to the internet using their VPN, their computer submits information to Websites through the encrypted connection created by the VPN. The VPN acts as an intermediary, that forwards the user's request to a Website and then sends the Website's response back to the VPN user.

Using a VPN allows multiple advantages. VPN provides anonymity and privacy to a user. It also protects a user's browsing history. Contemporary Web browsers along with ISPs have a record of a user's internet activity. They can use this information for targeted marketing. Since VPNs hide the user's IP address; this allows the user to connect to and browse the Web anonymously. Using a VPN prevents a user's search history data from being collected, or sensitive information from getting compromised.

[5]How does a VPN work? Fortinet, https://www.fortinet.com/resources/cyberglossary/how-does-vpn-work (accessed 9 June 2023).

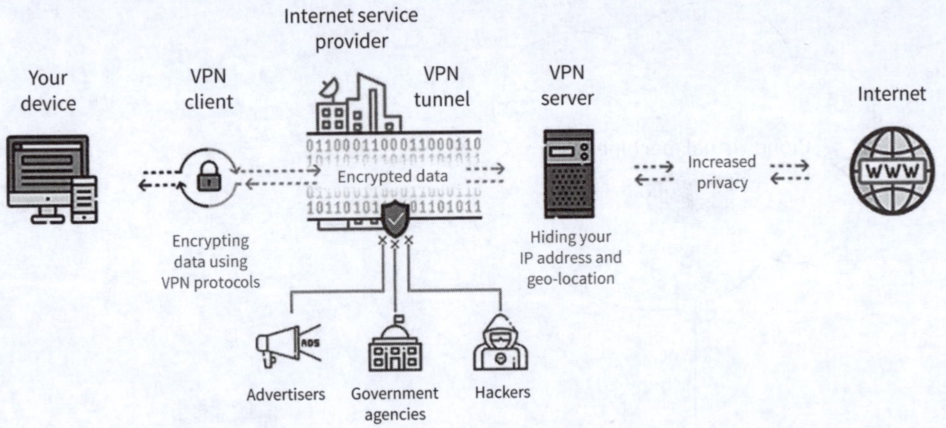

Fig. 17.2 Diagram on working of VPN systems.[6] Encrypted data flows back and forth from the user's device and the VPN server

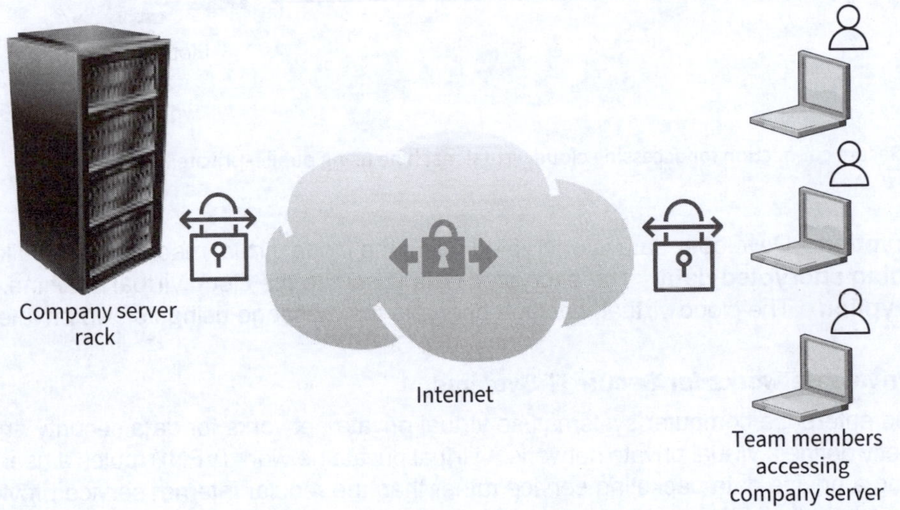

Fig. 17.3 VPN for establishing secure connection between company servers and several team members

Use of a VPN is not limited to anonymously browsing the internet. Enterprises and individual users can also install VPN clients on a variety of connected machines[7,8] to take advantage of privacy and security offered by VPNs. Figure 17.3 shows how an enterprise uses VPN to establish connectivity between users and the company server system.

[6]VPN encryption, https://www.cactusvpn.com/beginners-guide-to-vpn/vpn-encryption/ (accessed 6 June 2023).
[7]Zero config VPN, https://tailscale.com/integrations/ (accessed 10 June 2023).
[8]OpenVPN, https://openvpn.net/ (accessed 10 June 2023).

17.4 | Conclusion

The chapter presented commonly used cybersecurity terminology and then listed some commonly used techniques used by hackers to get access to sensitive business information. Ten recommendations from FCC are enumerated as means to prevent future attacks and reduce cyberattack surface. Businesses should consider the use of cryptographically generated keys and/or virtual private networks (VPNs) for secure data connectivity between users and company servers.

Exercises

A. State True/False

1. Cybersecurity is a concern only for large organizations.
2. Phishing is a type of cyberattack that uses e-mail or a malicious Website to infect your computer or system with malware or to collect sensitive information.
3. Unsecured IoT devices such as security cameras can lead to a data breach.
4. Training employees on cybersecurity does not help prevent cyberattacks.
5. Two factor authentication (such as one time password-OTP) is a good idea for secure logins.

B. Short-answer Questions

1. How does the use of virtual private networks (VPNs) provide anonymity and privacy to a web user?
2. Why is it recommended to regularly back up important data and business information on a different computer system?
3. Make a list of data that a small or medium scale business should regularly back up.
4. Give an example of a phishing e-mail or text message you may have received.
5. Why do hackers use e-mail as a way to breach cybersecurity of businesses and individuals?

C. Long-answer Questions

1. Prepare a report for a small business about things that can go wrong if it falls victim to a cyberattack.
2. Based on the recommendation presented in this chapter and your own research, prepare a checklist for a small or medium business to ward off cyberattacks.

D. Explore and Experiment

1. Setup up a secure VPN connection between two or more computers (or devices) by using options 7,8 mentioned in the footnote, or by using a VPN client of your choice.
2. In Figs. 17.4 and 17.5, we use Generative AI to learn more about VPN and public/private keys.

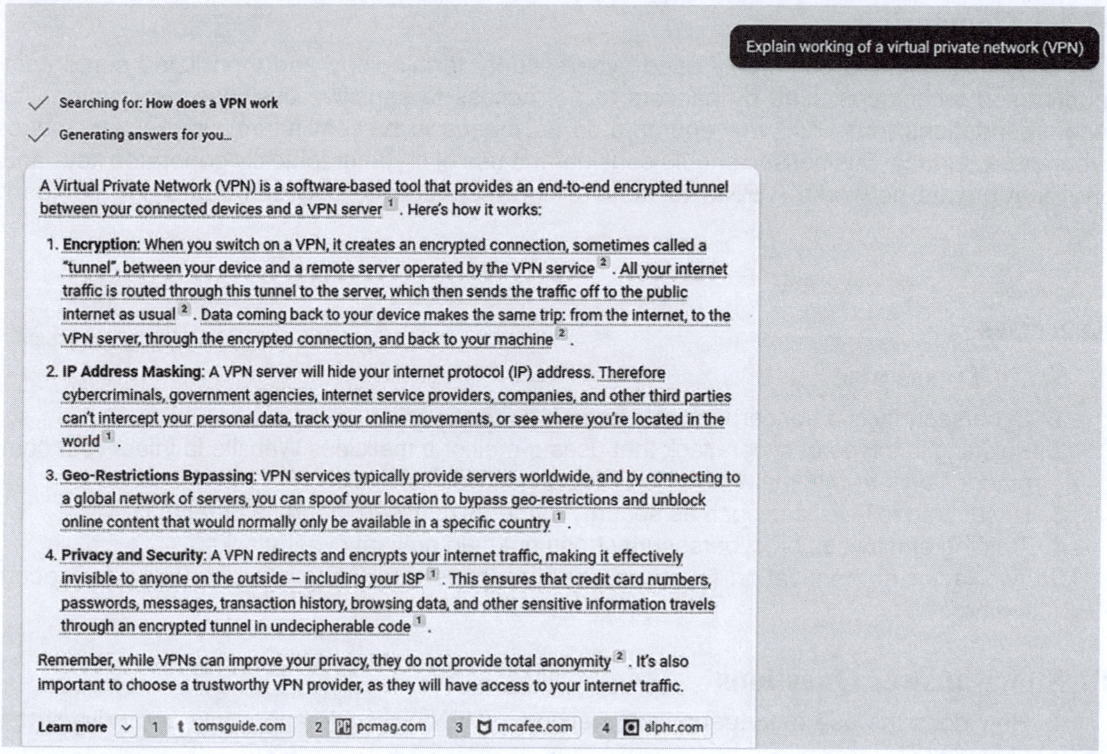

Explain working of a virtual private network (VPN)

Searching for: **How does a VPN work**

Generating answers for you...

A Virtual Private Network (VPN) is a software-based tool that provides an end-to-end encrypted tunnel between your connected devices and a VPN server [1]. Here's how it works:

1. **Encryption**: When you switch on a VPN, it creates an encrypted connection, sometimes called a "tunnel", between your device and a remote server operated by the VPN service [2]. All your internet traffic is routed through this tunnel to the server, which then sends the traffic off to the public internet as usual [2]. Data coming back to your device makes the same trip: from the internet, to the VPN server, through the encrypted connection, and back to your machine [2].
2. **IP Address Masking**: A VPN server will hide your internet protocol (IP) address. Therefore cybercriminals, government agencies, internet service providers, companies, and other third parties can't intercept your personal data, track your online movements, or see where you're located in the world [1].
3. **Geo-Restrictions Bypassing**: VPN services typically provide servers worldwide, and by connecting to a global network of servers, you can spoof your location to bypass geo-restrictions and unblock online content that would normally only be available in a specific country [1].
4. **Privacy and Security**: A VPN redirects and encrypts your internet traffic, making it effectively invisible to anyone on the outside – including your ISP [1]. This ensures that credit card numbers, passwords, messages, transaction history, browsing data, and other sensitive information travels through an encrypted tunnel in undecipherable code [1].

Remember, while VPNs can improve your privacy, they do not provide total anonymity [2]. It's also important to choose a trustworthy VPN provider, as they will have access to your internet traffic.

Learn more 1 tomsguide.com 2 pcmag.com 3 mcafee.com 4 alphr.com

Fig. 17.4 Main features of virtual private networks (VPNs)

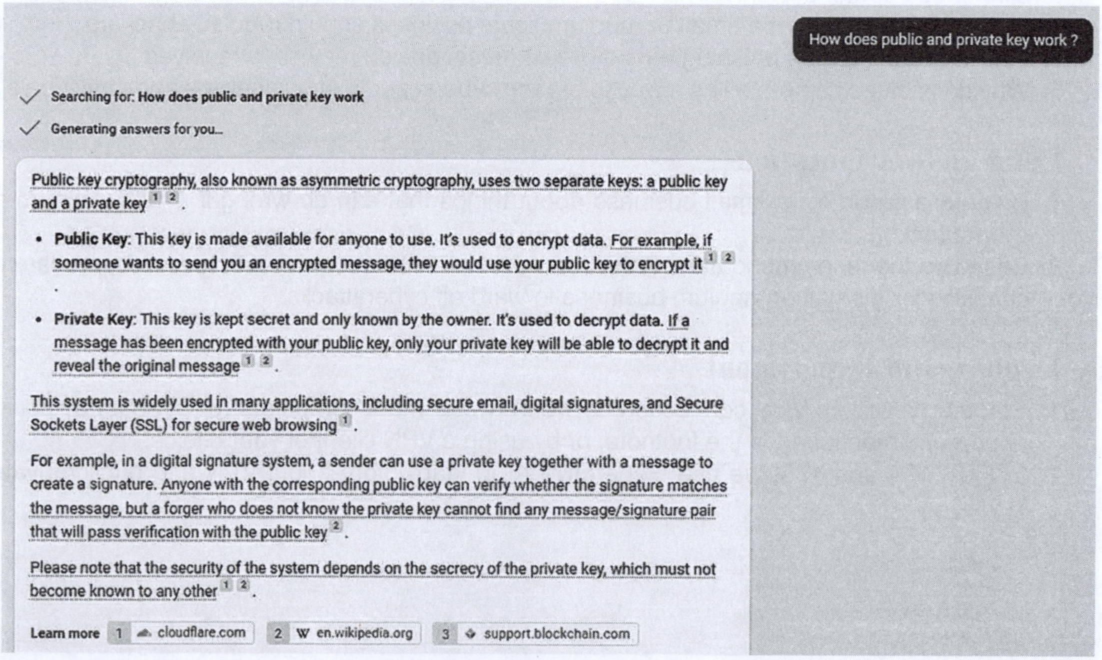

How does public and private key work ?

Searching for: **How does public and private key work**

Generating answers for you...

Public key cryptography, also known as asymmetric cryptography, uses two separate keys: a public key and a private key [1,2].

- **Public Key**: This key is made available for anyone to use. It's used to encrypt data. For example, if someone wants to send you an encrypted message, they would use your public key to encrypt it [1,2].
- **Private Key**: This key is kept secret and only known by the owner. It's used to decrypt data. If a message has been encrypted with your public key, only your private key will be able to decrypt it and reveal the original message [1,2].

This system is widely used in many applications, including secure email, digital signatures, and Secure Sockets Layer (SSL) for secure web browsing [1].

For example, in a digital signature system, a sender can use a private key together with a message to create a signature. Anyone with the corresponding public key can verify whether the signature matches the message, but a forger who does not know the private key cannot find any message/signature pair that will pass verification with the public key [2].

Please note that the security of the system depends on the secrecy of the private key, which must not become known to any other [1,2].

Learn more 1 cloudflare.com 2 en.wikipedia.org 3 support.blockchain.com

Fig. 17.5 Use of public/private keys to ensure data security

E. Generate Use Case on Cyberattacks and Ways to Prevent Them

Use Case: Understanding Cyberattacks on Small Businesses

Brief description: Cyberattacks come in multiple forms. A computer can get infected by downloading an innocuous file in an e-mail attachment, or clicking on a genuine looking weblink. Ransomware demands may be of the order of thousands of dollars, or large amount of money gets siphoned off from a bank account. Read the five use cases of cyberattacks mentioned in the resources and come up with a comprehensive use case on how technology and simple commonsense can help in thwarting such attacks.

Resources

https://www.nist.gov/itl/smallbusinesscyber/cybersecurity-basics/case-study-series

Template for Creating Use Case on Cybersecurity

Define goal and purpose	Goal statement
	Identify stakeholders
	Define scope
Details to include in use case	Capture how technology helps business process
	Keep use case findings description textual, with a few simple flowcharts if needed
	Focus on describing how technology benefits the use case
Future applications	Mention any new applications that can leverage the technology used

Suggested Reading

1. Sam Grubb, How Cybersecurity Really Works: A Hands-On Guide for Total Beginners, Paperback, No Starch Press.

CHAPTER 18

Synthesizing Ideas

CHAPTER OUTLINE

18.1 Ride-Sharing
18.2 Logistics
18.3 Digital Payments
18.4 E-Governance
18.5 Smart Cities Using Technology
18.6 Precision Agriculture Using Technology
18.7 Creating Your Own Disruptive Application Using Technology

LEARNING OBJECTIVES

After reading this chapter, you will be able to:

- comprehend contemporary use-cases enabled by emerging technologies
- understand steps to create a new application using emerging technologies

Effective Management Using Multiple Emerging Technologies

Real world applications use one or more technologies. For example, ride sharing uses multiple technologies under the hood. You may have heard the quote "the whole is greater than the sum of its parts". Similarly, business innovators need to understand and utilize multiple technologies for creating disruptive applications.

It is now time to understand how ideas are realized by the use of technology. We will present few well-known use-cases to understand how technology helps bringing these ideas to life. Before we get started with our discussion, let us review our journey so far. The technologies we have discussed are summarized in Table 18.1. Different technologies, when used together in an application

Table 18.1 Review of technologies from earlier chapters

Technology	Use
Big Data	Store and query data in different formats such as structured, unstructured or as a binary large object
Internet of Things	Connect and share information with devices spread across large areas
Cloud Computing	Provides scalable and on-demand compute resources and managed services
Blockchain	Useful distributed ledger technology to create secure transaction records
Machine Learning	Algorithms to cluster, classify, and predict data. Example: Decision tree
Deep Neural Networks	Multilayer networks configurable for a variety of applications such as classification and regression
Computer Vision	Classify, detect, and segment objects using convolutional neural networks
Text Analytics	Perform classification of text such as sentiment analysis and carry out meaningful dialogue
Edge Computing	Work on data capture, analysis, and action at the data source
Sensors	Myriad of sensors such as radio frequency identification (RFID), QR codes that enable sensing of physical parameters or encoded information
Drones and Robotics	Drones allow monitoring and ferrying of objects to hard-to-reach areas. Robots carry out tedious and hazardous tasks with accuracy
Cybersecurity	Allows secure exchange of data between users

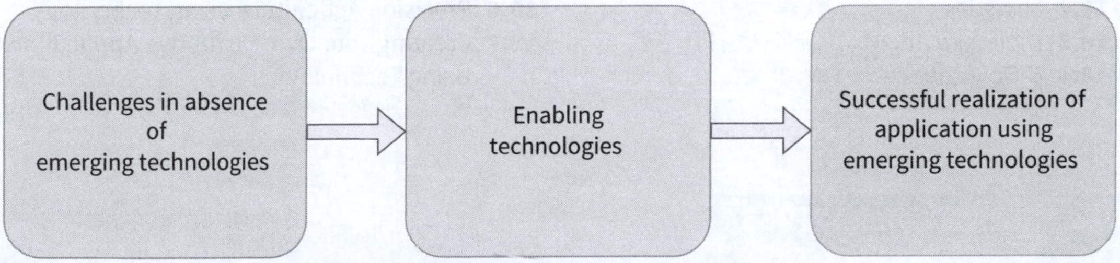

Fig. 18.1 Role of emerging technologies in realizing contemporary applications

form the technology stack for that application. We will present a simplified technology stack for the applications we discuss.

Even though we have not explicitly discussed the advances in computing, storage, communication, and mobile devices; they are the cornerstone for other technologies. In our discussion of use-cases, we will identify components from emerging technologies that make the use-case a reality. Figure 18.1 shows the pivotal role of enabling technologies.

18.1 | Ride-Sharing

The idea of ride sharing originated in Paris in 2008. This is when the founders of Uber had a difficult time hailing a taxi and thought of creating a ride-sharing phone app. The rest as they say is history. Ride sharing caught on throughout the world. It provides employment opportunities, pickups and drop-offs to precise locations, shows the movement of the taxi and also provides an estimate of the arrival time at the destination. All this would have been difficult to implement a decade before 2008. The technology elements to create the ride-sharing service were all mature in 2009 and the ride-sharing app harnessed it all. The centerpiece of the ride-sharing app is the smartphone and its location sensor. The smartphone communicates with a cloud server using cellular connectivity and updates the user on pricing and ride options. Let us discuss the underlying technologies used in a ride-sharing application.

Enabling Technologies for Ride-Sharing

The enabling technologies that have made ride-sharing more efficient, convenient, and accessible are presented as a technology stack in Fig. 18.2.

Mobile applications Mobile applications are at the heart of ride-sharing services. Users download and install ride-sharing apps on their smartphones to request rides, track drivers, and make payments. The apps provide a seamless user experience and enable real-time interaction between riders and drivers.

GPS and navigation systems GPS technology plays a crucial role in ride-sharing services by providing accurate location information. GPS enables drivers to locate riders and navigate to their pick-up and drop-off locations efficiently. Navigation systems integrated into ride-sharing apps offer turn-by-turn directions, optimizing route planning and minimizing travel time.

Real-time matching and dispatching algorithms Advanced matching and dispatching algorithms analyze the location, availability, and preferences of both riders and drivers in real-time. These algorithms consider factors, such as distance, estimated time of arrival, traffic conditions, and driver ratings to optimize the matching process and minimize waiting times for riders.

Digital payments and wallets Digital payment systems are integrated into ride-sharing apps and enable cashless transactions between riders and drivers. Users can link their payment methods, such as credit cards or mobile wallets, to their ride-sharing accounts. Some countries, such as India also offer the option to make cash payments.

Rating and feedback systems Ride-sharing platforms incorporate rating and feedback systems that allow riders to rate drivers and provide feedback on their experiences. This helps maintain

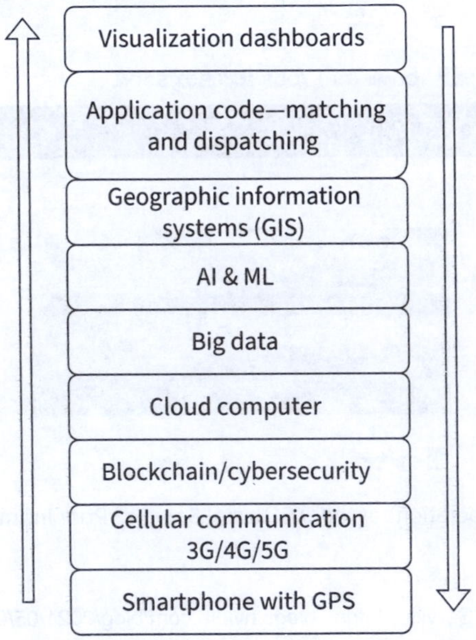

Fig. 18.2 Technology stack for typical ridesharing use-case. The arrows indicate data flow in both directions

service quality, ensures driver accountability, and helps riders make informed decisions when selecting drivers.

Safety and security features Ride-sharing services implement safety and security features to provide a secure experience for riders and drivers. This includes features, such as driver background checks, real-time tracking of rides, emergency assistance buttons, and ride-sharing insurance policies.

Big data analytics Ride-sharing companies collect and analyze vast amounts of data generated by their platforms. Big data analytics enables valuable insights regarding rider preferences, driver behavior, traffic patterns, and demand fluctuations. These insights help optimize service offerings, pricing, and operational efficiency.

Technology-Enabled Ride-Sharing Solution

Enabling technologies have transformed the ride-sharing industry. It allows for efficient matching of riders and drivers, convenient payment options, enhanced safety features, and data-driven decision-making. They have made ride sharing a viable and popular transportation option for many people world-wide. There are chances you have used Uber, Ola, Lyft, or a similar ride-sharing service.

18.2 | Logistics

It is easy to take logistics for granted. You order an item from Amazon and it usually arrives in a day or two. It is rarely misplaced or late. In a typical logistics application, each time an item reaches a transit node on the way to its destination, a timestamp is registered and accessible via the logistics operator's Website. Let me share a personal example on insight provided by a logistics operator. Some time back, I drove across the Golden Gate bridge. A camera at the bridge's toll booth recognized my car's license plate and used my car's registration information to send me a bill. An AI-based computer vision-based sorting machine at the postal department, scanned this bill in transit and let me know a day in advance by sending me an e-mail (Fig. 18.3).

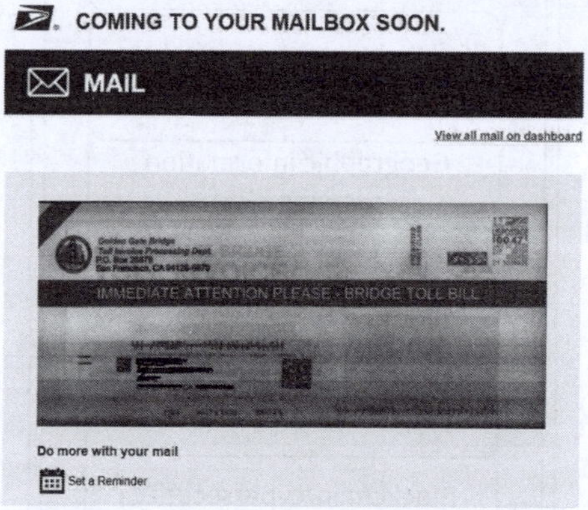

Fig. 18.3 An example of AI-based operations at the U.S. Postal Service.[1] Prior intimation of post arriving the next day!

[1]Nvidia Blog, AI Apps for US Postal Service, https://blogs.nvidia.com/blog/2021/05/06/edge-ai-usps/ (accessed 10 June 2023).

Enabling Technologies for Logistics

Let us discuss the key enabling technologies for logistics. These technologies are mentioned as building blocks of the technology stack shown in Fig. 18.4. Like other technology stacks in this chapter, the logistics stack is indicative and not comprehensive.

Internet of Things (IoT) IoT devices, such as sensors and RFID tags are used to track and monitor assets, inventory, and shipments in real-time. IoT technology provides visibility into the location, condition, and movement of goods throughout the supply chain. It enables proactive monitoring, reduces loss or damage, and improves overall supply chain efficiency.

Big data analytics The logistics industry generates vast amounts of data, including shipment details, inventory levels, transportation routes, customer preferences, and market trends. Big data analytics tools help analyze this data to derive insights, optimize operations, predict demand, and improve decision-making across the supply chain.

Artificial intelligence (AI) and machine learning (ML) AI and ML technologies are used in logistics for various applications. They can optimize route planning and scheduling, predict demand, forecast inventory requirements, and detect anomalies or potential disruptions in the supply chain. AI-powered chatbots and virtual assistants also improve customer service and provide real-time support.

Fulfilment center Fulfilment centers use various kinds of warehouse/industrial robots and automation systems to locate, collate, and pack items ordered by the customer.

Cloud computing Cloud-based platforms provide scalable and flexible infrastructure for storing, accessing, and processing logistics data. Cloud computing helps in real-time collaboration, data sharing, and integration among various stakeholders in the supply chain, including shippers, carriers, and customers.

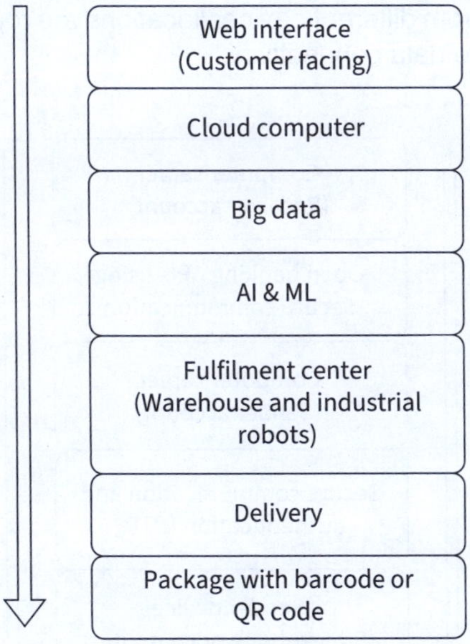

Fig. 18.4 Technology stack for a typical logistics use-case. Arrow indicates dataflow of a Web order getting processed. Sensors are used to track shipment and to indicate proof of delivery

Mobile technologies Mobile devices and applications play a crucial role in logistics operations. Mobile apps enable real-time communication, order tracking, proof of delivery, and electronic documentation.

Technology-Enabled Logistics Solution

Several enabling technologies mentioned above have transformed the logistics industry. It has helped companies to optimize processes, reduce costs, enhance customer experience, and respond to market dynamics more effectively. The integration of these technologies continues to drive innovation and reshape the future of logistics. You are likely to have used logistic services from Amazon, Zomato, DoorDash, or similar providers.

18.3 | Digital Payments

Digital payment provides the ability to electronically transfer money. There are several examples of financial transactions that use digital payment. Paying for an airline or train ticket when booking through a Website, paying for food at a restaurant using a credit card, sending your share of money to a friend after a picnic or paying for groceries to the neighborhood vegetable vendor using a QR code. For all the above-mentioned transactions, physical money does not exchange hands. Money is transferred electronically from the sender's account or credit card to the receiver's account.

Although the digital transfer of money seems intuitive and simple, there is considerable technology that makes this happen securely and correctly every time.

Enabling Technologies

Some key technologies have played a significant role in the advancement and widespread adoption of digital payments. Figure 18.5 shows information flow when a digital transaction (such as paying a utility bill online) takes place. A more generic digital payment scenario is seen in Fig. 18.6. Here transactions originating from different devices/locations are routed to respective servers using Open banking APIs and secure data connectivity.

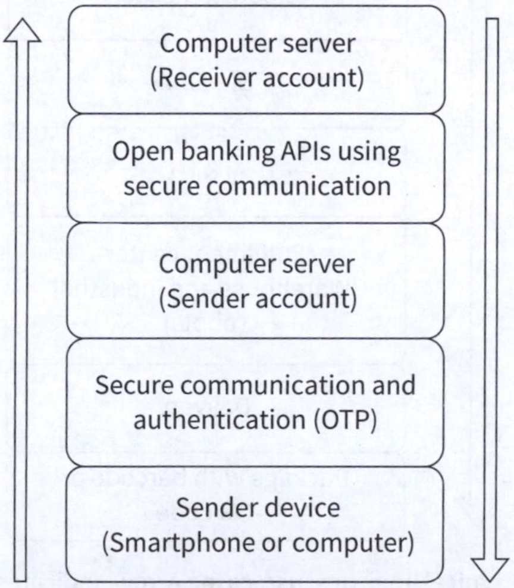

Fig. 18.5 Data flow for a digital payment use-case. Bidirectional data flow ensures transaction details to be communicated to the sender and receiver

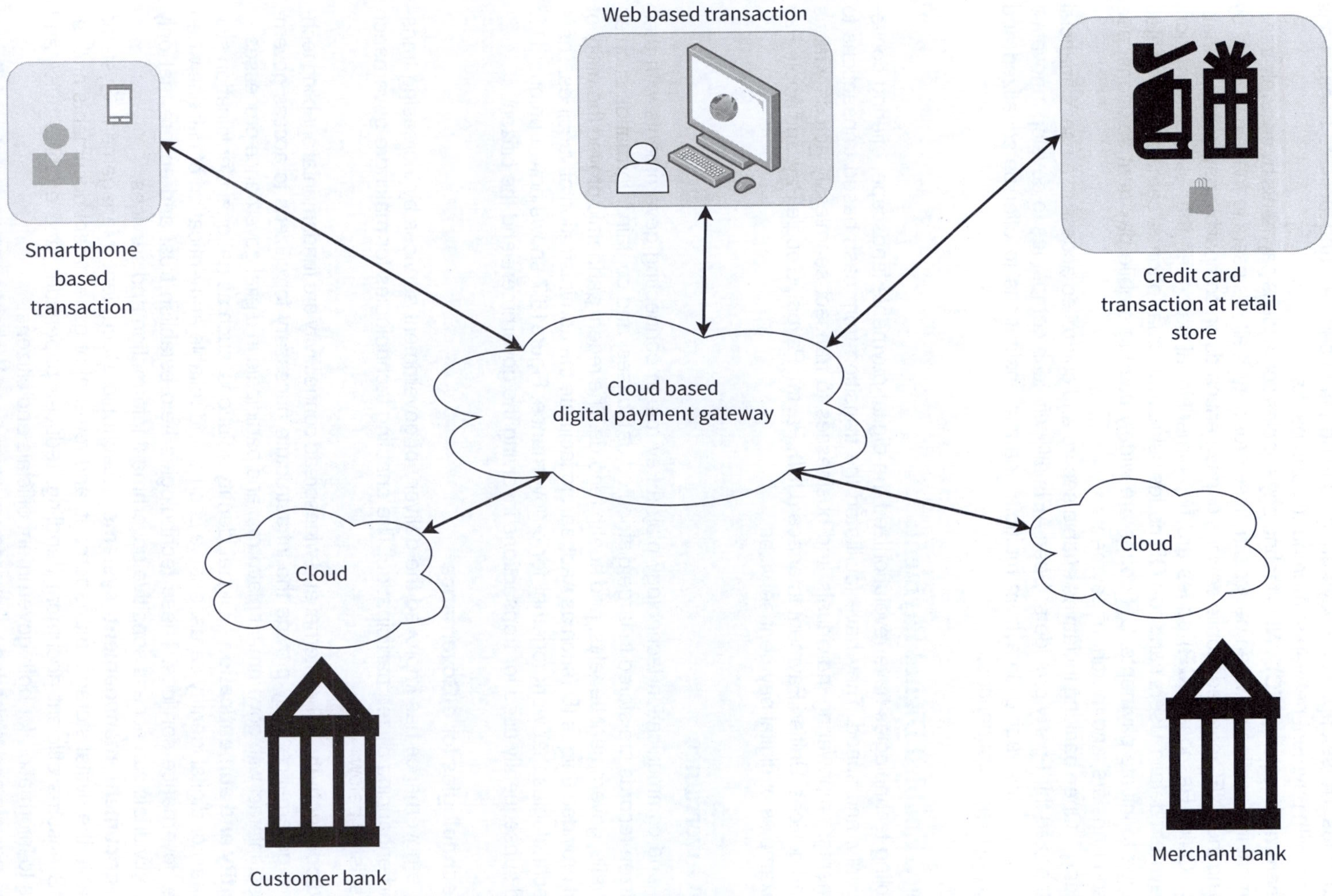

Fig. 18.6 Data flow between customer and merchant banks when a purchase is carried out

Mobile payment applications Mobile payment applications allow users to make payments using their smartphones. These apps store payment card information securely and facilitate transactions by connecting with payment networks, merchants, and banks.

Near-field communication (NFC) NFC technology enables contactless payments by securely transmitting payment information between devices in close proximity. It allows users to make payments by simply tapping their NFC-enabled mobile devices or payment cards on compatible payment terminals.

QR codes Quick Response (QR) codes are two-dimensional barcodes that store information, including payment details. Users can scan QR codes using their smartphones' camera or dedicated scanning apps to initiate payments. QR codes are widely used in mobile payment solutions, person-to-person transfers, and merchant payments.

Open banking Open banking initiatives enable secure and controlled access to a user's financial data by authorized third-party providers. Open APIs allow fintech companies to develop innovative payment solutions, leveraging data from multiple financial institutions to offer personalized and streamlined payment experiences.

Technology-Enabled Digital Payment

These enabling technologies have revolutionized the digital payments landscape, offering convenience, security, and speed. They have facilitated the transition from cash-based transactions to digital payments, empowering individuals and businesses to transact seamlessly across various channels and devices. Unified Payment Interface (UPI), Paytm, Paypal, Google Pay, and Apple Pay are some examples of digital payment services.

18.4 | E-Governance

Information and communication technology play a key role in connecting governments with their citizens. Citizen records are stored in large distributed databases, and contain information such as property details, government benefits, and health records. The recent pandemic proved the utility of government provided unique ID (such as Aadhaar) to facilitate the administration of vaccines. There are many technologies that work together for e-governance. Figure18.7 shows how a unique ID is created and subsequently used for transactions involving the government and the citizen.

Enabling Technologies for e-Governance

World over, e-governance has improved the delivery of government services by increasing transparency, and enhancing citizen participation. The enabling technologies for making e-governance a success is listed below.

Internet and connectivity The internet and widespread connectivity are fundamental enabling technologies for e-governance. They provide the infrastructure necessary for citizens to access government services, interact with government platforms, and participate in digital governance processes.

Digital identity and authentication Digital identity solutions, such as national identification systems (Aadhaar) or digital identity cards, enable secure and reliable authentication of citizens when accessing e-governance services. These technologies help establish trust and ensure that only authorized individuals can access sensitive government information and services.

Electronic document management systems Electronic Document Management Systems (EDMS) enable the digital storage, management, and retrieval of government documents and records. EDMS ensures efficient document handling, reduces paperwork, and enables quick and easy access to information for both government officials and citizens.

Government portals and Websites Government portals and Websites serve as central platforms for citizens to access a wide range of e-governance services. These portals provide a user-friendly

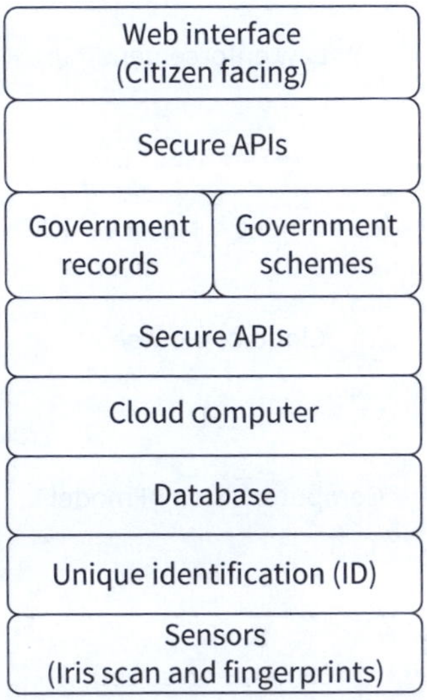

Fig. 18.7 Creation and use of unique id for e-governance

interface, allowing citizens to access information, submit applications, make payments, and interact with government agencies.

Online service delivery Enabling technologies facilitate the delivery of various government services online, including tax filing, license applications, permit issuance, and social welfare programs. Online service delivery streamlines processes, reduces bureaucracy, and improves the efficiency and accessibility of government services.

Mobile applications Mobile applications play a crucial role in e-governance by providing convenient access to government services through smartphones and tablets. Mobile apps allow citizens to access information, receive notifications, make payments, and submit applications from anywhere, enhancing the reach and accessibility of e-governance services.

Digital payment systems Digital payment systems enable citizens to make secure online payments for government services, such as taxes, fees, or fines. Integration with various payment options, such as credit/debit cards, mobile wallets, or online banking, ensures convenient and efficient payment processing.

Data analytics and big data Data analytics and big data technologies help governments derive meaningful insights from large volumes of data generated through e-governance platforms. Analyzing this data enables evidence-based policy-making, resource optimization, and identification of trends and patterns for better governance.

In India, Aadhaar[2] has proved to be a robust tool for implementing different e-governance schemes. Aadhaar is an important part of India's digital public infrastructure (DPI).

18.5 | Smart Cities Using Technology

As more population migrates from villages to urban areas, proper management of cities has become a necessity. Managing cities includes making sure the citizens get access to clean water,

[2]Aadhaar Technology and Architecture, March 2014, Planning commission, https://ia800108.us.archive.org/17/items/Aadhaar-Technology-Architecture/AadhaarTechnologyArchitecture_March2014.pdf (accessed 25 June 2023).

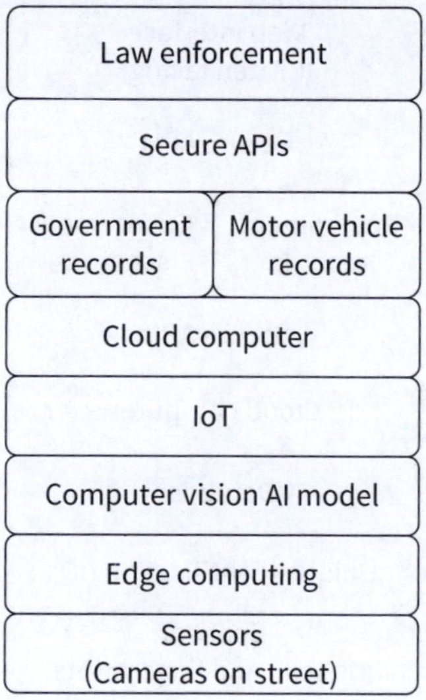

Fig. 18.8 Monitoring street safety using cameras and edge-based computer vision models

reliable electricity, good infrastructure, safe roads, and the environment. All this involves collecting a large amount of data, planning, and implementation. It is important to keep in mind that technology for the most part, provides information and insights. Humans or officials have to timely act on this information/insight to make a positive difference.

Smart cities have systems to monitor traffic, garbage disposal, real-time citizen safety using a large deployment of closed-circuit television cameras (CCTV). Figure 18.8 shows the technology stack of a camera on a street intersection. Vehicles that cross the intersection at a red light are identified using computer vision. A picture of the incident gets stored on the edge device and using IoT, the details of the vehicle's license plate are transferred to a cloud computer. A letter mentioning the fine amount along with the picture of the incident is sent to the registered owner of the vehicle and to law enforcement records. This is all managed using the technology stack shown in Fig. 18.8.

The example of traffic monitoring is one of the services provided by a smart city technology ecosystem. There are numerous such services that are enabled by multiple technologies.

Internet of things (IoT) The IoT forms the backbone of smart cities by connecting various devices, sensors, and systems. IoT devices collect and transmit data from physical assets, such as infrastructure, buildings, vehicles, and utilities. This connectivity enables real-time monitoring, data analysis, and automation of city operations.

Big data analytics Smart cities generate vast amounts of data from diverse sources. Big data analytics technologies allow cities to process and analyze this data to extract insights and make data-driven decisions. Advanced analytics techniques, including ML and AI, help identify patterns, predict trends, optimize resource allocation, and enhance service delivery.

Cloud computing Cloud computing provides scalable and on-demand access to computing resources, storage, and software applications. Smart cities utilize cloud computing to store and manage the massive amounts of data generated by IoT devices. Cloud-based platforms offer the computational power and flexibility required for data processing, analysis, and hosting smart city applications.

Artificial intelligence (AI) AI technologies, including ML, natural language processing, and computer vision, play a crucial role in smart cities. AI enables intelligent automation, predictive analytics, and autonomous decision-making. It helps optimize traffic flow, energy consumption, public safety, and other aspects of city operations.

Edge computing Edge computing brings computation and data storage closer to the data source, reducing latency and bandwidth requirements. Edge computing enables real-time processing and analysis of data at the edge of the network, closer to IoT devices and sensors. It helps handle the massive data volumes generated by smart city applications while ensuring rapid response times.

Geospatial technology Geospatial technologies, such as Geographic Information Systems (GIS) and satellite imagery, are critical for smart cities. GIS systems enable the collection, integration, analysis, and visualization of location-based data. These technologies support urban planning, infrastructure management, transportation optimization, emergency response, and environmental monitoring.

Sensor networks Sensor networks provide real-time data on various parameters, including environmental conditions, traffic flow, air quality, energy consumption, and water usage. These sensor networks capture data from across the city and enable monitoring, analysis, and optimization of resources and services.

Cities across the world are embracing technology to make the lives of their citizens easier by providing right amenities and security.

18.6 | Precision Agriculture Using Technology

Food security is a big challenge for countries across the world. Feeding a growing population requires efficient use of finite arable land present in many parts of the world. This requires optimum use of fertilizers, herbicides, irrigation, and harvesting methods. Unchecked use of groundwater for irrigation is a major concern for planners. Precision agriculture technology provides the ability to leverage GPS, drones, and remote sensing imagery to get information on crop health, nutrient levels, and pest infestations. This data enables targeted interventions, optimized resource usage, and improved yield. Let us enumerate how emerging technologies assist precision agriculture. The use of emerging technologies for agriculture provides best results, when implemented by cooperatives or large farm owners.

Internet of Things (IoT) IoT devices are used extensively in agriculture to monitor and collect data from various sources. Sensors placed in fields, livestock, and machinery capture information on soil moisture, temperature, humidity, crop growth, livestock health, and equipment performance. This data helps farmers make informed decisions, optimize resource allocation, and automate processes.

Artificial intelligence (AI) and machine learning (ML) AI and ML technologies are used in agriculture to analyze vast amounts of data and derive actionable insights. These technologies can identify patterns, predict crop diseases, optimize irrigation and fertilizer use, and suggest personalized recommendations for farmers. AI-powered systems can also automate processes like sorting, grading, and packaging.

Data analytics and cloud computing Data analytics and cloud computing enable farmers or governments to store, process, and analyze large volumes of agricultural data. Cloud-based platforms provide access to advanced analytics tools and databases for data-driven decision-making. Farmers can identify trends, analyze historical data, and gain valuable insights for improved crop management and resource optimization.

Smart irrigation systems Smart irrigation systems use real-time data from sensors and weather forecasts to optimize water usage. These systems can automatically adjust irrigation schedules based on soil moisture levels, weather conditions, and plant requirements. Smart irrigation helps conserve water, reduce costs, and maintain optimal crop health.

Advanced countries use computer vision technology for selectively spraying[3] weeds in the field, or robots to harvest fruits. Each country needs to figure out the agriculture technology that is best suited for their local condition and economy.

18.7 | Creating Your Own Disruptive Application Using Technology

So far, we have talked about technologies and how it has realized several disruptive applications. Suppose, you have a great idea in mind and are convinced it is the next big thing. How do you go about realizing this application? Here are some pointers to get you started.

Define requirements of your application Observe pain points of people around you. If you discover something that affects a lot of people, dive a little deeper and think of a solution. Talk to people about the solution and the perceived problem. If people shrug the problem or the solution, maybe it is time to reevaluate your strategy. On the other hand, if your idea resonates with people who are likely to use the service, you should start putting together basic requirements of the application.

Identify technologies to realize the application Do a quick feasibility check about realizing the application. As we have seen in the disruptive applications discussed earlier, many technologies may have to work cohesively. Consult a subject matter expert to get advise on technology that will get the application to work.

Create a minimum viable product (MVP) Put together a simple MVP that you can put in the hands of a test group. Use the internet, to discover the details about the MVP's created by Uber, Airbnb and Dropbox. Once you have the MVP and have positive feedback from paying customers, maybe it is time to start thinking about how to scale up the application.

Leverage best practices and gather feedback to improve As you scale up your operations, keep your eyes open to leverage technological best practices across the world and use them to optimize your setup. The great thing about most technology is its uniformness across the world.

18.8 | Conclusion

In this chapter, we presented some well-known applications, such as ridesharing, logistics, digital payment, e-governance, smart cities and precision agriculture to demonstrate the power of emerging technologies. There are many more applications such as content/code creation using Generative AI technology, and massive open online courses (MOOCs) that are now feasible using technology. It is worth reiterating that technology by itself is powerless. In all the applications we discussed in the chapter, we see that technology is harnessed to create and run meaningful, scalable applications that benefit a large number of people.

Exercises

A. State True/False

1. All disruptive applications use only one technology.
2. Data analytics is a technology used in most applications.
3. Creating an MVP is an important step in application building process.
4. Ride sharing application relies heavily on the GPS sensor.
5. India's Aadhaar ID is used by government sponsored programs.

[3]John Deere See and Spray, https://www.deere.com/en/sprayers/see-spray-ultimate/ (accessed 25 June 2023).

B. Short-answer Questions

1. Explain how ride-sharing application provides safety to its users.
2. How do logistics companies provide location of a package with the help of tracking number?
3. Enumerate citizen services in India that are linked to Aadhaar card.
4. Mention a new citizen service that you think can make good use of the Aadhaar card.
5. Provide examples of transactions where you have used digital payment.

C. Explore and Experiment

1. Generative AI helps identify different technologies and layers that enable applications such as ride sharing and smart city (Figs. 18.9, 18.10). Experiment with Generative AI to learn more about the technologies that power your favorite use case.

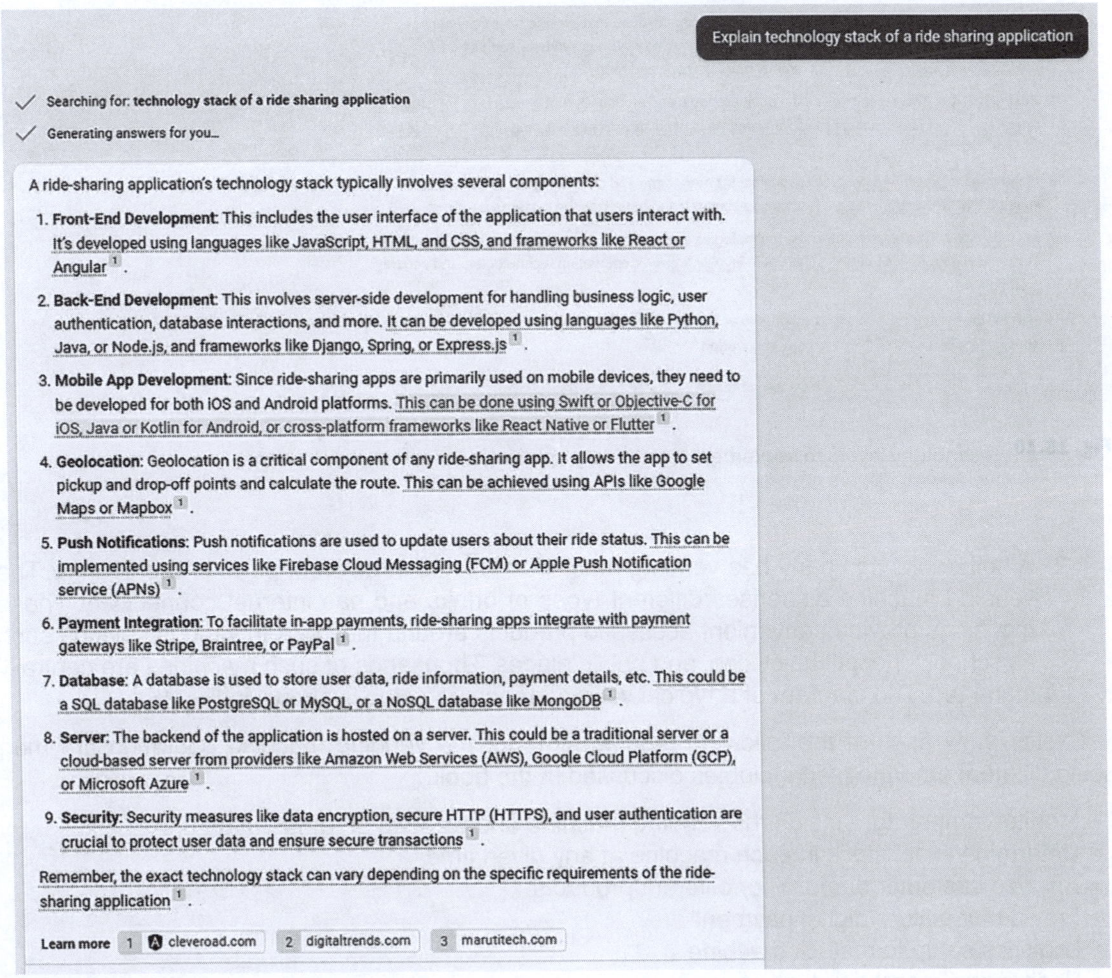

Fig. 18.9 Technologies used for a ride sharing application

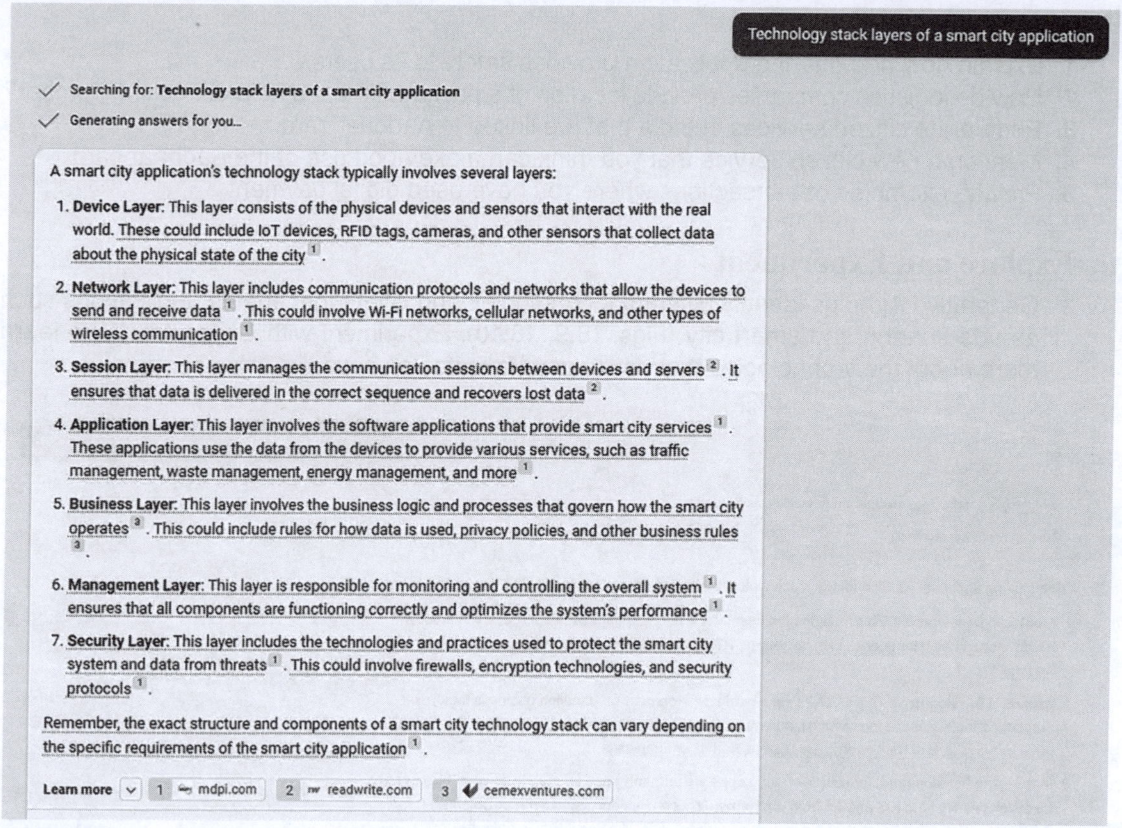

Fig. 18.10 Technology layers to implement a smart city application

2. A soft drinks company has vending machines located in different parts of the country. The vending machine dispenses different types of drinks and has internet connectivity. These machines provide convenient access to products around the clock in various settings such as schools, hospitals, offices, and public places. Thousands of such machines are centrally managed. The diagram of a typical vending machine setup is shown in Fig. 18.11.

Explain how each of the following requirements for the vending machine operation are met, using different emerging technologies discussed in the book.

- Monitor temperature inside the vending machine and working of refrigeration unit
- Determine exact stock in each machine at any given time
- Analyze customer demand for different products
- Provide for secure digital payment
- Logistics setup to restock machine
- Record and report any kind of vandalism

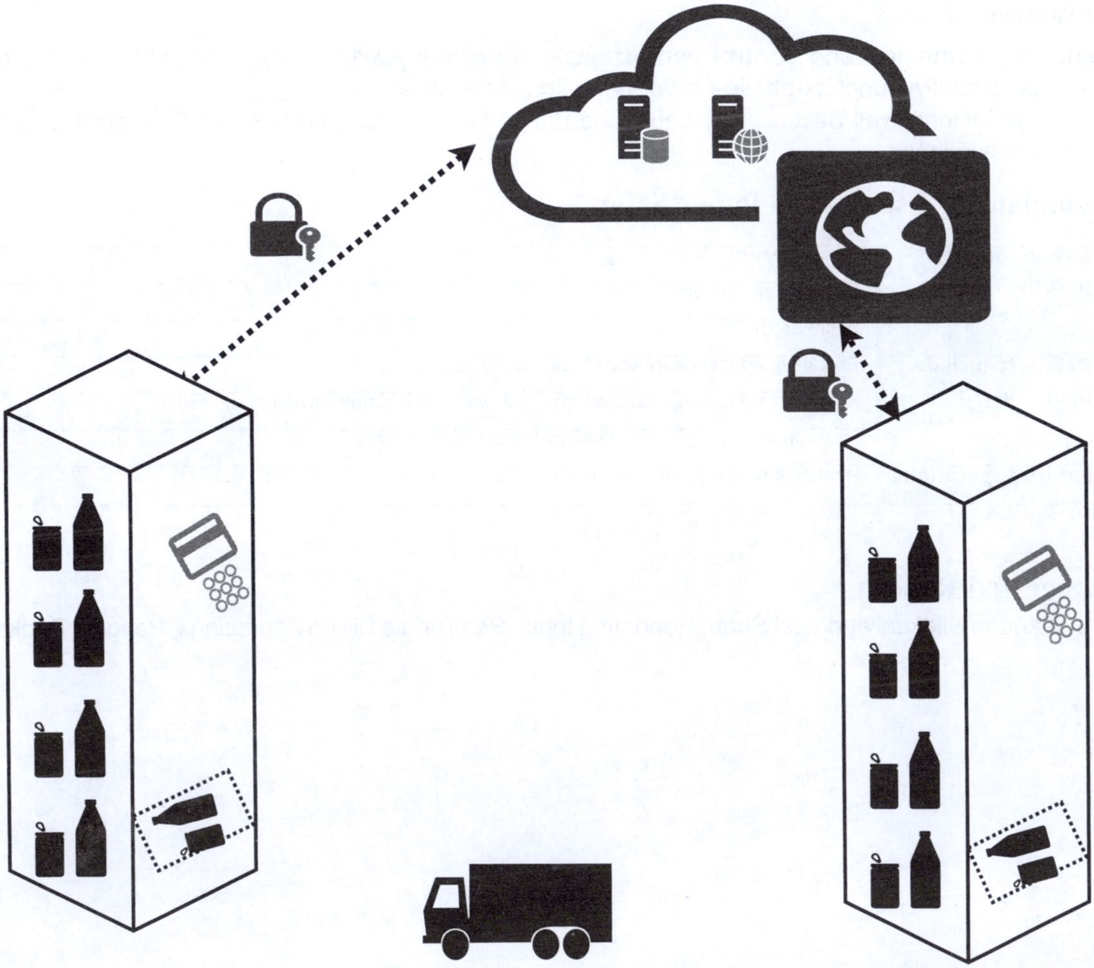

Fig. 18.11 A typical vending machine setup consisting of digital payment interface, secure internet connectivity with a cloud computer and surveillance camera. The job of the logistics van is to restock the machine as and when needed

D. Generate Use Case on Synthesizing Technology for Public Safety

Use Case: Safe City Project

Brief description: Bangalore has initiated a safe city project that envisages use of video cameras, AI, and call boxes for emergencies. Though the project is in its nascent phases, the project plan shows the use of several emerging technologies. Use the resource mentioned below and other sources from the internet to create a use case for citizen safety using emerging technologies.

Resource

Safe city command and control center: https://www.honeywell.com/in/en/press/2023/03/honeywell-successfully-launches-phase-one-of-bangalore-safe-city-project
Honeywell, Honeywell Successfully Launches Phase One Of Bangalore Safe City Project, March 2023 press release

Template for Use Case on Public Safety

Define goal and purpose	Goal statement
	Identify stakeholders
	Define scope
Details to include in use case	Capture how technology helps business process
	Keep use case findings description textual, with a few simple flowcharts if needed
	Focus on describing how technology benefits the use case
Future applications	Mention any new applications that can leverage the technology used

Suggested Reading

1. Nandan Nilekani and Viral Shah, Rebooting India: Realizing a Billion Aspirations, Penguin Books.

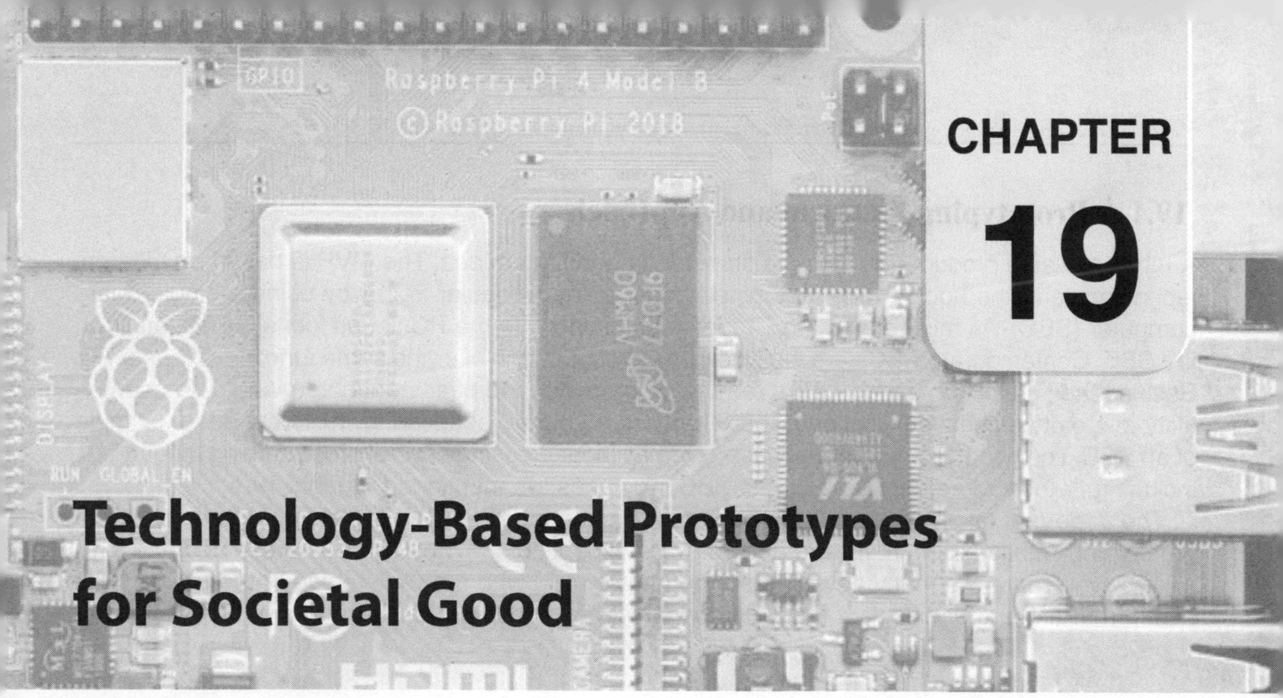

CHAPTER 19

Technology-Based Prototypes for Societal Good

CHAPTER OUTLINE

- **19.1** Prototyping Platform and Approach
- **19.2** Automated Car Parking Garage
- **19.3** Locally Saving and Remotely Querying Data
- **19.4** Sensors for Grain Silo
- **19.5** Machine Learning Models for Grain Quality
- **19.6** Connecting Grain Silos to Control Room (IoT)
- **19.7** Computer Vision for Traffic Safety
- **19.8** Dashboard for Location Information
- **19.9** Edge Computing for Street Safety
- **19.10** Drone for Search and Rescue
- **19.11** Precision Agriculture
- **19.12** Crowd Control

LEARNING OBJECTIVES

After reading this chapter, you will be able to:

- Recognize the need for prototyping ideas
- Understand scope of a prototype from eleven use cases
- Correlate hardware–software interface for realizing functionality

Effective Management Using Prototyped Solutions

Prototyping is a practical way to check the feasibility of an idea. It provides insights into possible things that can go wrong, aspects of the system that are not practical, or the cost-effectiveness of the solution. Prototyping also encourages teamwork. Different members of the team focus on different parts of the system. One member may be a subject matter expert on databases, while other team members may bring in domain knowledge in other areas.

19.1 | Prototyping Platform and Approach

A minimal viable product (MVP) is the first step in proving an idea. The MVP is based on different technologies in the book and is prototyped either using a regular PC or by using a single-board computer (SBC). As most of you are already acquainted with the PC, let us focus our attention on the SBC. Contemporary SBCs are the size of a credit card and offer the same functionality as a PC. Besides their small form factor, SBCs require lower power and offer input/output and data connectivity to prototype most applications. The Raspberry Pi board (seen in Fig. 19.1) is a good example of an SBC. The board is programmed for a given application using several programming languages, including Python. More details about the SBC interfaces are mentioned in Table 19.1.

The important takeaway from this chapter is to get a block level or systems perspective of the prototyping solution. Both hardware and software aspects of the prototype are presented at a simplified level. There are many developers around the world who are well-versed in the use of SBC and in realizing prototypes. If you are not technically inclined and are keen to create a prototype,

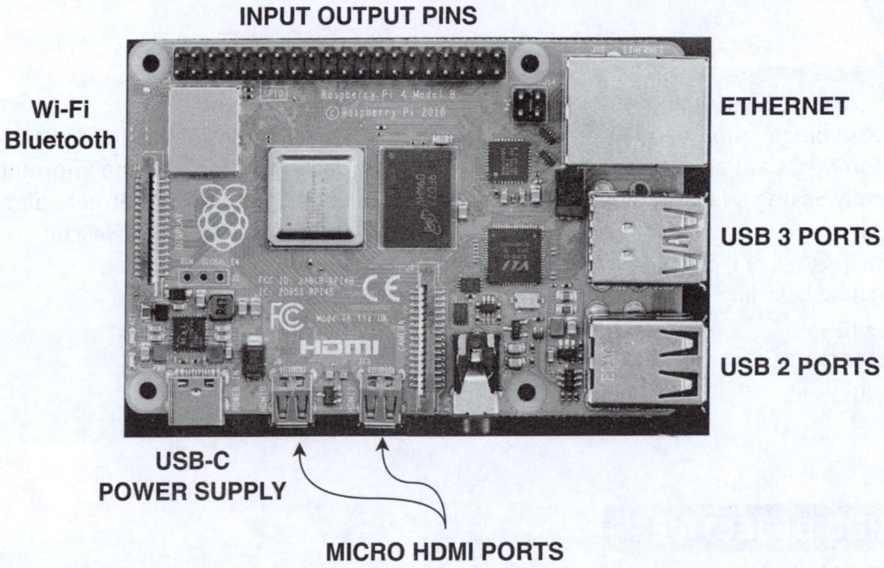

Fig. 19.1 Layout of a credit card-sized single-board computer (SBC), the Raspberry Pi. It provides conventional interfaces and uses the Linux operating system

Table 19.1 Some hardware features of a Single-Board Computer (SBC), Raspberry Pi 4

Hardware	Functionality
64-bit Microprocessor with Linux Operating System	Support for wide number of programming languages such as Python, C, Java, and many others
Bluetooth and Wi-Fi Connectivity	Easier to connect to Internet and Bluetooth-based devices
HDMI connector	Use as graphical user interface terminal or dashboard display
Ethernet connectivity	Useful for reliable wired communication
USB-2 and USB-3 ports	Interface to variety of sensors, peripherals, and cameras
40 pin input/output connector	Connection of physical devices such as relays, pushbuttons, lights, and sensors

look around. You are likely to find someone in your city/university or company. In this chapter, we will discuss eleven ideas and their prototypes. All ideas have wide application, as they are in the domain of societal good.

19.2 | Automated Car Parking Garage

The prototyping scheme of the automated car parking solution from chapter 1 is shown in Fig. 19.2. In the diagram, multiple entry/exit stations are considered. Each station consists of an SBC, which connects to a camera, payment gateway, and barrier gate. The camera reads the license plate of the vehicle at entry and exit and operates the gate. Before opening the gate at the exit, it checks for successful payment.

The functionality of the prototype is better understood by going through the hardware–software components of the solution given in Table 19.2.

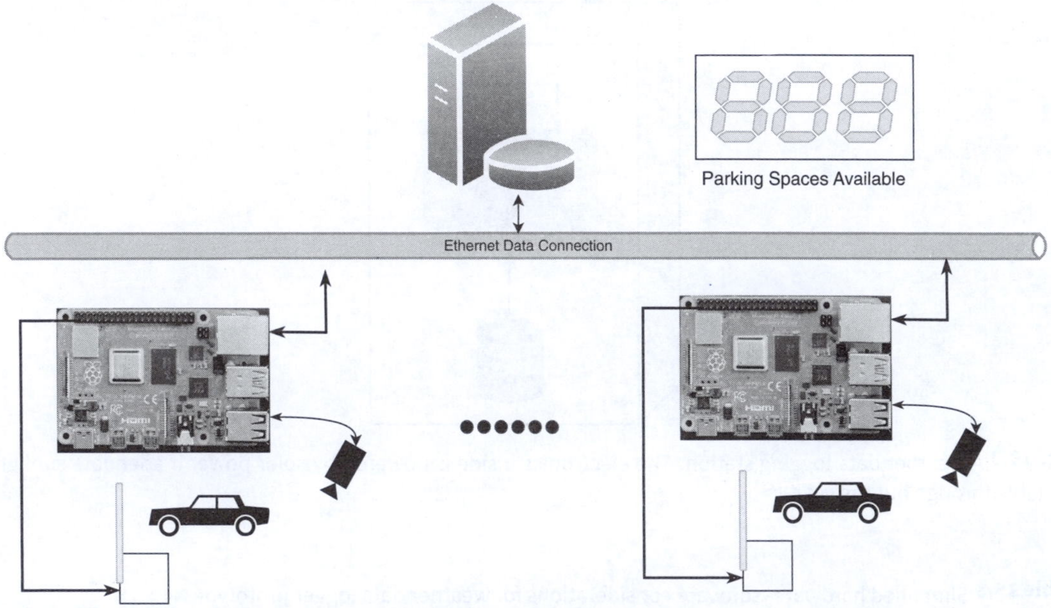

Fig. 19.2 Two entry stations are seen here. The details of each vehicle is recorded before it enters. A digital display at the entrance displays updated count of available parking spaces

Table 19.2 Simplified hardware–software considerations for automated car parking prototype

Hardware	Software	Functionality
Camera at entry and exit	Code to read license plate of car	Store license plate details of each car in parking garage
Barrier gate	Signal to open the gate at entry and exit	Open gate after reading plate at entry and open gate after payment check on exit
Digital display of number of available spaces at entry of garage	Calculate the number of cars in garage by subtracting the number of cars that have exited from the number of cars that have entered	Aid for users to enter the parking garage only if sufficient space is available. Data on garage occupancy is valuable for data analytics
Payment kiosk	Offer variety of payment options for user	Collect money based on duration of vehicle stay without human intervention

19.3 | Locally Saving and Remotely Querying Data

Our next idea is a weather station data logger. The data logger provides storage of weather conditions such as wind speed, temperature, humidity, and precipitation. This information is used for weather forecasting models and to monitor prevailing weather conditions. The weather data logger prototype is shown in Fig. 19.3 and a brief summary of its functionality and role of hardware–software is mentioned in Table 19.3.

A weather-proof enclosure is used to house the SBC, which connects to different sensors of the logger and stores the data on a hard drive with date and time stamp.

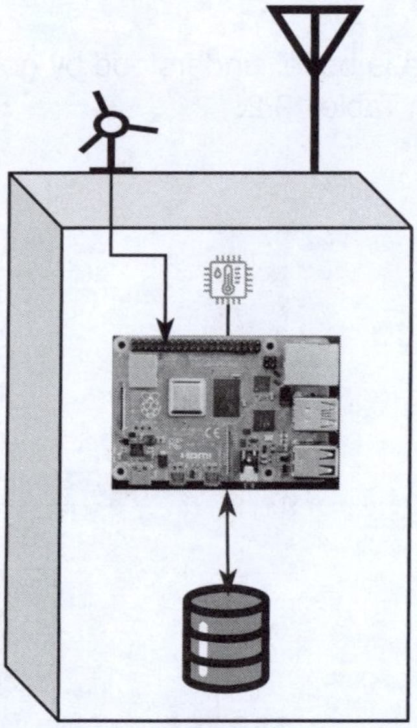

Fig. 19.3 A weather data logging station. The electronics inside is powered by solar power if adequate sunlight is available through out the year

Table 19.3 Simplified hardware–software considerations for weather data logger prototype

Hardware	Software	Functionality
Sensors such as wind speed, temperature, humidity, and precipitation	Periodically read sensor values and store in database	Store values for providing data on current weather conditions and for modeling
Solid state hard disk drive	Save data values in permanent storage using a SQL table	Respond to remote SQL queries to provide weather data
Internet connection gateway	Secure data protocols using cellular or satellite connectivity	Ability to access weather data loggers located at remote locations

19.4 | Sensors for Grain Silo

It is becoming a challenge to grow grains due to climate change. As a result, grains need to be stored safely after harvesting. The harvested grains are usually stored in grain storage silos or godowns. During storage, grains are periodically checked to see if they are going bad. Sensors

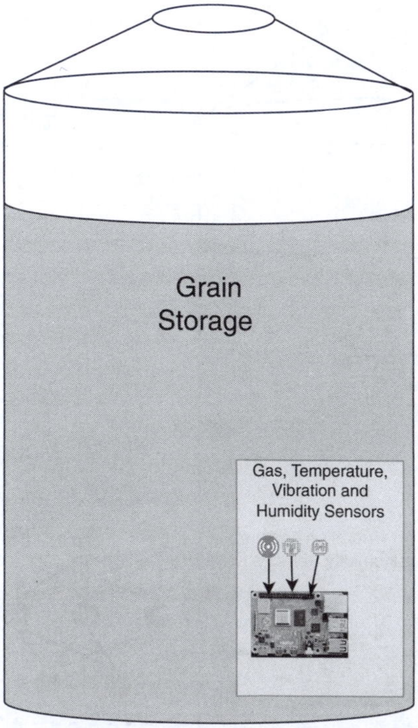

Fig. 19.4 Use of sensors inside a grain silo for monitoring grain quality during storage

such as humidity, temperature, and gas sensors help in monitoring the quality of grains. Fig. 19.4 is an aid to better understand grain silos and sensors.

Based on the size and the design of the grain storage, one or multiple sets of sensors are embedded at different locations in the silo and are connected to a compute device such as SBC to monitor different parameters. Table 19.4 enumerates the hardware–software aspects of sensors in grain silo.

19.5 | Machine Learning Models for Grain Quality

The data obtained from different sensors in the silo is used to train a machine learning or a neural network model. Trained model correlates the quality of the grains using data from the sensors. This model is hosted by the same compute device (SBC) that is connected to the sensors. Using real-time data from the sensor node, the quality of the grain in each silo is determined multiple times every day. Figure 19.5 shows the model hosted in the compute device to monitor grain quality.

To know more about the model details and use of human-in-the-loop, refer to Table 19.5.

Table 19.4 Simplified hardware–software considerations for grain silo sensor prototype

Hardware	Software	Functionality
SBC and sensors such as gas, temperature, humidity and vibration	Obtain readings from these sensors on a periodic basis	Values obtained from sensors reveal storage conditions and of possible rot
Bluetooth and Internet connectivity Gateway	Gather data from multiple sensor nodes and communicate them to control room	Use data for training machine learning or neural network model

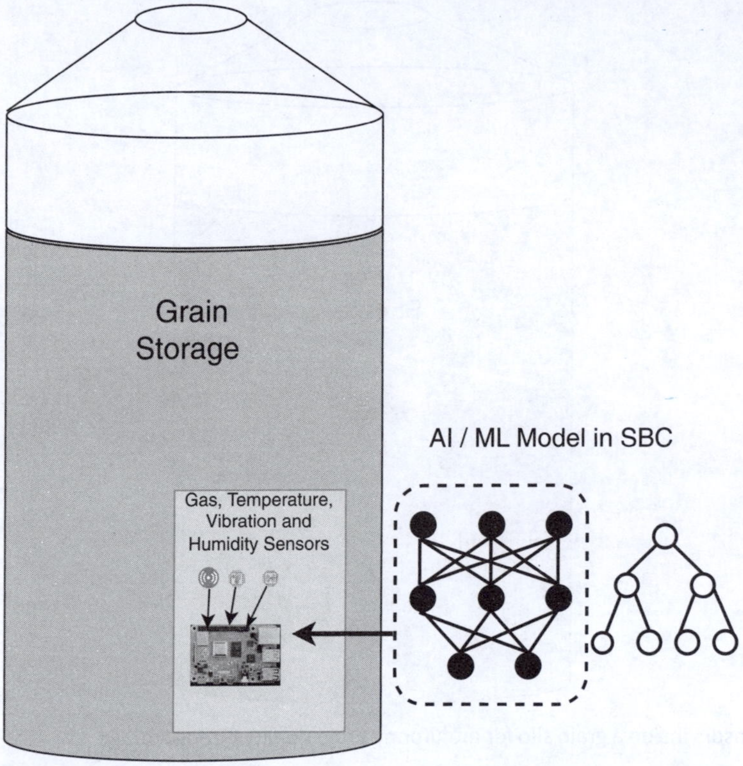

Fig. 19.5 A tiny AI/ML models runs on the data obtained from the sensors to determine the quality of the grain in the silo

Table 19.5 Simplified hardware–software considerations for determining grain quality in silo

Hardware	Software	Functionality
Gateway connected to multiple sensor nodes in silo	Gateway runs model inference using data from different nodes	The output of the inference is an indication of grain quality
Built-in outlets for grain sampling	Human randomly visits different silos to cross check model output	Check if the AI/ML model is working correctly

19.6 | Connecting Grain Silos to Control Room (IoT)

Grain quality determined by the AI/ML model is not just stored locally. It needs to be communicated or shared. This information is important if the grain is starting to go bad. Rodent infestation is also possible in some grain storage areas. Grain quality details from thousands of silos are aggregated at a control room, using internet connectivity. The internet-based (IoT) grain storage monitoring setup is shown in Fig. 19.6.

In the event, a silo shows deteriorating grain quality, the control room team takes required action to check and remedy the conditions in the silo. More details of how the setup works are mentioned in Table 19.6.

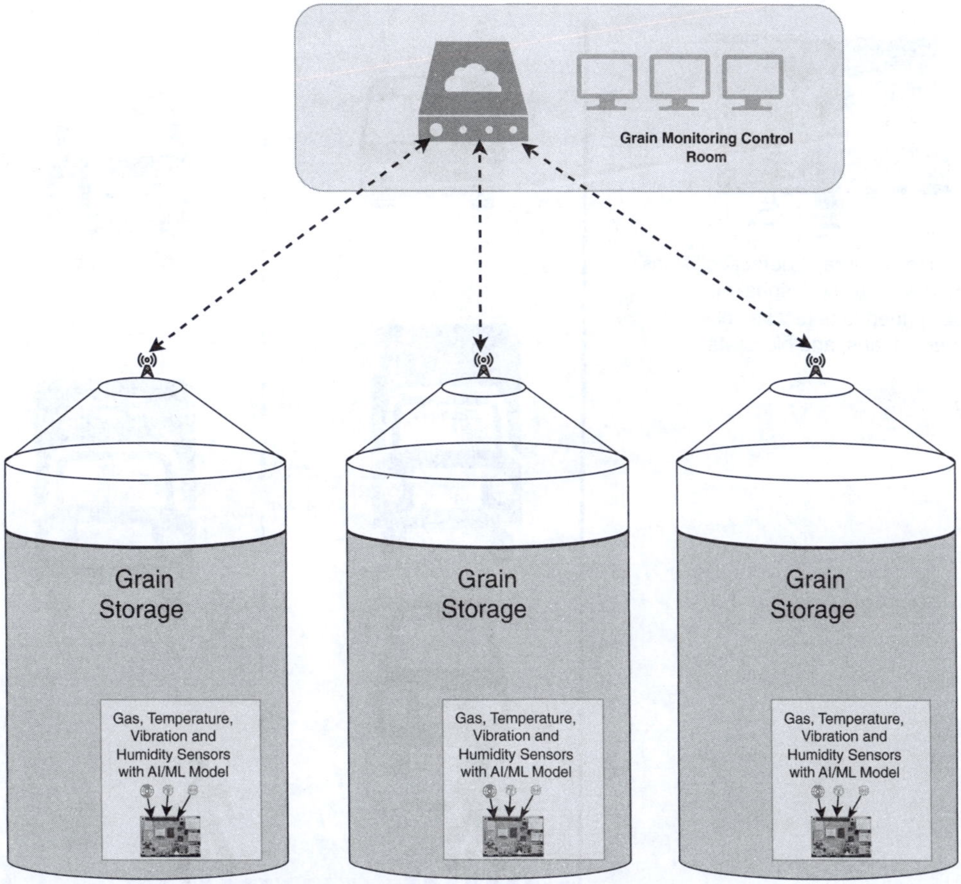

Fig. 19.6 A central control room monitors real-time conditions inside numerous grain silos using IoT. Any incipient rot or rodent infestation is caught in time to salvage large amount of grain.

Table 19.6 Simplified hardware–software considerations for wide area grain silo monitoring

Hardware	Software	Functionality
Internet Gateway at each grain silo	Periodically gather grain quality data and transmit to control room	Keep watch over grain in thousands of silos located in far-flung regions of the country
Local display and alarm at silo	Display grain quality data outside the silo and sound alarm if quality deteriorates	Back-up solution in case internet connectivity fails.

19.7 | Computer Vision for Traffic Safety

Road accidents are growing across the world. Distracted and tired drivers in cars, trucks, and buses are partially to blame for this. The situation is remedied by the use of computer vision technology. It notifies the driver of the motorized vehicle if pedestrians, bicyclists, or other vehicles are in close proximity. A camera mounted on the front windshield of the vehicles keeps a continuous watch on the road. Figure 19.7 illustrates a typical scenario where such an advanced driver-assistance system (ADAS) is useful.

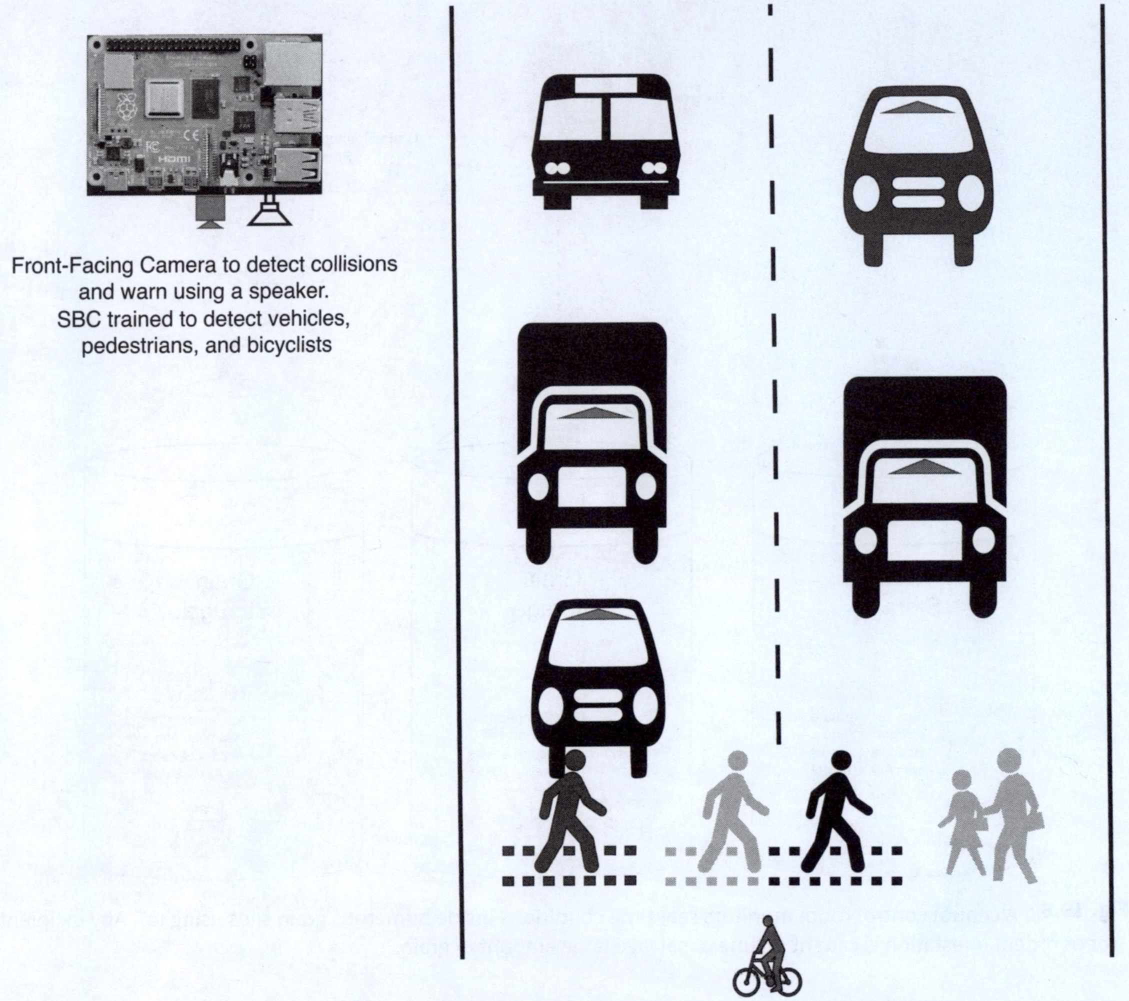

Fig. 19.7 A computer vision-based ADAS system. Many modern vehicles have an ADAS as a standard feature. It is possible to create an external ADAS system and install it in older vehicles

Table 19.7 Simplified hardware–software aspects for vehicle traffic safety

Hardware	Software	Functionality
Forward-looking camera connected to SBC	Computer vision software to analyze movement of people and vehicles	A second set of eyes looking at the traffic
Audible alarm connected to SBC	Alert driver if object comes very close	Prevent collisions from taking place.

The ADAS system can sound an audio alarm to alert the driver or can activate the brakes to prevent a collision. Table 19.7 gives more details about the setup.

19.8 | Dashboard for Location Information

We are surrounded by dashboard displays of different kinds. There are dashboards in fast food restaurants, containing details of the order being prepared or served. Dashboards on the airplane

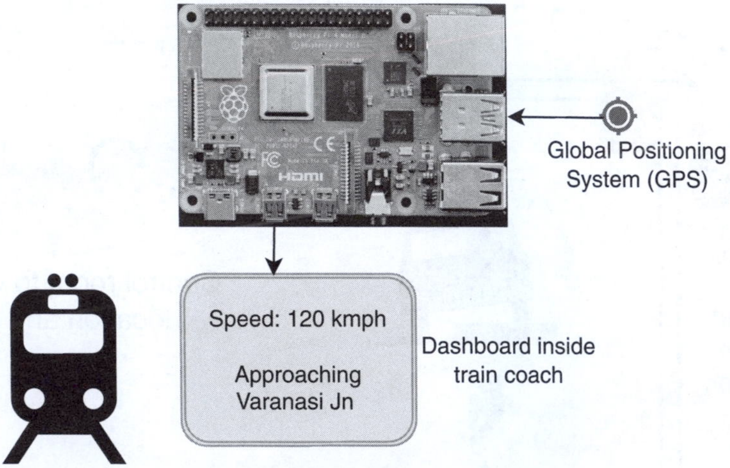

Fig. 19.8 A GPS-based train dashboard displaying speed and upcoming destination

Table 19.8 Simplified hardware–software aspects of a simple dashboard on trains

Hardware	Software	Functionality
GPS connected to SBC	Poll GPS to obtain latitude and longitude data	Convert latitude and longitude data to location on map
Dashboard display	Calculate speed based on change in location and estimate distance to next location	Inform passengers about the speed of the train and distance to the next station

show the location of aircraft at any given point of time. Many trains and buses also have dashboards to display speed and upcoming destination. In Fig. 19.8, we show the dashboard mounted in a train coach.

I recall my childhood train journeys, when some people in the coach were unsure about the next station or the station the train had stopped. These days, this information is easily available on a dashboard. The computer inside the dashboard uses location data from the ubiquitous global positioning system and calculates the speed of the train and its location. More details are mentioned in Table 19.8.

19.9 | Edge Computing for Street Safety

Keeping citizens safe is a big responsibility for cities and towns. A street light pole provides a good vantage point to monitor streets. Video and audio sensors on these poles detect accidents or cries for help. A city control room gets information about an incident and dispatches needed help. In the scenario described, the edge computer triggers an event for the control room based on local processing of its audio and video data. More details of the setup are shown in Fig. 19.9.

As most street light poles have similar hardware–software requirements, one robust design is replicated at thousands or millions of locations. Table 19.9 gives more details about how the setup works under the hood.

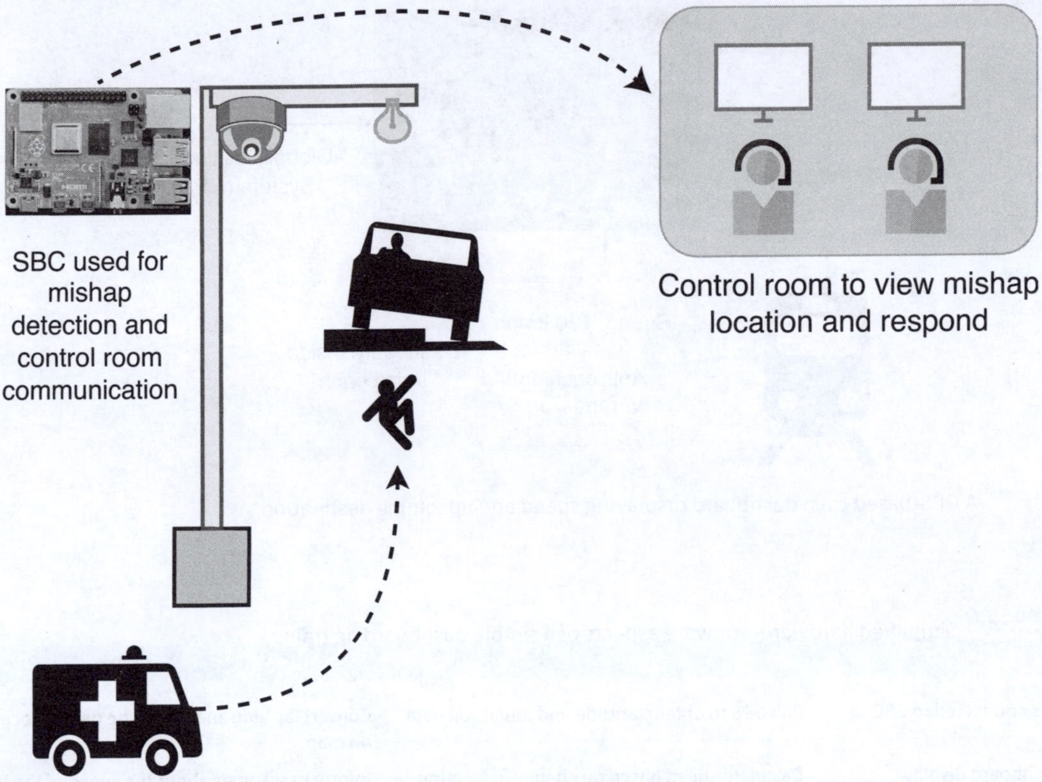

Fig. 19.9 An accident scenario in a smart city. Light pole mounted edge compute device informs the control room of the accident and help arrives quickly

Table 19.9 Simplified hardware–software aspects of city street safety

Hardware	Software	Functionality
Audio sensor connected to SBC	Acquire and analyze audio data for crash or cries for help	Generate event for control rooms in case of accident or distress
Video camera connected to SBC	Use computer vision to identify crashes or unusual activities	Generate notification for control room to investigate
Internet connectivity from SBC to control room	Locally store routine data, but transmit data based on events	Filter and send actionable data to the control room

19.10 | Drone for Search and Rescue

Drones serve as eyes in the sky. They can fly at high altitudes and check for objects, such as missing people in a forest or missing boats in the sea. Using computer vision and location is a low-cost tool for search and rescue operations. A simple illustration of this is seen in Fig. 19.10.

The battery and communications capability of the drone determines its range of operation. We take a closer look at this idea in Table 19.10.

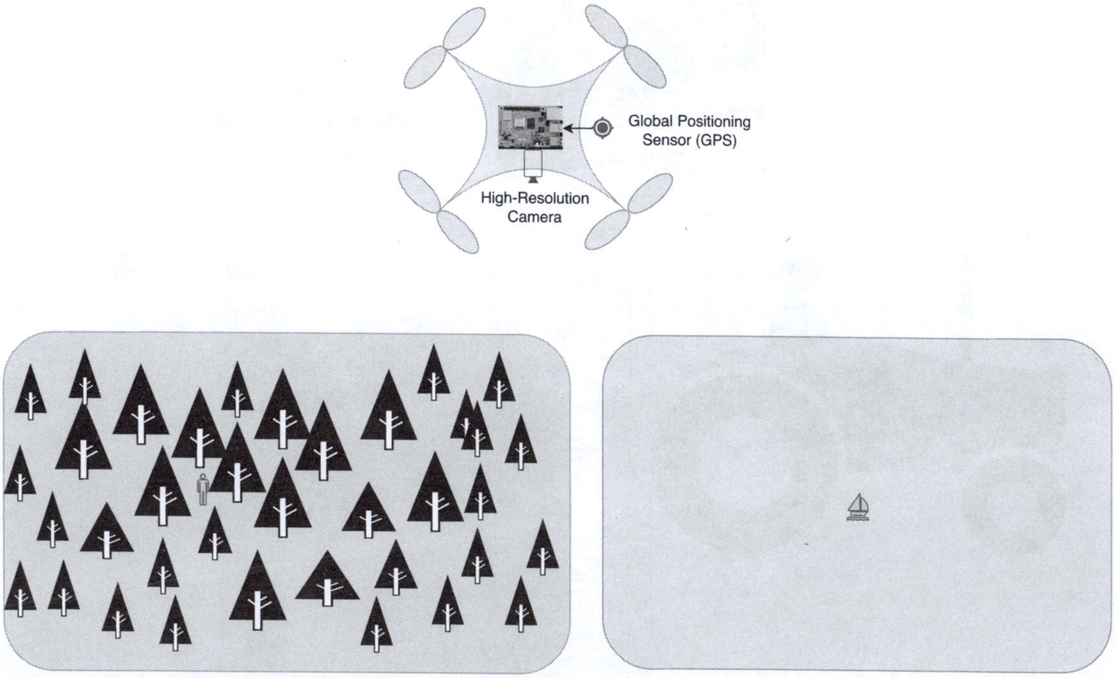

Fig. 19.10 Drone payloads such as high-resolution cameras and on-board object detection AI models assist in locating people lost in the wilderness

Table 19.10 Simplified hardware–software aspects of drone-based search and rescue

Hardware	Software	Functionality
GPS connected to drone SBC	• Guide drones to a desired general location. • Communicate GPS location if an object of interest is detected	• Control movement of drone. • Also obtain location of object of interest to carry out rescue.
Camera connected to drone SBC	Actively be on the lookout for object of interest, e.g., person or boat	Seach vast areas with ease using large field of view advantage

19.11 | Precision Agriculture

Each year fertile soil gets degraded by large amounts of herbicides to control unwanted weeds. A system that can accurately detect and destroy weeds in the farm saves the soil and herbicides. This is now possible with advances in computer vision technology and computer systems. In Fig. 19.11, we see two cameras that are used to detect weeds in different sections of the field. An accurate nozzle then sprays the required amount of herbicide on the weed.

More details on how this system weed detection and control works are outlined in Table 19.11. For creating your own system using Raspberry Pi, refer to the OpenWeedLocator (OWL) project[1].

1 Reference: Coleman, G., Salter, W. & Walsh, M. OpenWeedLocator (OWL): an open-source, low-cost device for fallow weed detection. Sci Rep 12, 170 (2022). https://doi.org/10.1038/s41598-021-03858-9, https://github.com/geezacoleman/OpenWeedLocator

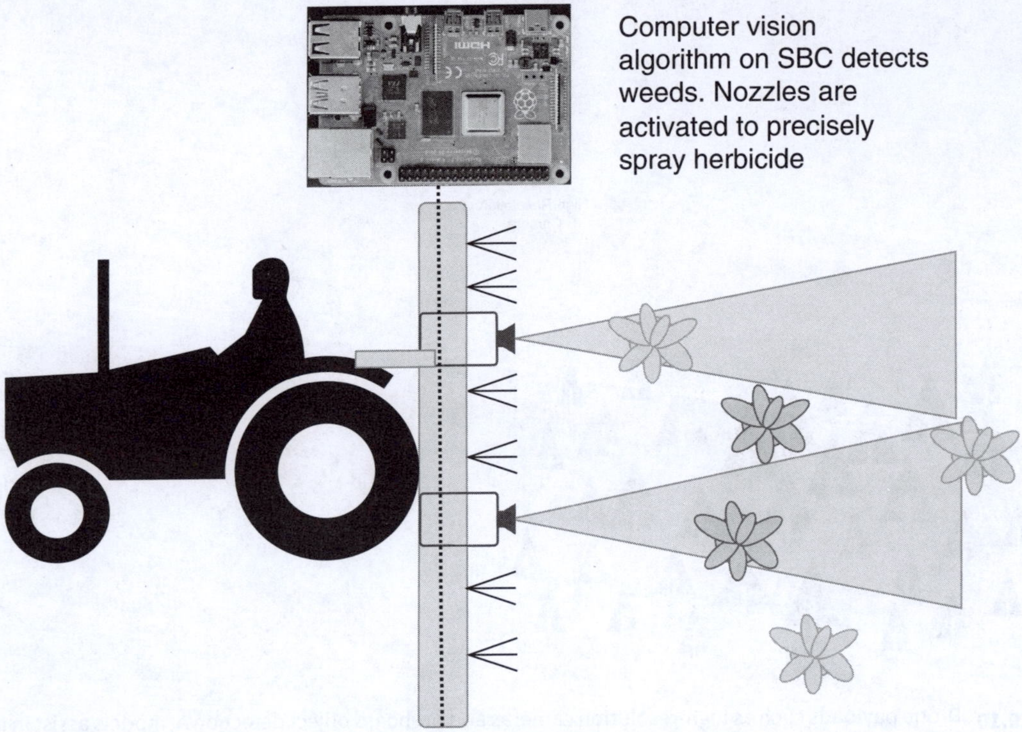

Fig. 19.11 Weed control by means of a computer vision model and precisely controlled herbicide nozzle. A computer system uses two cameras to detect weeds and then signals the nozzle to turn on

Table 19.11 Simplified hardware–software aspects of precision weed control

Hardware	Software	Functionality
Camera connected to SBC	Computer vision software to detect weeds of different types	Check the field for weeds
Herbicide spray nozzle connected to SBC	Turn on appropriate nozzle for a finite time to spray herbicide on weed	Precision use of herbicide to target the weed

19.12 | Crowd Control

Many events attract crowds in large numbers. These could be music concerts, sports, religious, or other kinds of events. If crowds are not adequately monitored and controlled, it can lead to stampedes. Figure 19.12 shows three gates through which crowds are entering an event. A smart camera with people detection AI model is mounted on a tall post and has complete view of the crowd. When the crowd becomes large, a red indication becomes active. This is seen on Gate Number 3. Crowd control team intervenes at this time to stop people from entering. Real-life crowd control is usually more complex than what is described. The basic setup of a crowd control system is mentioned in Table 19.12.

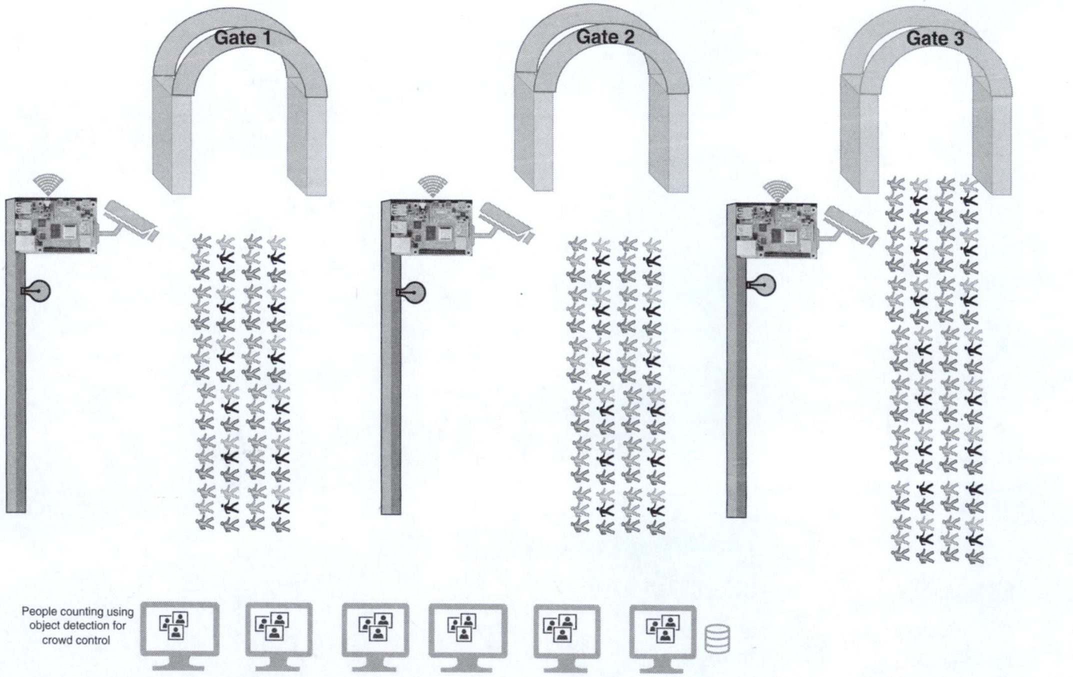

Fig. 19.12 Real-time monitoring of the number of people entering or exiting multiple gates of a venue

Table 19.12 Simplified hardware–software aspects of crowd control

Hardware	Software	Functionality
High-resolution Camera connected to SBC	AI people detection model to count people in the cameras field of view	Check if the number of people in any area exceed the prescribed threshold
Safety Indicator—Red or Green light	Indication to support crowd control team	Provide birds-eye perspective of crowd numbers and movement

19.13 | Conclusion

To create a solution using technology, the requirements of the problem and the role of technology need to be clearly articulated. Once this is in place, a simple prototype is created to check the feasibility of the technology-based solution. Most successful solutions start with a prototype or an MVP. This chapter provides eleven use cases and associated basic hardware and software details to put a prototype together.

Suggested Reading

1. Derek Molloy, Exploring Raspberry Pi: Interfacing to the Real World with Embedded Linux, Wiley 2016.

APPENDIX

A

Programming in Python—Quick Overview

OUTLINE

A.1 | Background

Python is a versatile interpreted language. It is suitable as the first programming language for students at all levels and also serves demanding applications such as machine and deep learning. These are some application areas and businesses where Python is used:

Web development Creating Web applications, with popular frameworks such as Django and Flask. For example, Instagram, a popular social media platform, was built using Django.
Data Science Useful for data analysis, machine learning, and artificial intelligence. Many popular data science libraries, such as NumPy, Pandas, and Scikit-learn are written in Python. Businesses, such as Amazon and Google use Python for data analysis and machine learning.
Finance Python is used in the finance industry for quantitative analysis and algorithmic trading. Financial institutions like JP Morgan and Morgan Stanley use Python to build trading algorithms and risk models.
Education Widely used as the first computer language to teach computer science concepts and programming skills. Many universities and schools use Python as the primary programming language in their computer science courses.
Healthcare Helpful in the healthcare industry for medical imaging, data analysis, and medical research. For example, the National Institutes of Health (NIH) uses Python for medical research.

These are just a few examples of how Python is used in industry and businesses. In this appendix, we will learn the basics of Python. The Python interpreter can be used in either *shell mode*, *script mode or Jupyter notebook mode*. We will use the shell mode to get started with simple Python

Table A.1 Python keywords

and	if
as	import
assert	in
break	is
class	lambda
continue	not
def	or
del	pass
elif	print
else	raise
except	return
exec	try
finally	while
for	with
from	yield
global	

constructs and syntax. The shell mode is an interactive mode recognized by the three Chevron symbols >>>. Python can be downloaded and installed on your local desktop from the Python's Website.[1]

Before we start with examples in Python, let us start with the keywords. Keywords are special reserved words that have specific meaning and purpose. They cannot be used as a variable name or any other purpose, other than what they are intended for. A subset of keywords supported by Python 3.8 is mentioned in Table A.1.

A.2 | Key Features of Python

Python is a strongly typed language (values and types are enforced). A programmer does not have to declare variables. The interpreter interprets variable type by parsing the assigned value. Variables are case-sensitive.

You can enter Python shell mode by typing python3.10 on the command line. If only a single version of Python exists on the machine, the command can be just *python*. The shell mode is like a calculator. One can use it for simple calculations or for trying out small snippets of code.

```
PS C:\Users\Rahul> python3.10
Python 3.10.8 (tags/v3.10.8:aaaf517, Oct 11 2022, 16:50:30) [MSC v.1933
64 bit (AMD64)] on win32
Type "help", "copyright", "credits" or "license" for more information.
>>> print ('Hello Emerging Technologies')
Hello Emerging Technologies
>>> variable = 2
>>> variable += 2 # add 2 to the variable value
>>> variable
4
```

[1]Python download, https://www.python.org/downloads/ (accessed 6 December 2022).

1. Python is an object-oriented language. If a user needs to find out how an object works, it can be found using *help(<object>)*. The object's methods can be found by *dir()*.

```
>>> text = "Emerging Technologies"
>>> type (text)
<class 'str'>
>>> dir(text)
['__add__', '__class__', '__contains__', '__delattr__', '__dir__',
'__doc__', '__eq__', '__format__', '__ge__', '__getattribute__',
'__getitem__', '__getnewargs__', '__gt__', '__hash__', '__init__',
'__init_subclass__', '__iter__', '__le__', '__len__', '__lt__',
'__mod__', '__mul__', '__ne__', '__new__', '__reduce__', '__re-
duce_ex__', '__repr__', '__rmod__', '__rmul__', '__setattr__',
'__sizeof__', '__str__', '__subclasshook__', 'capitalize', 'case-
fold', 'center', 'count', 'encode', 'endswith', 'expandtabs', 'find',
'format', 'format_map', 'index', 'isalnum', 'isalpha', 'isascii',
'isdecimal', 'isdigit', 'isidentifier', 'islower', 'isnumeric', 'is-
printable', 'isspace', 'istitle', 'isupper', 'join', 'ljust', 'low-
er', 'lstrip', 'maketrans', 'partition', 'removeprefix', 'removesuf-
fix', 'replace', 'rfind', 'rindex', 'rjust', 'rpartition', 'rsplit',
'rstrip', 'split', 'splitlines', 'startswith', 'strip', 'swapcase',
'title', 'translate', 'upper', 'zfill']

>>> text.upper()
'EMERGING TECHNOLOGIES'
>>> text.replace('Emerging', 'Existing')
'Existing Technologies'
>>>
```

Here we see the use of two string methods (upper and replace). In a similar manner, other string methods can also be used. Explore methods associated with integers, floats, Boolean, and lists.

2. The Python *syntax* does not require statement termination characters (such as in C programming); instead it makes use of indents to begin and close blocks. Statements such as conditional execution or function definitions end with a colon (:) and require an indent.
3. Python *data structures* consist of lists, tuples, and dictionaries. Simply put, *lists* are mutable one-dimensional arrays, *dictionaries* are associate arrays (like a lookup table), and *tuples* are immutable single-dimensional arrays. Dictionaries hold items in the format of a key-value pair (KVP). A KVP is a set of two linked data items—a key, which is a unique identifier for some item of data, and the value, which is either the data that is identified or a pointer to the location of that data. KVPs are frequently used in lookup tables, hash tables, and configuration files. Strings are also immutable arrays.

   The index of the first item in all array types is 0. Array ranges can be accessed using (:). When the first index is not defined, it is assumed as the first item. If the end index is not defined, it is assumed as the last item. The operator [x:y] returns the part of the string from the x-eth character to the y-eth character, *including the first but excluding the last*.

The list in Fig. A.1 is sliced to extract items using,

- mylist[:]   returns all items in mylist
- mylist[0:2]   returns items 0 to 1 from mylist

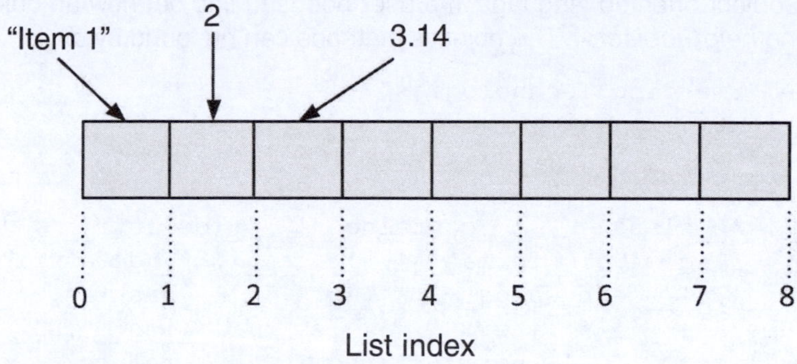

Fig. A.1 Location of *mylist* items for the earlier-mentioned example

```
>>> mylist = ["Item 1", 2, 3.14]
>>> print mylist[:]
['Item 1', 2, 3.14]
>>> print mylist [0:2]
['Item 1', 2]
>>> mylist[0]= "Changed item 1"
>>> print mylist[:]
['Changed item 1', 2, 3.14]
```

Python supports *flow control* statements, such as *if*, *for*, and *while*. It does not support the *switch* statement, that some of you may remember from the C programming language. All flow control statements end with a colon (:) and subsequent statements are indented. The code snippet below, shows use of the **for** and **if** statements. All **if** statements get evaluated sequentially. Try changing the second or third **if** statement to **elif** and see if the code is functional. Since this code consists of multiple Python statements, we now use the script mode instead of the shell mode.

```
rangelist = range (5,100,5)
for number in rangelist:
    remainder5 = number % 5
    remainder3 = number % 3
    if remainder5 == 0:
        print (number, "Is divisible by 5")
    if remainder3 == 0:
        print (number, "Is divisible by 3")
    if remainder5 == 0 and remainder3 == 0:
        print (number, "Is divisible by 15")
    else:
        pass
```

In this code, the range function generates numbers from 5 to 95 in increments of 5. Using the for loop, each generated number is checked for divisibility by 5,3 and 15. Now instead, the last two conditional if statements, are replaced by elif; the code would only check divisibility by 5 and not check divisibility by 3 and 15.

4. Python supports two types of functions—built-in and user-defined. Built-in functions should not be confused with methods, that are usually linked to a particular data type. These functions may work with multiple data types.

A
abs()
aiter()
all()
any()
anext()
ascii()

B
bin()
bool()
breakpoint()
bytearray()
bytes()

C
callable()
chr()
classmethod()
compile()
complex()

D
delattr()
dict()
dir()
divmod()

E
enumerate()
eval()
exec()

F
filter()
float()
format()
frozenset()

G
getattr()
globals()

H
hasattr()
hash()
help()
hex()

I
id()
input()
int()
isinstance()
issubclasss()
iter()

L
len()
list()
locals()

M
map()
max()
memoryview()
min()

N
next()

O
object()
oct()
open()
ord()

P
pow()
print()
property()

R
range()
repr()
reversed()
round()

S
set()
setattr()
slice()
sorted()
staticmethod()
str()
sum()
super()

T
tuple()
type()

V
vars()

Z
zip()

_
__import__()

In the following code snippet, we see the built-in ***len*** function being used to determine the length of a string (name) and of a list (seq).

```
>>> name = 'Rahul'
>>> len(name)
5
>>> seq = [1,2,'a', True]
>>> len(seq)
4
>>>
```

5. Python user-defined functions are declared using the *def* keyword. Variables inside a function are local. When the function terminates, the local variable is destroyed (becomes unavailable).

```
>>> def modulo(dividend,divisor):
        remainder = dividend % divisor
        return remainder

>>> print (modulo(5,3))
2
>>> print (modulo(7,2))
1
```

6. Lambda functions are ad hoc functions written as a single-line statement. The example below creates a function that returns the square of the input argument.

```
>>> s = lambda y: y ** 2; s(3)
9
```

The Python standard library comes with multiple built-in modules. This feature is often referred to as batteries-included. It is a big list and worth is checking out.[2]

In addition to the built-in modules, additional Python packages can be installed. Python packages are listed on the Python Package Index (PyPi)[3]. It has more than 400,000 packages and is continuously growing. It is advised to check and use packages created by trusted sources or companies.

Some popular computational packages are listed in Table A.2.

Just like the Linux package manager, Python package installer (pip) offers multiple commands. These commands are mentioned in Table A.3 below. Additional details on pip commands are available at the pip Website.[4]

Table A.2 Commonly used Python packages

Python Package Name	Functionality
NumPy	Fundamental package for numerical computation. It enables matrix operations
SciPy	A collection of numerical algorithms and domain-specific toolboxes including signal processing optimization, statistics, and much more
Matplotlib	Popular plotting package that provides publication-quality 2D plotting as well as simple 3D plotting
Pandas	Provides high-performance easy-to-use data structures
Keras, TensorFlow	Used for creating and testing deep learning architecture
IPython	A good interactive interface which allows for processing data and test ideas. IPython is used as a kernel by Jupyter notebook

Table A.3 Commonly used pip commands for Python packages

Environment Management and Introspection	
pip install	Install packages from PyPI or other sources
pip uninstall	Uninstall most installed packages
pip inspect	Inspect the content of a Python environment and produce a report in JSON format
pip list	List installed packages, in a case-insensitive sorted order
pip show	Show information about one or more installed packages
pip freeze	Output installed packages in requirements format (with version information), in a case-insensitive sorted order
pip check	Verify installed packages have compatible dependencies
Handling Distribution Files	
pip download	Download packages from PyPI or other sources
pip wheel	Build Wheel archives for your requirements and dependencies
pip hash	Compute a hash of a local package archive
Package Index Information	
pip search	Search for PyPI packages whose name or summary contains <query>

[2]Python standard library, https://docs.python.org/3/library/ (accessed 6 December 2022).
[3]Python Package Index, https://pypi.org/ (accessed 6 December 2022).
[4]Pip commands, https://pip.pypa.io/en/stable/cli/index.html (accessed 6 December 2022).

The following example makes use of built-in functions from Numpy and Matplotlib packages to demonstrate a sine wave plot (Fig. A.2). Numpy's *np.arange* function is used to generate a time base from 0.0 to 5.0 in increments of 0.01. Subsequently Numpy *np.sin* function is used to calculate sine value for five cycles.

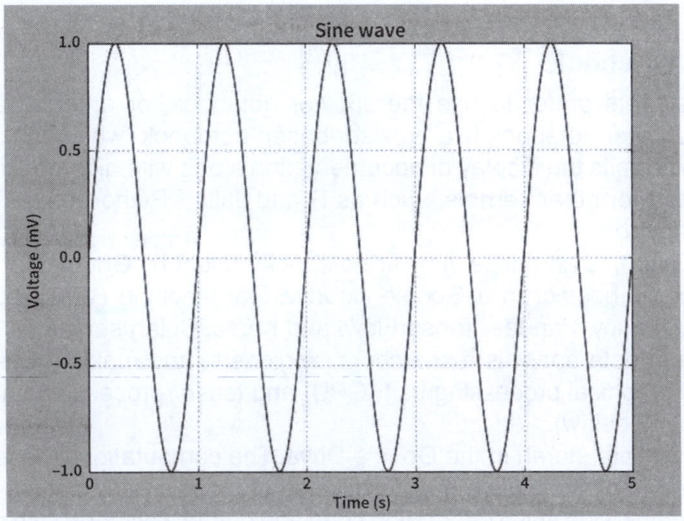

Fig. A.2 Sine wave plot using Python Numpy and Matplotlib packages

```
import matplotlib.pyplot as plt
import numpy as np

t = np.arange(0.0, 5.0, 0.01)
s = np.sin(2*np.pi*t)
plt.plot(t, s)

plt.xlabel('time (s)')
plt.ylabel('voltage (mV)')
plt.title('Sine wave')
plt.grid(True)
plt.show()
```

Python's Pandas package has numerous built-in functions to analyze the data. It uses data frame (df) for data manipulation and indexing

A.3 | Formatted Strings (F-Strings)

Formatted string literals begin a string with a **f** or **F** before the opening quotation mark. Inside this string, a Python expression between is written inside the { and } characters. The expression can refer to variables or literal values. The example below demonstrates how to increment the value of an integer and use the string method (upper) by f-string.

```
>>>a = 5
>>> print (f'The incremented value of a is {a+1}')
The incremented value of a is 6
>>> s = 'Emerging Technologies'
>>> print (f'Upper case "s" looks like {s.upper()}')
Upper case "s" looks like EMERGING TECHNOLOGIES
```

A.4 | Jupyter Notebook

Many Python developers prefer to use the Jupyter notebook for entering and debugging the Python code. The Jupyter notebook is a browser-based notebook, which makes it platform independent and it also permits the display of documentation along with different kinds of files. Jupyter also provides support for other kernels, such as R and Julia.[5] Python-based Jupyter notebooks have a file suffix *(*.ipynb)*.

Colaboratory[6] (Colab), is an online Jupyter notebook project by Google, for research and education.[3] Colaboratory is hosted on a Google cloud virtual machine (VM). There is inbuilt kernel support for Python, Numpy, Pandas, TensorFlow, and Keras. Colab serves as a good platform for machine learning and data analysis researchers, engineers, and makers. Besides CPU, it offers backend support of graphical processing unit (GPU) and tensor processing unit (TPU) for training AI models (see Fig. A.3 below).

All Colab notebooks are stored in the Google Drive. The computational-based interactive documents can be shared with others via e-mail just like other Google documents.

Figs. A.4 and A.5 show sine wave generation code and output waveform within Colab and Jupyter notebook environment. You can see the similarity in both environments.

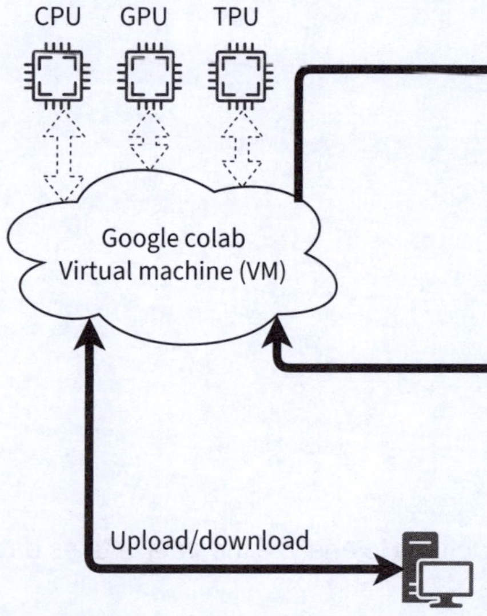

Fig. A.3 Working of Google Colab using cloud-based virtual machine. Two cloud-based machines (Colab and Google Drive) interact with one another to exchange data and files

[5] Jupyter, *Documentation*, available at http://jupyter.org/documentation (accessed 8 October 2018).
[6] Colaboratory, *Welcome to Colaboratory*, available at https://colab.research.google.com/notebooks/welcome.ipynb (accessed 8 October 2018).

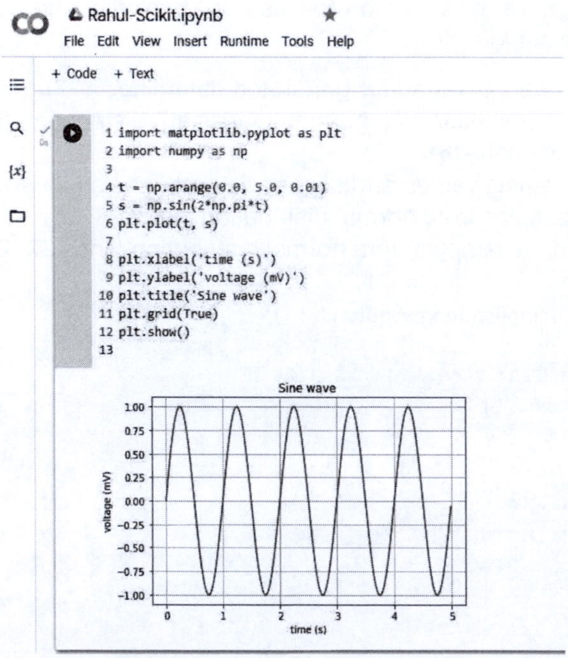

Fig. A.4 Sine wave generation in Colab notebook environment

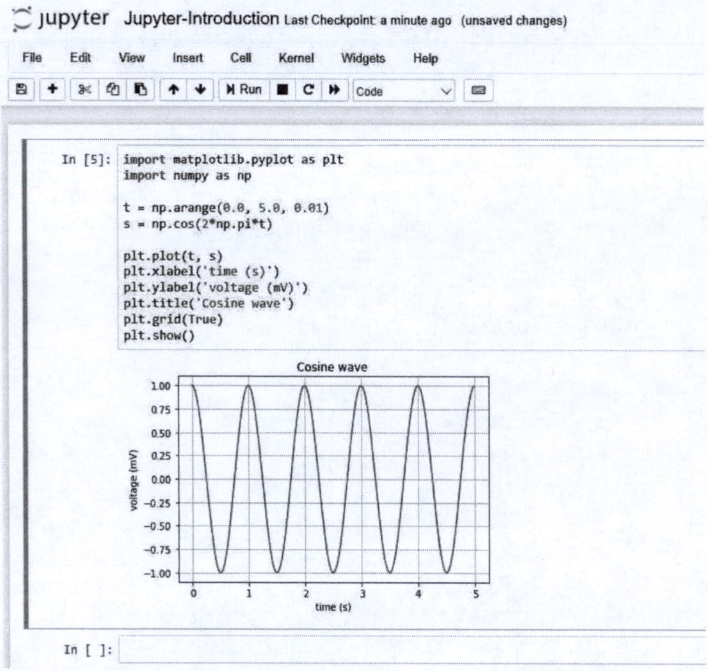

Fig. A.5 Sine wave generation in Jupyter notebook environment

Let us look at some more examples on the use of Matplotlib. The code in Listing A.1 shows plotting of different types of plots.

- Scatter plot using two sets of randomly generated data (lines 4–7)
- Histogram of random samples from a normal (Gaussian) distribution (lines 9–11)
- Bar plot of two lists (lines 13–16)
- Pie chart of a list containing values and second list with labels (lines 18–21)
- Box plot of random samples from normal distribution (lines 23–25)
- Display image of random samples from normal distribution (lines 27–29)

Listing A.1 Python code for demonstrating Matplotlib

```
01.  import matplotlib.pyplot as plt
02.  import numpy as np

03.  # plt.scatter(): Create scatter plots.
04.  x = np.random.normal(size=100)
05.  y = np.random.normal(size=100)
06.  plt.scatter(x, y)
07.  plt.show()

08.  #plt.hist(): Procedure to plot histograms.
09.  x = np.random.normal(size=1000)
10.  plt.hist(x, bins=30)
11.  plt.show()

12.  # plt.bar(): Command is used to plot bar charts.
13.  x = ['A', 'B', 'C', 'D']
14.  y = [3, 7, 1, 9]
15.  plt.bar(x, y)
16.  plt.show()

17.  #plt.pie(): Method to plot pie charts.
18.  x = [3, 7, 1, 9]
19.  labels = ['A', 'B', 'C', 'D']
20.  plt.pie(x, labels=labels)
21.  plt.show()

22.  #plt.boxplot(): Plot boxplots.
23.  x = np.random.normal(size=100)
24.  plt.boxplot(x)
25.  plt.show()

26.  #plt.imshow(): Display images.
27.  image = np.random.normal(size=(100, 100))
28.  plt.imshow(image, cmap='gray')
29.  plt.show()
```

A.5 | Working with Datasets and Pandas

Exploring datasets is a skill all business students should have. Some popular datasets to practice data analysis are available on the internet from Websites such as Kaggle, UCI Machine Learning Repository,[7] or can be obtained from other publicly available sources. Popular datasets for a business student include datasets mentioned in Table A.4.

We start our discussion with an overview of Pandas. Pandas is a Python library that is commonly used for data analytics. It provides a wide range of tools and functions for manipulating and analyzing data, including the ability to read and write data in various file formats, filtering and sorting data, handling missing or incomplete data, and computing summary statistics. Table A.5 summarizes the use of Pandas in a data analytics application,

We will first demonstrate the use of Pandas[8] to explore a dataset from vega datasets.[9] This package provides straightforward access in Python to the dataset available at vega datasets. Using a simple API, it returns the results in the form of a Pandas dataframe. Several datasets are bundled in the installation to allow dataset usage in the absence of an internet connection.

Table A.4 Typical data used to analyze business activities

Customer churn	Information about customers who have left a company and why they left
Stock market	Details about the stock prices of different companies over time
Sales	Sales data of different products in different regions
Marketing campaign	Data containing effectiveness of marketing campaigns for a product

Table A.5 Major areas where pandas helps in data analytics

Data cleaning	Clean and preprocess raw data such as removing duplicates, filling in missing data and transforming data into a usable format
Data exploration	Explore data by computing summary statistics, visualizing data and identifying patterns in data
Data analysis	Perform complex data analysis tasks such as computing correlations, regression analysis and time-series analysis
Data integration	Pandas can be used to integrate data from multiple sources and formats allowing for more comprehensive analysis

[7]University of California Irvine (UCI) machine learning repository, https://archive.ics.uci.edu/ml/index.php (accessed 1 June 2023).

[8]Pandas, https://pandas.pydata.org/ (accessed 3 June 2023).

[9]Vega datasets, https://pypi.org/project/vega-datasets/ (accessed 10 May 2023).

Listing A.2 Python code to demonstrate data exploration methods of Pandas

```
from vega_datasets import data
import pandas as pd

df = data.iris()

#head(): View the first few rows of a DataFrame.
print ('First 5 rows of dataframe')
print (df.head())

#tail(): View the last few rows of a DataFrame.
print ('Last 5 rows of dataframe')
print (df.tail())

#info(): View a summary of a DataFrame, including data types and missing
#values.
print ('Dataframe summary')
print (df.info())

#describe(): See the statistical summaries of a DataFrame.
df.describe()
```

In the code from Listing A.2, following Pandas commands are used to parse a dataset captured inside a dataframe(df).

- df.head() to view first 5 rows of a dataset
- df.tail() to view last 5 rows of a dataset
- df.info() to obtain a summary of dataset
- df.describe() to get statistical summary of a dataset

The vega dataset package locally installs several datasets. The package is installed using the command pip install vega_datasets. Datasets can also be imported directly from repositories such as UCI machine learning repository. Many datasets are available as Microsoft Excel (.xls) files. The .xls file is saved as a comma separated value (csv) file using the following steps.

a) In the Excel spreadsheet, click File.
b) Click Save As.
c) Click Browse to choose where you want to save your file.
d) Select “CSV” from the “Save as type” drop-down menu.
e) Click Save

Pandas read_csv command is used to convert a file containing csv data to a Pandas data frame. Here, we read in wine data from UCI machine learning repository and then print it out.

```
wine = pd.read_csv('https://archive.ics.uci.edu/ml/machine-learning-databases/wine/wine.data')
wine
```

Try different Pandas commands in the Colab notebook to know more about a given dataset.

A.6 | Reading and Writing to a Database Using Python DB-API

The Python standard library supports SQLite database by the help of sqlite3, which is a DB-API 2.0 interface for SQLite databases. SQLite is a lightweight disk-based database that does not require a separate server-client setup (MySQL database discussed in Chapter 2 supports server-client, multi-user configuration). Most smartphones use SQLite for internal data storage. SQLite can also be used to prototype an application, that can later be ported to a larger database.

Our example code in Listing A.3, demonstrates how to save contents of a comma separated values (csv) file to an SQLite database. To use this code, replace 'path_to_your_file.csv' with the path to your CSV file, 'database_name.db' with the name of your SQLite database, and 'table_name' with the name of the table you want to create in the SQLite database. This code does not consider scenarios such as appending data and error handling.

The next example in Listing A.4 shows a Python script that connects to an SQLite database called employee_database, creates a table named employees if it does not exist, inserts two records into the table, commits the transaction, selects all records from the table, fetches all the rows from the query result, prints each row, and finally closes the connection to the SQLite database. Several methods of Python DB-API 2.0 are exercised in this code. Execute the codes in Listing A.3 and A.4 with a specific CSV file and a real-world database.

Listing A.3 Python code to write a comma separated values (csv) file to a SQLite database

```
import pandas as pd
import sqlite3

# Load CSV file to a Pandas Dataframe df
df = pd.read_csv('path_to_your_file.csv')

# Create a connection to SQLite database
# If the database does not exist, this command will create it
conn = sqlite3.connect('database_name.db')

# Write records stored in a DataFrame to a SQL database.
df.to_sql('table_name', conn)

# Commit the transaction
conn.commit()

# Close the connection
conn.close()
```

Listing A.4 Creating an SQLite database, a table, writing values to the table and then retrieving it using Python DB-API 2.0

```
import sqlite3

# Connect to the SQLite database
# If the database does not exist, this command will create it
conn = sqlite3.connect('employee_database.db')
```

(Continued)

Listing A.4 *(Continued)*

```
# Create a cursor object
cursor = conn.cursor()

# Execute a SQL query
cursor.execute("CREATE TABLE IF NOT EXISTS employees(id INTEGER
PRIMARY KEY, name TEXT, salary REAL)")

# Insert a new record
cursor.execute("INSERT INTO employees VALUES(1, 'Rahul Dubey',
50000)")

# Insert a second record
cursor.execute("INSERT INTO employees VALUES(2, 'Raj Kumar', 45000)")

# Commit the transaction
conn.commit()

# Execute a SQL query
cursor.execute("SELECT * FROM employees")

# Fetch all the rows
rows = cursor.fetchall()

for row in rows:
    print(row)

# Close the connection
conn.close()
```

Exercises

A. Short-answer Questions

1. Which Python mode is better suited for simple calculations—shell or script?
2. Name two Python string methods.
3. What is the difference between a Python list and tuple?
4. List the data types on which the built-in Python len function works.
5. Name the command to list installed Python packages.
6. Name the Pandas method to get statistical summary of a dataset.
7. Name the built-in database used by Python.
8. Name the API used by Python to interact with SQL databases.
9. Name the Python package used for plotting graphs and charts.
10. Explain how a CSV file is saved to an SQLite database.

B. Explore and Experiment

1. Generate short Python code snippets by providing meaningful prompts. Check the AI-generated code in Python environment. In Fig. A.6, we use Generative AI to create Python code to access data from a SQL database, and then plot it using Matplotlib. This code needs to be suitably modified to execute correctly. Generative AI provides you with a reasonable starting point.

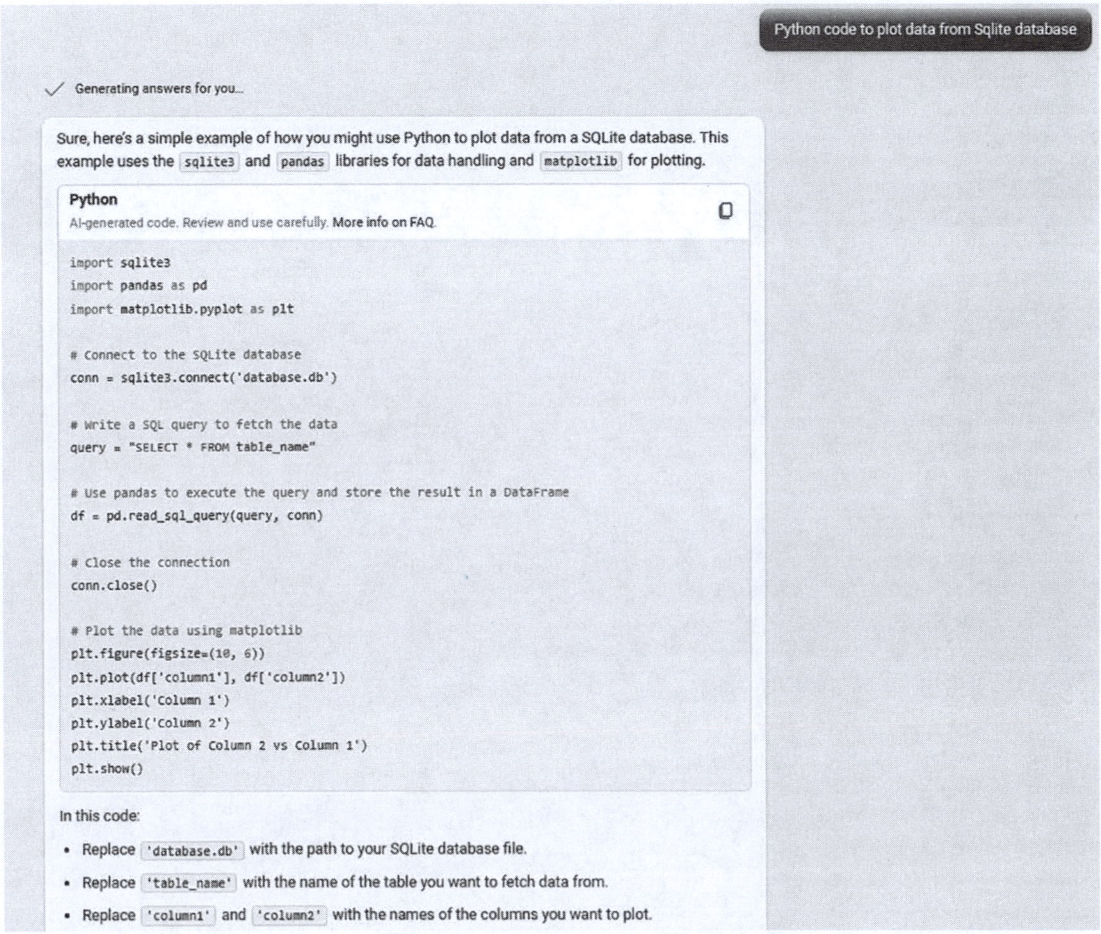

Fig. A.6 AI generated Python code snippet

Suggested Readings

1. Jeffrey Elkner, Allen B. Downey, and Chris Meyers, *How to Think Like a Computer Scientist*, 21 April 2012, available at http://openbookproject.net/thinkcs/python/english2e/ (accessed 8 October 2018).
2. Stavros Korokithakis, 'Tutorial-Learn Python in 10 Minutes', *Stavros's Stuff*, available at https://www.stavros.io/tutorials/python/ (accessed 8 October 2018).
3. Al Sweigart, *Automate the Boring Stuff with Python,* Free to read at https://automatetheboringstuff.com/ (accessed 26 March 2023).

Index